Human reliability in
quality control

Human reliability in quality control

Edited by

C. G. Drury
State University of New York at Buffalo
and
J. G. Fox
University of Birmingham, England

Taylor & Francis Ltd London

Halsted Press
a division of John Wiley & Sons Inc
New York—Toronto

1975

First published 1975 by Taylor & Francis Ltd, London
and Halsted Press (a division of John Wiley & Sons Inc.) New York.

© 1975 Taylor & Francis Ltd

Taylor & Francis ISBN 0 85066 088 2

Printed and bound in Great Britain by
Taylor & Francis (Printers) Ltd
Rankine Road, Basingstoke, Hampshire

Library of Congress Cataloging in Publication Data
Main entry under title:

Human reliability in quality control.

    Includes Indexes.
    1. Engineering Inspection. 2. Quality Control. 3. Errors.
I. Drury, C. G.   II. Fox, John Graham.
TS156.2.H85   1975   658.5   75–11695
ISBN 0–470–22315–4

Contributors

S. K. Adams is an associate professor in the Department of Industrial Engineering, Iowa State University, U.S.A. Previously he was with Eastman Kodak, N.A.S.A. and the School of Industrial Engineering and Management, Oklahoma State University. His interests include work design, product design and industrial safety.

R. W. Astley is a lecturer in ergonomics at the Lucas Institute for Engineering Production, University of Birmingham, England. His research and applied interests have centred on equipment and workplace design and industrial quality control.

G. Kemble Bennett is an associate professor in the Industrial Systems Department at the University of South Florida, U.S.A. He was formerly an assistant professor in the Department of Industrial Engineering and Operations Research at Virginia Polytechnic Institute and State University. His research activities include cost-based quality control and consumer protection systems.

J. R. Bloomfield is a Principal Research Scientist in the Life Sciences Section of the Systems and Research Center, Honeywell Inc., Minneapolis, Minnesota, U.S.A. His previous appointment was in the Department of Psychology, University of Nottingham, England. His professional interests are visual perception, particularly visual search and related topics such as peripheral visual acuity, target acquisition, displays and industrial inspection.

J. R. Buck is an associate professor in the School of Industrial Engineering, Purdue University, Indiana, U.S.A. His teaching and research takes him into the fields of ergonomics, biomechanics and engineering economics.

D. Elizabeth Chapman graduated in ergonomics at the University of Technology, Loughborough, England. She now has a teaching post in Bexhill, Sussex.

W. P. Colquhoun is in charge of the M.R.C. Applied Psychology Unit Outstation at the University of Sussex, England. He has a long professional record of interest in vigilance and its relation to industrial inspection; circadian rhythm, shift work and transzonal travel.

A. Craig is a Scientific Officer at the M.R.C. Applied Psychology Unit Outstation at the University of Sussex, England. His professional interests are in vigilance and inspection; and the role of decision strategies in target detection and recognition.

C. G. Drury is an assistant professor in the Department of Industrial Engineering, State University of New York, Buffalo, U.S.A. Previously he was Manager of the Ergonomics Section, Pilkington Brothers Ltd., Glass Manufacturers, England. His chief research interests are in applying mathematical models of human performance to the design of industrial jobs. Particular areas of interest are industrial inspection and the control of industrial vehicles.

W. E. Dunkel is currently with I.B.M. at East Fishkill, New York, U.S.A. He lists among his professional interests: manufacturing, from a technical and scientific point of view, of semi conductor components, hybrids and integrated circuits.

D. E. Embrey carries out research in the Department of Applied Psychology, University of Aston in Birmingham, England. His current work is in methods of training for perceptual skills and applying psychological methodology to industrial problems.

T. W. Faulkner is with the Human Factors section of Eastman Kodak in their Health and Safety Laboratory, Rochester, New York, U.S.A. His work is concerned with various facets of illumination, e.g. dark adaptation and inspection lighting.

J. G. Fox has recently joined the Directorate of Social Affairs of the Commission of the European Communities with responsibility for a programme of ergonomics and rehabilitation in the coal and steel industries of the Community. Previously he was a lecturer in ergonomics and Director of the Ergonomics Information Analysis Centre, Department of Engineering Production, University of Birmingham, England. His ergonomics interests have been in industrial quality control and equipment design: his research work has been centred on perceptual and vigilance problems.

H. A. Froot is currently with I.B.M. at East Fishkill, New York, U.S.A. Among his interests is the development of optical microscopic techniques for failure analysis and characterization of semi conductor components and thin films.

G. J. Gillies is Manager, Ergonomics Section, Pilkington Brothers Ltd., Glass Manufacturers, England. In this capacity he is responsible for a range of ergonomics activities including inspection, work in hot environments and man–computer interaction in process control.

J. Moraal is with the Institute for Perception, T.N.O., Soesterberg, The Netherlands. Previously he worked in the Psychological Department of the Royal Dutch Steel Industry, 'Hoogovens', Ijmuiden, The Netherlands. In general he is professionally concerned with various civil and military ergonomics problems including social psychological design, traffic research and motor skills.

T. J. Murphy is currently with Eastman Kodak, Rochester, New York, U.S.A. His doctorate is in industrial psychology. His interests are shift work, inspection and product design.

L. V. Rigby is an industrial psychologist at Sandia Laboratories, Albuquerque, New Mexico, U.S.A. He works on problems of human error, personnel selection and evaluation, and on motivation.

M. A. Sinclair is a lecturer in the Department of Human Sciences, Loughborough University of Technology, England. His range of professional interests is wide and currently include the effect of incentive schemes on salesmen, the ergonomics of intruder alarms, the movement of people around housing estates, the development of eye movement apparatus and the classification of the behaviour of inspectors.

G. L. Smith is an associate professor in the Department of Industrial and Systems Engineering, Ohio State University, U.S.A. His interests are in man–machine systems engineering, design methods and labour arbitration.

A. D. Swain is an engineering psychologist in the Systems Reliability Division, Sandia Laboratories, New Mexico, U.S.A., and a lecturer for Industrial and Commercial Techniques Limited, London, England. He has a broad range of interests in the fields of ergonomics, human reliability, systems safety and industrial processes. Among his qualifications he is a Certified Psychologist in the State of New Mexico and an A.S.Q.C. Certified Reliability Engineer.

E. L. Wiener is a professor of Management Science, University of Miami, Florida, U.S.A. His professional interests include human vigilance, aviation safety, vehicular safety, laboratory computers and ageing.

X. K. Zunzanyika is a Senior Engineer in the Quality Assurance Department of Carborundum, 2350 Main Street, Niagara Falls, New York 14305, U.S.A. His first degree was in Mathematics and he is now specialising in industrial engineering. His professional interests include human performance in industrial processes and the use of multi-variate analysis.

Contents

Preface

The quality control engineer who wishes to use realistic human error rates in designing quality control schemes has very few sources upon which to call to help in the task. Whilst many articles have appeared over the years showing that human error exists the net result seems to have been surprise at the magnitude of the error and a preoccupation with methods, such as zero defects programmes, to exhort humans to do better.

Yet there have been enough inspection studies in enough industries backed by theoretical and laboratory data to allow a much more fundamental and realistic approach to accounting for human error in quality control models. It was this point of view which led to the International Symposium on Human Factors in Quality Control held at the State University of New York, Buffalo, New York in 1974. This symposium in turn led to the present book. This book then is an attempt to collect together, systematize and organize the data that is available on human errors in quality control and to consider how they should be treated.

If a book were a sermon, the *Prologue* would be the text. Papers such as this represent not just a means of producing better quality control schemes and hence a more efficient industry, but are a challenge to the human factors engineer and ergonomist to produce realistic models of human work.

It is the intention of this current volume to extend the tools available for improving quality control systems by reviewing the major theoretical foundations upon which a theory of the industrial inspector might be based, backed up by examples of the use of these theoretical constructs in industrial situations. Thus the structure of the book unfolds itself. The *Prologue* and *Introductory Paper* consider the need for and the possibilities of an extension of tools for describing human performance and the three sections following give substance to the human factors engineer's claim to a contribution in building models for quality control systems.

Each of the three sections is essentially self contained. The first deals with the theoretical foundations of human factors in inspection, providing an example of the use of each in industrial situations. The second section deals with factors which can and do affect inspection performance. The final section emphasises the thesis that human inspection in many industries poses the same problems. The reader can tackle the book in serial order or pick out those areas of special interest. But it should be noted that, to avoid redundancy, in many of the industrial applications and performance papers reference is made to theoretical models covered in detail only in the first section.

Symbols, particularly p, P, β, appear frequently in the papers. An attempt has been made to standardize their use but this has not always been possible. However, in any particular context their meaning should be unambiguous and the reader need only be cautious as to his assumptions of their meanings.

The stimulus for this book was the International Symposium on Human Factors in Quality Control when the State University of New York, Buffalo was host to a gathering of human factors specialists in inspection problems and also industrial quality control engineers and managers. The practical viewpoint which we hope characterises the contributions of this volume are a direct result of the interaction of these groups made possible by this meeting. We must acknowledge our debt and our sincere thanks to the University for making this meeting possible. Particularly we would like to thank Dr. W. H. Baumer, *Chairman*, 'Conferences in the Disciplines Fund', Professor Warren Thomas of the Department of Industrial Engineering and Mr. Allan L. Canfield, the Assistant for Conferences. With the two editors separated by the Atlantic, expert secretarial help has been essential and the parts played in the eventual appearance of this book by Miss Phyllis Ketley in Birmingham, England and Mrs. Pat Doeing in Buffalo, U.S.A., cannot go unacknowledged.

J. G. Fox,
University of Birmingham,
England.

June 1974.

Inspection error: its influence on quality control systems

G. Kemble Bennett

1. Introduction

As any experienced quality control engineer can verify, inspection tasks are not error free. On the contrary, these tasks are often error prone contradicting the traditional design assumption that inspection is free of error. In fact, it is not uncommon to find error figures of twenty-five percent or higher for even the most experienced inspector personnel (Jacobson 1952).

Although inspection errors are unintentional they nevertheless can severely distort the quality objectives of any system design which has ignored their presence. Many a good quality control system has been rendered a failure when the system did not meet expectations. Designs have been checked and rechecked only to find that all calculations were mathematically correct. In such situations further investigation frequently reveals that inspection error is present in the system causing distorted figures to be produced.

Once it is known that inspection error is present the quality control engineer may use revised training procedures and even new equipment to reduce the inaccuracies. However, these actions alone will not erase them. Even under what may be considered ideal inspection conditions it is not uncommon to find extremely high error figures (Jacobson *op. cit.*). So what must be done to achieve quality objectives given that inspection error is to be ever present? The answer is simple. The quality control engineer must be able to accurately measure these errors and then be able to design for them. For it is only through the incorporation of inspection error into the design of a quality control system that management can hope to achieve its desired quality goals when its product is being submitted to error prone inspection tasks.

Measuring inspection error and designing for it represent two areas of challenging and fruitful research, each dependent upon one another. The content of this volume is specific to their discussion. However, the major purpose of this paper is to illustrate the drastic effects inspection error can have on sampling plan designs. This will be done by illustrating its effect on the performance measures: 'average outgoing quality' (AOQ) and 'average total inspection' (ATI). Also, the effects of inspection error on the design of single sampling plans based on the measures: 'lot tolerance percent defective' (LTPD) and 'acceptable quality limit' (AQL) will be considered. A method is also discussed whereby desired quality risks can be maintained even though sampling is subject to inspection error. These discussions are based on the work of Collins *et al.* (1973).

An additional purpose of the paper is to illustrate the economic effects of inspection error on sampling plan design. Economic design and justification of sampling plans is becoming increasingly more important to the quality control engineer. Therefore, it will be useful to investigate the economic consequences of inspection error. This discussion is based on the work of Bennett *et al.* (1974).

The equally important topics of how one accurately measures inspection errors and their causes are left for discussion by those more worthy. These are better treated by human factors personnel and are the subject of later papers.

2. Performance measures

Single sampling plans involving attribute inspection are characterized by two decision variables, the sample size, n, and the acceptance number, c. In these plans a sample of n items is drawn from a lot of size S and each item is inspected and classified as either good or defective. If the number of items classified as defective exceeds c the lot is rejected. Otherwise, it is accepted.

Two types of errors are possible in attribute sampling. An item which is good may be classified as defective (Type 1 error), or an item which is defective may be classified as good (Type 2 error).

Let

E_1 = the event that a good item is classified as a defective,

E_2 = the event that a defective item is classified good,

A = the event that an item is defective,

and

B = the event that an item is classified as a defective.

Then,

$$P(B) = P(A)P(\bar{E}_2) - P(\bar{A})P(E_1).$$

By defining the quantities

$p = P(A)$, true fraction defective,

$p_e = P(B)$, apparent fraction defective,

$e_1 = P(E_1)$, the probability that E_1 occurs,

and

$e_2 = P(E_2)$, the probability that E_2 occurs,

the expression for the apparent fraction defective may be more meaningfully expressed as

$$p_e = p(1 - e_2) + (1 - p)e_1.$$

2.1. *Probability of acceptance*

It has been shown by Hald (1960) that the binomial distribution is applicable to hypergeometric sampling. That is, if a lot of size S if formed from a binomial data generating process and a sample of n items is taken from the lot, then the number of defectives in the sample is described by a binomial mass function. Thus, assuming perfect inspection, the probability of lot acceptance is given by

$$P_a = \sum_{x=0}^{c} \binom{n}{x} p^x (1-p)^{n-x}$$

A plot of P_a as a function of lot quality, p, determines the sampling plan's operating characteristic (OC) curve.

The probability of acceptance when inspection error is present, Pa_e, is written in a similar manner by replacing the true fraction defective, p, by the apparent fraction defective p_e. Thus,

$$Pa_e = \sum_{x=0}^{c} \binom{n}{x} p_e^{x}(1-p_e)^{n-x}$$

To illustrate the effects of inspection error on the probability of acceptance let us consider a typical sampling plan which was selected and evaluated by Collins *et al.* (1973). Specifically, the lot size, sample size, and acceptance number were selected as $S = 4000$, $n = 150$, and $c = 5$, respectively. For this plan several error-pairs, (e_1, e_2) were used and their effects can be witnessed in Figure 1.

Figure 1. Probability of acceptance v incoming quality: $S = 4000$, $n = 150$, $c = 5$.

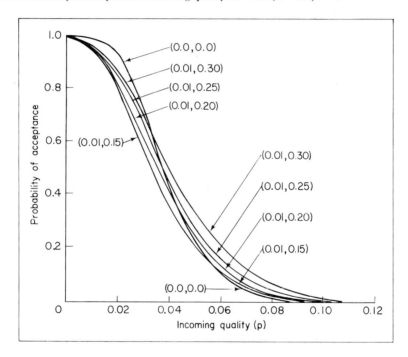

2.2. *Average outgoing quality*

The performance measure 'average outgoing quality' (AOQ) is defined by the ratio

$$AOQ = \frac{\text{expected number of defective items remaining after inspection}}{\text{total number of items in the lot}}$$

If we assume perfect inspection with replacement of defective items, the ratio becomes

$$AOQ = \frac{(S-n)p\,Pa}{S}.$$

When inspection error is present Collins *et al.* (1973) have shown that an expression for the AOQ with replacement can be written as

$$AOQ = [npe_2 + p(S-n)(1-p_e)Pa_e + p(S-n)(1-Pa_e)e_2] \div S(1-p_e).$$

The average outgoing quality without replacement is again the ratio of the number of defective items in the lot to the lot size; however, no defectives are introduced through replacement and there is no replenishment of lot size. For this case, the AOQ when inspection error is present is given by

$$AOQ = \frac{npe_2 + p(S-n)Pa_e + p(S-n)(1-Pa_e)e_2}{S - np_e - (1-Pa_e)(S-n)p_e}.$$

In Figure 2 the average outgoing quality as a function of fraction defective and inspection error is examined for the sampling plan given earlier. Incorrect classification of a good item reduces the average outgoing quality due to the

Figure 2. Average outgoing quality v incoming quality: $S = 4000$, $n = 150$, $c = 5$.

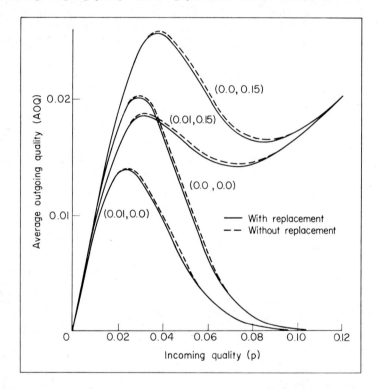

fact that more screening inspection takes place while incorrect classification of a defective item has the effect of causing higher AOQ values for all values of p. Type 2 error also causes a significant change in the shape of the AOQ curve. Near the point at which $Pa_e \to 0$, the AOQ curve rises due to the increased number of defective items classified good as p increases. Further, as $p \to 1$, the AOQ $\to 1$ as a limit. Therefore, for any given sampling plan encompassing Type 2 errors, the conventional concept of the AOQ is not meaningful.

2.3. *Average total inspection with replacement*

The average total 'inspection per lot' (ATI) represents the long run average of total items inspected per lot. It includes the original sample, the screened portion of rejected lots, and all items from the process inspected for replenishment of the lot. When inspection error is present the average total inspection with replacement can be written as Collins *et al.* (1973)

$$\text{ATI} = \frac{n + (1 - Pa_e)(S - n)}{1 - p_e}.$$

The average total inspection with replacement is just the average inspection per lot:

$$\text{ATI} = n + (1 - Pa_e)(S - n).$$

Figures 3 and 4 illustrate the average total inspection as a function of fraction defective and error for the replacement and nonreplacement policies respectively. As intuitively expected, the general effects of Type 1 and Type 2 errors are to

Figure 3. Average total inspection (without replacement) v incoming quality: $S = 4000$, $n = 150$, $c = 5$.

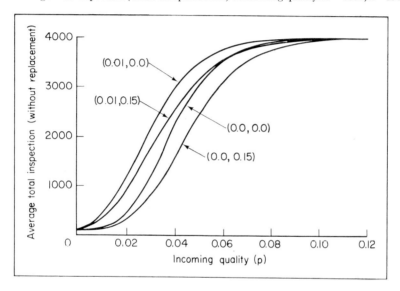

increase or decrease the ATI respectively for any specified incoming fraction defective.

For the example shown, the policy of replacement or nonreplacement does not significantly affect the AOQ. The distinguishing difference between the policies of replacement and nonreplacement is in the ATI values as the fraction defective increases. Under a nonreplacement policy, it can be seen that as $Pa_e \to 0$, $\text{ATI} \to S$. Thus, for large fractions defective and normal ranges of errors, the ATI essentially equals the lot size. Under a replacement policy, as observed, fraction defective $p_e \to 1$, $Pa_e \to 0$, and the ATI increases without bound. Since the policy chosen affects the ATI and thus the incremental quality costs, it will be desirable to consider both policies in the selection of an acceptable plan.

2.4. *Adjusting a single sampling plan*

Each single sampling plan has associated with it an operating characteristic curve. The design of single sampling plans is often based on the choice of two points on this theoretical curve. These points may be the AQL and LTPD, often

Figure 4. Average total inspection (with replacement) v incoming quality: $S=4000$, $n=150$, $c=5$.

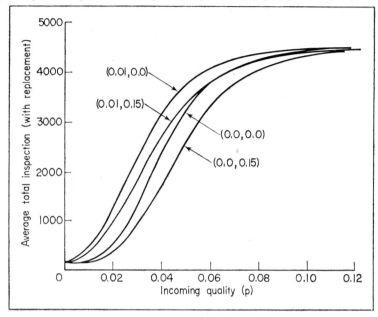

associated with the producer's risk and consumer's risk, respectively. For example, let us define AQL and LTPD as follows:

AQL $\quad=p_{1-\alpha}=$ the actual fraction defective considered to be an acceptable quality level and at which it is desired to accept $(1-\alpha)\times 100$ percent of such lots,

LTPD $=p_{\beta}\quad=$ the actual defective considered to be a lot tolerance limit and at which it is desired to have a $\beta\times 100$ percent probability of accepting such a lot.

Consider the selection of $p_{1-\alpha}$ and p_{β} and the development of a sampling plan assuming perfect inspection. Under conditions of inspection error, the desired AQL and LTPD fractions defective no longer have probabilities of acceptance of $1-\alpha$ and β, respectively. We may, however, force the actual OC curve to fit the desired points.

In order to actually attain levels of $p_{1-\alpha}$ and p_{β} it is only necessary to design the sampling plan for $p_{e,1-\alpha}$ and $p_{e,\beta}$ where

$$\mathrm{AQL}_e=p_{e,1-\alpha}=p_{1-\alpha}(1-e_2)+(1-p_{1-\alpha})e_1$$

and

$$\mathrm{LTPD}_e=p_{e,\beta}=p_{\beta}(1-e_2)+(1-p_{\beta})e_1.$$

If the observed OC curve then fits $p_{e,1-\alpha}$ and $p_{e,\beta}$, the actual OC curve will fit $p_{1-\alpha}$ and p_{β}.

3. Economic effects of inspection error

To examine the effects of inspection error on sampling plan design let us consider some of the results from the work of Bennett *et al* (1974). In particular, let us consider the situation where defectives in both the sample and rejected lots are repaired. For this case, the cost of the decision to accept a lot containing u defectives after n items are sampled and x defectives are found is,

$$T_a = c_i n + c_r x + c_a u$$

where c_i is the cost of inspecting an item, c_r the cost of repairing an item, and c_a the cost of accepting a defective item. The cost of the decision to reject a lot is given by

$$T_r = c_i S + c_r(u + x)$$

where S is the lot size.

When inspection error is present the above expressions become

$$T_a = (c_i + c_r e_1)n + (c_r \epsilon + c_a e_2)x + c_a u$$

and

$$T_r = (c_i + c_r e_1)S + (c_r \epsilon + c_a e_2)x + (c_a e_2 + c_r \epsilon)u$$

where

$$\epsilon = 1 - e_1 - e_2.$$

Table 1. Expected cost of the optimal sampling plan ($n = 126$, $c = 6$) for selected error pairs.

(e_1, e_2)	Cost of acceptance	Cost of rejection	Total cost C'_{TE}	Percentage error Δ_1
	$	$	$	
(0·00, 0·01)	870·51	886·56	1,757·07	0·70
(0·00, 0·03)	872·07	909·40	1,781·47	2·10
(0·00, 0·05)	1,049·36	752·67	1,802·03	3·28
(0·00, 0·10)	1,054·35	801·41	1,855·76	6·36
(0·00, 0·15)	1,059·33	850·16	1,909·49	9·43
(0·01, 0·00)	689·27	1,078·34	1,767·61	1·30
(0·01, 0·01)	689·84	1,091·47	1,781·31	2·09
(0·01, 0·03)	690·98	1,117·73	1,808·71	3·66
(0·01, 0·05)	875·01	939·45	1,814·46	3·99
(0·01, 0·10)	878·90	996·57	1,875·47	7·48
(0·01, 0·15)	882·80	1,053·69	1,936·49	10·98
(0·03, 0·00)	342·98	1,539·40	1,882·38	7·88
(0·03, 0·01)	343·19	1,555·68	1,898·87	8·83
(0·03, 0·03)	512·13	1,358·09	1,870·22	7·18
(0·03, 0·05)	512·88	1,387·66	1,900·54	8·92
(0·03, 0·10)	514·74	1,461·59	1,976·33	13·27
(0·03, 0·05)	516·60	1,535·53	2,052·13	17·61
(0·05, 0·00)	92·05	1,978·54	2,070·59	18·67
(0·05, 0·01)	92·07	1,996·91	2,088·98	19·72
(0·05, 0·03)	92·12	2,033·67	2,125·79	21·83
(0·05, 0·05)	92·17	2,070·42	2,162·59	23·94
(0·05, 0·10)	201·32	1,961·45	2,162·77	23·95
(0·05, 0·15)	201·79	2,048·97	2,250·76	28·99
(0·10, 0·00)	26·28	2,204·28	2,230·56	27·84
(0·10, 0·01)	26·28	2,223·14	2,249·42	28·92
(0·10, 0·03)	26·28	2,260·87	2,287·15	31·08
(0·10, 0·05)	26·28	2,298·61	2,234·89	33·24
(0·10, 0·10)	26·28	2,392·93	2,419·21	38·65
(0·10, 0·15)	26·28	2,487·26	2,513·54	44·05
(0·15, 0·00)	26·65	2,291·52	2,318·17	32·86
(0·15, 0·01)	26·65	2,310·39	2,337·04	33·94
(0·15, 0·03)	26·65	2,348·12	2,374·77	36·10
(0·15, 0·05)	26·65	2,385·85	2,412·50	38·26
(0·15, 0·10)	26·65	2,480·18	2,506·83	43·67
(0·15, 0·15)	26·65	2,574·51	2,601·16	49·07

Inspection error

Now let us consider the case where sampling inspection is hypergeometric and the number of defectives in an inspection lot can be described by a *Polya* distribution with parameters n' and x'. In particular, let us consider a specific example where the quality costs and prior parameters are

$$
\begin{aligned}
c_i &= \$2\text{·}00 & x' &= 3 \\
c_r &= \$1\text{·}90 & n' &= 60 \\
c_a &= \$40\text{·}00 &
\end{aligned}
$$

Substitution of these values into the error-free assumption model and optimizing for the minimum cost sampling plan yields the plan $(n = 126, c = 6)$ at an expected cost per lot of $1,744·87. See Bennett *et al.* (1974) for details on the optimization of the model.

Using the cost and distributional parameters above the model was evaluated at the optimal plan $(n = 126, c = 6)$ for various combinations of inspection errors (e_1, e_2). The results of these evaluations are listed in Table 1. These results show the effects of using the error-free sampling plan $(n = 126, c = 6)$ when error is present. Note that for several error pairs the effects are substantial. For example, if the inspection process includes errors of $(e_1 = 0\text{·}10, e_2 = 0\text{·}15)$ then the true expected total cost is $2,513·54, not $1,744·87 as one would be led to believe if he was unaware of existing inspection error. Also listed is the percentage error. For the error pair $(e_1 = 0\text{·}10, e_2 = 0\text{·}15)$ the percentage error is,

$$
\frac{\$2,513\text{·}54 - \$1,744\text{·}87}{\$1,744\text{·}87} \times 100 = 44\text{·}05\%
$$

In general, the percentage error is defined by

$$
\Delta_1 = \frac{(C'_{TE} - C_T)}{C_T} \times 100
$$

where

$C_T = \$1,744\text{·}87$, the expected total cost of the optimal sampling plan when the inspection process is error-free,

and

$C'_{TE} =$ the expected total cost of the optimal sampling plan under the assumption that the inspection process is error-free, when inspection error is present.

Table 2 lists the results obtained from optimizing the model when inspection error is acknowledged as being present. These results give the optimal sampling plan and its expected cost when inspection error is included into the design. Also provided is a measure of the error one suffers by having an inspection process which is not error free. This result is expressed as a relative percentage and is defined by the relation,

$$
\Delta_2 = \frac{(C'_T - C_T)}{C_T} \times 100
$$

where

$C'_T =$ the expected total cost of the optimal sampling plan when it is assumed that inspection error is present.

For example, if the inspection process includes errors of $(e_1 = 0\text{·}10, e_2 = 0\text{·}15)$ then $C'_T = \$1,945\text{·}78$.

Table 2. Optimal sampling plan for selected error pairs.

(e_1, e_2)	Optimal sample plan (n, c)	Cost of acceptance	Cost of rejection	Total cost C'_T	Percentage error Δ_2
		$	$	$	
(0·00, 0·01)	(117, 6)	958·52	797·97	1,756·49	0·67
(0·00, 0·03)	(117, 6)	960·15	819·07	1,779·22	1·97
(0·00, 0·05)	(110, 6)	1,036·46	764·68	1,801·14	3·22
(0·00, 0·10)	(101, 5)	1,145·07	707·57	1,852·64	6·18
(0·00, 0·15)	(77, 4)	1,265·69	632·47	1,898·16	8·79
(0·01, 0·00)	(117, 7)	959·07	793·88	1,752·95	0·46
(0·01, 0·01)	(117, 7)	959·88	804·43	1,764·31	1·11
(0·01, 0·03)	(115, 7)	982·38	804·58	1,786·96	2·41
(0·01, 0·05)	(110, 7)	1,037·81	770·52	1,808·33	3·64
(0·01, 0·10)	(101, 6)	1,146·39	712·61	1,859·00	6·54
(0·01, 0·15)	(77, 5)	1,266·76	636·69	1,903·45	9·09
(0·03, 0·00)	(117, 9)	961·80	806·79	1,768·59	1·36
(0·03, 0·01)	(115, 9)	983·45	796·47	1,779·92	2·01
(0·03, 0·03)	(110, 9)	1,038·82	762·62	1,801·44	3.24
(0·03, 0·05)	(109, 9)	1,051·63	770·99	1,822·62	4·46
(0·03, 0·10)	(84, 7)	1,163·03	708·52	1,871·55	7·26
(0·03, 0·15)	(76, 6)	1,283·99	629·83	1,913·82	9·68
(0·05, 0·00)	(110, 11)	1,038·99	744·93	1,783·92	2·24
(0·05, 0·01)	(110, 11)	1,039·84	754·72	1,794·56	2·85
(0·05, 0·03)	(109, 11)	1,052·63	763·14	1,815·77	4·06
(0·05, 0·05)	(105, 11)	1,100·05	736·24	1,836·29	5·24
(0·05, 0·10)	(81, 8)	1,208·34	674·79	1,883·13	7·92
(0·05, 0·15)	(71, 7)	1,363·56	560·25	1,923·81	10·26
(0·10, 0·00)	(105, 16)	1,102·43	717·11	1,819·54	4·28
(0·10, 0·01)	(103, 16)	1,126·74	702·88	1,829·62	4·86
(0·10, 0·03)	(101, 15)	1,152·17	696·73	1,848·90	5·96
(0·10, 0·05)	(81, 12)	1,210·16	657·54	1,867·70	7·04
(0·10, 0·10)	(76, 12)	1,287·75	621·88	1,909·63	9·44
(0·10, 0·15)	(64, 10)	1,479·96	465·82	1,945·78	11·51
(0·15, 0·00)	(101, 20)	1,156·15	695·69	1.851·84	6·13
(0·15, 0·01)	(81, 16)	1,212·71	648·38	1,861·09	6·66
(0·15, 0·03)	(77, 15)	1,272·92	605·76	1,878·68	7·67
(0·15, 0·05)	(76, 15)	1,289·38	605·71	1,895·09	8·61
(0·15, 0·10)	(69, 14)	1,401·55	531·43	1,932·98	10·78
(0·15, 0·15)	(62, 13)	1,517·09	447·45	1,964·54	12·59

It is also instructive to note the percentage error which results when the sampling plan ($n = 126$, $c = 6$) is used instead of the optimal sampling plan when inspection error is present. In this case the percentage error is defined by

$$\Delta_3 = \frac{(C'_{TE} - C'_T)}{C'_T} \times 100$$

These results are listed in Table 3. For example, if the inspection process includes errors of ($e_1 = 0·10$, $e_2 = 0·15$) then by designing for inspection error the total cost per lot can be reduced by $567·76.

4. Conclusion

A major purpose of this paper was to illustrate the effects, both statistical and economic, that inspection error can have on a quality control system. At this time the reader should be convinced that inspection error should not be taken lightly. It does, as we have seen, severely distort quality objectives and cause increased

Table 3. Percentage error realized by using plan ($n=126, c=6$) instead of the optimal plan when inspection error is present.

(e_1, e_2)	Total cost C'_{TE}	Total cost C'_T	Percentage error Δ_3
	\$	\$	
(0·00, 0·01)	1,757·07	1,756·49	0·03
(0·00, 0·03)	1,781·47	1,779·22	0·13
(0·00, 0·05)	1,802·03	1,801·14	0·05
(0·00, 0·10)	1,855·76	1,852·64	0·17
(0·00, 0·15)	1,909·49	1,898·16	0·60
(0·01, 0·00)	1,767·61	1,752·95	0·84
(0·01, 0·01)	1,781·31	1,764·31	0·96
(0·01, 0·03)	1,808·71	1,786·96	1·22
(0·01, 0·05)	1,814·46	1,808·33	0·34
(0·01, 0·10)	1,875·47	1,859·00	0·89
(0·01, 0·15)	1,936·49	1,903·45	1·74
(0·03, 0·00)	1,882·38	1,768·59	6·43
(0·03, 0·01)	1,898·87	1,779·92	6·68
(0·03, 0·03)	1,870·22	1,801·44	3·82
(0·03, 0·05)	1,900·54	1,822·62	4·28
(0·03, 0·10)	1,976·33	1,871·55	5·60
(0·03, 0·15)	2,052·13	1,913·82	7·23
(0·05, 0·00)	2,070·59	1,783·92	16·07
(0·05, 0·01)	2,088·98	1,794·56	16·41
(0·05, 0·03)	2,125·79	1,815·77	17·07
(0·05, 0·05)	2,162·59	1,836·29	17·77
(0·05, 0·10)	2,162·77	1,883·13	14·85
(0·05, 0·15)	2,250·76	1,923·81	16·99
(0·10, 0·00)	2,230·56	1,819·54	22,59
(0·10, 0·01)	2,249·42	1,829·62	22·94
(0·10, 0·03)	2,287·15	1,848·90	23·70
(0·10, 0·05)	2,324·89	1,867·70	24·48
(0·10, 0·10)	2,419·21	1,909·63	26·68
(0·10, 0·15)	2,513·54	1,945·78	29·18
(0·15, 0·00)	2,318·17	1,851·84	25·18
(0·15, 0·01)	2,337·04	1,861·09	25·57
(0·15, 0·03)	2,374·77	1,878·68	26·41
(0·15, 0·05)	2,412·50	1,895·09	27·30
(0·15, 0·10)	2,506·83	1,932·98	26·69
(0·15, 0·15)	2,601·16	1,964·54	32·41

costs. To assume error-free inspection for the sake of mathematically tractible model building just cannot be rationally justified. Designs must incorporate inspection error into the model building phases of analysis if quality control systems are to be accurately represented. This incorporation, however, cannot be achieved until we better understand the source of this error and are able to accurately measure it. Then and only then will we be truly on our way to accurate modelling of quality control systems. An attempt at better understanding of the source of this area is the major purpose of the papers which follow in this book.

References

BENNETT, G. K., CASE, K. E., and SCHMIDT, J. W., 1974, The economic effects of inspector error on attribute sampling plans. *Naval Research Logistics Quarterly*, **21**, 431–443.

COLLINS, R. D., CASE, K. E., and BENNETT, G. K., 1973, The effects of inspection error on single sampling inspection plans. *International Journal of Production Research*, **11**, 289–298.

HALD, A., 1960, The compound hypergeometric distribution and a system of single sampling plans based on prior distributions and costs. *Technometrics*, **2**, 275–340.

JACOBSON, H. J., 1952, A study of inspector accuracy. *Industrial Quality Control*, **9**, 16–25.

The imperfect inspector

C. G. Drury and J. G. Fox

1. Human factors and the inspector's errors

Statistical quality control schemes, as they have been designed almost exclusively in the past, have concerned themselves with perfect inspectors. Any quality control textbook will show an elaborate proliferation of schemes which have been based on the assumption of the 100% efficient inspector. *A priori*, or from practice, or from available psychological data, it is readily apparent that such an assumption is unwarranted. Intrinsically, man is rarely perfect in either detection or diagnosis and it can be said with confidence that operating as an inspector he has never been provided with the stringently controlled physical conditions for performing optimally in these respects. As a consequence the schemes are frequently found not to work in practice. This has led in recent years to studies which have demonstrated the effects inspector's errors can have on sampling plans and the need to take account of realistic values of inspector's errors. The *Prologue* represents one such study.

The mathematics of including human error in quality control schemes are not at all daunting. Even the calculation of numerical estimates of systems' performance for specific levels of human error is not difficult by hand. With electronic computers it is possible to turn the calculations into routines simple enough to be used as a matter of course in industry. Most textbooks on statistical quality control and probability theory have used examples of error prone inspection in teaching aids. The concepts are simple: the human inspector behaves like any other sampling scheme with its own Type 1 and Type 2 errors linked in series in the main sampling scheme. Equally the problems of physically designing inspection systems are rarely insurmountable. The technology of the hardware for most inspection tasks, where efficiency is almost totally dependent on the sensory and decision capacities of the inspector, is not often complex.

If the concepts, the mathematics, the calculations and the hardware to accommodate realistic evaluations of an inspector's behaviour are all relatively simple, then clearly the demand to take account of realistic values of inspector behaviour rests on an understanding and a means of accurate measurement of the inspector's errors. Understanding and measurement in their turn require the availability of theories and models of human behaviour and a data base of inspector performance under varying conditions of practice.

Some thirty years of concentrated human factors, or ergonomics, research on the many facets of human inspection activity have gone a considerable way to provide both the theories and the models and the data base: the latter from an ever increasing and complex matrix of tasks, ethnic groups and the sexes. It is no longer necessary to accept simplisticly that 'human nature' is the reason an inspector who consistently picks-up minute faults will occasionally lapse and miss one glaringly obvious, even to the layman. There is no reason that a quality control scheme should carry such an obvious handicap without taking account of it, either statistically or physically. The behaviour is predictable: its magnitude, cause and frequency can be described in some measure and estimated with significant accuracy from established data.

Of course, if it would be naive to accept 'human nature' as the root of the inspector's inaccuracies, it would be no less so to look to existing human factors data as the panacea for the ills the human being brings to quality control schemes. In another context he has been described as a 'vocal adaptive controller'. Such qualities give him tremendous advantages, but make him rather difficult to handle mathematically. For example, being 'adaptive' means on the one hand, he is flexible, adapting to a range of different situations or directives: on the other, it makes any description of him dependent on the particular situation and history in which he is embedded. Similarly 'vocal' means the operator can give useful information on subjective effects such as estimating magnitudes: and he can give early warning of overload and take appropriate action. But it also means that the operator will have his say about the situation as he finds it. The inspector will have his own views on whether the adaptation demanded of him is reasonable and in the limit these views can be expressed through the feet. Human satisfaction is among the numerous factors as yet not accounted for in human factors models and this will ensure that even the perfect conjoining of statistical quality control models with human performance models will not lead to 100% effective inspection systems.

Nevertheless, although zero errors may be a myth in human inspection systems, an injection of human factors data into standard quality control schemes can do much to reduce the error rates of 20–30% which are quoted. The human factors engineer may have yet to generate an exact model of the inspector's performance but he has moved us along the road from the situation of being forced to use unrealistic assumptions about human operators because of lack of any method of predicting his performance. It is now a question of predicting the changes in performance from a known baseline, attributable to the effects of many inputs to the human inspector. As with any of man's practical tools, methods of predicting inspection performance will be refined and sharpened over the years.

2. Human factors and the inspector's task
Giving it the briefest task description, the inspector's function is to search, recognize a fault and make a decision on its acceptability within the quality limits. In these crucial areas, human engineering data and theories have progressed to predictive models which have operational value. The inspector's performance cannot always be completely described simply by the search and decision models however. With prolonged periods of inspection it is commonly observed that fault detection deteriorates as a function of time. Thus human engineering data and models related to vigilance have relevance for predicting performance.

2.1. *Human search behaviour*
Inspection is often categorized as being 'with or without search'. In the final analysis it is difficult to maintain the distinction, for during inspection of even the smallest object either the eye or the object moves and essentially a search

pattern is produced. How intrinsic search is to inspection performance may be deduced from a report by Grindley and Townsend (1970) which suggests that with foreknowledge of specific fault characteristics the inspector will carry out some routine of activity analogous to visual search without eye movements which contributes to improved performance. The importance of the problem has been demonstrated most convincingly by Wallis and Samuel (1961) who presented very strong evidence that some parts of a display tend to be 'favoured' even although the appearance of faults is equiprobable everywhere. They suggested that scanning may incorporate biases away from the theoretically optimal search and may be the cause of surprising irregularities in the level of efficiency which appear from time to time.

Since the Wallis and Samuel study there have been many studies which have elucidated the mysteries of search performance. Among the most significant have been those by Howarth and Bloomfield (1969 and 1971) which have provided a framework in which solutions to practical search problems may be attempted. From known characteristics of the eye and a theory of visual search, an equation has been developed relating the extent to which a faulty item deviates from the ideal to the time to locate it. From the evidence they present, it should be possible to predict the proportion of faulty items detected as a function of the time allowed for search.

2.2. *Fault recognition and decision making*

A detailed examination of an inspector's failures reveal them to be of two types: failure to detect a fault and falsely reporting the presence of a fault. The 'false rejection' is not a casual process but appears to be related to fault detection efficiency. This relationship has led to the use of the theory of signal detection (TSD) as a model for the decision process.

Put briefly, this theory, which Swets (1964) translated from communication engineering to human behaviour, proposes that the human, functioning as a fault detection device, builds up in his neural system two distributions of activity: one relating to the probability of his accepting an item (P_A), the other to the probability of his rejecting it (P_R). The degree of separation of these two distributions is a measure of the inspector's *sensitivity* (or the *discriminability* of the defects) designated d' and available for mathematical treatment. Physically such sensitivity is determined by training to discriminate faults and to assess their probability of occurrence and by standard ergonomic factors in the viewing conditions of the workplace. It is hypothesized that two distributions will overlap and it is therefore necessary to superimpose a 'criterion level' which delineates the boundary between accept and reject, and which in doing so takes in some good items to be rejected and some faulty items to be accepted. The 'criterion level' introduces another mathematical measure, the *likelihood ratio* (β), which relates the relative costs and values of false rejects and correct detections, often simply called the *criterion*. The basic model with two variations applied to inspection is indicated in Figure 1. (It must be noted that for a strict mathematical treatment, it must be assumed that the P_A and P_R distributions have equal variances.)

The descriptive, explanatory and predictive value of the model is immediately apparent. It becomes clear that in all but the 'perfect situation', 100% fault detection cannot be expected: that false detection is an intrinsic part of the

Figure 1. The theory of signal detection applied to fault rejection.

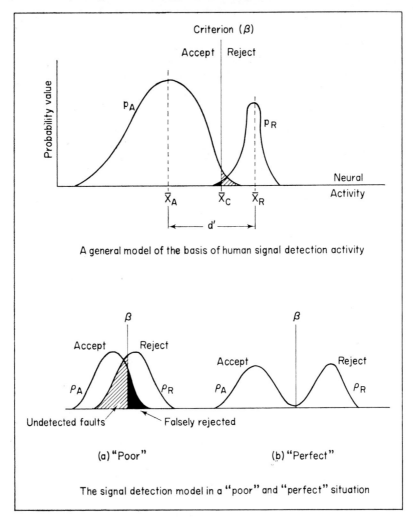

A general model of the basis of human signal detection activity

The signal detection model in a "poor" and "perfect" situation

activity: and that in 'normal circumstances' improved fault detection may only be achieved at the cost of an increase in the level of false scrap. The mathematical properties of the model being known, it is possible to determine the numerical values of true and false rejections for a given situation and prediction of performance can be made. This, of course, makes the model a most useful tool to management. Apart from providing a prediction of performance, it allows a selection of values to give the required A.Q.L. with knowledge of the cost in relation to false detections and hence the need or otherwise to carry out a further check on the rejects. If the cost involved in rejecting good items is high, the manufacturer may be inclined to send back the rejects for re-inspection. Eilon (1962) has analysed several models which indicate under which circumstances such a recirculation policy has value.

The exploitations of the theory of signal detection by human factors specialists in inspection problems are legion. However two developments are especially noteworthy. Wallack and Adams (1970) have developed their measurement philosophy in relation to measures based on Bayes' rule. In addition to supporting the theory by demonstrating that an inspector's efficiency is a function of the *a priori* probability of a fault appearing, they demonstrated that performance measures should be selected relative to performance evaluated objectives and that graphs describing sampling plans for ideal inspectors should be modified to reflect performance of real inspectors under actual conditions. Secondly, Drury and Addison (1973) have shown how the values of the TSD parameters d' and β can be extracted from production-inspection data.

2.3. *Vigilance*

An inspector's performance cannot be completely described by the decision and search models, however. With prolonged inspection periods it is commonly observed that fault detection deteriorates as a function of time. The rate of deterioration can be rapid: drops of 40% in 30 minutes have been reported. As many paced inspection tasks are carried out for periods well in excess of half-an-hour, the implication of the phenomenon for quality assurance can be serious and an understanding of its basis is correspondingly important. In the event, the interested quality engineer will find not one but several theories to explain this behaviour. For practical purposes it is unlikely that the engineer will look beyond that based on the theory of vigilance which essentially develops from the ideas of Hebb (1955). Whatever comparisons may be made between it and its rivals it does allow prediction of performance and suggests appropriate measures to prevent deterioration in performance.

Figure 2. Possible criterion factors determining the efficiency of visual inspection.

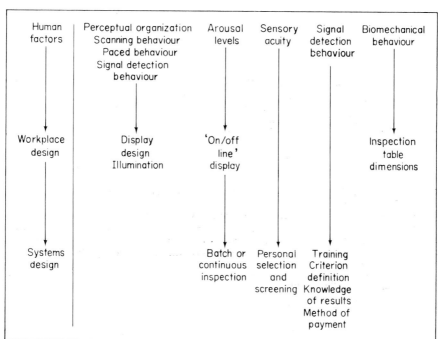

2.4. *The design of inspection systems*

Prediction and measurement of performance are, of course, in themselves only half the story for the practicing quality control engineer. With the measure or prediction of a system that is less than optimal his job may just be beginning. He must then turn his attention to the design of an improved system. Here in immediate practical terms, the work of human engineering specialists of the last thirty years which has produced the corrollaries to these theories is invaluable to the quality control engineer.

For example, search theory has its implications for the design of illuminating or pacing an inspection task: the theory of signal detection has relevance to training, or feedback of inspector's performance: the theories of vigilance may have their implications for the physical environment or job organization. Each particular inspection system will have its own particular facets which can be optimized by reference to the theories. A not atypical relationship between the theories and practical design is illustrated in Figure 2 which is taken from a study by Fox (1964) on the visual inspection of newly minted coins. From Figure 2 it will be seen that identifying the physical parameters involved in defining inspection performance is no small task and producing an integrated solution can be complex. Yet solutions to these problems by human factors specialists in recent years have been many and a perusal of a selection can give the key features to be attacked in future problems.

3. Conclusions

Human factors data, it is evident, have a significant contribution to make to industrial quality control. They lay the basis for the use of models which will allow prediction and measurement of performance and they give guidance for the design of improved inspection systems. The evidence for this claim has only been sketched out in this paper, the substance of the claim will come as the other papers of the volume unfold.

References

DRURY, C. G., and ADDISON, J. L., 1973, An industrial study of the effects of feedback and fault density on inspection performance. *Ergonomics*, **16**, 159–169.

EILON, S., 1962, Recirculation of products through an inspection station. *International Journal of Production Research*, **1**, 39–44.

FOX, J. G., 1964, The ergonomics of coin inspection. *Quality Engineer*, **28**, 165–169.

GRINDLEY, G. C., and TOWNSEND, V., 1970, Visual search without eye movement. *Quarterly Journal of Experimental Psychology*, **22**, 62–67.

HEBB, D. O., 1955, Drives and the C.N.S. (Conceptual Nervous System). *Psychological Review*, **62**, 243–254.

HOWARTH, C. I., and BLOOMFIELD, J. R., 1969, A rational equation for predicting search times in simple inspection tasks. *Psychonomic Science*, **17**, 225–226.

HOWARTH, C. I., and BLOOMFIELD, J. R., 1971, The application of visual search theory to industrial inspection tasks. *Paper to the Ergonomics Research Society Annual Conference, Cranfield.*

SWETS, J. A., 1964, *Signal Detection and Recognition by Human Observers.* (New York: WILEY.)

WALLACK, P. M., and ADAMS, S. K., 1970, A comparison of inspector performance measures. *AIIE Transactions*, **11**, 97–105.

WALLIS, D., and SAMUEL, J. H., 1961, Some experimental studies in radar operating. *Ergonomics*, **14**, 155–168.

1. Models of inspector performance

Theoretical approaches to visual search

J. R. Bloomfield

1. Introduction

1.1. *Eye movements and visual search*

Our eyes move constantly. We focus them on one point then another, never lingering in one place. The time taken for an eye movement is very short. It moves through an angular distance of 15° in approximately 1/20 second (Yarbus 1967). We make many discrete fixations. On average, there are three fixations per second, or 180 per minute.

From a series of brief pictures of relatively small areas, we arrive at a complex perceptual experience where a very large visual field is 'seen' in clear detail and in depth. This vivid impression of the real world, is reconstructed from a succession of brief retinal images; we do not see the whole scene at a glance. This is also the case when we are searching or are inspecting an object, whether it is a steel sheet or a transistor.

1.2. *Peripheral visual acuity*

When we fixate on a point, we see with maximum sensitivity down the line of sight. We are progressively less sensitive as points successively farther away from the line of sight are considered. The decrease in sensitivity is linear, as Figure 1 shows. This plotted data was obtained from Wertheim's (1894) classic study using a low contrast target in a uniform background.

Unfortunately, visual acuity is often defined as the reciprocal of the minimum resolvable angle, measured in minutes of arc. This has led to the erroneous view that peripheral acuity decreases rapidly initially as one moves away from the fovea, then more slowly as the far periphery is reached. Low (1951), Weymouth (1958) and Bloomfield (1972b) have pointed out that a more accurate picture of peripheral acuity is obtained if the minimum resolvable angle itself is plotted against eccentricity. To summarize, peripheral acuity falls off gradually and approximately linearly, as one moves from the fovea into the periphery, and in the far periphery it falls off more rapidly.

In studies of visual search, it has been shown that search performance and peripheral acuity are related. The correlation has been found with targets presented amongst competing nontargets (Smith 1961, Erickson 1964, Johnston 1965, Bloomfield and Howarth 1969), for targets presented against a plain background (Bloomfield 1970), and for textured targets embedded in a textured background (Bloomfield *et al.* 1974).

On the basis of these findings, one would expect correlations between inspection performance and peripheral visual acuity. However, Harris and Chaney (1969,

Figure 1. Wertheim's (1894) peripheral acuity data shown in terms both of the visual angle sub-tended at the eye and of its reciprocal (adapted from Low 1951).

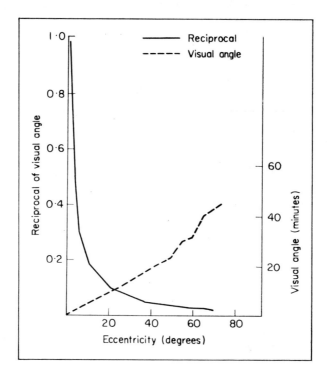

p. 171) state that 'little has resulted from attempts to predict inspection performance from measures of visual acuity'. This statement is accurate, but also misleading. Measures of visual acuity are typically made on the line of sight, at the fovea. Because of this, the target must be very small or very dim; it has to be at the limits of the observer's performance. The discrimination that has to be made is usually very different from that required in inspection tasks. However, if the same visual discrimination is required when making both measurements, it should be possible to demonstrate a relationship between inspection performance and peripheral visual acuity.

1.3. *Investigations of visual search*

There are two methods for investigating search. First, the materials and conditions of the real environment may be used either directly, by field trials, or indirectly, by simulation. Second, we can abstract those features of the task which seem important, and perform laboratory studies in which these parameters are examined. Most theories of search have been developed with laboratory studies.

Because of the variety and complexity of search tasks and processes, it is not easy to theorize about them. However, this is no excuse for the lack of thought and rigour that have distinguished some search models.

2. Theoretical approaches to visual search

2.1. *Ideal search*

Ideal observer. At the National Academy of Sciences 'Symposium on Visual Search' (1960) Tanner and Jones presented what they hoped was a 'general model of an ideal observer applicable to any search problem'. Their model was derived from statistical decision theory, and was derived with all the mathematical skill one has come to expect from Tanner. However, they did not show the way in which the ideal observer model is to be applicable to 'any search problem'. Edwards (1960) states 'Tanner throws away both searching and the searcher'. He also points out that Tanner and Jones treat the observer as being equivalent to an ideal observer faced with a lower signal-to-noise ratio than is actually present. Thus, noise becomes an intervening variable. This would be acceptable, except that Tanner and Jones did not suggest how this might be related to the situational variables. In fact, the paper does no more than present a slightly different version of decision theory's ideal observer, leaving all the work of applying the idea to search, assuming that it can be applied, to someone else.

Ideal strategies. Harris (1960) in the same symposium also discussed the ideal strategies for various search problems. He followed Tanner directly, and the contrast must have been quite striking, since Harris approached the problems of search head on.

He considered the visual detection lobe, i.e. the three dimensional region within which a target can be seen. He pointed out that the size of this region changes with adaptation level of the eye, target shape, size, pattern and motion, fixation duration, background factors and atmospheric transmission.

Harris described the ideal strategies in plain, uniform backgrounds for the detection of a target that is stationary, one that is moving radially towards the observer, and one that is moving laterally with (i) known velocity and direction, (ii) unknown velocity and direction. For these situations, he described the method by which the upper limit of search performance can be achieved, in fact, going some way towards what Tanner and Jones attempted to do.

2.2. *Descriptive models*

Three other theoretical approaches, made at the same symposium, have certain common points. All depend on the idea of search intervals and how they are related. But, they are descriptive models and are in no way related to target/background characteristics.

Search acts. Miller and Ludvigh (1960) suggested that search proceeds in 'search acts'. They derived the probability of a detection occurring on the nth search act, in terms of p, the probability of success in a single search act, the obtained search time, reaction time and the time for a search act. By arbitrarily assuming reaction time and search time values they were able to derive p. This procedure allows comparisons between conditions. However, Miller and Ludvigh treated their derived ps as though they were meaningful enough to allow them to dismiss the hypothesis that search was systematic and exhaustive for their observers. This last step is a dubious one.

Random delays. McGill (1960) proposed a model involving two random delays, one for reaction time, the other for what he described as 'active searching' ('active' sits uneasily with the idea of randomness). This model, which as McGill suggested is probably too simple, leads to the same equations as a, perhaps, more realistic model. In this, the search area is divided by the observer into small regions, which are searched in turn. Since the targets are positioned randomly with respect to the observer's fixation pattern, and since McGill assumed that the time needed to search each region has an exponential density function, it is possible to reduce the complex search delay function to the simpler one. For both models McGill obtained the equation:

$$f(t) = \frac{\alpha\beta}{\beta-\alpha} [e^{-\alpha t} - e^{-\beta t}] \tag{1}$$

where $f(t)$ is the search time distribution and α and β are the constants associated with the reaction time and search time respectively. The mean of this equation is given by:

$$t = \frac{1}{\alpha} + \frac{1}{\beta} \tag{2}$$

By plotting the cumulative distributions for his increasing density (and number) competition task on semilog scales and fitting straight lines, McGill obtained estimates of $-\alpha$ and $1/\beta$ from the gradient and intercept values respectively. The agreement between mean search time, t, predicted from equation (2) with these obtained α and β values, and the actual time is quite good. Interestingly the ratio of α to β is virtually constant for all four of McGill's display densities.

As well as being unrelated to the target discrimination task the observers must carry out, this model is non-predictive, except in the very general sense that one might expect cumulative search time distributions to be roughly exponential in form. But we knew already that they were.

Exponential glimpse theory. Krendel and Wodinsky (1960) used a more traditional model. Based on some ideas of Lamar (1946), its basic unit was the fixation pause or glimpse. If glimpses are independent of each other, and p_s is the probability that the target will be detected in a single glimpse, then the probability that the target will be located within a time, T, since search began is:

$$P_T = 1 - (1 - p_s)^{T/t_s} \tag{3}$$

where t_s is the fixation duration. (This notation is not the same as Krendel and Wodinsky's. Also they included the time between fixations in the term that t_s replaces. This is omitted here as it is small relative to t_s.)

Plotting search time against percentage of targets detected should produce an exponential curve. On the other hand, a strategy involving exhaustive coverage of the display, with no overlap between glimpses, should produce a linear cumulative distribution on linear coordinates. The exponential function provides a better fit to Krendel and Wodinsky's data.

Assuming that their curves have a common origin with each other and the 100% detected point of the vertical axis, which they do not in some cases, they derived mean times from the semilog plots of their cumulative distributions (the mean, in this case, being the reciprocal of the gradient). They did not compare these derived times with the obtained ones, in the many cases where this was possible. Again the model is descriptive, unrelated to search display characteristics, and non-predictive.

2.3. *Lobes and glimpses*

Early formulation. Another type of theoretical model was presented at the 'Visual Search Techniques' symposium. Here, Lamar (1960) updated his 1946 formulations. Using the contrast threshold data of Craik (1946), he produced equations to define the visual detection lobe. These were used in combination with an exponential glimpse model. Lamar's final equation is

$$P(x,y) = 1 - \exp\left[(1/vT) \int_{y}^{ym} \log(1-g)\, dy\right] \qquad (4)$$

where $P(x,y)$ is the probability of detecting the target by the time it has reached a position identified by its x and y coordinates, v is target velocity, T fixation time, and g the glimpse probability related both to search area and the visual lobe equations.

Lamar was in error, when he said that a reduction in T, the fixation time, leading to more fixations per unit time, will increase $P(x,y)$. As Harris (1960) mentioned, lobe size varies with fixation time. A reduction in T will be associated with a reduction in g. Under these circumstances $P(x,y)$ may or may not vary. Lamar's formulation, unlike the others discussed so far, can be used predictively. He was able to fit flight data for air-to-air and air-to-sea situations, though he assumed very large fixation times to do it: values so large (1·65 seconds) that they are unrealistic.

Lobe calculations. Gordon (1964) showed how similar calculations to those of Lamar can be made from more recent data than Craik's. These calculations are, however, not checked against any empirical data.

Recent work. The most extensive work along these lines is by Davies (1965, 1968 a and b, and Davies and Smith 1969). His primary interest is in predicting air-to-ground detection performance. For visual lobe calculations, Davies made use of the Tiffany (Blackwell 1946) eight position search data, with an appropriate degradation constant, for foveal thresholds, combined with the peripheral threshold data of Taylor (in Linge 1961). He treated the visual lobe as if it has a 'hard shell', i.e. as if it has a boundary, such that if the target falls within that boundary it will be detected, whereas if it falls outside no detection will occur. He took the 0·5 isopter as that boundary—a not unreasonable procedure. Search was again treated as a series of independent glimpses, and an equation similar to equation (3) was used. Assuming fixation times *cf* 0·33 to 0·67 second, Davies (1968a) achieved close agreement between theoretical predictions and the empirical data for Krendel and Wodinsky (1960). The theory is also consistent with data from a simulated aircraft approach-visual search experiment by Smith (1966).

Davies attempts to mould his theoretical ideas in accordance with empirical search and visual threshold data. The air-to-ground situation is very complex. As well as the complexities of natural backgrounds and velocity and altitude, which all affect search, navigation and briefing problems are also of great importance. It will take much more time and effort before prediction in this situation is possible with any great accuracy, as opposed to fitting obtained data.

2.4. *Systematic search*

Williams (1966) took a different theoretical approach. He started with the assumption that search is systematic, as opposed to the random fixation process

Figure 2. Hypothetical plot of the probability of detecting a target as a function of time for a systematic search model (from Williams 1967, Figure A2, p A6).

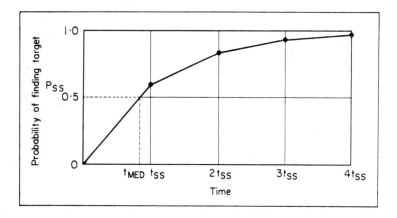

hat most others have assumed. His ideas have branched in two directions.

Limited search time. Both Krendel and Wodinsky (1960) and Davies (1965) point out that, for systematic and efficient search, where the coverage of the search area is exhaustive and there is no overlap of fixations, the cumulative probability of search times after time T, will be given by an equation of the form:

$$P_T = \frac{P_s T}{t_s} \qquad (5)$$

where P_s and t_s are the probability of detection in a single fixation and the fixation duration, respectively.

The exponential equation (3) was derived with the assumption that search was an essentially random process. Williams (1966), saying nothing about exhaustive coverage or overlap, manages to arrive at an exponential equation on the more realistic assumption that search was systematic. If P_{ss}, the probability that the target is detected after a single scan of the search display, is less than 1·0, a series of linear segments should be obtained on a normal cumulative plot, as shown in Figure 2. When P_{ss} is less than 0·6, there will be little difference between the linear segment curve and an exponential curve, based on the percentage detection points that coincide with the end of completed scans of the display. The equation has the form:

$$P_T = 1 - e^{(T/t_{ss}) \cdot \log (1 - P_{ss})} \qquad (6)$$

where P_T is the probability of detection after time T, and t_{ss} and P_{ss} are the time and probability of detection in a single scan.

The remainder of Williams' paper dealt with the special case of search in limited time. He made several predictions but they are in no way peculiar to his theoretical formulation. In a later paper (Williams 1967) he stated that P_{ss} is usually greater than 0·5, while his exponential formulation requires it to be less than 0·6.

Predicting search times. With his second theoretical attempt Williams (1967) goes back to Figure 2. From the geometry of the curve, for P_{ss} 'greater than

0·5 (as it typically is)', median search time can be expressed as a function of scan time and scan probability. This is then converted to:

$$t_{MED} = \frac{\Sigma\, Si}{2R} + D \qquad (7)$$

where t_{MED} is median search time, Si is the proportion of times that an object is expected to be fixated relative to the fixation rate of objects having the specified characteristics of the target, and R is the effective rate of fixation, that is the rate at which stimuli are fixated multiplied by the probability of identifying the target. D is a delay added to account for an orientation period at the beginning and/or verification period at the end of search.

Williams has shown this formulation to be of descriptive and predictive value (Williams *et al.* 1970). However, the concept of Si is not easy to handle in competition tasks where the target is the only object with the specified characteristics, as it is, for example, in the experiments by Smith (1962) and Bloomfield (1972), since it is difficult to obtain fixation rate data for the target. It does not handle tasks in which the observer can reject several nontargets in a single fixation. Nor can it deal with threshold task data.

The theory deals with the case in which for detection, as opposed to distinguishing objects with the specified target characteristic, the target must be fixated centrally.

2.5. *Search and peripheral acuity*

The linear relation between retinal eccentricity and target threshold size is shown in Figure 1. This relationship was used by Howarth and Bloomfield (1968, 1969) to derive equations relating search time to the physical characteristics of the search display. They dealt with a competition task, i.e. one in which the target can be confused with other nontarget objects that are within the search area. Their target was a disc smaller in size than the non-target discs. They show that mean search time t is directly related to physical measures, as follows:

$$t \propto \frac{1}{(d_B - d_T)^2} \qquad (8)$$

where d_B and d_T are the diameters of the nontarget background discs and the target disc respectively (see Figure 1, in Bloomfield 1974).

The equation can be adapted to other search situations. Not surprisingly, it describes the data when size differences with square targets and nontargets are used (Bloomfield *et al.* 1972). However, more interestingly, in the same study it was shown that a size and shape difference can be handled by the equation, which becomes

$$t \propto \frac{1}{(\sqrt{A_B} - \sqrt{A_T})^2} \qquad (9)$$

where A_B and A_T are the areas of the background squares and the rectangular targets respectively (see Figure 2, Bloomfield 1974).

A similar equation is found to describe data from threshold search experiments in which a low contrast target is presented against an unstructured background (Bloomfield 1970 see Figures 7 and 8, Bloomfield 1975). Most recently it has been extended to embedded target (or camouflage) search situations, i.e. situations in which the target does not emerge perceptually from the background because its internal pattern combines in some way with the background. Bloomfield *et al.* (1974) show that mean search time can be related to ratings of discriminability when texture targets that differ primarily in colour from a texture background are used (see Figure 4, Bloomfield 1974). With targets differing primarily in texture, the equation is less successful.

This approach has some predictive power (Bloomfield and Howarth 1969). However, it is conceived at a fairly crude level. It does not have the sophistication of Williams' approach. Nevertheless, it is likely to be of some use in considering inspection problems.

2.6. *Exhaustive but inefficient search*

Many theorists have assumed that observers use a random or independent glimpse search strategy. However, there is evidence that they do not. For example, Enoch (1960) found that observers repeat a similar pattern of eye movements from one trial to the next.

It seems reasonable to assume that observers aim to be systematic in their coverage of a search display. But, while they may set out to be systematic, they may not be very efficient. In fact, in many situations it is difficult, if not impossible to be efficient.

The most efficient strategy will occur under the following conditions. The distance that the eyes move from one fixation to the next should be short enough that no point on the display is missed. At the same time, the distance between fixation points should be large enough to minimize the overlap between the areas in which the target could be seen on either of the two fixations.

However, often the observer will not know the size of the area within which he can detect the target. In this case he will be lucky if he is efficient. Again, he may be looking for two or more targets that differ in discriminability. In this case the efficient strategy for one will be inefficient for the other.

2.7. *Summary*

Search theories have not progressed very far. Tanner and Jones do not even deal with search. Miller and Ludvigh, McGill, and Krendel and Wodinsky provide mathematical descriptions of their data. Harris demonstrates what strategies are needed for optimal search performance under various conditions and Gordon shows how to calculate visual lobes. Using threshold acuity data and exponential glimpse theory, Lamar and Davies have both been able to describe data from flight and simulated flight trials.

Williams, assuming search to involve systematic scanning, makes predictions for the specific competition-specification experiments he has performed. A cruder approach by Howarth and Bloomfield has produced equations that describe search performance in a variety of search situations. Finally, the problems relating to efficient search have been described.

3. Applications to inspection
3.1. *Search theory and inspection*

Theoretical approaches like those of Williams and Howarth and Bloomfield can be illustrated by flow diagrams. Drury (1973) produced a flow diagram

Figure 3. Flow diagram for visual search in inspection.

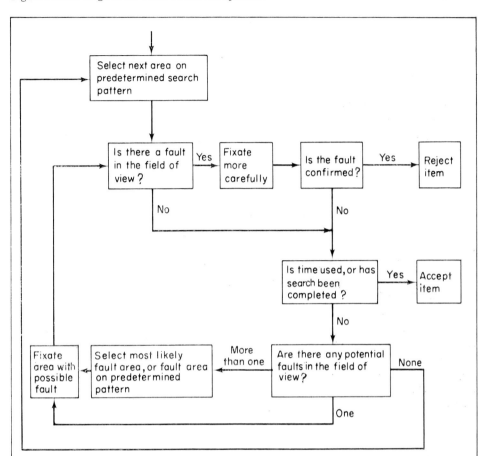

for inspection. This incorporated a simplified search routine. Figure 3 shows Howarth and Bloomfield's (1971) flow diagram for visual search adapted to cover inspection. In effect, it is also a more detailed version of Drury's diagram. The diagram is complex, but it can be related at its various stages to the observer's response and to the way he moves his eyes. Because of this, it is relatively easy to test. A more complete description of inspection performance would entail an expansion of some of the boxes in Figure 3. More detail of the selection, processing and decision operations should be included. However the figure could provide a framework within which the elements of a complete theory of inspection would be integrated.

3.2. *Recommendations*

The equations developed by Howarth and Bloomfield are all based on the correlation between search performance and peripheral visual acuity. All their equations can be reduced to

$$t \propto \frac{1}{D^2} \qquad (10)$$

or

$$\bar{t} \propto \frac{1}{\theta^2} \tag{11}$$

where $\bar{t}$ is average search time, D is the discriminability of the target or fault from the rest of the display, and θ is the extent into the periphery that discrimination can be made.

Knowledge of peripheral visual acuity could be used to improve inspection in terms of individual physical and organizational factors.

Individual factors-selection. An inspector should have good peripheral acuity. If he does not, he will not be able to search quickly and efficiently.

Individual factors-training. An inspector with good peripheral acuity may not perform well at the inspection task. But, he should be trainable. It should be possible to train him to scan the displayed material more efficiently.

Physical factors. An inspection task may be performed badly because insufficient time is given to the inspectors. We can measure the average amount of the display area that can be covered in a single fixation. Then, if we also know the average length of a fixation, it is possible to state how much time should be allowed for the inspector to do an efficient job.

Organizational factors. Faults differ in kind and degree, and will therefore differ in discriminability. Some faults may be more important than others. If the area within which an important fault can be detected in a single fixation is known, a search strategy appropriate for detecting that fault can be devised. With such a strategy, some less important faults, may be missed, because they require a finer search, while others will be located more slowly than they could be, because they can be found using a coarser strategy. However, the inspector will search for the important fault using a relatively efficient strategy.

References

BLACKWELL, H. R., 1946, Contrast thresholds of the human eye. *Journal of the Optical Society of America*, **36**, 624–643.

BLOOMFIELD, J. R., 1970, *Visual Search*. (PH.D. THESIS, UNIVERSITY OF NOTTINGHAM.)

BLOOMFIELD, J. R., 1972a, Visual search on complex fields: size differences between target disc and surrounding discs. *Human Factors*, **14**, 139–148.

BLOOMFIELD, J. R., 1972b, Peripheral acuity with complex stimuli at two viewing distances. In *Air to Ground Target Acquisition*, AGARD Conference Proceedings, No. 100. (Brussels: AGARD.)

BLOOMFIELD, J. R., 1975, Studies on visual search. In: *Human Reliability in Quality Control* (Edited by C. G. DRURY and J. G. FOX.) (London: TAYLOR AND FRANCIS.)

BLOOMFIELD, J. R., BECKWITH, W. E., EMERICK, J., MARMUREK, H. H., TEI, B. E., and TRAUB, B. H., 1974, *Visual Search and Embedded Targets*. (ARI TECHNICAL REPORT.) (In press.)

BLOOMFIELD, J. R., and HOWARTH, C. I., 1969, Testing visual search theory. In *NATO Symposium on Image Evaluation*. (Edited by H. W. LEIBOWITZ.) Pp. 203–214.

BLOOMFIELD, J. R., HOWARTH, C. I., and BONE, K. E., 1972, *Visual Search and Pattern Recognition*. (University of Nottingham Research Report on Contract M.O.D. (P.E.) No. AT/24 018/GC.)

CRAIK, K. J. W., 1946, In *Search and Screening*. (Edited by B. O. KOOPMAN.) (OEG REPORT 56.)

DAVIES, E. B., 1965, *Contrast Thresholds for Air to Ground Vision*. (R.A.E. TECHNICAL REPORT No. 65089.)

DAVIES, E. B., 1968a, *Visual Search Theory with Particular Reference to Air to Ground Vision*. (R.A.E. TECHNICAL REPORT No. 68055.)

DAVIES, E. B., 1968b, Visual theory in target acquisition. In *AGARD Conference Proceedings*, No. 41. (Brussels: AGARD.)

DAVIES, E. B., and SMITH, L. J., 1969, *A Comparison of Visual Search Theory and R.R.E. Experimental Data*. (R.A.E. TECHNICAL REPORT No. 69057.)

DRURY, C. G., 1973, The inspection of sheet materials: model and data. In *Proceedings of the 17th Annual Meeting of the Human Factors Society*. (Edited by M. P. RANC and T. B. MALONE.) Pp. 457–464.

EDWARDS, W., 1960. In *Visual Search Techniques*. (Edited by A. MORRIS and E. P. HORNE.) (Washington: NATIONAL ACADEMY OF SCIENCES.) Pp. 86–89.

ENOCH, J. M., 1960, Natural tendencies in visual search of a complex display. In *Visual Search Techniques*. (Edited by A. MORRIS and E. P. HORNE.) (Washington: NATIONAL ACADEMY OF SCIENCES.) Pp. 184–193.

ERICKSON, R. A., 1964, Relation between visual search time and peripheral visual acuity. *Human Factors*, **6**, 165–177.

GORDON, J. I., 1964, Visual search. *Applied Optics*, **3**, 591–596.

HARRIS, D. H., and CHANEY, F. B., 1969, *Human Factors in Quality Assurance*. (New York: WILEY.)

HARRIS, J. L., 1960, Factors to be considered in developing optimum visual search. In *Visual Search Techniques*. (Edited by A. MORRIS and E. P. HORNE.) (Washington: NATIONAL ACADEMY OF SCIENCES.) Pp. 69–83.

HOWARTH, C. I., and BLOOMFIELD, J. R., 1968, Towards a theory of visual search. In *AGARD Conference Proceedings, No. 41*. (Brussels: AGARD.)

HOWARTH, C. I., and BLOOMFIELD, J. R., 1969, A rational equation for predicting search times in simple inspection tasks. *Psychonomic Science*, **17**, 225–226.

HOWARTH, C. I., and BLOOMFIELD, J. R., 1971, Search and selective attention. *British Medical Bulletin*, **27**, 253–258.

JOHNSTON, D. M., 1965, Search performance as a function of peripheral acuity. *Human Factors*, **7**, 527–535.

KRENDEL, E. S., and WODINSKY, J., 1960, Visual search in unstructured fields. In *Visual Search Techniques*. (Edited by A. MORRIS and E. P. HORNE.) (Washington: NATIONAL ACADEMY OF SCIENCES.) Pp. 151–169.

LAMAR, E. S., 1946, Visual detection. In *Search and Screening*. (Edited by B. O. KOOPMAN.) (OEG REPORT 56.)

LAMAR, E. S., 1960, Operational background and physical considerations relative to visual search problems. In *Visual Search Techniques*. (Edited by A. MORRIS and E. P. HORNE.) (Washington: NATIONAL ACADEMY OF SCIENCES.) Pp. 1–9.

LOW, F. N., 1951, Peripheral visual acuity. *Archives of Ophthalmology*, **45**, 80–99.

McGILL, W. J., 1960, Search distributions in magnified time. In *Visual Search Techniques*. (Edited by A. MORRIS and E. P. HORNE.) (Washington: NATIONAL ACADEMY OF SCIENCES.) Pp. 50–58.

MILLER, J. W., and LUDVIGH, E., 1960, Time required for detection of stationary and moving objects as a function of size in homogeneous and partially structured visual fields. In *Visual Search Techniques*. (Edited by A. MORRIS and E. P. HORNE.) (Washington: NATIONAL ACADEMY OF SCIENCES.) Pp. 170–180.

SMITH, E. S., 1966, *Visual Search for Simulated Approaching Aircraft Targets*. (R.R.E. MEMORANDUM 2259.)

SMITH, S. W., 1961, Visual search time and peripheral discriminability. *Journal of the Optical Society of America*, **51**, 1462 (Abstract).

SMITH, S. W., 1962, Problems in the design of sensor output displays. In *Visual Problems of the Armed Forces*. (Edited by M. A. WHITCOMB.) (Washington: NATIONAL ACADEMY OF SCIENCES.) Pp. 146–157.

TANNER, W. P. JR., and JONES, R. C., 1960, The ideal sensor system as approached through statistical decision theory and the theory of signal detectability. In *Visual Search Techniques*. (Edited by A. MORRIS and E. P. HORNE.) (Washington: NATIONAL ACADEMY OF SCIENCES.) Pp. 59–68.

TAYLOR, J. H., 1961, reported in LINGE, A., *Visual Detection From Aircraft*. (GENERAL DYNAMICS/CONVAIR ENGINEERING RESEARCH REPORT ASTIA 270630.)

WERTHEIM, T., 1894, Über die indirekte sehschärfe. *Zeitschrift für Psychologie und Physiologie der Sinnesorgane*, **7**, 172–187. Cited in Low (1951).

WEYMOUTH, F. W., 1958, Visual sensory units and the minimal angle of resolution. *American Journal of Ophthalmology*, **41**, 102–113.

WILLIAMS, L. G., 1966, Target conspicuity and visual search. *Human Factors*, **8**, 80–92.

WILLIAMS, L. G., 1967, *A Study of Visual Search Using Eye Movement Recordings*. (HONEYWELL DOCUMENT 12009–IR2.)

WILLIAMS, L. G., FAIRCHILD, D. D., GRAF, C. P., JUOLA, J. F., and TRUMM, G. A., 1970, *Visual Search Effectiveness for Night Vision Devices*. (HONEYWELL FINAL REPORT. CONTRACT NO. DAAK02–67–C–0472).

YARBUS, A. L., 1967, *Eye Movements and Vision*. (Translated by B. HAIGH.) (New York: PLENUM PRESS.)

Studies on visual search

J. R. Bloomfield

1. Introduction

Harris and Chaney (1969) defined three basic categories of inspection tasks: those involving scanning, measurement and monitoring. This paper deals with only the first of these using data from both search and inspection studies: but using the terminology of inspection. The discussion covers type of inspection, individual factors and physical factors.

2. Studies related to types of inspection task

In inspection tasks, search or scanning is required when, for some reason, a fault cannot be located immediately. There are three main types of inspection task, that involve scanning: the inspection of simple items, multi-part items or sheets.

Within these three categories various studies of visual inspection have been carried out with particular emphasis on the role of visual search in inspection efficiency.

Figure 1. Relationship between mean search time and discriminability for two observers searching for disc targets among larger nontarget discs (from Howarth and Bloomfield 1969).

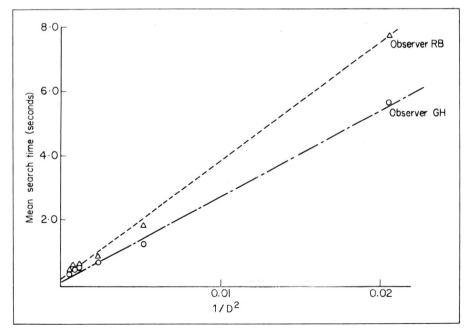

Studies on visual search

2.1. *Displays containing simple items*

In this first type of task the inspector is presented a set of similar small objects. His problem is to distinguish those items that have faults from the good product. The less obtrusive the fault, the harder is his task. In many inspection situations, the degree to which the various faults are different from the good items varies. There does not appear to be any inspection study in which discriminability itself has been investigated. However, it has been investigated in several studies of visual search. Search time can be related to discriminability by the following equation:

$$\bar{t} \propto \frac{1}{D^2} \qquad (1)$$

where $\bar{t}$ is mean search time and D is discriminability.

This equation can be used with targets that differ in size from the nontargets also present within the display area (Howarth and Bloomfield 1969). This is illustrated by Figure 1. The discriminability measure used here is the difference in diameter of the target and background discs. It can also be used with shape and size differences (Bloomfield *et al.* 1972). Figure 2 shows the relationship

Figure 2. Relationship between mean search time and discriminability for two observers searching for rectangular and square targets amongst square nontargets (from Bloomfield *et al.* 1972).

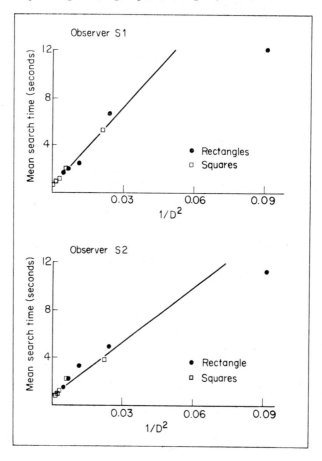

32

when square and variable rectangle targets were used amongst square non-targets. Discriminability here was the difference between the square roots of the areas of the targets and nontargets.

2.2. *Multi-part items*

In the second type of inspection task a single complex object is shown to the inspector. He has to search those features of the object that might be faulty. They may be very different in character from each other. He looks at these heterogeneous features, checking them for damage, dimensions and location. There may be as many as forty faults of various kinds.

Harris (1966) investigated the effect of increasing the complexity of the items. He used ten pieces of electronic equipment. They were rated for complexity, the judgment being made largely in terms of the number of major parts the pieces contained. Each piece was assessed for defects by a group of experts. Then it was inspected. At least eight experienced inspectors looked at each piece individually away from the normal work situation, but with the appropriate tools. They all took much longer than they usually did on routine inspections. Figure 3 shows that the percentage of defects found decreased with complexity. This was

Figure 3. Inspection performance as a function of equipment complexity (from Harris 1966).

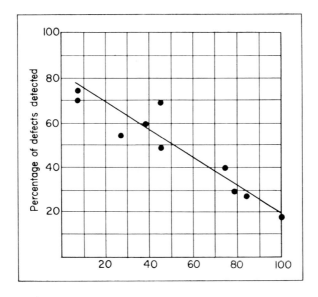

not a function of the number of defects present, since the correlation between percentage of defects detected and the number present was very small (-0.14).

One approach to studying multi-part inspection items would be to carry out a series of limited inspections. Take an item with three separate types of feature. Then 7 experimental conditions should allow: (1–3) inspection of one feature with the other two ignored, (4–6) inspection of two features with the third ignored, and (7) inspection of all three features together. A comparison of the results of all seven conditions would allow recommendations to be made about the way in which inspection should be carried out; whether one feature should be inspected first with the others following sequentially, whether when several inspectors are available they should each scan a different feature or whether they should all carry out a total inspection.

2.3. *Sheet materials*

In the inspection of sheets the inspector looks at a large expanse of material, e.g. cloth, glass, steel. Faults may be difficult to detect for one of three reasons.

Embedded fault. The fault fails to emerge perceptually from its immediate background. The failure being caused by the patterning of the background and the fault combining to obscure the fault.

Threshold fault. As with embedded faults, a near threshold fault does not emerge perceptually from its immediate background, the reason now being that there is a very low contrast difference between the fault and its background.

Relative size of the fault. Here the fault is clearly distinguishable from its immediate background, but it remains hard to detect because it is very small relative to the total area that has to be inspected.

With embedded and threshold faults, it can be very difficult to discriminate the fault from the background. A point may be reached at which a fault is so difficult to discriminate that we no longer consider it a fault at all. As a result, the inspection criteria need to be defined carefully.

There is limited data from inspection studies on the different discriminations outlined, but visual search experiments have been carried out in all these regions.

Bloomfield *et al.* (1974) investigated embedded target situations. They used one inch squares of vinyl floor tiles to form a background. The target was of similar texture but had a different colour mixture. Equation (1) was found to hold for this task with the discriminability scores being taken from rated estimates

Figure 4. Relationship between mean search time and rated discriminability for four observers searching an embedded target colour display (adapted from Bloomfield *et al.* 1974).

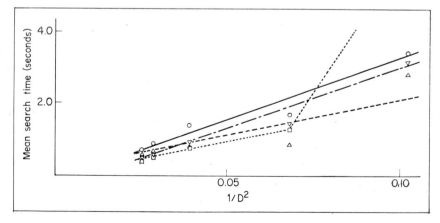

Figure 5. Log-linear plot of cumulative search times for targets of varying contrast in a homogeneous background (from Krendel and Wodinsky 1960).

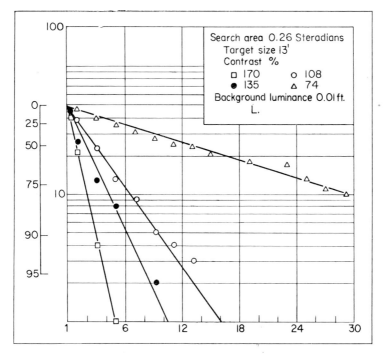

Figure 6. Relationship between search time and flaw size: data points averaged across four inspectors and four conditions (from Drury 1973b).

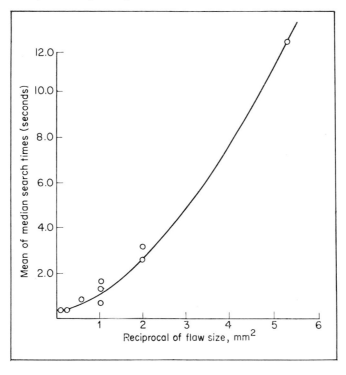

of discriminability. Figure 4 illustrates this finding. With black and white photographic textures, the equation was less successful.

Krendel and Wodinsky (1960) presented low contrast threshold targets against a plain unstructured background. They varied background luminance, target size and contrast, and the size of the search area. Figure 5 shows a typical plot of their cumulative time distributions. The figure shows 4 of the 256 conditions they investigated. In an inspection study, Drury (1973b) used sheets

Figure 7. Data from Miller and Ludvigh (1960) replotted to show the relationship between mean search time and discriminability for three observers searching for a low contrast target in a plain background (from Bloomfield 1970).

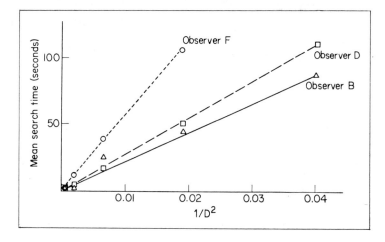

Figure 8. Relationship between mean search time and discriminability with search for a low contrast target in a plain background (adapted from Bloomfield 1970).

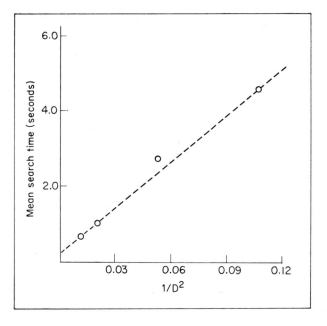

of glass containing faults from 0·19 mm² in area (measured from the shadow they cast on a shadowgraph). Figure 6 shows his results, with search time plotted as a function of the reciprocal of the area of the fault. Search time increases with the reciprocal but the relationship is not linear. However, each point appears to be the mean of the median of four observers searching each fault four times (but each time under different viewing conditions).

Using targets of low contrast in a plain background, Miller and Ludvigh (1960) and Bloomfield (1970), varied target size. Both experiments could be summarized by equation (1) as Figures 7 and 8 show. Discriminability here is the difference in diameter of the target and a threshold target presented at the fovea.

3. Studies of individual factors which influence visual search

Visual search *per se* influences inspection efficiency. But it in its turn is influenced by individual factors; and so the general conclusions drawn from studies relative to task type may have to be modified. Among the individual factors which have the greatest effect on inspection are eyesight, experience and age.

3.1. *Eyesight*

The two aspects of eyesight that are crucial to an inspector are his visual acuity; and the way in which he distributes his fixations over the inspection area.

Visual acuity. Peripheral acuity and its relation to search and inspection tasks were discussed briefly in the previous paper (Bloomfield 1975). There it was concluded that one would expect correlations between inspection performance and peripheral visual acuity if the same visual discrimination is required in both tasks.

Bloomfield (1972) suggested that, for viewing distances longer than six feet (two metres), peripheral visual acuity is independent of viewing distance. He reported no change in acuity when the viewing distance was increased from seven to 47 feet. Thus, Gillies' (1975) finding, that there was no appreciable difference in inspection performance when viewing distance was increased from 2·4 to 4·8 metres, was to be expected.

Eye fixations. During saccadic eye movements, the retinal image is blurred and there appears to be a reduction in visual sensitivity (Volkmann 1962). This finding largely explains, and justifies, the amount of attention that has been directed towards investigating fixation pauses.

Fixation duration increases as the difficulty of discriminating a target increases (Bloomfield 1970). It also appears to increase as the complexity of the stimulus materials increases. Enoch (1959) found that for small display areas (less than 9°) a high percentage of fixations fell outside the search area.

Schoonard *et al.* (1973) investigated eye movements with an inspection task. They presented slides showing integrated circuit chips. The visual angle of the chips was 18° (slightly smaller than when they are inspected normally through a microscope). They used eight inspectors, with between 3 and 13 months experience with these chips. There were eight possible faults (e.g. localized decrease in feature width, significant reduction in size or absence of hemisphere). There were 168 slides, 20% with faults.

They found that there were few fixations on the edges of the chips: that the duration of the fixations differed considerably when different features of the chips were fixated: that fixations were clustered where the chips were most complex: that there were few refixations.

They were unable to pick out repeated patterns of eye movements. Nor did they find differences in the patterns of the different inspectors. They found that the fastest inspectors were also the most accurate (i.e. had fewest mis-classifications). Table 1 illustrates this last finding.

Table 1. Comparison of scanning parameters for inspectors ranked according to accuracy (from Schoonard *et al.* 1973, Table 1).

Inspector	Overall error rate	Overall mean scanning time	Mean no. fixations per chip	Modal fixation duration in 50 millisecond intervals
1	10%	2·7 sec	9·4	250
2	12%	2·5 sec	9	200
3	13%	5·4 sec	15·3	200
4	15%	3·6 sec	14·4	200
5	16%	4·4 sec	15·2	200

The difference was due to the fast inspectors requiring fewer fixations (rather than shorter ones). One wonders whether the distance between fixations was greater for the two faster inspectors. If it was, they may have been scanning the inspection area more efficiently.

3.2. *Experience*

Although experience as an inspector is recognized as being an important variable, it has not been investigated in a systematic way. It may have positive or negative effects. A long-time inspector should be good. He knows his job. However, there may be occasions when he does it inefficiently. He may not have adapted to a change in the process because his inspection technique has become so ingrained.

In visual search studies, Baker *et al.* (1960) and Bloomfield (1970) have found that observers are able to search faster and with fewer errors after practice. Parkes (1967) found that skilled observers were significantly better than unskilled in locating targets on aerial photographs. Clearly inspection performance should improve with practice, with more practice necessary for complex tasks.

With experience, an inspector will build up expectancies. He will know what type of fault predominates, where it is likely to occur and what proportions of good and faulty items to expect. This is part of the reason why an inspector improves with experience. He need not worry about areas where no fault occurs, or types of faults that rarely occur. Sometimes, this may work against him: for example, where the product quality changes. If it changes abruptly he should notice the change quickly. However, if the change takes place gradually over a long period of time, he may be unaware of it, with the result that some faults are not detected.

3.3. *Age*

The effects of age are likely to be mediated through eyesight and experience. While performance might be expected to improve with experience, there may be decrement associated with reduced visual acuity.

Erickson (1964) with a group of 16 observers aged between 23 and 41 years, found no correlation between age and search performance, whether the latter was assessed with static or moving displays. Erickson's observers were searching for a Landolt 'C' placed amongst rings of similar size and contrast. Contrary to this finding, Sheehan and Drury (1971) report a decrease in inspection performance as a function of increasing age. Their inspectors were presented batches of hooks. The important difference from Erickson's study is that a larger age range was used; the inspectors ranged from 30 to 65 years. However, only five inspectors were used by Sheehan and Drury. More work will be needed before firm conclusions can be drawn.

4. Physical factors

Type of task and individual factors apart, visual search is also influenced by the physical conditions which prevail in the inspection situation. Methods of presentation of the item, display size and aids for inspection are factors which have been shown to be important.

4.1. *Rate of presentation*

There are several inspection studies addressing questions in this area.

Movement. Many inspection studies involve the use of a conveyor belt. Those in which the speed of the belt is varied are of interest here.

Perry (1968) found that performance improved the slower his conveyor moved. More small cracks round the sealing edge of the bottles that had to be inspected were detected when the time available per bottle was increased. Related visual search experiments have been carried out by Williams and Borow (1963), using alphabetic stimulus items, and by Erickson (1964), using a Landolt C target amongst nontarget rings. These two studies give quantified information. As the velocity of the moving display increases, the level of search performance decreases. For velocities below 7° per minute the decrease is small; i.e. in the range from 0 to 7° per minute movement is relatively unimportant.

Moder and Oswalt (1959) varied belt speed, but at the same time they changed the product density, so that a constant rate of presentation was maintained. They found that a belt speed of about 50 ft/min resulted in the best performance for several rates of presentation. Their inspectors had to pick faulty items from a moving belt. (*N.B.* their paper contains contradictory statements about whether the good or the faulty items had to be picked from the belt, however the weight of the evidence suggests it was the latter.) The quantities of items presented are given in pounds weight, while the results are given in terms of number picked out. It is not possible to gather from this the proportion of faults correctly rejected and incorrectly accepted. This makes interpretation difficult. With high densities and low speeds, slightly more items are detected as speed is increased (this effect is probably not significant). With low densities and faster speeds many fewer faults are detected as speed increases. Moder and Oswalt's suggestion that 50 ft/min is an optimal speed is not necessarily contradictory to the early studies with fixed density. The initial improvements as density is reduced and speed increased, are probably almost entirely due to density (remembering from the Perry, Erickson, and Williams and Borow studies that low velocities have little effect). The decrements as density is reduced still further while belt speed is increased, occur because the disadvantages due to increased speed now far outweigh the advantages of low density.

Static displays. Two studies involving the inspection of electronic circuit chips provide information on the effect of varying the time allowed for inspection. Schoonard and Gould (1973) photographically presented simulated integrated circuit chips to inspectors. They used a restricted field of view scanning procedure. Increasing the time available for inspection from 16 to 32 to 64 seconds reduced the overall error rate from 27% to 19% and 16%. In the second study, Schoonard *et al.* (1973) presented the chips via a microscope. They discovered the normal inspection time for each inspector. They used five time conditions; the five being the following multiples of the normal inspection time: 0·5, 1·0, 1·5, 2·0 and 3·0. Table 2 gives the percentage errors averaged over all error types and all observers.

Table 2. Percentage error rate as a function of time allowed for inspection of electronic chips (adapted from Schoonard *et al.* 1973).

Time available (multiple of normal time taken)	% Faulty chips missed	% Good chips rejected
0·5	29·6	1·8
1·0 (Normal)	23·2	2·2
1·5	16·5	2·1
2·0	18·0	3·1
3·0	16·4	2·6

Allowing more time per chip resulted in improvements. Considerably fewer faulty chips were missed, while the number of good chips rejected did not change significantly. There was an improvement in the detection of all types of fault. The error rate for the easiest fault (insufficient clearances at the edge of the chip) improved from 6·4% to 3·4% while for the hardest (two adjacent features touching where they should not, and localized decreases in the width of a feature) it improved from 56·0% to 46·0%, while the time available increased from 1·0 to 1·5 times the normal time.

These two studies with electronic chips show that increases in the time allowed for inspection do lead to improvements in error rate. Whether the improvements are sufficient to compensate for the cost of allowing more time for inspection is another question; one that needs to be answered after careful cost analysis of the inspection structure.

Density. With the inspection of displays containing several simple items, the density of items per unit area is important.

As already mentioned Moder and Oswalt (1959) varied the density of items inversely with increases in belt speed in order to maintain a constant rate of presentation. Given that we accept the Erickson and Williams and Bojow find-ings that low belt speeds are unimportant, their study can be interpreted as showing that reducing density leads to an increase in the number of correctly rejected faulty items.

Drury (1973a) reports two studies involving glass items. In the first, the items were presented on a belt that was moving at a ' very slow ' speed. The second is not strictly a density study; the items were presented in a stack containing work for one minute. However, both studies showed that as the time available per item was increased (i.e., for the first study, as density was reduced) the probability of a fault being rejected was increased. There was also an increase in the number of incorrectly rejected good items.

There is a considerable amount of work on the effects of density in visual search experiments. In these, typically, a single target is presented amongst a number of nontargets and the search time is unlimited. Search time increases as the number of items present is increased (Smith *et al.* 1962, Bloomfield 1973).

4.2. *Display size and shape*
Display size and shape have been investigated in several visual search experiments.

Display size. Size has been investigated in competition search situations. Increasing the display area (and the number of nontargets, with density constant) increases search time when the target differs from the nontargets in shape (Baker *et al.* 1960, Johnston 1965) and when it is a particular number in other digits, a letter pair in other letter pairs or is specified as a particular dial hand orientation amongst other dials (Cizkova 1967). The effect of increasing area with the number of nontargets constant (with density being reduced) is not clear.

With a low contrast target in an unstructured background, Krendel and Wodinsky (1960) found that search time increases with increases in the size of the search area.

When the search or inspection task involves display movement, an increase in the display area may increase the length of time a fault is present. This may increase the likelihood of it being detected.

Display shape. Bloomfield (1970) varied display shape. He compared search times with three shapes: a 4×1 vertical rectangle, a 2×2 square, and a 1×4 horizontal rectangle. There was no systematic difference in search times for a small target disc amongst larger nontarget discs. In a second experiment, letter stimuli and much more extreme examples of vertical and horizontal rectangles (including 30×1 and 1×30 rectangles) were used. The observers were required to search through the display for every item in turn. Here the vertical rectangle displays required more time for horizontally arranged letters. It seems that display shape is only likely to affect performance in static conditions, if the display contains material, like letters, to which the observer has developed stereotyped responses.

With moving displays, the shape of the display area may affect the length of time the material can be observed.

4.3. *Aids*
It has been suggested that partitions or sector markings might assist observers in scanning more efficiently. Eriksen (1955) with a competition search task, and Reilly and Teichner (1962), with a threshold search task, found that search

performance improves as the number of partitions is reduced, the opposite of the hoped for effect.

Using an overlay inspection mask, Teel *et al.* (1968) investigated the inspection of photographic marks used in the production of multilayer circuit boards. Ten observers used the overlays; ten did not. The possible defects were of two kinds: pad defects or line defects. Detection of the former was much better for the overlay group of inspectors. There was no significant difference in detection of the line defects. Clearly, the use of the overlay was indicated. Similar aids may be of use in other inspection tasks. They will need to be tailored closely to the requirements of the particular inspection task.

Using dimensioned drawings of simple parts with similar characteristics grouped together, Chaney and Teel (1967) found improvement in the detection of faults in four fabricated machine parts. Each part had approximately 100 characteristics to be inspected and there were 34 possible types of defect.

Townsend and Fry (1960) compared search performance, when the observer used an automatic scan marker, with free search. The targets were Landolt Cs placed on aerial map backgrounds. The free search condition gave faster detection times except with a very low contrast Landolt 'C' target.

Schoonard and Gould (1973) investigated the effect of restricting the amount of the electronic chip slides visible at one time. In one condition, a full view of the slide was presented. In the second, each quadrant of the slide was presented alone for a quarter of the allowed viewing time. In the third, the slide was divided into sixteenths, with each segment shown for a sixteenth of the viewing time. The total allowed time was varied (16, 32 or 64 seconds). While there were differences in performance attributable to changes in the time allowed no differences were obtained between the three restricted view conditions.

Schoonard *et al.* (1973) compared presentation of the electronic chips via a microscope and via a standard ground glass screen attachment to the microscope. Detection performance was better with the microscope for seven of the types of fault investigated. Detection of the easiest fault was slightly better with the screen. Over all eight faults, 5·6% more defects were detected with the microscope. Schoonard and Gould suggest that the screen could be worse because there is a loss in resolution when it is used, and/or that the inspectors had not had any experience with the screen, while they were trained with the microscope.

References

BAKER, C. A., MORRIS, D. F., and STEEDMAN, W. C., 1969, Target recognition on complex displays. *Human Factors*, **2**, 51–61.

BLOOMFIELD, J. R., 1970, *Visual Search*. (Ph.D. Thesis. UNIVERSITY OF NOTTINGHAM.)

BLOOMFIELD, J. R., 1972, Peripheral acuity with complex stimuli at two viewing distances. In *Air to Ground Target Acquisition*, AGARD Conference Proceedings No. 100. (Brussels: AGARD.)

BLOOMFIELD, J. R., 1973, Experiments in visual search. In *Visual Search* (Washington, D.C.: NATIONAL ACADEMY OF SCIENCES.) Pp. 1–25.

BLOOMFIELD, J. R., 1975, Theoretical approaches to visual search. In *Human Reliability in Quality Control*. (Edited by C. G. DRURY and J. G. FOX.) (London: TAYLOR & FRANCIS.)

BLOOMFIELD, J. R., BECKWITH, W. E., EMERICK, J., MARMUREK, H. H., TEI, B. E., and TRAUB, B. H., 1974, *Visual Search with Embedded Targets*. (ARI Technical Report.) (In press.)

BLOOMFIELD, J. R., HOWARTH, C. I., and BONE, K. E., 1972, *Visual Search and Pattern Recognition*. (University of Nottingham Research Report on Contract M.O.D. (P.E.) No. AT/24108/GC.)

CHANEY, F. B., and TEEL, K. S., 1967, Improving inspection performance through training and visual aids. *Journal of Applied Psychology*, **51**, 311–315.

CIZKOVA, J., 1967, Effect on the quantity and complexity of visual stimuli on operator's search activity. *Studia Psychologica*, **9**, 241–246.

DRURY, C. G., 1973a, The effect of speed of working on industrial inspection accuracy. *Applied Ergonomics*, **4**, 2–7.

DRURY, C. G., 1973b, The inspection of sheet materials—model and data. In *Proceedings of the 17th Annual Meeting of the Human Factors Society*. (Edited by M. P. RANC and T. B. MALONE.) Pp. 457–464.

ENOCH, J. M., 1959, Effect of the size of a complex display upon visual search. *Journal of the Optical Society of America*, **49**, 280–286.

ERICKSON, R. A., 1964, Visual search performance in a moving structured field. *Journal of the Optical Society of America*, **54**, 399–405.

ERIKSEN, C. W., 1955, Partitioning and saturation of visual displays and efficiency of visual search. *Journal of Applied Psychology*, **39**, 73–77.

GILLIES, G. J., 1975, Glass inspection. In *Human Reliability in Quality Control*. (Edited by C. G. DRURY and J. G. FOX.) (London: TAYLOR & FRANCIS.)

HARRIS, D. H., 1966, Effect of equipment complexity on inspection performance. *Journal of Applied Psychology*, **50**, 236–237.

HARRIS, D. H., and CHANEY, F. B., 1969, *Human Factors in Quality Assurance*. (New York: WILEY.)

HOWARTH, C. I., and BLOOMFIELD, J. R., 1969, A rational equation for predicting search times in simple inspection tasks. *Psychonomic Science*, **17**, 225–226.

JOHNSTON, D. M., 1965, Search performance as a function of peripheral acuity. *Human Factors*, **7**, 527–535.

KRENDEL, E. S., and WODINSKY, J., 1960, Visual search in unstructured fields. In *Visual Search Techniques*. (Edited by A. MORRIS and E. P. HORNE.) (Washington, D.C.: NATIONAL ACADEMY OF SCIENCES.) Pp. 151–169.

MILLER, J. W., and LUDVIGH, E., 1960, Time required for detection of stationary and moving objects as a function of size in homogeneous and partially structured visual fields. In *Visual Search Techniques* (Edited by A. MORRIS and E. P. HORNE.) (Washington, D.C.: NATIONAL ACADEMY OF SCIENCES.) Pp. 170–180.

MODER, J. J., and OSWALT, J. H., 1959, An investigation of some factors affecting the hand quality picking of small objects. *Journal of Industrial Engineering*, **10**, 213–218.

PARKES, K. R., 1967, *Visual and Televisual Detection Studies. Part 1. The Effect of Navigational Uncertainty and Target Difficulty on Detection Performance.* (University of Loughborough Technical Report.)

PERRY, G., 1968, *Lighting for Inspection.* (Technical Note No. 115. British Glass Industry Research Association.) (*Cited in* DRURY 1973*a*.)

REILLY, R. E., and TEICHNER, W. H., 1962, Effect of shape and degree of structure of the visual field on target detection and location. *Journal of the Optical Society of America*, **52**, 214–218.

SCHOONARD, J. W., and GOULD, J. D., 1973, Field of view and target uncertainty in visual search and inspection. *Human Factors*, **15**, 33–42.

SCHOONARD, J. W., GOULD, J. D., and MILLER, L. A., 1973, Studies of visual inspection. *Ergonomics*, **16**, 365–379.

SHEEHAN, J. J., and DRURY, C. G., 1971, The analysis of industrial inspection. *Applied Ergonomics*, **2**, 74–78.

SMITH, S. W., KINCAID, W. M., and SEMMELROTH, C., 1962, *Speed of Visual Target Detection as a Function of the Density of Confusion Elements.* (University of Michigan Memorandum 2900–235–R.)

TEEL, K. S., SPRINGER, R. M., and SADLER, E. F., 1968, Assembly and inspection of microelectronic systems. *Human Factors*, **10**, 217–224.

TOWNSEND, C. A., and FRY, G. A., 1960, Automatic scanning of aerial photographs. In *Visual Search Techniques*. (Edited by A. MORRIS and E. P. HORNE.) (Washington, D.C.: NATIONAL ACADEMY OF SCIENCES.) Pp. 194–210.

VOLKMANN, F. C., 1962, Vision during voluntary saccadic eye movements. *Journal of the Optical Society of America*, **52**, 571–578.

WILLIAMS, L. G., and BOROW, M. S., 1963, The effect of rate and direction of display movement upon visual search. *Human Factors*, **5**, 139–146.

Human decision making in quality control

C. G. Drury

1. Why decision making?

Control of quality implies knowledge of quality. It is essentially a choice between actions based on data about quality. It is this 'data about quality' and its collection and analysis which forms the bulk of textbooks on quality control (Grant and Leavenworth 1972, Duncan 1965).

Statistical quality control (SQC) is a procedure for making decisions on batches or lots based on information from a sample and the laws of probability. The information from the sample rests ultimately on decisions on individual sample items made by an inspection device, either a human inspector, a human inspector aided by mechanical and electronic equipment, or a completely automatic inspection device. Thus the whole SQC procedure is only as valid as its assumptions about the reliability of the inspection device which is subject to human error either in operating or setting up.

Of particular interest is the inspection device with a human component. The traditional assumption has been that it is perfect in its decisions on individual items, despite contrary evidence dating back before the widespread use of SQC (e.g. Juran 1935, Tiffin and Rogers 1941). Since that time many studies and reviews (e.g. McCornack 1961, Harris and Chaney 1969) have confirmed these earlier observations that the human inspector, with or without instruments, is not a perfect decision maker.

Recently, researchers have begun to study the effect of inspection error on single sampling SQC plans (Collins *et al.* 1973) and continuous sampling plans (Case *et al.* 1973). In these the inspector can make both Type 1 and Type 2 errors, defined as:

Type 1 error: a good item is rejected
Type 2 error: a faulty item is accepted

Corresponding to these two errors are the error probabilities:

e_1 = probability of a Type 1 error
e_2 = probability of a Type 2 error

It is equally convenient to think in terms of *performance* measures of the inspection device and to define the probabilities of correct decision:

$P_1 = 1 - e_1$ = probability that a good item is accepted
$P_2 = 1 - e_2$ = probability that a faulty item is rejected

Using these performance measures it is possible to express the apparent fraction defective (P_e) in a lot subject to imperfect inspection as:

$$P_e = PP_2 + (1 - P)(1 - P_1) \qquad (1)$$

where P is the actual fraction defective in the batch. Knowing P_1 and P_2 it is then possible to compute the actual operating characteristic curve of the SQC scheme (the probability of lot acceptance as a function of P). The two papers cited above go to the next stage, however, and show how to construct SQC schemes which give a desired operating characteristic curve for given values of P_1 and P_2.

The role of the human factors specialist in SQC schemes which are not completely automatic should thus be:

> to be able to predict P_1 and P_2 for a given inspection situation and,

> to know the variation of P_1 and P_2 with other systems variables (e.g. lighting, training, speed of working) so that management can be given clear and cost-effective ways of improving inspection performance.

This paper is a review of some of the methods by which performance can be predicted by considering the human inspection device as a decision maker.

In all of the models considered, the inspection device is modelled by analogy with a decision process from some other discipline, usually mathematics and the physical sciences. Thus for each model there is a normative model of how decisions should be made and a realistic or actual model describing how the human inspection device actually does operate.

2. Models of human decision making

2.1. *Bayesian decision models*

In the decision making task the human decision maker must decide between courses of action on the basis of input information. Logically this information arises not just from the item itself about which a decision is required but also from any prior information available to the decision maker, such as the expected probability of a faulty item and the expected costs of errors.

As a normative model for decision making in statistical inference, Bayesian decision theory relies on two assumptions:

> probabilities are best defined as 'personal probabilities' rather than relative frequencies;

> Bayes theorem is the optimum model for revision of opinion in the light of information.

Logically consistent and intuitively appealing arguments can be made for both of these assumptions (e.g. Savage 1962, Raiffa 1970). There is no serious argument against the use of Bayes theorem, which is derived directly from the definition of conditional probabilities. However, enough controversy exists among statisticians with respect to the use of subjective probabilities to make the publishing of elementary textbooks treating statistics in this way (e.g. Phillips 1973) something of a rarity.

A large research programme in the 1960's at the University of Michigan was based on the modelling of a human decision maker in a dynamic decision making system in which each new piece of information was integrated with previous information using Bayes theorem (e.g. Edwards 1965). This was based on previous research (e.g. Edwards 1955) which showed that human beings behaved in such a way as to maximize 'subjective expected utility' when choosing between risky courses of action with specific monetary payoffs contingent upon the outcomes of their choices.

The later studies showed that human decision makers do indeed modify their courses of action in the direction which Bayes theorem would suggest but that they are less than perfect in making maximum use of input information. This unwillingness to change opinions as much as Bayes theorem would suggest has been referred to as 'conservatism'. Whilst it appears to be a general human trait, it does not apply equally in all circumstances. In particular conservatism is less marked for simple events than for complex ones, so that to make maximum use of input information the human parts of a decision making system should provide the simple probability inputs and mechanical parts of the system should compute the final probabilities according to Bayes theorem. Such an allocation of function between humans and machines has been proposed by Edwards (1962) for probabilistic information processing systems in a military context.

Within a quality control framework Bayesian models of inspectors do not appear to have been used except to analyse results (Adams, following paper). However they do provide a well developed framework for the quantification of the combined effects of prior information (from standards, quality knowledge, probability of defect types, etc.) and information from the item itself.

2.2. *Theory of selective information*

The original quantification of information flowing through a communication channel (e.g. Shannon and Weaver 1949) was rapidly taken up by experimental psychologists as a model of human processing of information. Early studies found that within a range of laboratory tasks where a subject had to make a 'choice reaction', a model of man as a single information processing channel of limited capacity emerged (e.g. review by Welford 1968). The relationship could be described by

$$t = \frac{I}{K} \tag{1}$$

where t = time to process information (seconds),
I = amount of information transmitted (bits),
K = information processing rate (bits/second).

The information, I, is defined by the *set* of all possible messages which the channel can transmit and their probabilities. If there are n possible messages each with probability of occurring p_i $(1 \leqslant i \leqslant n)$ then

$$I = - \sum_{i=1}^{n} p_i \operatorname{Log}_2 (p_i) \tag{2}$$

For any *set* the amount of information is increased when the number of messages, n, increases, when their probabilities become more equal and when any sequential redundancy between messages is removed. Equation 1 shows that each of these conditions would require more time for the 'human information channel' to process the information.

In a quality control context the information transmitted can be equated with the inspector's choice between accepting or rejecting items. Thus, larger inspection times are associated with longer message *sets* (e.g. a number of categories into which items are sorted), with values of defective probability P closer to 0·50 and with greater independence between defects occurring in a sequence of items.

More importantly the measure of transmitted information increases with increasing quality of inspection performance as measured by P_1 and P_2. [A technique for measuring transmitted information which takes this into account is given in Welford (1968).] This means that the inspector can trade-off speed and accuracy against each other, and the particular trade-off should be fitted by equation 1. Hick (1952) found that this was true for laboratory experiments but no evidence of a test of this in a quality control situation has been found in the literature. It has been successfully applied to the analysis of a visual search task which has many features of industrial inspection tasks (Meudell and Whiston 1970). With its application to decision making and visual search tasks it may

Figure 1. Effect of standard size on decision making performance.

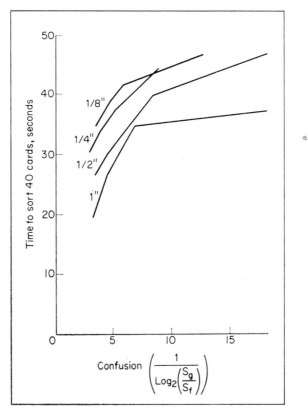

provide a unified metric for describing the inspection of sheet materials which requires both tasks. A model of such a task has been developed by Drury (1973a) to describe the speed/accuracy trade-off in a wide range of inspection tasks (Drury 1973b) but so far no information theory analysis has been attempted.

However there are a number of features of the theory of selective information as a human inspection model which potentially limit its usefulness. Firstly, the human information processing rate (K) is not constant. It varies between people and, more importantly, it varies with the specifics of the task and with the familiarity of the subject with the task. For example the discriminability between stimulii (i.e. between a good item and a faulty item) affects the time taken to decide and the errors made (Drury 1973a) but the only satisfactory treatment of this (Crossman 1953) is essentially *ad hoc* rather than a strict information theory derivation. Crossman's formula relates the decision time $t(d)$ to the difference between some dimension of good and faulty items by:

$$t(d) = k_1 \cdot \frac{1}{\left| \text{Log} \left(\frac{S_g}{S_f} \right) \right|}$$ (3)

where k_1 is a constant and S_g and S_f are the dimensions of some critical property of good and faulty items respectively. Even this is not a complete formulation as the absolute values of the dimensions also have an effect on decision time. Figure 1 shows data obtained in a laboratory task at SUNY at Buffalo where subjects had to sort cards containing spots of different diameters into good and faulty. Each curve in Figure 1 represents a different absolute spot size and the differences between spot sizes are significant at $p < 0.01$. As an example of the effect of training, Mowbray and Rhoades (1959) showed that choices between two stimulii or up to ten stimulii were not significantly different after 36,000 responses—a level of practice not uncommon among experienced inspectors.

The second feature not modelled by information theory is the meaning and value attached to the items and responses. It assumes that all errors are equally bad and says nothing about how inspectors can vary their decisions with the costs and payoffs inherent in the task.

2.3. *Theory of signal detection*

Probably the greatest impact of decision models on inspector performance has been the use of the theory of signal detection (Wallack and Adams 1969, Sheehan and Drury 1971). Electrical engineers in the early 1950's began to treat such topics as radar detection in terms of the detection of a specified signal in a background of random noise (e.g. Woodward 1953). From this and statistical decision theory arose the concept of the Ideal Signal Detector. This forms a normative model for the evaluation of real signal detectors (e.g. Swets 1964). The signal detector (analogous to an inspector) is seen as choosing between two alternatives (e.g. Accept or Reject) on the basis of noisy information. Performance is measured by two variables, derived from the assigned performance measures P_1 and P_2, thus

$$discriminability = d' = Z(P_1) + Z(P_2)$$ (4)

$$criterion = \beta = f(P_2)/f(P_1)$$ (5)

where $Z(P_1)$ and $Z(P_2)$ are the normal deviates corresponding to P_1 and P_2, and $f(P_1)$ and $f(P_2)$ are the ordinates of the normal curve at these points. The *discriminability* should remain constant for a particular individual in a particular task. It can also be expressed as an effective signal-to-noise ratio as in Table 1.

In particular d' should remain constant as the costs and payoffs are changed and as the prior probability of a faulty item (P) changes. These payoff matrix variables should influence the inspector by changing his chosen criterion so as to maximize his expected net gain in the long term.

49

Table 1. Relationship between d' and signal to noise ratios.

d'	Signal-to-noise ratio
1·0	−3·0 db
2·0	+3·0 db
3·0	+6·5 db
4·0	+9·0 db
5·0	+11·0 db

All of these factors have been seen in laboratory tasks to hold for human subjects and the model has recently been applied to studies of vigilance (e.g. Milosevic 1969) recognition memory (e.g. Wickelgren and Norman 1966) and inspection (e.g. Drury and Addison 1973). There are some difficulties with inspection applications however. In many cases inspection is not merely a one-stage process but an interaction between visual search and decision making. Thus, any attempt to apply this should be preceded by some form of task analysis (Meister 1971) to determine the sub-task to which it is applicable. Secondly, the Ideal Signal Detector should integrate information over time so that the d' value increases with time allowed for the decision thus:

$$d_t' = d_1' \sqrt{t} \tag{6}$$

where d_t' is the effective d' value after t seconds of observation and d_1' is the d' value after 1 second of observation. The evidence from laboratory tasks using

Figure 2. ROC curves based on data in Assenheim (1969).

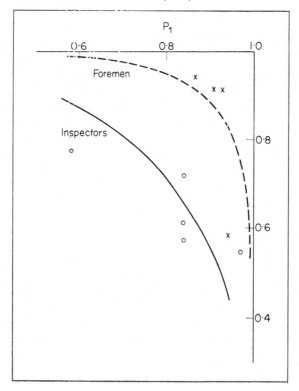

both a series of short exposures and a single long exposure of the item have shown that d_t' is somewhere between that predicted by equation (6) and a linear function of t.

Despite these objections the measures d' and β are particularly appealing as indices of inspector performance. They are based only on error data so that the inspection of different products can be measured on the same scale, opening up new possibilities for absolute measures of job difficulty as well as their diagnostic value in improving performance (Drury 1972). Usually performance is measured by P_1 and P_2 for a simple accept/reject decision so that d' and β are readily calculable. For example Assenheim's (1969) data on the accuracy of inspection of glass tableware can be interpreted as signal detection data. Figure 2 shows part of a plot of P_2 against P_1 (usually called a Receiver Operating Characteristic (ROC) Curve) where the performance of groups of foremen and inspectors are compared. It is apparent that while the two groups overlap considerably on both P_1 and P_2 values they are much more clearly separated along the two curves of constant d' shown in the figure.

Also, the theory of signal detection can be used to analyse and interpret data collected by having inspectors use more than two categories for their response. Egan *et al.* (1959) showed that the additional task of categorizing signals into four categories gave the same d' values as those obtained in a two-choice task. Milosevic (1969) showed that the d' values calculated for three different criterion levels dividing four response categories were essentially equal in a vigilance task. The advantage of using these n-category methods is that they provide $(n-1)$ points on the ROC curve from a single set of data.

3. Conclusions

Three different, but related, models of decision making have been surveyed for their potential utility in explaining and predicting human operator performance in a quality control task. Any model can be applied at three different levels.

1. As a normative model of how some Ideal Decision Maker would behave. This will usually represent an upper bound on actual human performance.

2. As a quantitative model for analysis and interpretation of field and laboratory data. Thus the theory of signal detection was used to analyse previous data (Sheehan and Drury 1971) and show that an inspector's age had an effect on *discriminability* even though it had no significant effects on P_1 or P_2 alone. Used in this way a model can unify the data and allow interpolation and extrapolation to new situations to proceed more confidently.

3. As a descriptive model to predict the direction of performance changes with alternative managerial or structural changes in the inspection task. For example the theory of signal detection would predict that increasing the proportion of faulty items in a batch (P) should increase the value of P_2 and decrease the value of P_1: an effect found in both laboratory and factory situations (Fox and Haslegrave 1969).

The next step in solving the problem referred to in the Introduction is to combine models of different aspects of the inspection task such as visual search, decision making and vigilance and use this combined model with the SQC

Figure 3. Flow chart for deriving SQC scheme with inspection error.

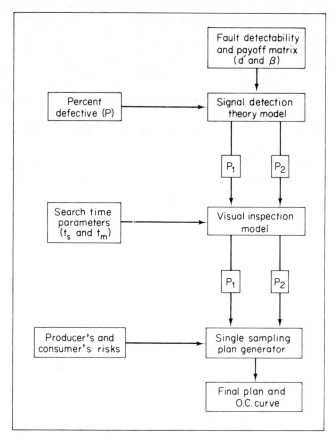

problem formulation to generate appropriate SQC schemes (usually defined by their OC curve) contingent upon the variables affecting the inspector and his performance.

A project aimed at this problem has been started at SUNY at Buffalo. This predicts the P_1 and P_2 values of inspectors as a function of time on task and defect probability (P) and uses the P_1 and P_2 values to derive an SQC single sampling plan with required consumer's and producer's risk. A flow chart of the computer programme is shown in Figure 3. The main problem at this level is not the fit of specific models to specific sub-tasks but finding an appropriate structure for combining the models. As this computer modelling proceeds, it is hoped to start factory experiments for its validation. Until we have adequate predictive models of inspection we can only ever improve the factory situation, never optimize it.

References

ASSENHEIM, G., 1969, Etude d'un systeme au travers d'un centre privilegie: un poste de controle en cristallerie. *Le Travail Humain*, **32**, 1–12.

CASE, K. E., BENNETT, G. K., and SCHMIDT, J. W., 1973, The Dodge CSP–1 continuous sampling plan under inspection error. *AIIE Transactions*, **5**, 193–202.

COLLINS, R. D., JR., CASE, K. E., and BENNETT, G. K., 1973, The effects of inspection error on single sampling inspection plans. *International Journal of Production Research*, **11**, 289–298.

CROSSMAN, E. R. F. W., 1953, Entropy and choice time: the effect of frequency unbalance on choice-response. *Quarterly Journal of Experimental Psychology*, **5**, 41–51.

DRURY, C. G., 1972, The measurement of inspection performance. *Paper presented to Glass Manufacturers Federation Symposium 'Inspection 72', Sheffield, England.*

DRURY, C. G., 1973a, The inspection of sheet materials—model and data. *Proceedings of 17th Annual Meeting of the Human Factors Society.* (Edited by M. P. RANC and T. B. MALONE.) Pp. 457–464.

DRURY, C. G., 1973b, The effect of speed of working on industrial inspection accuracy. *Applied Ergonomics*, **4**, 2–7.

DRURY, C. G., and ADDISON, J. L., 1973, An industrial study of the effects of feedback and fault density on inspection performance. *Ergonomics*, **16**, 159–169.

DUNCAN, A. J., 1965, *Quality Control and Industrial Statistics.* (Homewood, Illinois: IRWIN.)

EDWARDS, W., 1955, The prediction of decisions among bets. *Journal of Experimental Psychology*, **50**, 201–214.

EDWARDS, W., 1962, Dynamic decision theory and probabilistic information processing. *Human Factors*, **4**, 59–73.

EDWARDS, W., 1965, *Human Processing of Equivocal Information.* (Technical Report No. ESD-TDR–64–601, United States Air Force.)

EGAN, J. P., GREENBERG, G. Z., and SCHULMAN, A. I., 1961, Operating characteristics, signal detectability and the method of free response. *Journal of the Acoustical Society of America*, **33**, 993–1007.

FOX, J. G., and HALSEGRAVE, C. M., 1969, Industrial inspection efficiency and the probability of a defect occurring. *Ergonomics*, **12**, 713–721.

GRANT, E. L., and LEAVENWORTH, R. S., 1972, *Statistical Quality Control.* (New York: McGRAW-HILL.)

HARRIS, D. H., and CHANEY, F. B., 1969, *Human Factors in Quality Assurance.* (New York: WILEY.)

HICK, W. E., 1952, On the rate of gain of information. *Quarterly Journal of Experimental Psychology*, **4**, 1952.

JURAN, J. M., 1935, Inspectors' errors in quality control. *Mechanical Engineering*, **57**, 643–644.

McCORNACK, R. L., 1961, *Inspector Accuracy: A Study of the Literature.* (Report SCTM 53–61(14), Sandia Laboratories.)

MEISTER, D., 1971, *Human Factors: Theory and Practice.* (New York: WILEY.)

MEUDELL, P. R., and WHISTON, T. G., 1971, An informational analysis of a visual search task. *Perception and Psychophysics*, **7**, 212–214.

MILOSEVIC, S., 1969, Detection du signal en fonction du critere de response. *Le Travail Humain*, **32**, 81–86.

MOWBRAY, G. H., and RHOADES, M. V., 1959, On the reduction of choice reaction times with practice. *Quarterly Journal of Experimental Psychology*, **11**, 16–23.

PHILLIPS, L. D., 1973, *Bayesian Statistics for Social Scientists.* (Edinburgh: NELSON.)

RAIFFA, H., 1970, *Decision Analysis: Introductory Lectures on Choices Under Uncertainty.* (Reading, Massachusetts: ADDISON-WESLEY.)

SAVAGE, L. J., 1962, *The Foundations of Statistical Inference.* (London: METHUEN.)

SHANNON, C. E., and WEAVER, W., 1949, *The Mathematical Theory of Communication.* (Urbana: UNIVERSITY OF ILLINOIS PRESS.)

SHEEHAN, J. J., and DRURY, C. G., 1971, The analysis of industrial inspection. *Applied Ergonomics*, **2**, 74–78.

SWETS, J. A., 1964, *Signal Detection and Recognition by Human Observers: Contemporary Readings.* (New York: WILEY.)

TIFFIN, J., and ROGERS, H. B., 1941, The selection and training of inspectors. *Personnel*, **18**, 14–31.

WALLACK, P. M., and ADAMS, S. K., 1969, The utility of signal detection theory in the analysis of industrial inspector accuracy. *AIIE Transactions*, **1**, 33–44.

WELFORD, A. T., 1968, *Fundamentals of Skill.* (London: METHUEN.)

WICKELGREN, W. A., and NORMAN, D. A., 1966, Strength models and serial position in short-term recognition memory. *Journal of Mathematical Psychology*, **3**, 316–347.

WOODWARD, P. M., 1953, *Probability and Information Theory, With Applications to Radar.* (London: PERGAMON.)

Decision making in quality control: some perceptual and behavioural considerations

S. K. Adams

1. Introduction

Modern industrial technology with its ever-increasing demands for higher productivity and economy has caused a considerable amount of research in psychology and ergonomics to be directed toward improving work design in quality control tasks. Much of this research has been directed toward improving instrumentation (magnification, sensing devices) and task conditions (lighting arrangement, work rate) so that signals to the inspector are more likely to be well above perceptual thresholds. Traditionally, the inspection task is represented in terms of a simple flow chart or decision tree (Figure 1) in which the perceptual-decision process is represented by a box, incoming units and inspection criteria or instructions being represented by incoming arrows, and the action taken (representation of a decision) is represented by a set of outgoing arrows. A double or split box could be drawn indicating perception processes as separate and preceding decision processes. Thus one 'perceives' and then decides based on what he perceives.

Figure 1. Basic inspection task model. Adapted from Wallack and Adams (1969).

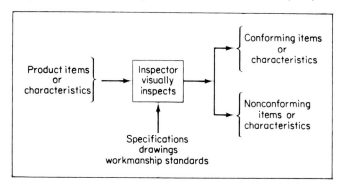

The analysis of perceptual ability in terms of threshold, response rate, or other basic measure is difficult to achieve without requiring the observer (inspector) to make decisions. Exceptions to this occur in perceptual research involving automatic responses such as galvanic skin response in place of voluntary (operant) responses. When operant behaviour is being emitted as a response to perceived stimuli, a dependent-independent variable relationship exists, responses being assumed to be emitted in a manner dependent upon the stimulus and the conditions under which it is presented. It is at this point that decision processes enter the picture because the inspector is forced to choose one of several alternatives in evaluating the product and to be answerable to the consequences of his decision. Thus, there is feedback for deciding correctly or incorrectly even though the feedback may not follow every decision made. Also implied in this concept of a decision model is that the decision to observe or not observe has been made (Smith and Barany 1970). Both the decision to observe and the decision regarding product classification following observation are modified by feedback in the form of past consequences of selecting each of the available alternatives given a similar perceptual display.

Thus, the inspector may decide to limit his perceptual-behavioural search processes as a result of associating first cues with a 'no defect' response which was made after observing these and additional cues. On the other hand, the inspector may decide to intensify his search (observing responses) as a result of detecting early cues which have been indicators of additional defects or of a more serious defect. These search-no search responses are, in turn, rewarded by the detection of additional cues or not rewarded by their absence. The inspector must also use criteria in deciding to report the presence or absence of a particular defect. These criteria, while they may be standardized in the inspection instructions, are likely to vary in the mind of the inspector as a result of recent past experience in using them. This can happen even when photographs or samples of defects are used as a basis for comparison by matching although such practice will generally result in improved performance since the inspector can 're-calibrate' his judgment criteria. The entire observing process can be summarized as shown in Figure 2, a chain of observe-search-decide responses occurring in iterative fashion with possible feedback dependent upon past responses. On a self-paced or complex task, selection of the next characteristic or unit of product to be inspected would constitute yet another decision in the model. When multiple alternatives are included the actual perceptual-behavioural sequence becomes highly variable and complex.

Inspection errors are typically defined as Type 1 (rejecting good units) or Type 2 (accepting bad units). As shown in Figure 3, the specification of a criterion lying within the region of perceptual overlap between good and bad items determines the relative amounts of Type 1 and Type 2 errors to be committed. Moving the criterion line X_c along the X axis causes corresponding increases and decreases in the two types of errors, thereby affecting inspection costs. In terms of this simple two choice task, the problem of controlling decisions is one of providing periodic feedback to the inspector so that he will maintain the criterion line in its proper position. As will presently be shown, a number of factors complicate this procedure, and raise questions regarding the observing process actually used during inspection.

2. Statistical decision models

Referring to Figure 1, let

$$I = p_0 I + q_0 I$$

where:

I = total input quantity (number of items inspected)

p_0 = fraction of nonconforming items

q_0 = fraction of conforming items = $1 - p_0$

A probability matrix (shown in Table 1) can be constructed.

Figure 2. Perceptual-decision processes occurring during a series of observations or inspections.

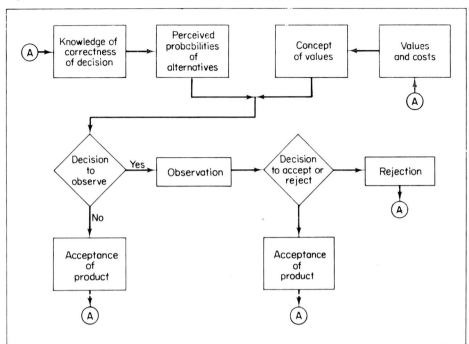

Figure 3. Overlapping distributions of perceptual input requiring the use of accept-reject criteria.

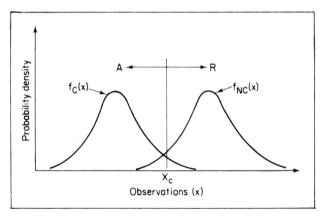

2.1. *Signal-detection theory*

Signal detection theory was derived in connection with applying Wald's theory of statistical decision making (Wald 1950) to radar system design. A paper by Swets *et al.* (1961) served as a basis for many additional studies and elaborations on the basic theory (Swets 1964), (Green and Swets 1966). Referring to the X_c criterion in Figure 3 both correct and incorrect decisions may be made in either accepting or rejecting a unit of product. If the two critical regions are designated A (accept) and R (reject), then one decision outcome may be a 'hit' $(NC \cdot R)$ corresponding to correctly rejecting a nonconforming unit, or a 'miss' $(NC \cdot A)$ corresponding to incorrectly accepting a nonconforming unit. The two other outcomes are correct acceptance of a conforming unit $(C{\cdot}A)$ and a 'false alarm' $(C{\cdot}R)$, the rejection of a conforming unit. The interdependence of the four probabilities is readily apparent. Increasing the probability of a hit, $P(NC{\cdot}R)$ is achieved only by accepting an increase in the probability of a false alarm, $P(C{\cdot}R)$ and a decrease in the other two probabilities.

Table 1. Definitions of probability statements.

Product mix	Decision based on inspection		
	Accept	Reject	Total
Conforming	$(1p_1)q_0$	$q_0(p_1)$	q_0
Nonconforming	p_2p_0	$(1-p_2)p_0$	p_0
Total	$(1-p_1)q_0+p_2p_0$	$q_0p_1+p_0(1-p_2)$	1

$q_0 = $ *A priori* probability of conforming product in an inspection lot
$p_0 = $ *A priori* probability of nonconforming product in an inspection lot $=(1-q_0)$
$1-p_1 = $ Probability of a correct acceptance decision for conforming product
$1-p_2 = $ Probability of a correct reject decision for nonconforming product

$$P(X|Y)=\frac{P(X \cdot Y)}{P(Y)}$$

$$P(\text{Accept}|\text{Conforming})=\frac{(1-p_1)q_0}{q_0}$$

$$P(\text{Reject}|\text{Nonconforming})=\frac{(1-p_2)p_0}{p_0}$$

$$P(\text{Reject}|\text{Conforming})=\frac{(q_0p_1)}{q_0}$$

$$P(\text{Accept}|\text{Nonconforming})=\frac{p_0p_2}{p_0}$$

Of particular interest are: the probability of rejecting, given a nonconforming unit, written as $P(R|NC)$ and the probability of acceptance, given a conforming unit, written $P(A|C)$. The other two probabilities are complementary to these since

$$P(R|C)=1-P(A|C) \text{ and } P(A|NC)=1-P(R|NC)$$

Conditional and joint probabilities are related since,

$$P(R|NC)=\frac{P(R{\cdot}NC)}{P(NC)}$$

$$P(A|C)=\frac{P(A{\cdot}C)}{P(C)}$$

where $P(NC)=$ *a priori* probability of occurrence of a faulty item.

It is then possible to define an expected value of an inspection decision in terms of value (V) and cost (K) as follows:

$$E(V)=V_{NC{\cdot}R}P(NC{\cdot}R)+V_{C{\cdot}A}P(C{\cdot}A)-K_{NC{\cdot}A}P(NC{\cdot}A)-K_{C{\cdot}R}P(C{\cdot}R)$$

Substituting *a priori* and conditional probabilities and collecting terms produces the result that maximizing $E(V)$ the expected value, is equivalent to maximizing

$$P(R|NC) - \beta P(R|C)$$

where

$$\beta = \frac{P(C)}{P(NC)} \left(\frac{V_{C \cdot A} + K_{C \cdot R}}{V_{NC \cdot R} + K_{NC \cdot A}} \right).$$

This value of β is equal to the value of the *likelihood ratio* or the probability of a 'hit' divided by the probability of a 'false alarm' in the former equation, but is a function of *a priori* probabilities and values of decision outcomes in the latter one.

If $P(R|NC)$ is plotted as a function of $P(R|C)$ a curve known as the Receiver Operating Characteristic or ROC curve is obtained. Figure 4 shows ROC curves for d' values of 1·0, 2·0 and 3·0 where

$$d' = \frac{\mu_{f_{NC}(x)} - \mu_{f_C(x)}}{\sigma_{f_C(x)}}$$

equals the number of standard deviations separating the populations of conforming and nonconforming product units. ROC curves for 'ideal' observers express theoretically optimal decision making under given perceptual and payoff conditions. Curves for 'real' (actual) observers have fewer hits per false alarm than those for ideal observers for a given value of d'.

In a study reported by Wallack and Adams (1969), industrial inspectors were pre-trained on a simple inspection task in which inspectors were required to identify nicks in small exposed stranded electrical conductors (Figure 5). Four levels of product defectiveness were used with p_0 equal to 5, 15, 25 and 35 %,

Figure 4. Receiver Operating Characteristic curves for one, two, and three standard deviations of observable product variance.

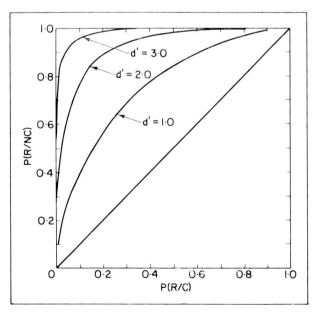

Figure 5. Test materials used in studies by Wallack and Adams (1969, 1970).

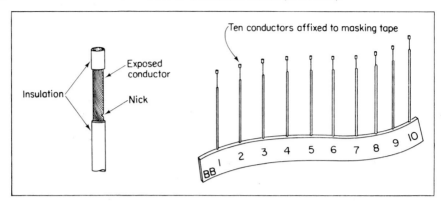

respectively. Selection of a value of p_0 for a particular lot (260 conductors each) was arbitrary in order to simulate industrial conditions.

Based on the outcome of tests, it was possible to classify inspector performance in terms of d', X_c and $E(V)$ for the decision process. Figure 6 shows the intersection of the two probability density functions with the criteria, X_c and d', given for each p_0. The reference point, X_c, indicated both the direction and magnitude of improvement needed. The criterion used when p_0 was 25% was lower than the others, for example. The reason for variations in X_c are not apparent, but did not appear to be the result of application of V and K values. These values were $+1$ for accepting good items or rejecting bad items, and -3 for accepting bad items or rejecting good items in this study. This means that V plus K was equal to four in all cases, so β was the ratio of $P(C)$ to $P(NC)$. Differences between this ratio and β are given in Table 2.

The greatest difference between used and optimal criteria occurred in the 5% sets. To produce a β equal to 19·00 for the given levels of V and K, X_c would have to be 2·465, based on a trial and error comparison of ratios of ordinates of normal curves with d' equal to 2·89. This would produce a Type 1 error rate of 0·007 and a Type 2 error rate of 0·335. Thus, defect detection would actually be poorer under an increased fraction of correctly identified conforming units. This concept of an inspection task is in contrast to the usual inspection objective of only maximizing the detection of defects.

Two distinct populations of inspectors were found to exist for the 5% test sample results. Differences among seven inspectors were analyzed using the χ^2 statistic and also in terms of signal detection theory. The latter method showed significant differences in the relative percentages of Type 1 and Type 2 errors. For Type 1, the percentages were 7·8 and 92·2 and for Type 2 they were 6·67 and 93·33, respectively for the two groups.

Problems in conducting this kind of industrial-laboratory experiment include the following.

1. Availability of inspector-subjects.

2. Establishment of payoff values V and K (reported to inspectors and supervisor). The values used were the result of consensus among quality control engineers, inspection supervisors, and a quality control manager.

3. Precise control of the introduction of the visual stimulus upon which decisions are based.

4. Knowledge of *a priori* probabilities. Signal detection theory presumes that the observer has such knowledge. The inspector usually does not have prior knowledge of the fraction defective. He is likely to be influenced by past experience.

5. Quantification of d' for an ideal observer is difficult, especially in working with industrial products. Signal/noise ratios depend upon many interacting factors when the visual stimulus is presented.

Figure 6. Illustration of d' and X_c for each p_0 in studies by Wallack and Adams (1969, 1970).

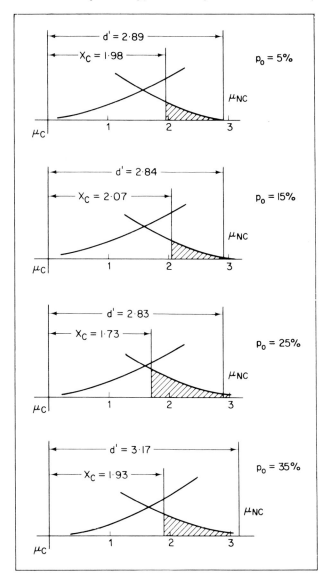

Table 2. Differences between ordinate ratio and β.　Adapted from Wallack and Adams (1969).

$f_{NC}(x)$	β	$f_{NC}(x)/f_{c}(x)$	Difference
5%	19·00	4·74	−14·26
15%	5·67	6·36	+0·69
25%	3·00	2·44	−0·56
35%	1·86	3·31	+1·45

Behavioural factors strongly affect the nature of the ROC curve and their effects can be shown to be largely independent of stimulus variables. *A priori* probabilities (lot fraction defective) and signal-noise ratios (detection effectiveness in terms of physical parameters and information feedback) affect the magnitude of d' for a real observer. These are primarily stimulus variables. Variables affecting primarily the response to be given include deprivation variables and the payoff structure. Deprivation variables (inspector sensitivity to knowledge of his performance and its consequences) and the outcome or payoff structure associated with correct and incorrect decisions affect the position along a particular ROC curve, representing the conservativeness or liberality of the inspector in committing a high false alarm rate in order to achieve more detections.

Behaviourally engineering an inspection task by taking these four variables into account and providing effective yet acceptable feedback poses some unique challenges in engineering psychology with respect to individual and group decision making and overall quality control systems design.

2.2. *Bayesian measures*

Applying Bayes' rule to an inspection task is another statistical approach useful in studying decision making in quality control. Under this approach,

$$P(C|A) = \frac{P(C) \cdot P(A|C)}{P(C) \cdot P(A|C) + P(NC) \cdot P(A|NC)}$$

where

$$C = \text{conforming item}$$
$$NC = \text{nonconforming item}$$
$$A = \text{decision to accept}$$
$$R = \text{decision to reject}$$

Referring to Table 1, this becomes

$$P(C|A) = \frac{q_0(1-p_1)}{q_0(1-p_1)+p_2 p_0} = \begin{array}{l}\text{conditional probability that an accepted}\\ \text{item is good.}\end{array}$$

Also

$$P(NC|R) = \frac{p_0(1-p_2)}{q_0 p_1 + p_0(1-p_2)} = \begin{array}{l}\text{conditional probability that a}\\ \text{rejected item is defective.}\end{array}$$

The effect of p_0 upon $P(C|A)$ and $P(NC|R)$ and $P(NC|R)$ in the study by Wallack and Adams (1970) is shown in Figure 7. The existence of an apparent plateau (from 15 to 25%) was supported by difference tests using the z statistic. Table 3 shows that the decision process is affected by the *a priori* probability of nonconforming product but the effect occurs more at extreme values of p_0 than at central values. Referring to Figure 7, it can be seen that at the 5% level few defective items are accepted, but many conforming items are rejected. These effects change at the 15% level, especially for $P(NC|R)$. More defects are accepted and fewer conforming items are rejected. Differences beyond the 15% level are not significant. The different trends in the curves representing $P(C|A)$ and $P(NC|R)$ are of interest in that they suggest that the ability to identify conforming and nonconforming product may vary with p_0.

Figure 7. Bayesian criteria versus p_0 (Wallack and Adams 1969, 1970).

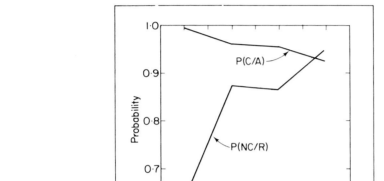

Table 3. Test of hypotheses for Bayesian criteria

Measure	H_0	H_1	Critical region	Decision
$P(C|A)$	$p_05 = p_015$	$p_05 > p_015$	$z > z_{.05}$	Reject H_0
	$p_015 = p_025$	$p_015 > p_025$	$z > z_{.05}$	Cannot reject H_0
	$p_025 = p_035$	$p_025 > p_035$	$z > z_{.05}$	Reject H_0
$P(NC|R)$	$p_05 = p_015$	$p_05 < p_015$	$z < -z_{.05}$	Reject H_0
	$p_015 = p_025$	$p_015 > p_025$	$z > z_{.05}$	Cannot reject H_0
	$p_025 = p_035$	$p_025 < p_035$	$z < -z_{.05}$	Reject H_0

It is possible that in some tasks cognitive processes associated with visual search may have an influence. For example, it takes longer to identify words in a list which do not contain a letter than to identify those which do (Neisser 1964). This is because only a rapid scan is needed to identify a target letter but every letter must be processed in some complex way when searching for words not containing the target letter.

Decision making

It is important that probable effect of p_0 on decision making be taken into account if feedback or instructions for purposes of controlling performance are to be effective. Compared with signal detection theory, Bayesian methods are limited in that they do not clearly indicate the direction of decision improvement needed.

2.3. *McCornack's measures*

McCornack (1961) suggested three measures of inspector performance. Referring to Table 1, these are

$$A_1 = (1-p_1)q_0 + (1-p_2)p_0$$
$$A_2 = (1-p_1)$$
$$A_3 = (1-p_2)$$

In using A_1, it is assumed that both correct decisions are equally important. The use of A_2 emphasizes the importance of maximizing the acceptance of conforming products. The use of A_3 emphasizes the need to reject nonconforming products. Thus A_2 emphasizes Type 1 errors and A_3 emphasizes Type 2 errors. Since damage caused by defects and waste caused by rejecting good items both affect inspection costs, A_1 is more generally useful. Plots of A_1, A_2, and A_3 as a function of p_0 are given in Figure 8. The results indicate, but less clearly than the Bayesian measures, that overall performance is affected by p_0.

Figure 8. McCornack's criteria versus p_0 (Wallack and Adams 1969, 1970).

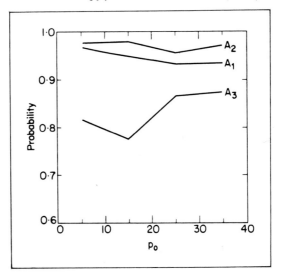

3. Examples of application

The foregoing discussion of the effectiveness of statistical measures of inspector error and performance used the study and analysis by Wallack and Adams as an example of application. The product used in this case was small pieces of stranded cable. Defects consisted of nicks in the cable. Several other successful applications of signal detection theory to industrial inspection have been demonstrated on a laboratory basis. Since the use of signal detection theory permits the study of both stimulus and response variables, the entire inspection task may, at least in theory, be studied. The use of ROC curves should permit the comparison of viewing conditions, inspectors, equipment used, or visual target used to signal a defect. In studies by the author, the use of signal detection theory has been one of controlling the experiment in the areas of subject selection (especially the exclusion of data showing too high a tendency to 'guess' or to reject good products) and in the analysis of response data.

3.1. *Microminiature inspection*

A study of microminiature inspection by Smith and Adams (1971) involved the use of a binocular microscope to detect standard Landolt rings among O-type rings in 8×8 and 7×7 patterns photographically reduced and placed on motion picture film for frame by frame analysis under the microscope. Earlier experiments using typed C's and O's presented on 35 mm slides had demonstrated the superiority of using 6×6 patterns over using 8×8 patterns in terms of time per correct inspection. The two time values were about $0 \cdot 10$ minute for the 8×8 pattern and about $0 \cdot 05$ minute for the 6×6 pattern. The distribution of the number of C's was approximately Poisson, varying from 0 to 6 for the 6×6 pattern ($2 \cdot 6$ average) and from 2 to 9 for the 8×8 pattern ($5 \cdot 4$ average). Magnification levels were varied in five increments from $\times 7$ to $\times 40$. An optimal level of magnification of $8 \cdot 3$ minutes of visual angle was clearly demonstrated. The experiments using Landolt and O-type rings indicated an optimal level of magnification at $\times 8(9 \cdot 3'$ visual angle) for both 7×7 and 8×8 patterns. Advantages of high levels of illumination were also demonstrated. The effect of magnification became less as the combined effects of illumination and pattern size presented easier viewing conditions.

In a third experiment, subjects were required to count defects and accept no C or one C but not two or more. The experiment was run under two sets of instructions: A (avoid false alarms) and B (avoid misses). The results were affected by levels of proficiency gained through practice, but demonstrated significant differences in d' and proved that factors affecting operator performance on detection are (or can be) independent of those affecting decision.

3.2. *Complex visual performance*

Signal detection theory has been used to simplify the analysis of tasks in which subjects are required to detect a target letter within a typed column or row of letters under normal viewing conditions but restricted time (Green 1970), (Adams 1970). These studies have been designed to compare visual search in a static field with visual search in a dynamic field, and to develop an overall theory helpful in the design of visual inspection tasks. Using signal detection theory, it was found possible to plot Type 1 and Type 2 error as a function of target position for various levels of target confusability and for several sizes of rows and columns. A significant 'tunneling effect' or restriction of accurate detection to a field of view no larger than 3 or 4 minutes of arc was observed for letter combinations with high confusability. This effect occurred primarily for Type 1 error (missed letters). Type 2 error was generally distributed uniformly with respect to target letter position. These experiments have been designed to study perceptual aspects of inspection rather than decision aspects. Signal detection theory provided a convenient tool for analyzing data and selecting subjects. The study of inspection of letter matrices could provide a basis for analyzing inspector decisions under controlled levels of perceptual confusability.

Much remains to be learned in applying signal detection theory to industrial inspection. Williges (1971), using as a stimulus programmed changes in brightness level on an electroluminescent panel, demonstrated that values of β and d' vary over time and with signal probability. When observers expected more signals, they detected more signals, but also produced more false alarms. Three levels of payoff relating to the importance of Type 1 and Type 2 errors were employed. It was found that signal probabilities rather than payoffs had the dominant effect in determining decision performance on a simple visual task.

(In the experiments by Williges and Jerison cited in this paper, β refers to the ratio of the height of the signal distribution ordinate to the non-signal distribution ordinate on the X_c criterion line.)

4. Other considerations

4.1. *Vigilance*

The use of signal detection theory presumes that an observing response (decision to observe) was made and that information was received and processed before the response to the stimulus is given. Stimulus intervals are also predefined. Thus, signal detection theory says nothing regarding attention by the inspector.

Jerison *et al.* (1965) performed an extensive set of experiments in which subjects observed changes in the regularity of movements of a small bar of red light (2 minutes × 18 minutes). They were able to define three levels of observing: alert observing, blurred observing and distraction. Alert observing generally follows the presumed fixed signal interval, highly attentive state assumed under signal detection theory. Blurred observing produces large increases in the variance of both noise and signal distributions. Distraction represents no responses to any stimuli and thereby reduces all response probabilities. The value of β is very high under this condition. The authors suggest the development and use of statistical analyses which take relative amounts of these three modes of observing into account.

4.2. *Behavioural modification*

Holland (1963), on the other hand, suggests that the central problem of analyzing vigilance tasks is that of defining the observing response. Using a simple pointer deflection test, Holland set up conditions making it necessary for the subject to press a key repeatedly in order to see the dial containing the pointer. Button pressing and hence responding to deflections was a function of the schedule of reinforcement (programmed schedule of deflections). Thus, 'attention' was transformed into a response which could be recorded. Holland demonstrated fixed interval, fixed ratio, and multiple schedule effects in a vigilance task. The implications of this study are that specific observing and reporting responses are beneficial in that they help to predefine stimulus intervals and to maintain alert observing by forcing the inspector to pay the price of making an effort to observe. Inspection becomes more active and less passive under these conditions.

Decisions are based upon actions and the result of actions and not upon a passive 'decision to observe'.

It seems likely that behavioural modification technology (operant conditioning) can be applied successfully in the area of inspector training. Improved response to stimulus conditions present and more importantly an improved observing behavioural scheme, both suggest improved decision making. Since response data can be quantified under such a scheme, accurate feedback to the inspector and the use of productivity incentives for good decisions should improve decision making in the inspection station.

Physically defining the observing response in order to quantify alert periods or 'decisions to observe' is not an entirely proven solution at this time. Jerison and Pickett (1963) pointed out that unless the switch used to illuminate the target area is difficult to operate (3 lb.), Holland's data 'cannot be duplicated'. Some criterion other than force applied to a button may allow this limitation to be overcome. It may be possible to behaviourally engineer some relatively simple psychomotor task into an inspection such that it generates the desired sensory monitoring processes. 'Tell me what you see' or 'tell me if anything is there' would, in many cases, produce more attentiveness than 'only tell me if you detect a rare occurrence'.

4.3. *Work-rest cycles, schedules*

The vigilance decrement in inspection performance has its onset after the first 30 to 40 minutes of monitoring a low probability signal detection task. This effort can and has been used to define work-rest schedules on inspection tasks, especially when advantage can be taken of batch production such as occurs when large rolls of film or paper are inspected one at a time. Since knowledge of results is important for improving decisions by the inspector, such knowledge could, in some cases, be obtained or reviewed during short rest breaks. Increasing signal probability as a function of time by using artificial signals, increasing the detecting sensitivity of the system through improved equipment, or increasing the speed at which the system operates to compress signals in time are all ways of modifying *a priori* signal probability. It is also possible to change the behavioural characteristics of the inspection task to require reporting of non-critical information to assure that observing is taking place. This practice is common in law enforcement when a local emergency develops and everyone representing a possible suspect or witness is questioned routinely. Thus, being required to make a decision more often for routine cases can help to assure that it will be made correctly when it is urgent.

5. Summary and recommendations

This paper represents an attempt to summarize some of the perceptual, statistical modelling, and behavioural aspects of decision making in industrial inspection. Some examples of applying signal detection theory to high signal probability tasks were given. Decision making was shown to be divided into several specific functions: the decision to observe (and what to observe) and the decision regarding the most economically advantageous alternative, given the process conditions and inspection plan being used. Maintaining effective control over both types of decisions depends strongly upon feedback to the inspector. This includes feedback from the task itself (technical feedback) and feedback from management or from other production functions. It seems likely that if effective measures of inspector performance can be applied in industry, that effective positive productivity incentive systems can be applied. This suggests some form of 'perceptual-decision work measurement'.

It seems likely that signal detection theory, behavioural modification technology, and improved definitions of observing responses will all be involved in the development of such an approach to inspection. While behavioural modification will very likely play a key role in this development, its application is not as simple as was at first presumed. Special studies in motivation on inspection tasks may provide the additional basic information needed to develop a better understanding of how and why individual decisions are made within intervals and over actual time periods.

At least one good start has been made in developing a comprehensive overall theory of vigilance tasks which incorporates behavioural modification and signal detection theory parameters. Russell Smith (1966) developed a comprehensive set of assumptions and experimental evidence for these assumptions and an overall mathematical model derived from them. Basic operational definitions in Smith's model include intrinsic (task induced) and extrinsic (management induced) motivation, simple (single signal, yes-no choice) and complex displays, monotony and conscientiousness. The model assumes that 'all individuals of normal intelligence and perceptual capacities are capable of continuously attending a simple vigilance display for one or two hours and detecting all signals' (Smith 1966, p. 11). The general mathematical model incorporates variables indicating the degree of monotony, time at the task, signal rates, probability of detection, and various constants. The function derived is of the negative exponential variety with asymptotic probability of detection for each signal rate over time. The model suggests an optimal signal presentation rate which will produce a maximum probability of detection by minimizing the degree of monotony. Monotony is higher and detection less probable on either side of this value. General postulates are made regarding the effects of task variety, motivation, rewards and punishment, coercion (threat of punishment), and identification with the 'influencer' (experimenter).

Evidence from reported studies in the literature is used to support proposed effects of signal rate, artificial signals, intersignal interval, false alarms, rest periods, knowledge of results, rewards and punishments (money earned and lost), coercion, and identification.

The theory contains a postulate with respect to artificial signals: that as long as artificial signals require the same simple acts, do not compete with real signals, and are considered as important as real signals, it does not matter if they are identical to or different from real signals. The effects of the two signals are identical. Neither published research literature nor industrial experience seem to offer encouragement to the idea of increasing signal rates by using artificial signals.

It appears possible to perform experiments on real or simulated industrial tasks to develop supporting evidence for the perceptual and decision making aspects of Smith's theory. Motivational variables present a greater challenge in industrial applications than in the laboratory. The theory and evidence supporting it suggest that work design, perceptual variables, decision making, and overall performance can be studied in terms of a combined model. The development of a taxonomy of industrial inspection tasks based on a unified theory appears to be a useful step toward the ultimate development of general standard data for inspection tasks.

References

ADAMS, S. K., 1970, Dynamic factors in the visual inspection of linear displays. *Paper presented at the Fourteenth Annual Meeting of the Human Factors Society, San Francisco.*

GREEN, D. M., and SWETS, J. A., 1966, *Signal Detection Theory and Psychophysics.* (New York: WILEY.)

GREEN, J. S., 1970, *Visual Search in a Dynamic Field.* (Unpublished Doctoral Dissertation (psychology), Oklahoma State University.)

HOLLAND, J. G., 1963, Human vigilance. In *Vigilance: A Symposium.* (Edited by D. N. BUCKNER and J. J. MCGRATH) (New York: MCGRAW-HILL.)

JERISON, H. J., and PICKETT, R. M., 1963, Vigilance: a review and re-evaluation. *Human Factors,* **5,** 211–238.

JERISON, H. J., PICKETT, R. M., and STENSON, H. H., 1965, The elicited observing rate and decision processes in vigilance. *Human Factors,* **7,** 107–128.

MCCORNACK, R. L., 1961, *Inspector Accuracy: a Study of the Literature.* (Sandia Corporation Technical Memorandum, SCTM 53–61 (14). Sandia Corporation, Albuquerque, New Mexico.)

NEISSER, U., 1964, Visual search. *Scientific American,* June, 2–9.

SMITH, G. L., and ADAMS, S. K., 1971, Magnification and microminiature inspection. *Human Factors,* **13,** 247–254.

SMITH, L. A., and BARANY, J. W., 1970, An elementary model of human performance on paced visual inspection tasks. *AIIE Transactions,* **2,** 298–308.

SMITH, R. L., 1966, *Monotony and Motivation: a Theory of Vigilance.* (Special report prepared for Dunlap and Associates, Inc., Santa Monica, California.)

SWETS, J. A. (ed.), 1964, *Signal Detection and Recognition by Human Observers, Contemporary Readings.* (New York: WILEY.)

SWETS, J. A., TANNER, W. P., and BIRDSALL, T. G., 1961, Decision processes in perception. *Psychological Review,* **68,** 301–340.

WALD, A., 1950, *Statistical Decision Functions.* (New York: WILEY.)

WALLACK, P. M., and ADAMS, S. K., 1969, The utility of signal detection theory in the analysis of industrial inspector accuracy. *AIIE Transactions,* **1,** 33–44.

WALLACK, P. M., and ADAMS, S. K., 1970, A comparison of inspector performance measures. *AIIE Transactions,* **2,** 97–105.

WILLIGES, R. C., 1971, The role of payoffs and signal ratios in criterion changes during a monitoring task. *Human Factors,* **13,** 261–267.

Vigilance: a review

A. Craig and W. P. Colquhoun

1. Introduction and summary of the evidence

The starting point for the consideration of 'vigilance' as a model for explaining performance in tasks of prolonged attention is generally taken as World War II, during which the frequency of reports of failures to detect various types of military target either by unaided vision or via the use of radar and similar devices reached the point at which research was commissioned to investigate the causes of what at the time was ascribed to 'mental fatigue'. A team at Cambridge under the direction of F. C. Bartlett, which was already examining fatigue in aircraft pilots and navigators, extended its programme to include studies of this phenomenon. Most prominent among the workers assigned to this project was N. H. Mackworth, whose experiments were eventually published in the now classic monograph *Researches in the Measurement of Human Performance* (Mackworth 1950).

Mackworth's approach was to present what he considered to be the essential elements of the actual operation in a relatively simple simulation of the task, performance of which was studied in the laboratory under a variety of conditions. The two main aims of this programme were: first, to identify those factors which contributed to the poor levels of efficiency observed; and secondly, to discover ways of improving these levels which could be of practical applicability in the field.

Using both visual and auditory displays, Mackworth quickly confirmed the findings from operational reports that detection of 'signals' declined to a considerable extent simply as a function of time on task, *even when environmental conditions were optimal*. This decline in detection rate has become known as the 'vigilance decrement' (see Figure 1) and a great deal of research effort has been expended by a large number of investigators in many countries to determine its basic cause. It would not perhaps be unfair to say that, despite this effort, no unique cause (if indeed there is a *single* basic cause) has yet been identified.

Mackworth identified a number of factors which tended to enhance the vigilance decrement. Among these were: unfamiliarity with the kind of work involved, a low signal rate, and the presence of adverse environmental conditions such as a high ambient temperature. To this list later research has added, among others, factors such as lack of sleep (Wilkinson 1960), night work (Colquhoun *et al.* 1969), depressant drugs (e.g. Colquhoun 1962a), and an inappropriately high expectancy of signal rate at the start of the session (Colquhoun and Baddeley 1964, 1967). Poor individual performance has been partly identified with personality variables, particularly extraversion (Bakan 1959), and low motivation in experimental subjects has been expressly cited as a major cause of pronounced decrement (see J. F. Mackworth 1970).

In his search for remedial measures, Mackworth found that the decrement was either abolished, or substantially reduced, by either: administering a stimulant drug beforehand; giving 'feedback' about performance during the task; or alternating 30-minute periods of work with rest-periods of similar length. Later research has demonstrated that the feedback need not necessarily be accurate (Weidenfeller *et al.* 1962), that the rest-period can be reduced to 5 minutes or less (Colquhoun 1959, Wilkinson 1959) and that the mere presence of a silent supervisor may be as effective as anything else (Fraser 1953). As might be expected from the list of detrimental factors given above, their 'opposites' have the reverse effect; thus the decrement is reduced when the expectancy of signal-probability is appropriate (Colquhoun and Baddeley *op. cit.*), and performance levels are higher in introverted subjects, particularly in the early morning (Colquhoun 1960, Colquhoun and Corcoran 1964). On the other hand, allowing the subject some control over the rate at which items are presented for inspection does not, as might perhaps have been expected, improve efficiency (Colquhoun 1962b, Wilkinson 1961). But an increase in the complexity of the task requirements (Adams *et al.* 1961, Monty 1962) can be beneficial, despite the fact that the work is thereby made more difficult.

Figure 1. The 'vigilance decrement': mean percentage of signals detected by a group of 36 subjects in a one-hour session of simple visual inspection, as a function of time on task.

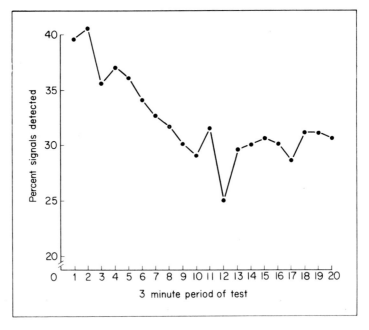

Two major criticisms that have been levelled at this research have been: (*a*) that the 'signal rates' employed in laboratory situations are unrealistically high in relation to, e.g., the typical defect incidence on an inspection line; and (*b*) that experiments have concentrated on the decline in efficiency with time to the neglect of the undeniably important fact that the *overall levels* of performance are always well below optimum. In fact Elliott (1960) claims that, in military watchkeeping tasks at least, within-session decrement is rarely observed; whether this be true of inspection operations or not, experiments which have involved repeated testing of subjects several times a day for up to 12 consecutive days (Colquhoun *et al.* 1968) have failed to observe any diminution in the on-task decrement with practice, despite the fact that performance at the beginning of each successive session returns to at least its initial level. To some extent this latter finding answers the further complaint that laboratory results are not applicable to people working in real-life situations because of the latter's extensive experience.

As regards the relative levels of 'signal rate' in laboratory and 'real-life' situations, it is true that in some jobs faults occur only with great rarity, but this does not hold in many production operations, and, in any case, although it must be admitted that extrapolation has its dangers, it is obviously a practical impossibility to experiment with signal rates which are so low as to give no measurable index of performance within a reasonable time period. It would seem that in this case it is safer to assume that laboratory findings with relatively high signal rates are in fact applicable to real-life situations with much lower rates than to dismiss the laboratory findings out of hand.

The importance of signal rate in determining the levels of efficiency observed is, in fact, the most generally accepted finding in vigilance research. Earlier workers (Jenkins 1959, Kappauf and Powe 1958) apparently showed that the fact that lower rates produced lower levels of detection efficiency than higher ones was due solely to an increased decrement over time in the former case. However, experiments by Colquhoun and Baddeley (1964, 1967) demonstrated that this was partly an artifact of the prior 'expectancy' of the subjects for a high rate, and that the greatest effect of rate was actually on the *overall level* of performance. Colquhoun (1961), in addition, showed that it is the conditional *probability* of a signal, given an 'event', that is the important factor, rather than the actual *frequency* of signals in time (though Jerison (1967) has argued that this does not necessarily apply at very low values). The general effect of signal probability is shown in Figure 2.

Increases in signal probability produce increases in detection rate, at the expense of a rise in the 'false report' rate (Baddeley and Colquhoun 1969). Thus it can be argued that, provided that false reports can be tolerated in the practical situation, improved detection efficiency could be achieved by the addition of 'artificial' signals to the input (Wilkinson 1964), particularly when the presumed 'true' signal rate is low (i.e., batch quality is high). However, apart from the practical difficulties of doing this in a real-life situation there is the distinct possibility that 'reject norms' that are known to arise over time in any actual inspection team (McKenzie 1958) may exert such a powerful influence on behaviour that the relationship between signal probability and detection rate observed in experimental situations would be obviated. More subtle approaches may be required to enable practical use to be made of the 'signal-probability effect' that appears so clearly in the laboratory.

It has been argued (Jerison 1966) that the 'signal-probability' effect, at least as observed by Colquhoun (1961), was due to a change in visual search patterns rather than to an alteration in detection efficiency *per se*. However Colquhoun (1966) has shown that the same effect occurs even when search is not required, and that there is no evidence that scanning behaviour alters as a function of

time on task (Colquhoun 1970). Nevertheless, it is true that differential probability of occurrence of signals in different parts of a large display has a definite
effect on detection efficiency (Nicely and Miller 1957), and that in many real-life
situations visual search is an important factor. But perhaps the most crucial
criticism of the practical relevance of research on vigilance has been the over-
riding tendency for experimenters to use uni-dimensional stimuli, and to define
'signals' or 'faults' in terms of a departure from the norm of fixed magnitude in
this single dimension. There is no doubt that this criticism is a valid one, and
that future research must aim to simulate more closely the real task, in which
defective items are identified more often in terms of a combination of variations
of different magnitude in several dimensions than by the presence or absence
of a fixed 'fault'. Nevertheless there is already evidence to suggest that the
possibility of faults having different magnitudes makes no difference to the
vigilance decrement, and that the latter is similar for each magnitude of fault
considered separately (Colquhoun 1967).

Figure 2. The 'signal-probability' effect: detection-rate and false report rate as a function of the
proportion of inspected items that are 'faulty'. (From Baddeley and Colquhoun 1969.)

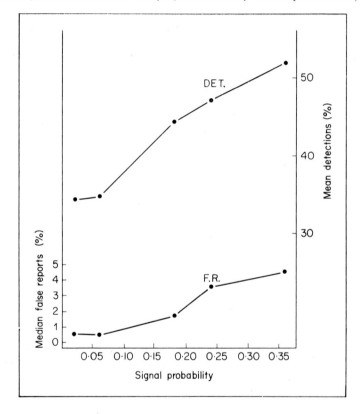

2. Explanatory theories

2.1. *Outline of theories*

Although numerous attempts have been made to account, in terms of theory,
for the vigilance phenomena described in the previous section, none has proved
entirely satisfactory, each theory having its own *bête noire* in some familiar

finding(s) for which it cannot account. It is arguable however, that the various explanations are complementary in character, rather than in opposition to each other, and in this way one can with few exceptions account for almost the entire body of evidence.

The predominant theories which have motivated much of the research during the past two decades and which, individually, can cope with large chunks, but not all, of the data, are based respectively on the notions of arousal (activation), inhibition (extinction), orienting response habituation, filtering (observing responses) and expectancy.

According to the arousal theory (Hebb 1955) the central nervous system requires some minimal level of activity in order to maintain a reasonable level of efficiency, and this activation level, which is dependent on the variation in external stimulation, will be low when man is in a monotonous, unstimulating environment. In vigilance, the argument runs, where the conditions are conducive to low arousal, the efficiency of performance will be low and will deteriorate as exposure to the monotonous environment continues (Zuercher 1965).

From the viewpoint of the inhibition theory, which was regarded by N. H. Mackworth (1950) as providing the least unsatisfactory explanation, the vigilance process is seen as analogous to those animal studies in which a behavioural response is experimentally extinguished by depriving the animal of any reward or reinforcement for making the response. One may argue that in the typical vigilance task, responses to the repetitive sequence of non-target events are extinguished since they are not reinforced and that this inhibitory state generalises to the response to signal items, since the latter normally share several features in common with the non-signal items.

Yet another approach argues that the decrement is the result of the habituation, not of an overt *motor* response, but of the orienting response which is a short-lived neurophysiological response to a discrete stimulus, especially a novel one, and which gradually habituates (i.e. disappears) to repeated presentations of the stimulus (Sokolov 1963). Proponents of this view (J. F. Mackworth 1969, Jerison 1970) entertain the possibility that the orienting-response is necessary to provide the internal 'evidence' on whose basis the observer decides that a 'signal' has been presented, but that this 'evidence' declines as the response habituates, most probably to the repetitive sequence of background events.

This same reduction in stimulus novelty as a consequence of the large number of repetitions involved was also held to be important by Broadbent (1958) who proposed that the vigilance phenomena might be explained by the operation of a filter, through which all information to be processed must pass, and which has a constant bias in favour of novel events. The progressive decline in novelty of the input from the task would lead the observer to attend less and less to the task itself, while causing him to become more easily distracted by other sources of stimulation. The filter approach links up very closely with certain views about the role of observing-responses, although the proposed mechanisms differ. Jerison (1967) has suggested that although there is a need to observe constantly throughout a vigilance task, over time the effort for sustained attention declines because the 'costs' of maintenance are too high. Inhibition of observing responses directed to the task develops from the long series of non-signal stimuli which go completely unrewarded, while other 'rewards' accrue for being attentive to stimulation other than that provided by the display itself.

From the brief sketches given of these four theories it seems clear that for them, despite the differences in their proposed mechanisms, the explanation for the reduced performance rests in each case on the repetitive, monotonous stimulation which is an essential feature of the vigilance task. And it must be admitted that the idea that performance falls off because of the boring nature of the task situation is one which carries intuitive appeal for anyone who has ever worked on an industrial inspection line, operated a radar console for a couple of hours, or taken part in a laboratory vigilance task.

The notion of reduced efficiency under conditions of low stimulation receives substantial support from the studies on sensory deprivation (Bexton *et al.* 1954, Vernon *et al.* 1959), in which subjects who were isolated from the normal level of background environmental stimulation by being confined in a small cubicle and whose vision, hearing, limb movement, and sense of touch were restricted, exhibited impaired performance as a result of their isolation in the monotonous environment on almost every item in a battery of tests of mental performance. In addition, some of these measures showed a progressive deterioration as the period of deprivation was extended, a finding which seems a close parallel to the decrement observed in a great many vigilance studies.

By way of contrast, the expectancy approach (Baker 1963) suggests that performance might benefit if the structure of the task was made even less varied, and that a major reason for the reduced efficiency during vigilance lies in the great uncertainty about signal arrival times which necessarily exists in a situation where very few of these critical events occur during a lengthy period of time. The low response rate, claims expectancy theory, is merely a reflection of the estimate of the low signal rate, an estimate which is based on past experience. Accordingly if an observer fails to detect a few of the signals early on in the sequence, because of his inability to anticipate accurately their arrival time, he will be even less certain about the arrival times of signals later in the run; in addition, he may revise his opinion about the overall signal probability so that on both of these counts he will become less likely to report any subsequent signals.

From the outlines which have been given it will be apparent that there are marked contrasts between expectancy theory and the others in some of the predictions which may logically be drawn, and these will be considered in the following section in which the evidence relating to the theories is discussed.

2.2. *Discussion of the theories*

Whereas evidence in favour of expectancy theory can only come indirectly from the interpretation of the experimental results, the arousal account has received rather more direct support from studies in which electrophysiological measures of the concomitant activity in the nervous system have accompanied the performance measures. Thus, for example, Dardano (1962) and Andreassi (1966) both report studies in which skin conductance, often cited as an index of arousal, declined during the vigil, and in both studies the greatest decline in the arousal measure was obtained from those individual subjects whose performance suffered most during the run. In a related finding, Tarriere and Hartemann (1964) reported within-session reductions in levels of heart-rate, another indicant of arousal, the declining levels again being accompanied by decrements in performance. It may be argued, however, that these results do not necessarily imply a direct causal chain, in which the links are: monotonous stimulation→low physiological arousal→reduced performance; the changes in both activation and performance levels could be independent of each other and merely derivative of changes in some other factor of mutual influence which is itself affected by the task conditions. This is the old, familiar problem of being unable to specify a causal connection between two correlated sets of data. The same criticism may be levelled at those studies in which the administration of amphetamines— drugs which are known to stimulate the nervous system—has resulted in the detection decrements being reduced to a non-significant level. Prior opinion held that this was strong evidence favouring the role of arousal, but again it is conceivable that the effect on performance is mediated by, for example, observing-responses, which are themselves increased by the stimulant drug (Weiner and Ross 1962). A more serious objection to the arousal interpretation is that the ampheta-mines do not improve the initial level of performance (J. F. Mackworth 1965) whereas, if the interpretation were correct, one would have expected them to do so. To offset these criticisms, the separate reports by Jenkins (1958), by Blake (1971) and by Colquhoun (1971) which appear to show time-of-day effects on both the initial level and the extent of the decrement are difficult to account for by any mechanism other than activation, in which a diurnal rhythm is a well established phenomenon (Conroy and Mills 1970). The time-of-day effect on vigilance performance is illustrated in Figure 3 which also shows the rhythm in body temperature.

The first group of theories contain so many points of common reference that it is rather difficult to differentiate between them when considering the evidence. For example, the beneficial effects of providing knowledge of results may be regarded as due to increased arousal, disinhibition, dishabituation or increased attention to the task. They might equally well be called to reinforce acceptance of the expectancy model, since knowledge of results must aid the observer in arriving at his estimate of the signal probability and in anticipating the arrival time of the next signal in the event sequence. Nevertheless, two experiments, one by Weidenfeller *et al.* (1962), another by J. F. Mackworth (1964) demon-strated that performance could benefit even when the knowledge of results was false, a finding for which expectancy theory cannot account. It is of particular interest that in the Mackworth experiment, and in a later one by the same investi-gator (J. F. Mackworth 1965), the false knowledge of results increased the overall level of performance *from the beginning of the session* but did not reduce the decrement in detections, which suggests that at least some part of the effect of providing true knowledge of results may be due to an initial increase in arousal or alertness.

The reduced decrement following a brief rest pause (Colquhoun 1959, Wilkinson 1959) and 'recovery' between testing sessions (Adams *et al.* 1962) may also be attributed to any of the proposed mechanisms of response to monotony, but without affording distinctions between them. Again, these effects are difficult to explain by means of expectancy theory, for which the renewed appearance of a decrement within each subsequent session (Colquhoun *et al.* 1968) is a particular problem.

Despite the remarks made in the preceding paragraphs about the equivalence of the former group of theories, there exists some evidence which is specific to the role played by observing responses. Weiner and Ross (1962) examined the effects of the non-signal rate on observing-responses in a task where the occurrence of an event could only be seen if an observing-response (the pressing of a lever) was made. They found that the observing responses *increased* as the non-signal rate was increased, which is in direct opposition to predictions based on the views of either Broadbent or Jerison, who would have anticipated a *decline* in the observing responses as the incidence of the 'unwanted' signals increased. Furthermore, the higher rate of the responses was achieved by a manipulation which would probably have resulted in a lower detection rate, either because of the increased event rate (Jerison 1967) or because of the reduced probability of a signal (Colquhoun 1961). A related finding is reported by Baker (1960), who photographed subjects engaged on a monitoring task and found that they were invariably observing the signal source when the signal appeared, despite the fact that the usual reduction in detection rate occurred, although to a non-significant extent. These two experiments, in combination, cast serious doubts on theories concerned with the role of overt observing-responses. If further evidence were needed, it is surely provided by Broadbent himself, who found that the observing

Figure 3. The arousal effect: mean detection rate and body-temperature level of a group of 12 subjects as a function of the time of day at which the measures were taken.

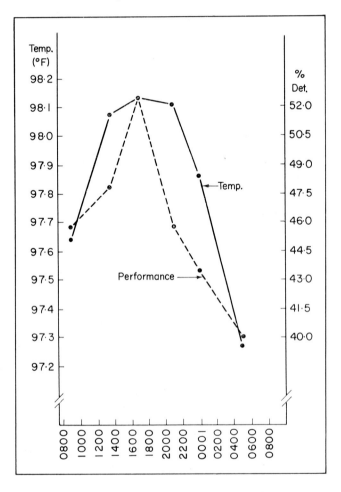

response rate increased during the session, even although efficiency (as measured by the response latency) was declining (Broadbent 1963).

It may prove useful to pause at this stage to consider the conclusions so far. Evidence has been discussed which seemed favourable to the arousal theory, as distinct from any of the others; consideration was made of two sets of results which could not be explained by the expectancy theory; and finally, three experiments have been mentioned from which it would appear that the observable action of making a 'looking-response' directed towards the display, is unrelated to detection efficiency at the task. Otherwise the evidence has not proved critical in distinguishing between the several theories. To redress the balance, in the paragraphs which follow, experiments will be discussed which offer substantial and exclusive support for the expectancy view and which pose serious problems for the other theories.

Proponents of expectancy theory consider that the response to a signal becomes more likely if the signal is more probable, and that the observer's estimate of the probability is derived from his prior experience of signal incidence (Baker 1963). The previously cited work by Colquhoun and Baddeley (1967) provides the most direct evidence favouring this hypothesis. They studied the effects of the signal probability level used during training on subsequent performance in the test session and found (as Figure 4 illustrates) that the overall level of performance

Figure 4. The expectancy effect: mean detection rate as a function of the signal probability experienced during practice and that obtaining during the subsequent test session. (From Colquhoun and Baddeley 1967.)

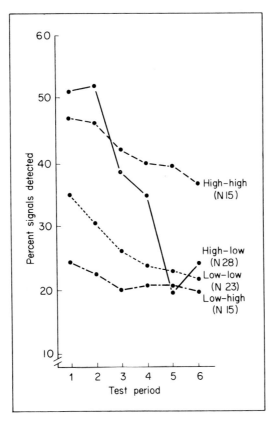

was higher when an appropriately high signal probability had been used during training, than when an inappropriately low one was used; the interpretation being that subjects who had trained under the low probability were not anticipating the higher relative frequency at which the signals were presented during the test run. They also found (see the figure) that, for a low test probability, the extent of the vigilance decrement was greater when an inappropriately high signal probability had been experienced during training. These results offer direct support for the expectancy hypothesis and cannot be explained by any of the 'under-stimulation' theories, since the decisive factor was what occurred during training and this could not have influenced habituation or inhibition during the subsequent test session. But it should be noted that a decrement still existed even when the appropriate training levels of signal probability had been used.

A previous study by Colquhoun (1961) had also emphasized the importance of signal probability. There, he had presented signals at two different rates and at two levels of signal probability and the results clearly showed that it was the *probability*, not the rate which determined the efficiency of performance, a finding in accord with the expectancy theory but one which runs counter to the predictions of the alternative class of theories, all of which point to event rate as an important variable in the determination of performance.

Another set of results which also are clearly contrary to 'understimulation' predictions was reported by Baker (1959). Using the clock task which had earlier been devised by N. H. Mackworth, he achieved a marked reduction in the decrements, bringing them to a non-significant level, by reducing the variability in the times between signal arrivals, while retaining the same average interval between signals as had been used in the earlier Mackworth studies. Baker's findings are directly opposed to the 'understimulation' predictions because by reducing the temporal variability in the task's structure, he had in effect increased the repetitive nature of the task and consequently performance ought to have been even worse. However, if one considers the results in the light of the expectancy hypothesis, then it is clear that they are as predicted; performance improving owing to the reduced uncertainty in the task, since the observers were more able to predict or to anticipate the moment at which the next signal would arrive. Baker (1963) reports further evidence complementing this study. Subjects who had been trained with a particular distribution of signal arrival times were later more likely to detect a signal when it arrived at the mean of these times, but less likely to detect it when it arrived relatively early or late. Baker's results clearly demonstrate that temporal uncertainty is an important determinant of efficiency.

As mentioned in Section 1, spatial uncertainty has also been shown to influence performance, but it is not clear whether this is a direct effect, in line with the expectancy theory, or whether the effect is mediated by the differential 'costs' of scanning over several locations.

As stated earlier, the expectancy theory accounts for the *decrement* in performance by reasoning that if a signal is missed, then this will lower the subjective estimate of the signal probability and distort acquired knowledge about inter-signal arrival times. That is to say, there develops a vicious circle in which missing a signal makes it more probable that a subsequent signal will be missed, and so on. Although the various studies already cited in this section could reasonably support this argument, the theory does not explain why the decrement should continue to occur after several sessions, with each subsequent session beginning with at least the same level of performance (Loeb and Binford 1964, Colquhoun *et al.* 1968), nor can it account for the perplexing result of Colquhoun (1967) who found that the decrement was unrelated to signal strength (although Colquhoun's result conflicts with an earlier one reported by N. H. Mackworth 1950). The expectancy hypothesis would predict that the stronger the signal and hence the greater its discriminability, the more knowledge the observer should possess about the structure of the task and consequently the less the fall off in performance should be. To this same end, the 'understimulation' interpretations would predict that with a stronger signal, that is with a higher level of stimulation, the decrement in performance should be less than that with a weaker, less stimulating signal. Colquhoun's result is therefore unaccountable by either class of theory.

The possibility that the theories may refer to complementary features of the vigilance process is suggested by the studies of Wilkinson (1964) and Jerison (1967). As noted in Section 1, Wilkinson demonstrated that the introduction of artificial 'signals' to the event sequence improved the overall performance level, which is in accordance with expectancy predictions, since the inclusion of the extra 'signals' raised the overall probability level for target items in the task. But he went on to show that a decrement still occurred, unless *full* knowledge of results was given, and as was noted previously, this effect may be seen as a prediction from, for example, the inhibition theory. In Jerison's study on the effect of event rate, it was shown that the significant effect on performance of signal probability, predicted by the expectancy hypothesis, only occurred at the higher event rates. Since event rate has what may be termed 'arousal potential' (Berlyne 1960), Jerison's study suggests that arousal and expectancy may complement each other.

A further link between the expectancy and the 'understimulation' theories arises in regard to orienting-responses. Sharpless and Jasper (1956) and Haider *et al.* (1964) suggested the view, later adopted by J. F. Mackworth (1969), that the vigilance decrement might be explained by the habituation of cortically induced orienting-responses such as evoked responses or CNV's (contingent negative variation) and indeed, Haider *et al.* (1964) produced evidence which would appear to offer direct support for this idea. They observed a reduction in detections as the orienting-response habituated. Furthermore, they noted that the response to missed signals had a lower amplitude than that to detected signals, which does suggest that the occurrence of an orienting-response is related to task efficiency. Further support comes from Eysenck's (1963) suggestion that introverts habituate more slowly than extraverts, a suggestion which, within the present context, meets agreement with the findings that introverts maintain performance better than do extraverts. However, the results of other studies suggest that such slow wave potentials (CNV's) vary directly with subjective probability or expectancy of signal occurrence (Walter 1967) and consequently the onset of 'habituation' might, instead, be indicative of declining expectancy.

From the discussion of this section it would seem safest to conclude that the only mechanisms for which involvement in the vigilance phenomena has been conclusively demonstrated are expectancy and physiological arousal. Between them these theoretical constructs can account for almost the entire body of evidence. But it must be pointed out that whereas the expectancy mechanism operates in a well defined manner, the relationship between physiological activation and performance levels is not as well defined as those studies which were cited make it appear, and contradictory evidence is not too difficult to find. For example, Wilkinson (1960) reported that sleep deprivation had a detrimental effect on performance, whereas an electrophysiological study by Malmo and Surwillo (1960) had previously shown that skin conductance, heart rate, and other activation measures rose under conditions of sleep deprivation. A combination of these findings could lead to such conclusions as: sleep deprivation is arousing, or, arousal is detrimental to vigilance performance. If the Wilkinson result were ignored, one could argue that since sleep deprivation is arousing, as indicated by the rising activation levels, and since arousal is held to benefit vigilance performance, observers should be sleep deprived in preparation for their watch. This facetious example is included to demonstrate that the relation between performance and physiological arousal is very complex and that interpretations based on a simplistic notion that the two are directly related could well lead to erroneous conclusions which could have serious consequences if put into practice.

3. The decision-theory approach

A conclusion of Section 1 was that the signal-probability effect was one of the few which had withstood the test of repeatability and it is not perhaps surprising that the discussion of Section 2 should point favourably to a theory of vigilance in which signal-probability as it influences subjective expectancy has a crucial role in accounting not only for the low, overall level of performance but also for the familiar decrement in that level.

This conclusion that the lowered performance reflects lowered subjective estimates of the probability than an event is a 'signal', is bolstered by the numerous, more recent, findings in which performance has been analysed in terms of decision theory and which on the whole agree that the performance decrement is most likely due to a shift in the decision criterion rather than to any *real* decline in the observer's ability to identify the 'target' events.

The most widely used decision model, following a report of its successful application to vigilance data by Broadbent and Gregory (1963), is signal detection theory, which views performance, measured by both the detection rate and the false positive rate, as reflecting the interplay between two independent processing mechanisms of the brain. On the one hand there is a sensory discrimination process which determines the capacity of the observer to distinguish between 'signal' and 'non-signal' events, or between 'signal' events and some background noise level. With the exception of studies by J. F. Mackworth (1965) and by Mackworth and Taylor (1963), the consensus would support the view that the level of sensory discriminability remains undiminished throughout the vigilance run. On the other hand a second process, which has to do with the observer's decision to make a report of a signal, does seem to be subject to a pronounced change within the session, in such a way that the observer becomes progressively less likely to make a report. In the parlance of signal detection theory, his 'decision-criterion' shifts in the direction of increased caution.

These two processes are separately identified by the measures d' (for the sensory processes) and β (for the decision processes) and the findings relating to their use in studies of vigilance performance are well summarised by J. F. Mackworth, in her book *Vigilance and Attention* (1970), and by Broadbent, in the third chapter of *Decision and Stress* (1971). In terms of the measures, the typical finding is that d' remains relatively constant while β increases during the run.

Signal detection theory should not be regarded as providing a new theoretical explanation of the vigilance decrement for in reality it only provides a new way of *describing* the performance changes, and it in no way replaces those earlier explanatory theories which were discussed in the preceding section. But it does add substance to these interpretations. The β measure, for example, is supposed to be directly related to $(1 - P)/P$, where P is the probability of a signal, so that it makes a great deal of sense, from an expectancy standpoint, to see β increasing during the run. Similarly, J. F. Mackworth's (1965) report that d' declined during the run makes sense for the habituation model when it is remembered that the *presence* of an orienting-response facilitates discrimination (Sokolov 1963).

The measures also seem to make intrinsic sense in that, for example, exhorting subjects to be more cautious does indeed produce an upward shift in β without influencing d' (Colquhoun 1967); changes in signal probability similarly have been shown to affect β but not d' (Baddeley and Colquhoun 1969); while changes in the difficulty of signal-discrimination bring about the expected changes in the d' level (Mackworth and Taylor *op. cit.*).

Despite these favourable comments, a word of caution is in order. Most of the studies mentioned are based on a set of untested assumptions about the applicability of the signal detection theory model, and the model is unfortunately rather sensitive to violations of these assumptions. Schulman and Greenberg (1970), for example, have shown in a psychophysical task that increases in signal probability can have a depressing effect on d', as it is usually measured, *even although the theory states that this is not possible*. But they went on to show that *detectability* had not in fact been affected, and that the apparent effect was due to the inappropriateness of the d' measure in analysing data where strict accordance with the assumptions had not been realised. Clearly, then, one must be careful about drawing inferences as to what is or is not changing during a run, when assumptions of the model have not been adequately tested.

Perhaps, also, attention should be drawn to the criticisms of Jerison and his colleagues (Jerison *et al.* 1965) who have pointed out that in vigilance, the d' measure tends to be lower, and the β measure much higher, than in comparable psychophysical studies where the observer only performs at the task for a few minutes at a time and, normally, is given frequent rest breaks. Jerison argues that whereas the decision theory analysis assumes that not reporting a signal when it is in fact present is due to the caution exercised by the observer in making his judgment, the same effect could result if the observer was not looking at the display at the appropriate moment. He then proceeds to demonstrate that in theory such failures to attend properly to the display might indeed affect the analysis so that the calculated d' would be lower than it ought to be, and the β measure higher. Although the argument is hypothetical, it clearly is one which could apply in real life, particularly to those tasks which involve an element of visual search.

Nevertheless, sight must not be lost of the basic fact that decision-processes and the operator's confidence in his judgments are involved in vigilance performance. One has only to look at the evidence presented by Broadbent and Gregory, to be aware of this. They used the 'rating method' technique, which allows subjects to rate the confidence of each report they make, and it is clear from their data that there was a progressive shift in the stated confidence of the judgments during the run. This, of course, is a result which stands, irrespective of whether one 'believes' in signal detection theory or not.

4. Conclusions

There can be little doubt that the problem of vigilance, which to some extent remains an unresolved issue, is one which is becoming increasingly important as the demands of improved technologies, and of automation in particular, increase the extent to which the role of the human operator is one of monitoring for rare or unusual events.

This account of vigilance research has shown that several factors, each of theoretical relevance, are important in determining inspection efficiency. These include *environmental conditions*, such as the ambient temperature, or whether the task is being performed during the day or at night; *personality variables*, of which the most important, so far, seems to be extraversion–introversion; *task related factors* such as the probability that an item will be defective and the spatial location of the fault itself; and, finally, the *decision-making processes* of the observer.

No unique theory has emerged which would explain the role played by each of these factors in contributing to the two main problems of vigilance: first, the low overall level of performance, and secondly, the fall-off in efficiency over time. The most acceptable ideas would seem to be that the vigilance phenomena are due either to the observer's *expectancy* for signals, on the one hand, or to his *physiological state* on the other, and it was indicated that these two factors could operate independently or in conjunction to account for most of the findings.

Questions may have arisen as to the relation between theory and research in the vigilance field, since it must be obvious that whereas Mackworth's pioneering work was directed primarily towards answering empirical questions, much of the more recent work referred to has been motivated by theoretical issues. It is of course the case that theory-motivated research furthers understanding of the problem, and that the greater this understanding the more possible it becomes to make predictions about any specific case; for example, about the effects on performance of a particular change in the task situation. The net effect, therefore, of the theoretical research has undoubtedly been to make more valuable the potential contribution of applied work. This may sound platitudinous, but it does seem worth stating when one considers that Mackworth anticipated, by fully 20 years, much of the contemporary knowledge about which factors are important in determining monitoring efficiency.

One may also consider here how far the laboratory research findings can be generalised to inspection tasks in the real world. To reiterate the comments made in Section 1, the main criticisms of the laboratory work have been that: unrealistically high signal rates are used; the observers are insufficiently practised/ experienced; and the tasks are too simple to be of any relevance. In response to the first criticism, it was argued that the higher rates used in the laboratory are necessary to provide sufficient data for analysis and that some data is surely better than none at all. The second criticism was seen to apply to a limited extent only, since observers entering their 48th session can hardly be called unpractised, yet, according to the results of Colquhoun *et al.* (1968), even they continued to produce a decrement. That the tasks are of limited relevance because the stimulus material used is too simple, was seen as a valid criticism; but even here progress is being made which lessens the strength of that criticism. In our own laboratory at Sussex experiments have been run in which the items for inspection vary from a 'standard' item by different amounts, on two separate attribute dimensions. The task thereby more closely resembles the real industrial ones where the inspectors are required to judge not only whether a defect of type A or of type B exists, but also whether its severity (or, in conjunction, their combined severity) makes it worth reporting as a 'fault'. So far, there are no signs that the greater complexity involved in these tasks eliminates the presence of the 'vigilance decrement'. It therefore seems fair to conclude that, in general, criticisms about the appropriateness of vigilance research for industrial or military application are not as well founded as they might at first sight appear.

As a final reflection, one may ponder the extent to which it comforts the manager's mind to know that the declining detection efficiency of his inspectors is most probably due to a shift in their decision criteria, and that their *real* ability to detect faults has not changed at all!

References

ADAMS, J. A., STENSON, H. H., and HUMES, J. M., 1961, Monitoring of complex visual displays II. Effects of visual load and response complexity on human vigilance. *Human Factors*, **3**, 213–221.

ADAMS, J. A., HUMES, J. M., and STENSON, H. H., 1962, Monitoring of complex visual displays III. Effects of repeated sessions on human vigilance. *Human Factors*, **4**, 149–157.

ANDREASSI, J. L., 1966, Skin conductance and reaction-time in a continuous auditory monitoring task. *American Journal of Psychology*, **79**, 470–474.

BADDELEY, A. D., and COLQUHOUN, W. P., 1969, Signal probability and vigilance: a reappraisal of the 'signal rate' effect. *British Journal of Psychology*, **60**, 169–178.

BAKAN, P., 1959, Extraversion–introversion and improvement in an auditory vigilance task. *British Journal of Psychology*, **50**, 325–332.

BAKER, C. H., 1959, Attention to visual displays during a vigilance task II. Maintaining the level of vigilance. *British Journal of Psychology*, **50**, 30–36.

BAKER, C. H., 1960, Observing behaviour in a vigilance task. *Science*, **132**, 674–675.

BAKER, C. H., 1963, Further towards a theory of vigilance. In *Vigilance: A Symposium*. (Edited by D. N. BUCKNER and J. J. McGRATH.) (New York: McGRAW-HILL.) Pp. 127–153.

BERLYNE, D. E., 1960, *Conflict, Arousal and Curiosity*. (New York: McGRAW-HILL.)

BEXTON, W. H., HERON, W., and SCOTT, T. H., 1954, Effects of decreased variation in the sensory environment. *Canadian Journal of Psychology*, **8**, 70–76.

BLAKE, M. J. F., 1971, Temperament and time of day. In *Biological Rhythms and Human Performance*. (Edited by W. P. COLQUHOUN.) (London: ACADEMIC PRESS.)

BROADBENT, D. E., 1958, *Perception and Communication*. (London: PERGAMON PRESS.)

BROADBENT, D. E., 1963, Some recent research from the Applied Psychology Research Unit, Cambridge. In *Vigilance: A Symposium*. (Edited by D. N. BUCKNER and J. J. McGRATH.) (New York: McGRAW-HILL.)

BROADBENT, D. E., 1971, *Decision and Stress*. (London: ACADEMIC PRESS.)

BROADBENT, D. E., and GREGORY, M., 1963, Vigilance considered as a statistical decision. *British Journal of Psychology*, **54**, 309–323.

COLQUHOUN, W. P., 1959, The effect of a short rest pause on inspection efficiency. *Ergonomics*, **2**, 367–372.

COLQUHOUN, W. P., 1960, Temperament, inspection efficiency, and time of day. *Ergonomics*, **3**, 377–378.

COLQUHOUN, W. P., 1961, The effect of ' unwanted ' signals on performance in a vigilance task. *Ergonomics*, **4,** 41–51.

COLQUHOUN, W. P., 1962a, Effects of hyoscine and meclozine on vigilance and short-term memory. *British Journal of Industrial Medicine*, **19,** 287–296.

COLQUHOUN, W. P., 1962b, Effets d'une faible dose d'alcool et de certains autres facteurs sur la performance dans une tâche de vigilance. *Bulletin du C.E.R.P.*, **11,** 27–44.

COLQUHOUN, W. P., 1966, The effect of ' unwanted ' signals on performance in a vigilance task: a reply to Jerison. *Ergonomics*, **9,** 417–419.

COLQUHOUN, W. P., 1967, Sonar target detection as a decision process. *Journal of Applied Psychology*, **51,** 187–190.

COLQUHOUN, W. P., 1970, Practice effects on a visual vigilance task with and without search. *Human Factors*, **12,** 537–545.

COLQUHOUN, W. P., 1971, Circadian rhythms in mental efficiency. In *Biological Rhythms and Human Performance*. (Edited by W. P. COLQUHOUN.) (London: ACADEMIC PRESS.)

COLQUHOUN, W. P., and BADDELEY, A. D., 1964, Role of pretest expectancy in vigilance decrement. *Journal of Experimental Psychology*, **68,** 156–160.

COLQUHOUN, W. P., and BADDELEY, A. D., 1967, Influence of signal probability during pretraining on vigilance decrement. *Journal of Experimental Psychology*, **73,** 153–155.

COLQUHOUN, W. P., BLAKE, M. J. F., and EDWARDS, R. S., 1968, Experimental studies of shift-work II: stabilized 8-hour shift systems. *Ergonomics*, **11,** 527–546.

COLQUHOUN, W. P., BLAKE, M. J. F., and EDWARDS, R. S., 1969, Experimental studies of shift-work III: stabilized 12-hour shift systems. *Ergonomics*, **12,** 865–882.

COLQUHOUN, W. P., and CORCORAN, D. W. J., 1964, The effects of time of day and social isolation on the relationship between temperament and performance. *British Journal of Social and Clinical Psychology*, **3,** 226–231.

CONROY, R. T. W., and MILLS, J. N., 1970, *Human Circadian Rhythms.* (London: J. & A. CHURCHILL.)

DARDANO, J. F., 1962, Relationship of intermittent noise, inter-signal interval, and skin conductance to vigilance behaviour. *Journal of Applied Psychology*, **46,** 106–114.

ELLIOTT, E., 1960, Perception and alertness. *Ergonomics*, **3,** 357–364.

EYSENCK, H. J. (Ed.), 1963, *Experiments with Drugs.* (London: MACMILLAN.)

FRASER, D. C., 1953, The relation of an environmental variable to performance in a prolonged visual task. *Quarterly Journal of Experimental Psychology*, **5,** 31–32.

HAIDER, M., SPONG, P., and LINDSLEY, D. B., 1964, Attention, vigilance and cortical evoked potential in humans. *Science*, **145,** 180–181.

HEBB, D. O., 1955, Drives and the C.N.S. (Conceptual Nervous System). *Psychological Review*, **62,** 243–254.

JENKINS, H. M., 1958, The effect of signal rate on performance in visual monitoring. *American Journal of Psychology*, **71,** 647–661.

JERISON, H. J., 1966, Remarks on Colquhoun's 'The effect of 'unwanted' signals on performance in a vigilance task'. *Ergonomics*, **9,** 413–416.

JERISON, H. J., 1967, Activation and long term performance. *Acta Psychologica*, **27,** 373–389.

JERISON, H. J., 1970, Vigilance: a paradigm and some physiological speculations. In *Attention and Performance III*. (Edited by A. F. SANDERS.) (Amsterdam: NORTH-HOLLAND.)

JERISON, H. J., PICKETT, R. M., and STENSON, H. H., 1965, The elicited observing rate and decision processes in vigilance. *Human Factors*, **7,** 107–128.

KAPPAUF, W. E., and POWE, W. E., 1959, Performance decrement on an audio-visual checking task. *Journal of Experimental Psychology*, **57,** 49–56.

LOEB, M., and BINFORD, J. R., 1964, Vigilance for auditory intensity change as a function of preliminary feedback and confidence level. *Human Factors*, **6,** 445–458.

McKENZIE, R. M., 1958, On the accuracy of inspectors. *Ergonomics*, **1,** 258–272.

MACKWORTH, J. F., 1964, The effect of true and false knowledge of results on the detectability of signals in a vigilance task. *Canadian Journal of Psychology*, **18,** 106–117.

MACKWORTH, J. F., 1965, The effect of amphetamine on the detectability of signals in a vigilance task. *Canadian Journal of Psychology*, **19,** 104–109.

MACKWORTH, J. F., 1969, *Vigilance and Habituation.* (Harmondsworth: PENGUIN BOOKS.)

MACKWORTH, J. F., 1970, *Vigilance and Attention.* (Harmondsworth: PENGUIN BOOKS.)

MACKWORTH, J. F., and TAYLOR, M. M., 1963, The d' measure of signal detectability in vigilance-like situations. *Canadian Journal of Psychology*, **17,** 302–325.

MACKWORTH, N. H., 1950, *Researches in the Measurement of Human Performance.* (M.R.C. Special Report 268. London: H.M.S.O.)

MALMO, R. B., and SURWILLO, W. W., 1960, Sleep deprivation: changes in performance and physiological indicants of activation. *Psychological Monographs*, **74,** 502.

MONTY, R. A., 1962, Effects of post-detection response complexity on subsequent monitoring behaviour. *Human Factors*, **4,** 201–208.

NICELY, P. E., and MILLER, G. A., 1957, Some effects of unequal spatial distribution on the detectability of radar targets. *Journal of Experimental Psychology*, **53**, 195–198.

SCHULMAN, A. I., and GREENBERG, G. Z., 1970, Operating characteristics and a priori probability of the signal. *Perception and Psychophysics*, **8**, 317–320.

SHARPLESS, S., and JASPER, H. H., 1956, Habituation of the arousal reaction. *Brain*, **79**, 655–680.

SOKOLOV, E. N., 1963, *Perception and the Conditioned Reflex*. (London: PERGAMON PRESS and MACMILLAN.)

TARRIERE, C., and HARTEMANN, F., 1964, Investigation into the effects of tobacco smoke on a visual vigilance task. *Ergonomics Supplement* (Proceedings of 2nd I.E.A. Congress, Dortmund), 525–530.

VERNON, J. A., McGILL, T. E., GULICK, W. L., and CANDLAND, D. K., 1959, Effects of sensory deprivation on some perceptual and motor skills. *Perceptual and Motor Skills*, **9**, 91–97.

WALTER, W. G., 1967, Slow potential changes in the human brain associated with expectancy, decision, and intention. In *The Evoked Potentials*. (Edited by W. COBB and C. MOROCUTTI.) (Amsterdam: ELSEVIER.)

WEIDENFELLER, E. W., BAKER, R. A., and WARE, J. R., 1962, Effects of knowledge of results (true and false) on vigilance performance. *Perceptual and Motor Skills*, **14**, 211–215.

WEINER, H., and ROSS, S., 1962, The effects of 'unwanted' signals and d-amphetamine sulphate on observer responses. *Journal of Applied Psychology*, **46**, 135–141.

WILKINSON, R. T., 1959, Rest pauses in a task affected by lack of sleep. *Ergonomics*, **2**, 373–380.

WILKINSON, R. T., 1960, The effect of lack of sleep on visual watchkeeping. *Quarterly Journal of Experimental Psychology*, **7**, 36–40.

WILKINSON, R. T., 1961, Comparison of paced, unpaced, irregular and continuous display in watchkeeping. *Ergonomics*, **4**, 259–267.

WILKINSON, R. T., 1964, Artificial 'signals' as an aid to an inspection task. *Ergonomics*, **7**, 63–72.

ZUERCHER, J. D., 1965, The effects of extraneous stimulation on vigilance. *Human Factors*, **7**, 101–106.

Vigilance and arousal: a key to maintaining inspectors' performance

J. G. Fox

1. Performance decrement in industrial inspection

In an analysis of inspection performance it immediately becomes clear that it is impossible to consider the inspector's fault detection capacity as limited only by his sensory threshold and the viewing conditions of the workplace. With prolonged inspection periods it is commonly observed in such analyses that fault detection deteriorates as a function of time. The rate of deterioration can be rapid—drops of 40% in 30 minutes have been noted. As many paced inspection tasks are carried on for periods well in excess of half-an-hour, the implications of the phenomenon for quality assurance are serious and some understanding of its basis is correspondingly important.

It has been suggested that the phenomenon is more demonstrable in the laboratory than in practice. Indeed Smith and Lucaccini (1969) have expressed the opinion that there is little or no evidence to indicate that the oft-found decrement with time in laboratory studies of inspection has a parallel in industry. However, among the earliest studies of the phenomenon was that by Lindsley (1944) which was occasioned by the signal detection decrement in operational radar duties. This would seem to make the point that the problems of sustaining acceptable performance levels have practical implications. In fact more recent studies allay Smith and Lucaccini's doubts: among them being Badalamente and Ayoub (1969) and Fox and Embrey (1972) and to some extent Belt (1971) and Tickner and Poulton (1973). Also Murrell (see Bhatia and Murrell 1969) and Hanhart (1954) in pursuing the question of fatigue in a more generalized production scene would appear to be considering the same phenomenon in an industrial context. On balance it can be concluded that in a practical quality control situation, a call for sustained performance by the inspector will lead to a significant reduction in fault detection.

That these decrements do not demonstrate themselves in industry as frequently as might be predicted from laboratory studies may simply be a function of the fact that many inspection tasks are carried on within the limits of reasonable vigilance conditions. Even in inspection in continuous automated processes, which might be thought to be ripe for vigilance decrement, the inspection may be carried on 'off-line' with frequent breaks so that vigilance is not at risk. However, with increasing automation, it becomes tempting to build inspection functions into the continuous process and in such conditions there is no doubt that vigilance decrement will appear and there will be a need for an understanding of its cause.

2. The role of vigilance

An examination of the inspector's failures with time reveals that they are of two types: failure to detect a fault and falsely reporting the presence of a fault. This causal relationship has most recently led to performance decrement being considered as a function of changes in decision criteria with time so that signal detection theory has been a convenient vehicle for analysis.

Earlier analyses, however, concerned themselves with an explanation of the phenomenon in terms of the operator's vigilance characteristics, i.e. his ability to sustain attention for a prolonged period, and several basic mechanisms, e.g. arousal, inhibition, habituation, filtering and expectancy have been explored to account for vigilance decrement in monitoring tasks.

Among them, the concept of arousal, which follows from the ideas of Hebb (1955), seems to have offered the most effective model for operationally offsetting this potential decrement with time.

The pre-eminence of arousal as a key to vigilance problems has, perhaps, been overtaken by the use of signal detection theory on such problems. However, it is far from complete eclipse. Rather it is a case of 'horses for courses'.

In absolute terms, signal detection theory must recommend itself to the research scientist. Its ability to handle phenomena in greater breadth with quantitative elegance would not make it otherwise. In application, however, an analysis which might be more qualitative and lacking in rigour can be more relevant if it serves to give reasonable explanations in every day contexts.

Such would seem to be the status of arousal. It gives a psycho-physiologically determinable mechanism explaining levels of monitoring performance under normal conditions, varying temperature, sleep loss, time of day, stress and so on (see Poulton 1973): and allows a plausible and readily appreciated organization of work and design of environment to combat reduced monitoring performance with time.

3. The arousal mechanism and fault detection

The phenomenon of decrement with time in terms of arousal essentially develops from the ideas of Hebb (1955). Efficiency in continuous inspection demands sustained attention or vigilance. Now, following Hebb's argument, inputs to the human Central Nervous System have a dual task: to provide information for subsequent actions; and to provide stimuli to non specific cortical areas (the reticular activating formation) which in turn determine the level of vigilance, or arousal, to sense, identify or interpret further inputs. The feature of the incoming stimuli which is pertinent to this second role is the variation in successive aspects of the stimuli: so that a series of uniform repetitive inputs, particularly those demanding no action, will eventually reduce the human's ability to handle such inputs effectively. As this latter condition leading to reduced ability is fulfilled by virtually all inspection tasks the decrement in fault detection with time finds an explanation.

To offset this potential decrement, some 'variations in the successive aspects' of the inspector's input must be provided.

4. Application of the theory

Various strategies have been tested to this end with some success. They have been applied to paced inspection tasks where the pacing has been real or implicit, say in an inspection incentive bonus scheme.

4.1. *Job enlargement*

As a consequence of the theory it would be predicted that as a job becomes more amenable to the description, 'passive, repetitive and short cycled', the more it is likely to be susceptible to performance decrement with time. Conversely, if the short-cycled passive repetitive nature of the job can be reduced in any of these facets it might be predicted that the slope of the performance decrement with time would be reduced and lead to a better over-all performance.

Macro work cycles can be lengthened and repetition reduced in inspection by combining several aspects of the quality control function within one job description: or by combining quality control functions with other functions.

Fox (1964) (reported in Fox 1975) tested this notion in determining the design of equipment, work organization, and plant layout for the efficient visual inspection of newly minted coins. Two alternative proposals were being put forward: one which gave continuous inspection on a conveyor belt direct from the stamping process, the other proposed inspection of small batches, each drawn from store, inspected and returned to store before the cycle was repeated. In as much as the first proposal led to a continuous two hour passive inspection period it was predicted that it would lead to poorer over-all fault detection than the second where a fourteen minute period of inspection was bracketed by two four minute periods fetching the coins and loading or unloading the conveyor belt hopper.

A study using twelve industrial inspectors upheld this prediction. Batch inspection showed an over-all 6% improvement in fault detection over continuous inspection in a six week period. This result had strong statistical significance ($p < 0.01$).

It seems most reasonable to attribute the improvement to the more acceptable vigilance conditions offered by the batch method. Both conditions provided the same environment, display presentation and physical conditions for the inspection. The single difference was that the batch inspection provided more acceptable vigilance conditions in that the inspection period was within limits.

It could be argued that the job enlargement offered by fetching and carrying is counter productive. If throughput is the criterion then this cannot be denied: but accuracy is usually more important in quality control.

This example of job enlargement may be considered rather crude. Other situations will certainly allow more elegant solutions. But it demonstrates that often there is a need to temper straightforward industrial engineering decisions with human factors data. In this instance, it resulted in the 'off line' system gaining favour over the 'on line' continuous process resulting from industrial engineering considerations.

4.2. *Extraneous stimulus*

The arousal model allows alternatives to such job enlargement where such a technique is not possible and continuous vigilance is unavoidable. Among these alternatives is supplementing the monotonous inspection input with a more variable input. If these supplementary inputs are in a different modality from that involved in inspection and intrinsically have no attention gathering value, then they can serve the purpose of providing the stimuli for the non specific reticular system and so vigilance, which can be applied to the inspection task, can be maintained.

Following the arousal model such extraneous stimuli should be relatively rare events in the human input programme or else they become just another series of uniform, repetitive inputs which will, in fact, contribute to a reduced capacity to handle the primary inspection input effectively. A parallel approach by Murrell (1962, 1966, 1970) in relation to the use of rest pauses applied to the more general problem of monotonous repetitive tasks in 'light work' indicates that there would be considerable benefit from timing the occurrence of the extraneous stimulus with the onset of the drop in arousal. This is, in fact, what might be predicted from following Hebb's hypothesis. The results of many vigilance experiments are such that in practice it would mean the appearance of the extraneous stimulus at 30 minute intervals.

There is no reason to believe that bursts of white noise would not provide effective extraneous stimuli. However, in practice, for other reasons, a more socially acceptable supplementary variable input would have more chance of success. A possible stimulus with this quality is music.

A number of studies have used music in the context of vigilance and arousal (e.g. Tarriere and Wisner 1962, Poock and Wiener 1966, Lucaccini 1968, Wokoun 1968) but none appear to have extended the philosophy to use the music on a time schedule synchronized with the predicted point of drop-off in arousal. All the studies showed, however, that the music had influenced fault detection positively.

More recently Fox and Embrey (1972) have incorporated the intermittent scheduled stimulus concept into a study of the effect of music on inspection efficiency.

Three of the experiments in the study seem to have direct relevance for the present discussion: giving strong support to the value of the notion of arousal in operationally maintaining inspection performance.

Experiment 1

One experiment took place in a factory manufacturing among other things metal fasteners. The job used as the vehicle for testing the effectiveness of the background music was the visual inspection of batches of metal fasteners for the purpose of separating out any defective articles which had resulted from the production process. Three main types of defect were searched for: two of which modified the line of the metal part in some degree and a third which grossly mis-shaped the part. To examine the batch the inspectors spread-out handfuls of fasteners on a table and visually scanned the resulting display: picking out the defects if there were any present and putting them on one side. No optical aids were used in the inspection.

Five females normally employed in this task by the manufacturing company were used as the inspectors during the study. All gave acceptable audiometer records indicating their hearing was within acceptable limits.

The inspection was carried out under three auditory conditions.

Normal working conditions which had a continuous ambient noise background of 83 dBA: this has been designated the 'noise' condition.

Normal working conditions with background vocal music relayed for 10 minutes at 30 minute intervals: the ambient noise and music produced a total background of auditory stimulus of 86 dBA: this is designated the 'noise plus music' condition.

In a room where the background noise level was 60 dBA : this is designated the silence' condition.

Each inspector examined a single test batch on three consecutive days under the noise condition. These batches were actually fed into the normal throughput to the inspection benches and the inspectors were unaware of their appearance. On each of another three days immediately before or after dealing with the test batch in the noise condition, the inspectors searched through batches for defects in what has been described as the silence condition. The bench layout and the illumination to do this task were the same as for the noise condition. One week later the same group again inspected a single batch of fasteners on three consecutive days when the batches were again fed into the normal throughput to the inspection benches. In the interim two days, a systematic programme of 10 minute periods of background music at 30 minute intervals had been implemented and continued throughout the period of these tests. There were no other changes in the work arrangements or the official rest pause schedule of 15 minutes morning and 15 minutes afternoon breaks. The inspection therefore took place in what has been designated the noise plus music condition.

Figure 1. The influence of music on fault detection when inspecting metal fasteners.

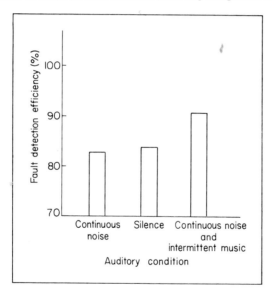

The overall results of the experiment are shown in Figure 1. Although the increase in fault detection is quite large (7·1%) its statistical significance in this study was small ($p < 0.1$). The low significance achieved was of little consequence for the study was one of a series conducted both in the laboratory and in industry and the over-all results confidently upheld the prediction from the arousal hypothesis on the effect of music on inspection efficiency. The points of interest are the small difference between the continuous noise and silence conditions and the changes in fault detection efficiency brought about by superimposing intermittent music on the continuous noise. This is what the arousal concept would predict for a group habituated to noise. Continuous noise adds nothing to the variability or novelty in successive inputs and would not be expected to raise flagging levels of arousal. The music by its intermittency, albeit a cyclic intermittency, has the necessary quality for restimulating the arousal mechanism and so maintains vigilance and performance. The implication of the use of the intermittent stimuli, such as music in this context, is that it will raise flagging levels of vigilance and maintain fault detection levels when they are likely to drop in the latter stages of an inspection period. If the arousal concept has any real relevance then this should be demonstrable. The second and third experiments in the study, in fact, demonstrated this.

Experiment 2

The second experiment was carried out in a factory where eight inspectors, whose normal job it was, carried out a quality control inspection of rubber seals of a variety of shapes and sizes. Test sessions lasted 30 minutes at any one time and the job was done either with no music or with a lively programme played during the 15th–20th minute of the session. It was known that the defect rate was 1 in 100 and that the detection efficiency was normally 47%.

The design of the experiment was essentially a replica of that used in the metal fastener study without the requirement for special arrangements for a noise *versus* silence comparison.

A summary of the results is given in Table 1. Again the use of music shows a pronounced effect in improving the detection scores. This time the source of the improvement emerges more clearly. It comes from stemming the fall-off in fault detection with time. The difference in detection efficiencies is statistically significant at $p < 0.025$: and the difference between the second half decrements for the two conditions is significant at $p < 0.02$.

Table 1. Mean detection efficiencies and decrements in performance over 30 minutes in an industrial inspection task with and without music.

	No music (Silence)	Lively music programme
Mean detection efficiency	51%	69%
Decrement in second 15 minutes of task compared with first 15 minutes	27%	18%

Experiment 3

The third experiment was one of a group of supporting laboratory studies, where conditions could be more easily manipulated. In this experiment it was possible to demonstrate even more clearly under more varied conditions the relevance of the hypothesis to the over-all effect. The results are shown in Figure 2 where detection efficiencies are related to decrements in performance in the second half of the test. Again in the two music conditions under consideration the improved over-all detection scores are a result of stemming the fall-off in subjects' performance in the second half of the experiment. The differences between detection scores are significant at $p < 0.01$.

Figure 2. Results of an experiment showing inspection performance being sustained with the use of music.

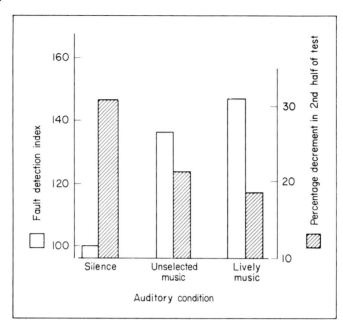

Though it is not over important in the present discussion, this experiment shows the importance of the nature of the content of the extraneous stimulus. It might be expected that 'lively music' would be more effective: and so it was. 'Unselected' music had too high a proportion of items which could be described as unstimulating and hence had a reduced effect.

The important result, however, is the difference between the 'silence' and both music conditions with reference to fault detection. On this comparison, the difference between the types of music is insignificant.

5. Conclusion

These results, essentially from Case Studies, give strong support for the value of the concepts of arousal theory as a framework for considering the vigilance aspects of signal detection tasks. It seems reasonable to conclude that in an industrial inspection task where faults are easily identified and defined then the notion of a decrement over time due to changes in the state of the inspector's arousal is meaningful and a significant phenomenon to be considered in an attempt to improve inspection performance.

Two methods of applying the theory to advantage have been outlined. They by no means exhaust the possibilities. The value of straightforward rest pauses should not be discounted, for example. Nor are the methods mutually exclusive. For example, a two-pronged attack might be made by way of job enlargement and rest pauses: or by rest pauses and music.

In research, classical vigilance studies have given way to consideration of decision processes in the evaluation of inspector's performance over time. In the less rigorous world of practice it seems still to have something to offer. Perhaps, it 'works' not quite for the reasons we ascribe: but it does 'work'.

References

BADALAMENTE, R. V., and AYOUB, M. M., 1969, A behavioral analysis of an assembly line inspection task. *Human Factors*, **11,** 339–352.

BELT, J. A., 1971, *The Applicability of Vigilance Laboratory Research to a Simulated Industrial Inspection Task.* (U.S. Government Report No. AD–728 490.)

BHATIA, N., and MURRELL, K. F. H., 1969, An industrial experiment in rest pauses. *Human Factors*, **11,** 167–174.

FOX, J. G., and EMBREY, E. D., 1972, Music: an aid to productivity. *Applied Ergonomics*, **3,** 202–205.

FOX, J. G., 1975, The inspection of newly minted coins. In *Ergonomics Case Studies.* (Edited by H. G. MAULE and J. S. WEINER.) (London: TAYLOR & FRANCIS.)

HANHART, A., 1954, *Die Arbeitspause im Beitrieb.* (Zurich: OESCH-VERLAG.)

HEBB, D. O., 1955, Drives and the CNS (Conceptual Nervous System). *Psychological Review,* **62,** 243–254.

LINDSLEY, D. B. (Ed.), 1944, *Radar Operator ' Fatigue ', the Effects of Length and Repetition of Operating Periods on Efficiency of Performance.* (Report No. OSRD 33334, Office of Scientific Research and Development.)

LUCACCINI, L. F., 1968, *Vigilance and Irrelevant Stimulation: a Test of the Arousal Hypothesis.* (Ph.D. Thesis, University of California.)

MURRELL, K. F. H., 1962, Operator variability and its industrial consequences. *International Journal of Production Research,* **1,** 39–55.

MURRELL, K. F. H., 1966, Performance decrement—a tentative explanation. In *Proceedings of the 2nd Seminar on Continuous Work.* (Edited by F. F. LEOPOLD.) (Eindhoven: INSTITUTE OF PERCEPTION RESEARCH.)

MURRELL, K. F. H., 1970, Temporal factors in light work. In *Measurement of Man at Work.* (Edited by W. T. SINGLETON, J. G. FOX and D. J. WHITFIELD.) (London: TAYLOR & FRANCIS.)

POOCK, J. L., and WIENER, E. L., 1966, Music and other auditory backgrounds during visual monitoring. *Journal of Industrial Engineering,* **17,** 318–323.

POULTON, E. C., 1973, The effect of fatigue on inspection work. *Applied Ergonomics,* **4,** 73–83.

SMITH, R. L., and LUCACCINI, L. F., 1969, Vigilance research: its application to industrial problems. *Human Factors,* **11,** 149–156.

TARRIERE, C., and WISNER, A., 1962, Effets des bruits significatifs ou non significatifs oa cours d'une epreuve vigilance. *Le Travail Humain,* **25,** 1–28.

TICKNER, A. H., and POULTON, E. C., 1973, Monitoring up to 16 synthetic television pictures showing a great deal of movement. *Ergonomics,* **16,** 381–401.

WOKOUN, W., 1968, *Effects of Music on Work Performance.* (Technical Memo 1–68, U.S. Army, Human Engineering Laboratory, Aberdeen, Maryland.)

Models of inspector performance

The inspection task broadly follows four stages: search, fault acquisition, fault recognition and quality decision. At each stage in the sequence it would appear that well developed current theories are available for discussing the relevant phenomena: though, of course, the stages of inspection and the theories are not necessarily mutually exclusive. Many inspection tasks have to be undertaken under conditions of sustained vigilance: and here again there are numerous theoretical formulations which can elucidate the problem.

The body of knowledge must give considerable confidence to those human factors specialists who would take up the challenge given in the *Prologue*, even if it must be accepted that fundamental research and the theoretical models of inspector performance currently still leave us short of the goal of including mathematical descriptions of human parameters in quality control models.

Despite theoretical disputes, visual search theories agree in so far as obtaining industrially acceptable estimates of probability of detection as a function of time: but the methods employed by Bloomfield to bring in the variables of interest need considerable extension if a direct estimation of performance is to be made.

Presenting something of a paradox, data from vigilance studies, while providing a firmer basis for preventing decrement in performance with time, are making some of the current vigilance theories less supportable as theoretical constructs. That they all, despite their current strengths and weaknesses, point to methods that were shown by Mackworth 30 years ago to be effective in preventing the decrements indicates that there is more than a germ of understanding of the phenomena available.

It will be clear on going through this volume that the theory of signal detection is currently the favoured vehicle for the analysis and description of inspector's performance. It must be recognized that the theory is a different class of construct from those of search or vigilance. It, of course, only offers an analysis and description of performance: devoid of truly psychological or physiological basis it does not provide a fundamental explanation of behaviour. As Craig points out, it adds nothing new to existing explanations in operational terms. Its advantages are that it brings together the operational variables and allows their separate and interactive effects to be treated comprehensively in mathematical terms. Though it is to be cautioned that the necessary assumption that the underlying distributions are of equal variance may not always obtain in every inspection situation. It has been said that in many visual inspection situations we might expect the signal to noise variance ratio to be of the order of two to one. However, the advantages of the model are not to be under-rated. It is a potentially powerful predictive tool and is most attractive as the vehicle for integrating human factors data with established quality control models. It also appears to be a strong contender as the model for drawing together the parameters of visual search and vigilance theories. In passing it might be commented that it might be more realistic and fruitful to follow the only line suggested by the various psychological and physiological theories of vigilance and to interpret the phenomenon in relation to changes in d' rather than, as is more fashionable, in terms of movements in β. Certainly in attempting to conceptualize the role of the physical and organizational factors discussed in the next section it is invaluable and provides a rationale which makes the importance of these factors indisputable.

2. Factors affecting inspection performance

Individual and group differences in inspection

E. L. Wiener

1. Introduction

Several years ago this author (Wiener 1969) lamented that the vigilance literature and theories reflected a 'signal-oriented rigidity' with a plethora of papers on signal properties such as rate, probability, intensity, pacing, and schedule. This has been to the exclusion of the 'softer' side of the problem, considerations such as motivation, incentives, training, personnel selection, social environment, and individual and group differences. The same is true of the scanty literature on industrial inspection. The likely reason is that there are limitless attractive signal and display variables, which are so easy to program experimentally, and they usually can be counted upon to yield significant results. Certainly the same cannot be said of the soft variables.

The extent to which laboratory vigilance data are applicable to inspection activities remains an open question which shall be examined at various places in this paper. The strongest argument against the laboratory studies comes from Smith and Lucaccini (1969), who even doubt the existence of the oft-reported time decrement, stating that it occurs only in laboratories and not in the real world. This is a serious accusation, as the phenomenon of time decrement is generally uncritically accepted by vigilance researchers. The matter of applicability defies a simple review; the reader's attention is invited to excellent summaries by Poulton (1973), Carroll (1969) and Harris and Chaney (1969).

2. Personnel selection

Since the recognition of the importance of industrial inspection coincided with the golden era of psychometric personnel selection, it was inevitable that such techniques would be applied to inspectors. The earlier papers deal almost entirely with selection devices, with occasional attempts at training, motivation, and very rare considerations of what we would call ergonomics—usually consisting of improving the lighting. The lure was great, as psychological testing had scored conspicuous success, at least in the eyes of its practitioners, on the assembly line.

Though post-war critics would later write unkindly of the statistical casualness exhibited in claims for test validity, it appeared at the time that, given any job description, there must be a psychometric device that would divide good prospective employees from poor. There was no apparent reason why inspection tasks should fare any differently from assembly tasks. But there were some important differences that emerged as various test techniques were applied, almost always resulting in low predictive validity. Primarily, the criteria were highly contaminated: as actual measures of inspector accuracy were (and still are) rare, most test scores were validated against supervisors' ratings. Such criteria are questionable in any task, and especially in inspection, where even the supervisor may be totally unaware of the work quality of individual inspectors. His ratings are probably based on perceptions of earnestness and cooperation, and the correlation between these attributes and actual inspection performance is unknown. If some tests seemed to increase inspection efficiency, it was probably due to the vagaries of bonus validity, that fortuitous correlation between predictor and ultimate criterion.

2.1. *Aptitude tests—inspection tasks*

The first mention of aptitude tests that we have found was a study by Link (1920) on munitions inspectors, in which he reports correlations of the order of 0·50 for three tests: card-sorting, number-cancelling, and number group checking. His criterion was rate of output, not accuracy, however. Wyatt and Langdon (1932) reported correlations between 0·25 and 0·40 for four tests predicting eight inspection tasks. Dorcus and Jones (1950) abstract 23 studies using over 100 scales which attempt to correlate selection devices with inspector performance and ratings. Most of the predictor devices were standard aptitude tests, or tests of visual skills. Wartime work in the U.S.A. was exemplified by Sartain's study (1945) on selection of inspectors in the aircraft industry. He reports a rather high multiple correlation, $R=0·79$, between seven tests and

Table 1. Summary of aptitude and other tests.

Author	Predictor	Criterion	Results
Chaney and Harris 1966	5 tests, incl. HIT	Errors	4 of 5 signif. Best 2, $R=0·75$
Harris 1964	HIT	Errors—4 tasks, and supervisor's ratings	3 of 4 signif. correlation: no correlation with ratings
Harris 1968	HIT	6 visual tasks	5 of 6 signif. (max $r=0·86$)
Kelley 1955	Review of 16 papers		Low predictive validity
McKenzie 1958	Review of older papers		
Nelson and Barany 1969	Dynamic visual acuity Reaction time	Visual insp. errors Visual insp. errors	$r=0·84$ $r=0·03$
Tiffin and Rogers 1941	Review of 1940 era		Low predictive validity
Sartain 1945	7 standard industrial tests	Supervisor ratings	$R=0·79$; best 3, $R=0·78$
Ghiselli 1942	Numerous standard tests	Supervisor ratings	Best 4, $R=0·72$ Best 2, $R=0·65$ Best 1, $r=0·57$
Link 1920	Card sorting	Output rate	$r=0·50$ (approx.)
Wyatt and Langdon 1932	4 tests	8 visual tasks	$r=0·25$ to 0·40. Highest was letter cancellation test
Schuman 1945	Otis B (form A) Minn. paper form Bennett mech. comp.	Supervisor ratings Supervisor ratings Supervisor ratings	$r=0·52$ $r=0·50$ $r=0·66$
Ayers 1942	4 visual items	Visual accuracy	$R=0·75$ to 0·88 (various criteria)

supervisory ratings. Ghiselli (1942) reported $R = 0.72$ between aptitude tests and supervisory ratings of inspector-packers. Schuman (1945) correlated three tests with supervisors' ratings and found correlations of $r = 0.52$, 0.50, and 0.66. Intercorrelations and R were not reported. Tiffin and Rogers (1941) found near-zero correlations in their test battery, the one exception being $r = 0.34$ between the *Purdue Hand Precision Test* and detection of an off-weight condition. Finally, Kelley's brief history (1955) reviewed 16 previous papers on selection tests, finding low validity.

In summary, the aptitude tests of the pre-ergonomics era showed either low correlation with inspector accuracy measures, or high correlation with questionable measures such as supervisory ratings. One may reasonably ask why the correlations with supervisory ratings are so high, as the reported values of R would indicate greater success than one usually encounters in industrial aptitude testing. It is not an easy question to answer, partly because the early studies lack the statistical documentation required in publications today. But if this reviewer had to guess, he would attribute the success to the fact that the aptitude tests primarily measured manipulation skills, as well as general suitability for production-line employment. The supervisors, in turn, based their ratings, not on inspector accuracy, which was probably unknown, but on their perceptions of workers' merits, which likely also had a high dexterity component and a general measure of industrial adaptability. Perhaps the selection devices and the supervisors were measuring the same thing, with neither measuring inspector accuracy. Whether hard criteria of inspector accuracy and supervisors' ratings are correlated remains to be seen. I commend the question to those with access to production line data.

2.2. *Recent developments*

It is astonishing that the renewed interest in industrial inspection has not spawned new tests. Those used so far were 'standard' industrial aptitude tests; none was tailor-made for predicting inspection proficiency. The current edition of the bible of test selection, Buros' *Mental Measurement Yearbook* (1972), does not list inspector in its job titles. The one exception that we are aware of is the *Harris Inspection Test* (*HIT*), a paper-and-pencil test that can be administered in 10–20 minutes. Harris reports rather remarkable results for the test. In an early paper (1964) he found significant validity coefficients between the *HIT* (not to be confused with *Holtzman Inkblot Technique*) and three out of four electronic inspection tasks ($r = 0.39$, NS; $r = 0.51$, 0.58, and 0.86, $p < 0.05$). But Chaney and Harris (1966) reported negative results. Unfortunately, neither this author nor Harris (*personal communication* 1974) is aware of any other attempts to validate the *HIT*, even though it is now commercially available. Inquiries to the publisher have gone unanswered.

Recently articles appeared in the U.S.A. press about a test for resistance to distraction ('mind would not wander') and, inevitably, the stories made rather extravagant claims for the device. There is no formal report of this work, only a test manual (Rutten and Block 1973). The task involves searching a matrix for the location of numbers which must be reported in order. No validation is reported, however the manual indicates that the test is in use with the Dutch National Railroad system, and Block (*personal communication* 1974) indicates that the test is now being used with a trucking firm and a chemical manufacturer to see if it is predictive of accidents. The authors have made no claim for the test in connection with inspection activities.

Antrobus *et al.* (1967) selected subjects who scored on the extremes of a scale of predisposition to daydreaming. The groups showed no differences on an auditory detection test. Unfortunately, the task had apparently not been correctly calibrated, since detection rates were about 0·96, making it impossible to produce an experimental effect. Resistance to distraction, if it can be easily measured, has at least face validity in selecting inspectors; the construct may bear watching.

The field is ripe for development of new industrial selection devices for inspection tasks. If traditional paper-and-pencil tests will not do the job, perhaps an apparatus test can be developed. With the availability of solid-state circuitry, a light, small, low-cost piece of apparatus, perhaps a vigilance-like task, is not out of the question. Even a slide projector-based task would seem reasonable. If someone does not at least see the intellectual challenge, he should certainly see the commercial possibilities.

2.3. *Visual tests*

Visual capability is unquestionably related to visual inspection performance, at least in the extremes where the applicant has serious, though perhaps correctable, visual deficiencies. Mitten (1957), writing on a team approach to an industrial inspection problem, revealed that the team's optometrist found the workers using their magnification device not as a magnifier, but as a corrective lens for poor vision. Ayers (1942), Tanalski (1956), and Nelson and Barany (1969) all found strong relationships between visual measures and various measures of inspector efficiency, as do many of the authors summarized in Dorcus and Jones (1950). Ayers reports R values between 0·75 and 0·88 with four criteria. Tanalski describes an off-colour detection task very similar to that used in the laboratory by Colquhoun (1961), and Nelson and Barany (1969) demonstrate the 'predictive accuracy' of a dynamic visual acuity test used, correlated with accuracy of students in simulated inspection. Their paper is an excellent summary of visual testing. High correlations between visual measures and visual tasks are not particularly surprising, and do not provide an inviting basis for personnel selection, except to do the obvious and screen out those lacking the sensory capability to do the job, or reroute those who have remediable problems.

2.4. *Personality scales—inspection tasks*

One would think that a wide variety of personality scales would have been employed to select industrial inspectors, owing to the general popularity of such scales in the post-war years. We are unable to uncover a single case where personality tests were used to select inspectors. The closest would be the work of Colquhoun (1959, 1960), but these should be discussed under vigilance tasks even though he uses the word 'inspection' in the titles. In the 23 studies summarized by Dorcus and Jones (1950), no use of personality tests is reported. But what is peculiar is that none of the literature since then reports investigation of personality scales on the industrial front. Perhaps would-be practitioners were discouraged by the results encountered in vigilance experiments, which we shall examine next.

2.5. *Personality scales—vigilance tasks*

Experiments in human vigilance have produced two highly repeatable findings. First, extreme individual differences, often going from zero to 100% detection among even a small group of subjects. The second finding is stability of performance from session to session, with reliability coefficients usually in the 0·70s and 0·80s (see Buckner *et al.* 1960). These two conditions set the stage for personnel selection devices. Furthermore, since the vigilance task appears to require so little perceptual ability, reasoning, or skill, personality or temperament variables seem to offer promising results. Given what appear to be ideal conditions for the application of psychometric devices, it is astonishing that so little work has been done, and the results have been so unimpressive.

Much of the research (see Table 2) has centred about the personality construct of introversion-extroversion (hereafter referred to as *I-E*). This construct was first applied to the area of vigilance by Eysenck (1957) and Broadbent (1958), and experimentally examined by Bakan (1959). The interest of these experimenters and the many who followed in the use of the various *I-E* scales was not in prediction of vigilance performance for selection purposes, but in validating the arousal theories of vigilance. Eysenck and others postulated that *I-E* scales measure an internal arousal mechanism. *I*'s are likely to be aroused by internal stimuli, and be less dependent on the external world for arousal. *E*'s require a greater external excitation, or richness of stimuli. The theory would predict that *E*'s would make poor inspectors or monitors, due to the constrained variety of input.

But the experimental results are somewhat disappointing, both to the arousal theorists and to those concerned with the practical matter of selecting persons for jobs of low stimulus variety. Few studies show a clear-cut superiority of *I*'s over *E*'s, though none show the opposite. *I*'s may have an increased resistance to time decrement, even if main effects are non-significant. The most curious result was that of Colquhoun who, after finding no correlation between *I-E* and performance in one study (1959), performed further experiments (Colquhoun 1960, Colquhoun and Corcoran 1964) which found a diurnal effect—*I* performance was superior in the morning, *E* in the afternoon. Other experiments using the *I-E* scales are summarized by J. Mackworth (1969).

Only two studies have extensively explored selection devices for vigilance tasks: Dobbins *et al.* (1961), and McGrath *et al.* (1960). Both used a wide variety of scales—personality, aptitude, attitude, and biographical, and therefore are difficult to summarize briefly. In Dobbins *et al.*, army personnel drove a truck around a closed course while maintaining a watch over a panel-mounted light. The results are summarized in Table 2. No scale correlated with either detections (*D*) or false alarms (*FA*) for both day and night. Generally poor results were also found with the non-personality predictor variables.

The work of McGrath *et al.* is by far the most extensive and sophisticated to date. Their population was naval personnel assigned to sonar school, and since sonar is a bimodal display, they used both a visual and auditory vigilance task, scoring the usual *D* and *FA*, as well as deriving several measures such as within-session decrement. The predictor variables were navy classification (aptitude) tests, special aptitude tests which the investigators judged to measure skills required of watchkeepers, and the following personality tests

Table 2. Personality tests in vigilance experiments.

Author	Task	Results
Bakan 1959	Aud.-numbers	*I* slightly better than *E*
Claridge 1960	Bakan task	*I* showed no decrement, *E did*
Bakan 1963	Same	*E* and normals more decrement
Keister and McLaughlin 1972	Bakan task	*E* showed decrement, not *I*
Purohit and Hardikar 1971	Vis.-CRT	*Hi* anxiety grp. more detections
Purohit 1972	Vis.-light bulbs	*I* detected more signals, fewer *FA*
Gale *et al.* 1972	Bakan task	No diff. *I v E* or Neuroticism *v* Normals
Colquhoun 1960	Vis.-colour patches	*I* better in A.M., *E* in P.M.
Colquhoun and Corcoran 1964	Letter cancellation	Same as above
Colquhoun 1959		No correlation with *I-E*
Hogan 1966	Vis	*I* superior to *E*.
Stroh 1971	Vis	*I–E*—no correl. with *d'* or *β* Same for Neuroticism Psychotocism—inverse relation to *d'*
Tarriere and Hartemann 1964	Vis	*I* superior
Davies and Hockey 1966	Digit checking	*E* showed decrement, not *I*
Antrobus *et al.* 1967	Aud	'Resistance to Daydreaming' test— no diffs.
Wilkinson 1961	Vis	*I-E* no diffs.
Tune 1966b	Aud	*I* 'more cautious'; correl. with *d'*=0·28, *β*=0·40
Dobbins *et al.* 1961	Vis (while driving)	Army self-descrip. inventory *r*= −0·38 with *FA*, daytime only gen. adjustment *r*=0·33 with *D*, day Mech. test *r*=0·26 with *D*, night 6 attitudinal scales—all non-signif.

1. Five scales of the *Guilford–Zimmerman Temperament Survey*: General Activity, Restraint, Ascendance, Sociability, and Emotional Stability.
2. Three scales of the *Minnesota Multiphasic Personality Inventory (MMPI)*: Manifest Anxiety (degree of guardedness in responding), and *L* (falsification in responding).
3. *Willingness-to-Guess*, a made-to-order test which the authors hypothesized would correlate with *FA*.

Of the 90 possible correlations between predictors and visual criteria, only five were significant, and none was a personality scale. Nineteen out of 90 correlations with auditory criteria were significant, the only personality variables being the *K* scale ($r = -0.49$ with *D*), *GZTS* Ascendance ($r = -0.32$ with *D*), and *GZTS* General Activity ($r = 0.41$ with a decrement measure).

In conclusion, personality scales employed to date show little promise in distinguishing between good and poor monitors. Before we despair of such techniques, however, more personality scales should be examined. I am astonished that some bold experimenter, armed with a large computer, has not at least tried the *MMPI*, correlating not only the scales, but each of the 560-odd items with measures of vigilance performance.

As to what direction further research should take, the author would defer to more competent authority in the field of personality theory. Further testing of specific aptitudes may be a *cul-de-sac*, and work on scales of temperament are risky, though potentially productive. I would like to see someone develop a scale of 'stick-to-it-tive-ness', perseverance in the face of boredom.

2.6. Sex

There is a paucity of information on the intriguing question of sex and inspecting performance. The literature indicates that both male and female inspectors abound in industry, but seldom working on the same line. We have no industrial data to report on comparisons between male and female operatives. There is a stereotyped view that males should assemble things and females should inspect them. Perhaps the whole question is irrelevant, for in the new world of 'equal opportunity' laws, industries could not select inspectors on this basis without rather substantial proof of differences, and finding such evidence seems unlikely.

Vigilance experimenters have examined the question, usually on campuses where both sexes are available as subjects. The popular misconception that women are better at dull jobs can probably be dismissed as a piece of what today would be called male chauvinist 'pap'. Of all the studies we have examined, six found no significant differences at all (Waag *et al.* 1973, R. Smith *et al.* 1966, Gale *et al.* 1972, Kappauf *et al.* 1955, Kirk and Hecht 1963, McCann 1969), two found men superior (Neal and Pearson 1966, Heimstra *et al.* 1967), and three report non-significant main effects of sex, but significant interactions with other variables (Bakan and Manley 1963, Krkovic and Sverko 1967, Whittenberg and Ross 1953).

Experimenters on college campuses may wish to statistically remove sex as a source of variance, and if they test it, no doubt occasional significant contrasts will appear. This reviewer sees little point, practical or theoretical, in pursuing this matter. Perhaps someone will soon write a thorough review of the findings and then dismiss it once and for all.

2.7. Age

Research into the aging process has generally established a slowing of response time, and deterioration of sensory and perceptual skills (Welford 1958). There is scanty information on age from the industrial inspection world. Drury and Sheehan (1969) and Sheehan and Drury (1971) report a decline in D with age (range from 30 to about 65), and a significant negative correlation between d' and age, with d' declining about 0·2 units per 10 years of age. The authors point out that in each study there were only five subjects, and therefore urge caution in any conclusions about age effects. Indeed, in Jamieson's interesting study of electronics inspection (1966), three groups of subjects (age to 60) showed the opposite, negative correlations ($-0·49$, $-0·87$, $-0·70$) between age and inspection errors. Jacobson (1953) found increasing accuracy of electronic inspectors up to age 34 ($D=0·90$), then a decline to age 55 ($D=0·75$), and Evans (1951) reported no age effect.

Vigilance experiments have usually shown either no age effect or weak negative effects with aging. Tune (1966a, b) reports no differences in D, but significantly higher FA rates with age. Surwillo and Quilter (1964) found no differences in the first 45 minutes of an hour's run, but a significantly greater decrement in the older monitors in the last 15 minutes. They attempted to relate monitoring performance, age, and skin potential (1965), but the interpretation of the results is unclear. Griew and Davies (1962) compared old and young industrial workers' performance in three experiments using an auditory task, with significant differences in only one, favouring younger workers. A follow-up experiment yielded no age differences (Davies and Griew 1963). York (1962), and Neal and Pearson (1966) found no significant age effect. Thompson *et al.* (1963) found no significant age main effects, but an interaction with stimulus presentation rate. Older subjects' performance suffered compared to younger ones at the highest of three input rates. This is consistent with other research on the elderly, which indicates no age effect as long as the input is below a certain rate, supporting the wisdom of placing older workers on unpaced inspection lines.

In summary, we see no conclusive results due to age effects. Therefore, it would be ill-advised and, in many states of the U.S.A., illegal to discriminate against workers on the basis of age. Except for line-paced tasks, older inspectors can probably be counted upon to produce quality work, though management would be wise to keep a check on their visual capabilities. In all likelihood, attitudinal set, experience, and orientation toward work, more than compensate for sensory deficiencies in aging workers.

2.6. Intelligence

There is a persistent belief that monotonous tasks are better performed by persons of low intellectual capability ('dull persons for dull jobs'), who enjoy a (putative) built-in resistance to boredom. To be sure, there have been conspicuous successes in using educable retardates in some repetitious industrial jobs, so it is reasonable to inquire about their suitability for inspection. First, we have no recent experimental evidence collected in an industrial setting. The older studies as reviewed in Dorcus and Jones (1950) give little guidance.

In the vigilance literature there are about a dozen studies, the best review being in Davies and Tune (1969). Of the papers we have examined, only one, Kappauf and Powe (1959) reports a significant intelligence effect, a positive correlation. Other experimenters found no intelligence effect (Wilkinson 1961, Ware 1961, Ware *et al.* 1962, Sipowicz and Baker 1961, N. Mackworth 1950, Solandt and Partridge 1946, Jenkins 1958, McGrath *et al.* 1960). While most studies examined the intelligence dimension over a wide 'normal' range, such as one might find in military recruits, the work of Ware *et al.* (1962) took an extreme course of comparing normals to retardates. In one study, 'trainable mental deficients' were compared to the performance of army recruits with no differences in performance. Ware (1961) had previously reported similar results with both visual and auditory displays.

So intelligence, in the range into which job applicants would fall, is not a promising basis by which to select inspectors. We would caution that all of these studies involved experimentation of very short duration. On almost any task, persons of higher intelligence will perform better than others, for the simple reason that they profit from instructions, perceive the reason behind the test, and perhaps have a general ego orientation that makes them competitive and goal-directed, and eager to cooperate with the experimenter. Whether they can maintain this difference over a long period of performing monotonous tasks remains a valid question. Before we close the books on intelligence, this reviewer would like to see a long-term assessment of its influence.

2.9. *Other group differences*
Several papers have compared the performance of subjects coming from various pre-defined (as contrasted with experimentally-contrived) groups. For example N. Mackworth (1950) found no differences between sonar operators and other naval personnel, and similarly for Jerison and Wallis' study (1957) of students from two very different colleges. But Tickner and Poulton (1973) found that police did better than civilians in simultaneously monitoring numerous TV screens. Tarriere and Hartemann (1964) report that smokers outperformed non-smokers in a visual task. Johnston (1966) also compared smokers and non-smokers in a rather confusing experiment in which rates of improvement were the dependent variable. Lion *et al.* (1968) reportarts students made fewer errors than science students in a belt-driven simulated inspection task. Little has been written about the potential of handicapped inspectors, although the experience with handicapped production workers has generally been extremely good. Riggs (1967) writes favourably of the use of handicapped and even blind inspectors, and this may be a worthwhile line of inquiry.

Also numerous investigators have sought to explain monitoring performance in terms of various physiological parameters, a recent example being Gale *et al.* (1972), and O'Hanlon and Horvath (1973). Rather than attempt to review findings in that area, I shall defer to the description in J. Mackworth (1969), and Loeb and Alluisi (1970). The quest for physiological correlates will undoubtedly be an area of increasing activity in the future, as such research is in vogue, and the possibility of finding electro-physiological correlates of vigilance intrigues many investigators. But the findings to date are something of a jumble, and offer little help in understanding watchkeeping or inspection behaviour, let alone selecting operators.

2.10. *Conclusion*
The generally discouraging, or at best inconclusive, picture which is conveyed by a review of individual and group differences, would recommend that those interested in improving inspection and monitoring performance look elsewhere. At this stage, one would be hard put to justify any variety of selection device, and those offering advice to industry might consider other approaches. Training, motivation, and job design appear to be strong candidates.

The legal situation, as well as recent court decisions, impact on test selection techniques. First, there are various legislative protections against non-discrimination in hiring with respect to age and sex. But even more important to our profession is the recent unanimous Supreme Court decision in the case of *Griggs vs. Duke Power Co.* (1970). In *Griggs*, a class action suit was filed on behalf of black labourers who were denied access to better jobs for lack of a high school degree. The plaintiff claimed that there was no real requirement for high school education in these jobs. The Supreme Court held that requirements for obtaining or being promoted to a job must demonstrably be related to success on the job. In short, selection devices must have predictive validity.

3. Motivational variables

A thorough discussion of motivation is beyond the possible scope of this paper, but we shall examine certain illustrative studies. There has been little investigation of motivational variables in inspection, which is surprising, in view of the popularity that motivational constructs enjoy in industry. There is almost nothing which a critical reader would regard as an adequately controlled study. Many quality control journals have papers with enticing titles and disappointing contents. Stok (1965) has written an entire book on his studies of enhancing feedback of knowledge of results (KR) to the inspector, but with this and a few other exceptions, this reviewer finds little to discuss. Perhaps the problem again is one of productivity measurement—inspectors can be exhorted to be more diligent, offered various incentives (positive or negative), and cajoled with catchy slogans such as 'zero defects', but if there is no direct measurement of their accuracy, the value of the incentives is questionable, in both senses of the word.

3.1. *Financial incentives*

Here we consider financial payoffs to the operators, usually based on an explicit or implied payoff matrix, with positive incentives for D and possible penalties for FAs and misses. No doubt there have been more attempts to influence inspector behaviour than the literature suggests; perhaps the results lurk in company files. Collin (1960) discovered that an offer of a 'substantial financial reward' did not significantly influence inspector accuracy. Murrell (1965) (p. 424) explains the failure of financial rewards thus.

> 'It must be realized that inspection is largely a perceptual task and that, provided the inspector is not deliberately making decisions which he knows to be wrong, it seems that an attempt to put an inspector on bonus must cause difficulties since successful perception is not a process which can be readily influenced by an incentive, however great.'

We have no quarrel with this rather strong statement as long as one confines the discussion to financial incentives. But if 'incentive' can be extended to other areas, such as provision of KR, we can find numerous exceptions. For example, Mitten (1957) reports that female inspectors of roller bearings were offered, in place of bonus pay, time off for high performance. As soon as a week's inspection bogey was achieved, the inspector could take the rest of the time off and receive a full week's pay. This was particularly attractive to these workers, who were mostly young, unmarried girls living at home, more easily incentivated by free time than extra money. Though this study was performed in the early 1950s, it may be a harbinger of things to come. Recent sociological studies of the younger workers in the American work force (I do not know if this applies to other countries) shows that they are not so economically oriented, and less a slave to the traditional work ethic, than previous generations. More work for more money may have less motivational impact than less work for the same money. This should suggest some interesting research possibilities and practical alternatives, with the caveat that many serial production lines presently installed in industry are intolerant of missing workers. Some re-engineering may be required before such a plan could be implemented.

In vigilance studies, financial incentives have generally yielded unimpressive results, as reviewed by Wiener (1969), whose experiment also produced negative results. As suggested, perhaps the price was not right, for the review reveals relatively modest potential payoffs, yet there is no evidence to suggest that more generous bonuses would have produced the desired effect. There have been numerous studies in recent years, owing largely to the popularity of the theory of signal detection (TSD) and 'Game Theory', which attempt to manipulate the subject's criterion by changing the values in the payoff matrix (Williges 1971, 1973). Williges (1971) showed that the fraction defective (P_0) was more effective than payoff values in achieving this. Finally, we should take note of the suggestion by Wallack and Adams (1969) that a payoff matrix in actual industrial inspection should not be arbitrary numbers, but ought to reflect the values and costs of the inspector's decisions. This author firmly agrees, but also recommends that TSD measures in vigilance experiments be applied with austere scepticism, if at all. Authors should consider some of the limitations of TSD before blindly stepping off the d' end.

3.2. *Knowledge of results* (*KR*)

It has long been recognized, both in laboratories and on production lines, that 'closing the loop' and furnishing the operator with knowledge of results about his own performance has both informational and motivational properties. This review will sidestep any theoretical considerations of just how *KR* functions, as the matter has been discussed in works too numerous to reference. Suffice it to say that on the production line, or inspection station, feedback of results almost invariably results in elevated performance, probably due to both the informational properties which enable self-guidance, and the motivational properties which energize the will to achieve commendation and to avoid criticism. Stok (1965) discusses in detail experiments which enhance the feedback loop, but unfortunately his results do not make an unambiguous case for *KR*. Chaney and Harris (1966) also discuss the effects of *KR*, but again, clear-cut results are not offered. Van Beek (1964) attributes improved accuracy to faster provision of *KR* in an industrial task, and Poulton (1973) stresses the benefits of immediate *KR*. The actual implementation of a feedback system is not easy—it calls for ingenuity and behavioural engineering skills that would tax the most able practitioners.

In vigilance experiments, providing immediate *KR* is generally found to be beneficial, both in increasing D and in decreasing FA, or increasing d' (Williges and North 1972). Any recent review of vigilance will provide a plethora of examples. Since there is so little informational content in most vigilance tasks, most requiring the observation of a unitary event on a display, a motivational interpretation is quite reasonable. Experimenters have usually invoked the law of effect: *KR*, particularly in the case of detections, reinforces observing responses, attentiveness, or whatever behaviour was appropriate to detecting the signal.

One may question the practical significance of *KR*, in that if the system were able to furnish this information then it would be cognisant of the presence of a signal, and the human monitor would be unnecessary. Several experimenters (Wiener 1963, and Annett 1966) have answered this justifiable criticism by showing that *KR*'s benefits were not short-lived, but resulted in positive transfer to conditions where the *KR* was withdrawn. Thus, they see *KR* not as something available in a system under true watchkeeping conditions, but programmable in a training device or simulator. Wiener (1967) showed that training with *KR* on one task transferred to another monitoring task. (For a review of transfer effects of *KR* in vigilance, see Wiener 1968.)

3.3. *Signal schedule*

One point of convergence between inspection and monitoring tasks is the importance of signal schedule. From the time of N. Mackworth's (1950) pioneering work, numerous vigilance experiments (e.g., Jenkins 1958) have shown that D is positively related to the signal rate. Similar results were seen in the inspection tasks of Drury and Addison (1973) and Fox and Haslegrave (1969), but not in Smith and Barany (1970). In brief, very infrequent signals are more difficult to detect.

Whether these results should be interpreted in motivational terms is contentious, but such an interpretation cannot be dismissed. Jerison *et al.* (1965) and others have described vigilance in terms of decision theory. The detection of a signal is seen as reinforcing observing (v non-observing, attention-wandering, etc.) behaviour. Higher signal rates increase the utility of making an observation. Whether or not one accepts the utility-theoretic argument is less important than the obvious practical implications. In those plants which are fortunate enough to have high quality manufacturing, there may be low fault detections at the inspection stations. In the extreme, consider certain monitoring tasks where signals virtually never occur—radar watching for enemy missile launches, scanning serological samples for extremely rare conditions, or watching aircraft instruments for conditions a pilot must guard against, yet will probably never see in a lifetime in the cockpit, e.g., an asymmetric ('split') flap indication. This has led some authors to suggest the possibility of inserting dummy signals into the display at pre-programmed intervals to essentially elevate the apparent P_0 (Garvey *et al.* 1959, Wilkinson 1964). Given the proper precautions against an artificial signal causing a grave commissive error, or slipping through the system as an omissive error, such a scheme may be applicable on the shop floor. If defective items could be inserted into a lot, prior to inspection, they would serve not only to keep the operator more alert, but could also be used administratively as a proficiency criterion, and as the known-signal necessary for implementing a training system with *KR*. Surely the ingenuity shown by some investigators (e.g., Badalamente and Ayoub 1969) in keeping track of experimenter-induced defectives, could be useful on an actual inspection line.

3.4. *Pre-task instructions*

Further evidence supportive of a motivational interpretation comes from three studies of pre-task instructions (Neal 1967, Lucaccini *et al.* 1968, and Tolin 1971). In each of these, the instructions were varied in such a way that the seeming importance of the task was either diminished or enhanced. In the

Lucaccini study, only one word was changed ('challenging' *v* 'monotonous'), and subjects receiving the more positively-toned instructions detected more signals. These experiments are interesting, and encouraging both from the point of view of motivation theory and from the general attractiveness of viewing operatives, not as mere tools, but rather as humans capable of taking an interest in the meaning of their labours, even in the most monotonous situations.

However, this reviewer would caution against over-interpretation of these findings and their potential applicability in industry. Certainly the practice of impressing workers with the importance of their own work is well founded. This is a basic tool of legitimate industrial psychologists and engineers, and regrettably also, of many self-styled motivational experts whose credentials are apocryphal to say the least. A single word, or even an entire set of instructions, which may be effective during the transient conditions of a laboratory experiment, could not be depended upon in the world of employment where, day after day, workers must perceive monotonous work as socially important. In closing, it is intriguing to contrast these results with those reported in Section 3.1. Apparently, perceived importance of the work is more effective than cold cash, a conclusion consistent with many theories of industrial motivation, e.g. Herzberg (1966).

4. Social factors

Here we consider the fact that inspection does not take place in a social vacuum, but that peer pressures, as well as administrative pressures, may effect the inspector's decisions. Many of these pressures result from the direct economic impact of the pass/reject decision upon the company, fellow workers, and possibly the inspector himself (McKenzie 1958).

4.1. *Social pressure—inspectors and peers*

Belbin (1957) describes peer influence in a knitwear factory. He discovered that inspectors were unable to resist the pressure from the knitters to pass their work, since rejects resulted in lost pay. Similarly, Jamieson (1966) found a higher quality of inspection when the inspectors were spatially separated from the production workers in an electronic plant. He remarks 'It is perhaps worth noting that anecdotal evidence from the inspectors in the present investigation revealed that they felt freer to report faults when they were isolated from production; in their new setting they developed a corporate identity which, they believed, had a beneficial effect on their standards' (p. 303). Colquhoun (1964) also found that inspectors experienced peer pressure to pass items, and that it was maximized when they were in close proximity with the production workers. But Van Beek (1964) raises an interesting point in opposition to separating producers and inspectors. He reports that the quality of production increased when inspectors were nearby, attributing the reason to the immediacy of *KR* available under such a plant layout.

Thus we encounter an intriguing conflict. The quality of inspection may be improved if peer pressure is relieved by isolating the inspectors. But this may be a sub-optimization, as the true goal is a high average outgoing quality level (AOQ), and it could be beneficial at the production end to have inspectors nearby. Close at hand, they represent to the production worker both a constant reminder that his output is being examined and, if Van Beek is correct, also a source of *KR*, and perhaps remedial information. There is an old and honoured aphorism in quality control, that quality must be manufactured into an item, not inspected into it. Those of us who are interested in effectiveness of inspection must be mindful of the danger of optimizing over the wrong goal.

4.2. *Social pressures—supervisors and experimenters*

Since the much-quoted Hawthorn studies (Roethlisberger and Dickson 1939), the role of the supervisory atmosphere has been well recognized. In a vigilance experiment, Fraser (1950) discovered accidently that merely having an experimenter present in the room with the subject elevated *D*. A later experiment (1953), planned to deliberately test the effect of experimenter presence, confirmed the early finding. Other experimenters (Bergum and Lehr 1963, Ware *et al.* 1964) have reported the same results. The performance of such an effect is an open question, and we have some doubt as to the long-term applicability of this finding in industry. McKenzie (1958) discusses the conflict between supervisory pressure to maintain tight inspection, and peer pressure to be lenient. In his studies, there was an additional force acting on the inspector. This particular line called for rectifying inspection, and the rectification was performed, not by the production workers, but by 'repairmen' who apparently exerted some influence on the inspectors to find defects in order to provide ample work. This unusual social-financial setup put the inspector in a most unenviable position, trapped between three conflicting forces as well as his own self-esteem. All of which illustrates the inseparability of social milieu, physical layout, and wage incentive plans.

When rectifying inspection is performed, the defect is usually returned to the line where it was produced, and if possible, to the responsible worker. This provides *KR* (*Anon* 1974), and also, since typical work rules call for the worker to rectify the defect on his own time, it is a form of financial penalty. Providing a professional repairman, as described by McKenzie, is rare, and it is not unusual for the inspector himself to perform minor rectifications, providing he has the tools and know-how.

Recently the author visited a computer mainframe manufacturer to observe the production and inspection processes. At the point where circuit boards were gathered and connected to make up the computer, the machine was inspected by a fellow assembly worker, not the one who did the actual assembly. Defects were noted and corrected on the spot. One might label this approach 'peer inspection'. Unfortunately, there were no measures of the effectiveness of the system, or of its social ramifications.

5. Training

Probably the most sorely neglected area is the training of inspector personnel. There are few cases reported in the literature, and most papers consist of exhortations for better training, seldom discussing any systematic efforts. One gains the impression that most inspectors came up through the production ranks, which, indeed, may (or may not) be the proper path to the inspection station. Since there are so few studies from the industrial world, we are forced to draw many of our conclusions from vigilance experiments, and even there, training has never been one of the most popular lines of inquiry.

5.1. *Industrial studies*

Most discussions of industrial training contain rather sketchy details of the regime, accompanied by enthusiastic claims for cost savings. For example, Tanalski (1956) reported on a training programme in the aircraft industry, providing no data, but claiming somewhat modestly that the training paid for itself. Thresh and Frerichs (1966) review their human factors efforts, claiming a 100% gain in accuracy, an average 80% gain in productivity, and a cost reduction of $210,000, all for an investment of $48,000. Eidukonis and Kidwell (1967) outline a training programme whose entire cost was recovered in a few months. A learning effect over two sessions is reported by G. Smith and Adams (1971), and over six sessions by Lion *et al.* (1968).

A more detailed account can be found in the work of Chaney and Teel (1967), who introduced both a training programme and improved visual aids over a six-months period. Compared to a control group of inspectors, both training and visual aids paid off, and the combination of the two was most effective. Tiffin and Rogers (1941) also report considerable success with both the training of new inspection personnel and the upgrading of old ones. In each of these cases, the primary training mechanism was providing immediate feedback (*KR*) to the inspectors. This author will leave it to the theoreticians to argue whether *KR* is a motivational or informational mechanism: the important point is that providing *KR* works, and no other device has been as effective.

Stressing the motivation aspect of *KR* is not to belittle its informational content. Certainly the training of the inspector, particularly in difficult perceptual discriminations (e.g., reading X-rays) requires a high degree of understanding the nature of the signal. Thomas and Seaborne (1961) and Thomas (1962) provide an interesting discussion of what they term 'contextual information', in which feedback is employed to aid the inspector in building his own standard for a defect. These papers argue that an inspector must develop a model of perceptual organization which delineates the boundaries between defective and effective items. They further stress the importance of the inspector understanding the underlying manufacturing process in order to assess defects. This view is consistent with prevailing industrial practices of drawing inspectors from the ranks of production personnel, as well as this author's example of 'peer inspection'. Indeed, there is striking similarity between Thomas's (1962) view of the formation of perceptual standards for inspection, and Annett's (1966) notion that training a monitor consists of building a mental template by which to judge signals *v* non-signals.

5.2. *Training for vigilance*

We need not dwell on the subject of training for vigilance, as several comprehensive reviews have accompanied recent experiments (Annett 1966, Annett and Paterson 1967, Colquhoun 1966, Wiener 1967, 1968). First, there is conflicting evidence on practice effects. Wiener (1967) reviewed a number of studies and wrote that practice alone cannot be relied upon to produce learning effects, but Colquhoun and Edwards (1970) have come to the opposite conclusion. Recent personal communication between this author and Colquhoun leaves the matter still unresolved: Colquhoun always obtains practice effects, and Wiener almost never does.

Be that as it may, many authors have found success with transfer of training designs, offering subjects training aids which enhance D and suppress FA, finding that these trends continue in later sessions when the aids are withdrawn. Wiener (1963) demonstrated the use of KR as a training aid, and later (1967) demonstrated that the effect could be transferred from one monitoring task to another quite different one. Annett (1966) has reported similar results with KR, but found greater transfer effects with pre-signal cueing (alerting). Wiener and Attwood (1968) were unable to obtain transfer with cueing. Colquhoun (1966), and Williges and Streeter (1971) have had considerable success with transfer of training designs.

The practical importance of these studies should not be overlooked. If a monitor must perform his vigil under the most perceptually difficult conditions, i.e., no KR, no cueing, low signal rate, and poor signal conspicuity, then his performance may be enhanced by training programmes which allow him to practice under less severe conditions, with training aids which may be unavailable in the real world of watchkeeping. The use of the autotutorial devices, including computer-based systems, in which the monitor can retrain himself, has been recommended by Attwood and Wiener (1969), who found considerable performance enhancement with a modest amount of time spent on a self-training device. This type of training would be most beneficial in those monitoring tasks in which signals rarely occur.

Recently Wiener (1973) and Wiener and Keeler (1974) have shown the efficacy of employing adaptive, or self-adjusting vigilance tasks, using a computer-based system. The size of the signal, relative to the non-signal stimulus was performance-adjusted: if the subject detected fewer signals than the target value of D, the size of the signal was increased, and vice versa. Figure 1 shows that a near-constant D was maintained, with the usual vigilance decrement seen as an increasing signal width (W) over the 48-minute run. Such a system could probably be advantageously employed in the training of inspectors. Given a specified target value of D, the inspector would be trained with a device which gradually decreased the conspicuity of the defect as the inspector became more proficient. Thus the size of the defect which he could spot, a required fraction of the time, would be the measure of his ability, and might dictate where in the inspection process he should be assigned. As he became more proficient, he would be deployed at a station requiring more exacting skills, instead of staying at the same job and catching a larger percentage of defects.

A careful reading of the literature devoted to training for vigilance should suggest many techniques that might be of value in training inspectors. As before, we caution that training techniques cannot be separated from incentive systems or the supervisory and social climate in which the inspector must work.

6. Conclusions

This review has revealed with regard to individual or group differences that there is little in the current state of the art in inspection or laboratory studies of vigilance that can be put to work in the industry without further research. Personnel selection, long a favourite of industrial management, offers little promise at the present, though there is no reason to believe that this is a closed issue. But it seems unlikely that even highly developed psychometric devices will effect large cost savings and great improvements in quality assurance.

This reviewer has no objection, technical or philosophical, to attempting to match workers to jobs; it just appears to be an approach of dubious potential payoff.

More attractive possibilities may reside in the murky areas of employee motivation and social atmosphere. These are forbidding territories, which unfortunately attract over-simplifiers and cliché merchants. A more aggressive approach toward research, in industrial settings, especially in combining direct, financial incentives with knowledge of results and other non-monetary rewards, offers great promise. As one particular line of inquiry, we would recommend further exploration of what this reviewer has called 'peer inspection'. We would

Figure 1.   Percent of signals detected is shown in the upper portion. The parameter K_{out} refers to the size of the outward adjustment in signal width (W), making it larger in the event of poor recent performance. $K_{in} = 16$ in both groups.   The lower portion plots the size of the signal against time, with vigilance decrement seen as increasing W in order to maintain a fixed detection rate. Data from Wiener and Keeler (1974).

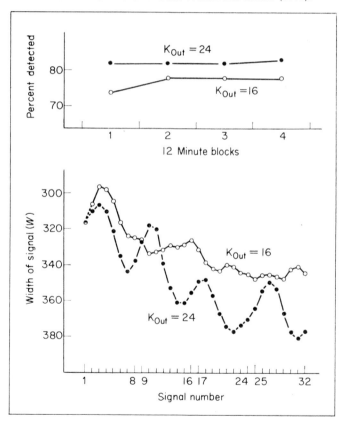

like to see some plant take it a step further and cross-train production employees and inspectors, then alternating the two activities. This form of peer inspection not only capitalizes on Thomas's (1962) suggestion that inspectors understand the manufacturing processes of the goods they are passing judgment over, but could also be regarded as a form of 'job enrichment'. This notion, popular in modern industry today, is a reaction to the over-specialization and separation from the total product which was an inevitable consequence of serial line manufacturing. Despite our nostalgia for the pre-Industrial Revolution work style, we will never see a return to direct contact between manufacturer and ultimate consumer, but experiments with job enlargement (one form of which is popularly called the '*Volvo* plan') may be a worthwhile compromise.

Finally, we stress the importance of training, and its high potential for dollar payoff. The modern training technologies, such as computer-assisted instruction, and sophisticated audio and visual devices have made little impact on the world of quality control. Since even modest manufacturing facilities have, or will soon have, some manner of digital computer on location, very sophisticated training devices can be interfaced with low incremental costs. It will be up to human factors specialists to devise the training 'software' and demonstrate its usefulness.

Lest anyone think that the monitoring and inspection problem is solved, or is unimportant, let him consider two cases from the real world. First, Yerushalmy (1969), summarizing a lengthy series of studies of the performance of a highly skilled group of inspectors called radiologists, reports that over 20% of the 'defects' present in the 15,000 chest X-rays examined, were overlooked. One must view with some discomfort the implications to public health of these findings, especially if he notes the fact that the radiologists in this study were particularly well qualified. As the second example, take the tragic case of *Eastern* 401, a Lockheed L–1011 inbound to Miami just a year and a half ago. The pre-landing cockpit check revealed an unsafe landing gear indication, and the crew initiated a *go-around* flying away from the airport at an assigned altitude of 2000 feet while they went through steps to ascertain the true situation of the gear. Several minutes later, the aircraft went into a slow, descending turn, crashing into the Everglades, killing 101 persons. With a full panel of cockpit instruments, as well as extra-cockpit cues, and even an auditory chime which sounded warning of the premature descent, the crew never raised a restraining finger. As the NTSB report read:

> 'The National Transportation Safety Board determines that the probable cause of this accident was the failure of the flight crew to monitor the flight instruments during the final 4 minutes of flight, and to detect an unexpected descent soon enough to prevent impact with the ground. Preoccupation with a malfunction of the nose landing gear position indicating system distracted the crew's attention from the instruments and allowed the descent to go unnoticed.'

This work was supported by a P.H.S. Research Grant No. R01–OH–00346 from the National Institute of Occupational Safety and Health. The author is grateful for the assistance of Anne K. Manchester.

References

ANNETT, J., 1966, Training for perceptual skills. *Ergonomics*, **9**, 459–468.

ANNETT, J., and PATERSON, L., 1967, *The Use of Cueing in Training Tasks: Phase III.* (Technical Report, NAVTRADEVCEN 4717–1, Orlando, Florida.)

ANON, 1974, Defect tags inspire quality. *Industrial Engineering*, **6**, 22–23.

ANTROBUS, J. S., COLEMAN, R., and SINGER, J. L., 1967, Signal-detection performance by subjects differing in pre-disposition to daydreaming. *Journal of Consulting Psychology*, **31**, 487–491.

ATTWOOD, D. A., and WIENER, E. L., 1969, Automated instruction for vigilance training. *Journal of Applied Psychology*, **53**, 218–223.

AYERS, A. W., 1942, A comparison of certain visual factors with the efficiency of textile inspectors. *Journal of Applied Psychology*, **26**, 812–827.

BADALAMENTE, R. V., and AYOUB, M. M., 1969, A behavioral analysis of an assembly line inspection task. *Human Factors*, **11**, 339–352.

BAKAN, P., 1959, Extraversion-introversion and improvement in an auditory task. *British Journal of Psychology*, **50**, 325–332.

BAKAN, P., 1963, Time-of-day preference, vigilance and extraversion-introversion. In *Vigilance: A Symposium.* (Edited by D. N. BUCKNER and J. J. McGRATH.) (New York: McGRAW-HILL.)

BAKAN, P., and MANLEY, R., 1963, Effect of visual deprivation on auditory vigilance. *British Journal of Psychology*, **54**, 115–119.

BAKER, C. H., and HARABEDIAN, A., 1962, Performance in an auditory vigilance task while simultaneously tracking a visual target. In *Studies of Human Vigilance, Technical Report 740–2.* (Goleta, California: HUMAN FACTORS RESEARCH, INCORPORATED.)

BELBIN, R. M., 1957, New fields for quality control. *British Management Review*, **15**, 79.

BERGUM, B. O., and LEHR, D. J., 1963, Effects of authoritarianism on vigilance performance. *Journal of Applied Psychology*, **47**, 75–77.

BROADBENT, D. E., 1958, *Perception and Communication.* (London: PERGAMON PRESS.)

BUCKNER, D. N., HARABEDIAN, A., and McGRATH, J. J., 1960, A study of individual differences in vigilance performance. In *Studies of Human Vigilance, Technical Report, No. 2.* (Goleta, Calif: HUMAN FACTORS RESEARCH INCORPORATED.)

BUROS, O. K., 1972, *Mental Measurement Yearbook (7th Ed.).* (Highland Park, N.J.: GRYPHON PRESS.)

CARROLL, J. M., 1969, Estimating errors in the inspection of complex products. *Transactions of Industrial Engineering*, **1**, 229–235.

CHANEY, F. B., and HARRIS, D. H., 1966, Human factors techniques for quality improvement. *Paper presented at 20th Annual American Society for Quality Control Technical Conference, New York City.*

CHANEY, F. B., and TEEL, K. S., 1967, Improving human performance through training and visual aids. *Journal of Applied Psychology*, **51**, 311–315.

CLARIDGE, G. S., 1960, The excitation-inhibition balance in neurotics. In *Experiments in Personality, Volume* 2. (Edited by H. J. EYSENCK.) (New York: PRAEGER.)

COLLIN, D. A., 1960, personal communication, referenced in *Human Performance in Industry*, by K. F. H. MURRELL, 1965 (New York: REINHOLD.)

COLQUHOUN, W. P., 1959, The effect of a short rest-pause on inspection efficiency. *Ergonomics*, **2**, 367–372.

COLQUHOUN, W. P., 1960, Temperament, inspection efficiency, and time of day. *Ergonomics*, **3**, 377–378.

COLQUHOUN, W. P., 1961, The effect of unwanted signals on performance in a vigilance task. *Ergonomics*, **4**, 41–51.

COLQUHOUN, W. P., 1964, Recent research in the psychology of inspection. *Textile Institute and Industry*, 252–255.

COLQUHOUN, W. P., 1966, Training for vigilance: a comparison of different techniques. *Human Factors*, **8**, 7–12.

COLQUHOUN, W. P., and CORCORAN, D. W. J., 1964, The effects of time of day and social isolation on the relationship between temperament and performance. *British Journal of Social and Clinical Psychology*, **3**, 226–231.

COLQUHOUN, W. P., and EDWARDS, R. S., 1970, Practice effects on a visual vigilance task with and without search. *Human Factors*, **12**, 537–545.

DAVIES, D. R., and GRIEW, S., 1963, A further note on the effect of aging on auditory vigilance performance: The effect of low signal frequency. *Journal of Gerontology*, **18**, 370–371.

DAVIES, D. R., and HOCKEY, G. R. J., 1966, The effects of noise and doubling the signal frequency on the individual differences in visual vigilance performance. *British Journal of Psychology*, **57**, 381–389.

DAVIES, D. R., and TUNE, G. S., 1969, *Human Vigilance Performance.* (New York: AMERICAN ELSEVIER.)

DOBBINS, D. A., SKORDAHL, D. M., and ANDERSON, A. A., 1961, *Predictions of Vigilance: AASHO Road Test.* (APRO Technical Research Note 119, Washington.)

DORCUS, R. M., and JONES, M. H., 1950, *Handbook of Employee Selection* (New York: McGRAW-HILL.)

DRURY, C. G., and ADDISON, J. L., 1973, An industrial study of the effects of feedback and fault density on inspection performance. *Ergonomics*, **16**, 159–169.

DRURY, C. G., and SHEEHAN, J. J., 1969, Ergonomic and economic facts—an industrial inspection task. *International Journal of Production Research*, **7**, 333–341.

EIDUKONIS, E. R., and KIDWELL, J. L., 1967, The inspection training program. *Industrial Quality Control*, **23**, 622–628.

EVANS, R. N., 1951, Training improves micrometer accuracy. *Personnel Psychology*, **4**, 231–242.

EYSENCK, H. J., 1957, *The Dynamics of Anxiety and Hysteria.* (New York: PRAEGER.)

FOX, J. G., and HASLEGRAVE, C. M., 1969, Industrial inspection efficiency and the probability of a defect occurring. *Ergonomics*, **12**, 713–721.

FRASER, D. C., 1950, The relation between angle of display and performance in a prolonged visual task. *Quarterly Journal of Experimental Psychology*, **2**, 176–181.

FRASER, D. C., 1953, The relation of an environmental variable to performance in a prolonged visual task. *Quarterly Journal of Experimental Psychology*, **5**, 31–32.

GALE, A., BULL, R., PENFOLD, V., COLES, M., and BARRACLOUGH, R., 1972, Extraversion, time of day, vigilance performance, and physiological arousal: Failure to replicate traditional findings. *Psychonomic Science*, **29**, 1–5.

GARVEY, W. D., TAYLOR, F. V., and NEWLIN, E. P., 1959, *The Use of 'Artificial Signals' to Enhance Monitoring Performance*. (USN NRL Report 5269, Washington.)

GHISELLI, E. C., 1942, Tests for the selection of inspector packers. *Journal of Applied Psychology*, **26**, 468–476.

GRIEW, S., and DAVIES, D. R., 1962, The effect of aging on auditory vigilance performance. *Journal of Gerontology*, **17**, 88–90.

Griggs, et al., versus Duke Power and Light Co., 1970, Supreme Court of the United States, No. 124 October Term.

HARRIS, D. H., 1964, Development and validation of an aptitude test for inspectors of electronic equipment. *Journal of Industrial Psychology*, **2**, 29–35.

HARRIS, D. H., 1968, Effect of defect rate on inspection accuracy. *Journal of Applied Psychology*, **52**, 377–379.

HARRIS, D. H., and CHANEY, F. B., 1969, *Human Factors in Quality Assurance*. (New York: JOHN WILEY AND SONS.)

HEIMSTRA, N. W., ELLINGSTAD, V. S., and DEKOCK, A. R., 1967, Effects of operator mood on performance in a simulated driving task. *Perceptual and Motor Skills*, **25**, 729–735.

HERZBERG, F., 1966, *Work and the Nature of Man*. (New York: WORLD PUBLISHING CO.)

HOGAN, M. J., 1966, Influence of motivation on reactive inhibition in extraversion-introversion. *Perceptual and Motor Skills*, **22**, 187–192.

JACOBSON, H. J., 1953, A study of inspector accuracy. *Engineering Inspection*, **17**, 2.

JAMIESON, G. H., 1966, Inspection in the telecommunications industry: A field study of age and other performance variables. *Ergonomics*, **9**, 297–303.

JENKINS, H. M., 1958, The effect of signal rate on performance in visual monitoring. *American Journal of Psychology*, **71**, 647–661.

JERISON, H. J., PICKETT, R. M., and STENSON, H. H., 1965, The elicited observing rate and decision processes in vigilance. *Human Factors*, **7**, 107–128.

JERISON, H. J., and WALLIS, R. A., 1957, *Experiments on Vigilance, II: One-Clock and Three-Clock Monitoring*. (USAF WADC Technical Report No. 57–206; AD 118171.)

JOHNSTON, D. M., 1966, Effect of smoking on visual search performance. *Perceptual and Motor Skills*, **22**, 619–622.

KAPPAUF, W. E., CROWDER, W. F., McDIARMID, C. G., and DAVIES, J. D., 1955, *Performance During Prolonged Watchkeeping at a Visual Detection Task Involving Search* (University of Illinois Memor. Report H–10, Urbana.)

KAPPAUF, W. E., and POWE, W. E., 1959, Performance decrement at an audio-visual checking task. *Journal of Experimental Psychology*, **57**, 49–56.

KEISTER, M. E., and McLAUGHLIN, R. J., 1972, Vigilance performance related to extraversion–introversion and caffeine. *Journal of Experimental Research in Personality*, **6**, 5–11.

KELLEY, M. L., 1955, A study of industrial inspection by the method of paired comparisons. *Psychology Monograph*, **69**, No. 394.

KIRK, R. E., and HECHT, E., 1963, Maintenance of vigilance by programmed noise. *Perceptual and Motor Skills*, **16**, 553–560.

KRKOVIC, A., and SVERKO, B., 1967, Characteristics of performance on a new variety of vigilance task. *Acta Instituti Psychologici Universitatis Zagrabiensis*, No. 54.

LINK, H. C., 1920, *Employment Psychology*. (New York: McMILLAN).

LION, J. S., RICHARDSON, E., and BROWNE, R. C., 1968, A study of the performance of industrial inspectors under two kinds of lighting. *Ergonomics*, **11**, 23–34.

LOEB, M., and ALLUISI, E. A., 1970, Influence of display task and organismic variables on indices of monitoring behaviour. In *Attention and Performance III*. (Edited by A. F. SAUNDERS.) (Amsterdam: NORTH-HOLLAND.) Pp. 343–366.

LUCACCINI, L. F., FREEDY, A., and LYMAN, J., 1968, Motivational factors in vigilance: effects of instructions on performance in a complex vigilance task. *Perceptual and Motor Skills*, **26**, 783–786.

MACKWORTH, J. F., 1969, *Vigilance and Habituation*. (Baltimore: PENGUIN BOOKS.)

MACKWORTH, N. H., 1950, *Researches on the Measurement of Human Performance*. (MRC Report Series No. 268, Cambridge.)

McCANN, P. H., 1969, The effects of ambient noise on vigilance performance. *Human Factors*, **11**, 251–256.

McGRATH, J. J., HARABEDIAN, A., and BUCKNER, D. N., 1960, An exploratory study of the correlates of vigilance performance. In *Human Factor Problems in Anti-Submarine Warfare, Tech. Rep.*, 4. (Los Angeles: HUMAN FACTORS RESEARCH.)

McKenzie, R. M., 1958, On the accuracy of inspectors. *Ergonomics*, **1**, 258–272.

Mitten, L. G., 1957, Research team approach to an inspection operation. In *Introduction to Operations Research*. (Edited by C. W. Churchman, R. L. Ackoff, and E. L. Arnoff.) (New York: Wiley.)

Murrell, K. F. H., 1965, *Human Performance in Industry*. (New York: Reinhold.)

National Transportation Safety Board, 1973, *Aircraft Accident Report NTSB-AAR-73-14 Eastern Airlines, Inc. I.–1011 N310EA, Miami, Florida, December* 29, 1972. (Washington: NTSB.)

Neal, G. L., 1967, *Some Effects of Differential Pretask Instructions on Auditory Vigilance Performance*. (HumRRO, Professional Paper 34–67. Alexandria, Virginia: George Washington University.)

Neal, G. L., and Pearson, R. G., 1966, Comparative effects of age, sex, and drugs, upon two tasks of auditory vigilance. *Perceptual and Motor Skills*, **23**, 957–974.

Nelson, J. B., and Barany, J. W., 1969, A dynamic visual recognition test for paced inspection tasks. *Transactions of Industrial Engineering*, **1**, 327–332.

O'Hanlon, J. F., and Horvath, S. M., 1973, Interrelationships among performance, circulating concentrations of adrenaline, noradrenaline, glucose, and the free fatty acids in men performing a monitoring task. *Psychophysiology*, **10**, 251–259.

Poulton, E. C., 1973, The effect of fatigue upon inspection work. *Applied Ergonomics*, **4**, 73–83.

Purohit, A. K., 1972, Personality types and signal detection. *Indian Journal of Psychology*, **47**, 161–164.

Purohit, A. K., and Hardikar, S., 1971, Manifest anxiety and visual signal detection. *Indian Journal of Experimental Psychology*, **5**, 98–99.

Riggs, W. L., 1967, Use of the blind and visually handicapped in inspection. *Industrial Quality Control*, **24**, 7–8.

Roethlisberger, F. J., and Dickson, W. J., 1939, *Management and the Worker*. (Cambridge: Harvard University Press.)

Rutten, J. W., and Block, J. R., 1973, *Test Manual for the Attention DiagnosticMethod (ADM)*. (Hempstead, N.Y.: Instrumental Psychological Methods, Inc.)

Sartain, A. Q., 1945, The use of certain standardized tests in the selection of inspectors in an aircraft factory. *Journal of Consulting Psychology*, **9**, 234–235.

Schuman, J. T., 1945, The value of aptitude tests for factory workers in the aircraft engine and propeller industries. *Journal of Applied Psychology*, **29**, 156–163.

Sheehan, J. J., and Drury, C. G., 1971, The analysis of industrial inspection. *Applied Ergonomics*, **2**, 74–78.

Sipowicz, R. R., and Baker, R. A., 1961, Effects of intelligence on vigilance: a replication. *Perceptual and Motor Skills*, **13**, 398.

Smith, G. L., and Adams, S. K., 1971, Magnification and microminiature inspection. *Human Factors*, **13**, 247–254.

Smith, L. A., and Barany, J. W., 1970, An elementary model of human performance on paced visual inspection tasks. *Transactions of Industrial Engineering*, **2**, 298–308.

Smith, R. L., and Lucaccini, L. F., 1969, Vigilance research: Its application to industrial problems. *Human Factors*, **11**, 149–156.

Smith, R. L., Lucaccini, L. F., Groth, H., and Lyman, J., 1966, Effects of anticipatory alerting signals and a compatible secondary task on vigilance performance. *Journal of Applied Psychology*, **50**, 240–246.

Solandt, D. Y., and Partridge, R. C., 1946, Research on auditory problems presented by naval operations. *Journal of Canadian Medical Services*, **3**, 323–329.

Stok, T. L., 1965, *The Worker and Quality Control*. (Ann Arbor, Michigan: The University of Michigan.)

Stroh, C. M., 1971, *Vigilance: the Problem of Sustained Attention*. (Oxford: Pergamon Press.)

Surwillo, W. W., and Quilter, R. E., 1964, Vigilance, age, and response-time. *American Journal of Psychology*, **77**, 614–620.

Surwillo, W. W., and Quilter, R. E., 1965, The relation of frequency of spontaneous skin potential responses to vigilance and to age. *Psychophysiology*, **1**, 272–276.

Tanalski, T. G., 1956, The eyes have it—At Convair. *Industrial Quality Control*, **12**, 9–10.

Tarriere, C., and Hartemann, F., 1964, Investigation into the effects of tobacco smoke on a visual vigilance task. *Ergonomics Supplement* (Proceedings of 2nd I.E.A. Congress, Dortmund), 525–530.

Thomas, L. F., 1962, Perceptual organization in industrial inspectors. *Ergonomics*, **5**, 429–434.

Thomas, L. F., and Seaborne, A. E. M., 1961, The sociotechnical context of industrial inspection. *Occupational Psychology*, **35**, 36–43.

Thompson, L. W., Opton, E., and Cohen, L. D., 1963, Effects of age, presentation speed, and sensory modality on performance of a vigilance task. *Journal of Gerontology*, **18**, 366–369.

THRESH, J. L., and FRERICHS, J. S., 1966, Results through management application of human factors. *Paper presented at 20th Annual ASQC Technical Conference, New York.*

TICKNER, A. H., and POULTON, E. C., 1973, Monitoring up to 16 synthetic television pictures showing a great deal of movement. *Ergonomics*, **16**, 381–401.

TIFFIN, J., and ROGERS, H. B., 1941, The selection and training of inspectors. *Personnel*, **18**, 14–31.

TOLIN, P., 1971, Instruction effects on watch keeping in a 'simple' vigilance task. *Perception and Psychophysics*, **9**, 227–228.

TUNE, G. S., 1966a, Age differences in errors of commission. *British Journal of Psychology*, **57**, 391–392.

TUNE, G. S., 1966b, Errors of commission as a function of age and temperament in a type of vigilance task. *Quarterly Journal of Experimental Psychology*, **18**, 358–361.

VAN BEEK, H. G., 1964, The influence of assembly line organization on output, quality and morale. *Occupational Psychology*, **38**, 161–172.

WAAG, W. L., HALCOMB, C. G., and TYLER, D. M., 1973, Sex differences in monitoring performance. *Journal of Applied Psychology*, **58**, 272–274.

WALLACK, P. M., and ADAMS, S. K., 1969, The utility of signal-detection theory in the analysis of industrial inspector accuracy. *Transactions of Industrial Engineering*, **1**, 33–44.

WARE, J. R., 1961, Effects of intelligence on signal detection in visual and auditory monitoring. *Perceptual and Motor Skills*, **13**, 99–102.

WARE, J. R., BAKER, R. A., and SIPOWICZ, R. R., 1962, Performance of mental deficients on a simple vigilance task. *American Journal of Mental Deficiency*, **66**, 647–650.

WARE, J. R., KOWAL, B., and BAKER, R. A., 1964, The role of experimenter attitude and contingent reinforcement in a vigilance task. *Human Factors*, **6**, 111–115.

WELFORD, A. T., 1958, *Ageing and Human Skill*. (London: OXFORD UNIVERSITY PRESS for the Nuffield Foundation.)

WHITTENBURG, J. A., and ROSS, S., 1953, *A Study of Three Measures of Perceptual Efficiency during Sustained Vigilance.* (University of Maryland Tech. Rep. 14, College Park.)

WIENER, E. L., 1963, Knowledge of results and signal rate in monitoring: A transfer of training approach. *Journal of Applied Psychology*, **47**, 214–222.

WIENER, E. L., 1967, Transfer of training from one monitoring task to another. *Ergonomics*, **10**, 649–658.

WIENER, E. L., 1968, Training for vigilance: Repeated sessions with knowledge of results. *Ergonomics*, **11**, 547–556.

WIENER, E. L., 1969, Money and the monitor. *Perceptual and Motor Skills*, **29**, 627–634.

WIENER, E. L., 1973, Adaptive measurement of vigilance decrement. *Ergonomics*, **16**, 353–363.

WIENER, E. L., and ATTWOOD, D. A., 1968, Training for vigilance: Combined cueing and knowledge of results. *Journal of Applied Psychology*, **6**, 474–479.

WIENER, E. L., and KEELER, F. L., 1975, Adaptive strategies in vigilance research. *Ergonomics*, in press.

WILKINSON, R. T., 1961, Comparison of paced, unpaced, irregular and continuous display in watchkeeping. *Ergonomics*, **4**, 259–267.

WILKINSON, R. T., 1964, Artificial 'signals' as an aid to an inspection task. *Ergonomics*, **7**, 63–72.

WILLIGES, R. C., 1971, The role of payoffs and signal ratios in criterion changes during a monitoring task. *Human Factors*, **13**, 261–267.

WILLIGES, R. C., 1973, Manipulating the response criterion in visual monitoring. *Human Factors*, **15**, 179–185.

WILLIGES, R. C., and NORTH, R. A., 1972, Knowledge of results and decision making performance in visual monitoring. *Organization Behavior and Human Performance*, **8**, 44–57.

WILLIGES, R. C., and STREETER, H., 1971, Display characteristics in inspection tasks. *Journal of Applied Psychology*, **55**, 123–125.

WYATT, S., and LANGDON, J. N., 1932, *Inspection Processes in Industry.* (Industrial Health Research Board Report 63, London.)

YERUSHALMY, J., 1969, The statistical assessment of the variability in observer perception and description of roentgenographic pulmonary shadows. *Radiologic Clinics of North America*, **VII**, 381–392.

YORK, C. M., 1962, Behavioural efficiency in a visual monitoring task as a function of signal rate and observer age. *Perceptual and Motor Skills*, **15**, 404.

Training the inspector's sensitivity and response strategy

D. E. Embrey

1. Training objectives

One of the most noticeable characteristics of the human factors and ergonomics literature on industrial inspection is the paucity of data on the training of operatives for this task. A possible reason for the lack of research interest in training for inspection may be in the concentration on motor learning in most applied studies rather than the perceptual skills predominating in quality control situations. Whatever the reason, the neglect of this area by research workers in industrial inspection is particularly regrettable since it has several attractions from an applied research standpoint. One important consideration is that training is the essential intervening variable between the sophisticated theoretical models relevent to inspection and their application in a real life situation.

An inspector's performance can be considered from two separate standpoints. The first of these, the inspector's intrinsic sensitivity for defects, can be regarded primarily as a function of peripheral and central factors such as visual acuity and the inspector's knowledge of the distinguishing characteristics of acceptable and non-acceptable items. The inspector's criterion, his bias towards responding 'defect' as opposed to 'acceptable' is, on the other hand, essentially a decision making procedure defined by the *a priori* probability of a defect occurring and the costs and values of the various types of incorrect and correct decisions.

There is however, another more subtle aspect of performance which, though related to those considered up to now, is an entity in its own right and which has been neglected in the typically static tasks usually investigated in the laboratory. This is the question of the inspector's reaction to change during the task itself, specifically his reaction to changes in the probability of defects which might occur at any point in the task. Consider an inspector examining products produced in a continuous flow process. If, for example, one of the production units suddenly goes out of limits and starts to produce a higher incidence of defects, how will the inspector react in such a situation? Or if an inspector is transferred from a situation where a high defect density is the norm to a more fault free product, how quickly will he adjust to the new situation? In order to maintain optimal performance in terms of the theory of signal detection (TSD) he should lower his criterion to one appropriate to the new defect probability and make a greater number of 'defect' responses. But this adjustment presupposes that the inspector has a perfect knowledge of the new defect probability and that he is able to act on this knowledge by adjusting his criterion to the appropriate degree. It is clear that the first of these conditions will not occur. An accurate estimate of the new probability would only be available if the inspector was able to discriminate perfectly between defects and non-defects and if a sufficiently large sample were available. His subjective estimate of the degree of change in fault density will clearly be a function of his intrinsic sensitivity for defects. We also know that human beings are very conservative interpreters of evidence as far as the revision of subjective probabilities is concerned (Edwards 1962). Bayes' theorem tells us the optimal degree to which subjective probability estimates should be revised on the basis of evidence, but experiments show that subjects do not generally do this to the optimal degree.

These two factors, the limited evidence available due to the finite sensitivity of the operator and his innate conservatism, mean that his subjective estimate of the defect probability will lag behind the actual probability. The ability of the inspector to adjust his response bias to the new probability can be regarded as a completely separate attribute to his skill at estimating this probability. There is no guarantee that he will utilise this information in the optimal way. In summary then, we can establish three desirable objectives for a training scheme to be applied in the area of industrial inspection. The inspector's sensitivity, that is his ability to detect defects, should be maximized. His decisions as to whether items should be accepted or rejected should be compatible with the ongoing defect incidence and the cost and values of his decisions to the inspection system. Finally, the inspector should be able to modify his strategy if the costs and values of his decisions are changed, or if the defect incidence changes abruptly: essentially there is the requirement that the inspector be as sensitive as possible to change in the incidence of defects.

2. Training for sensitivity

Although little work appears to have been done specifically on training for industrial inspection, a wide range of literature exists in two areas which seem relevant to training an inspector's sensitivity to defects and his criterion: training for sonar detection and training for vigilance. Although the auditory modality used in sonar training is not often required in inspection tasks, nevertheless it seems likely that many of the techniques evolved for training the sensitivity of sonar operators would be applicable to inspection, bearing in mind the similarity between the two tasks, in that they both involve the detection of a random infrequent signal. Similarly, although vigilance may be only one factor in inspection many experimental vigilance tasks have resembled true inspection situations.

Two heavily subscribed techniques for promoting perceptual learning in these contexts are cueing, or prompting techniques, associated with the work of Annett (1959, 1961) in sonar detection and knowledge of results (KR) advocated by Wiener (1963, 1968) and others in connection with vigilance tasks.

Knowledge of results has been defined as 'knowledge which an individual or group receives relating to the outcome of a response or group of responses'. Some of the forms of KR include, in the detection context, immediate feedback as to whether a response was a correct detection or false alarm, giving missed signal information or giving any or all of this information in a summary form after a number of responses. KR is the classical learning paradigm, exerting its action in accordance with the *Law of Effect*. KR can be said to reinforce observing responses and maintain alertness via its motivational effect. The efficacy of KR as a component of training has been well established in the area of motor skills. Gibson (1953) has suggested however that perceptual learning may not necessarily be analogous to motor learning and that different training techniques may therefore be appropriate.

Work by Annett (1959, 1961) has seemed to confirm this view. He found that the technique of cueing seemed more effective in promoting learning in sonar training than KR. Cueing has been defined as ' the provision of stimulus information before or during a response such that the response is made more effective or more likely to occur than would be the case without such information'. Cueing is said to exert its effect by the simple association in time of the signal characteristics and the associated response. Later experiments by Annett indicated that there was little to choose between KR and cueing although subjects trained using KR tended to obtain increased detection scores at the expense of increased false alarms, implying that at least part of the change was attributable to a more lax response criterion.

Annett postulated that the degree of perceptual learning that occurred was a function of the number of 'authenticated' samples of the signal provided during training and the amount of information that could be gained concerning the distribution of the signal. Although he did not express it in TSD terms the first of these requirements can be looked upon as being necessary in order that the subject learns the characteristics of the signal, thereby enhancing his sensitivity. A knowledge of the signal distribution is necessary in order that the response strategy or criterion adopted is the optimal one.

In theory both cueing and KR provide the signal specification and distribution information required. However Annett suggests that in some situations cueing has certain specific advantages in that pre-warning the subject that a stimulus is about to occur lowers his threshold for the signal and gives him a greater chance to learn its characteristics.

By contrast Wiener asserts that KR is the most effective method of training for perceptual tasks and cites as evidence several experiments (Wiener 1968), including a vigilance task involving the detection of an occasional extra large deflection of a voltmeter. In this experiment KR was clearly superior to both cueing and a cueing plus KR condition in promoting a transfer of training. These apparently contradictory results can be explained to some extent by the different nature of the signals used in each case. The voltmeter deflection was clear and unambiguous and required very little learning, whereas the auditory signal used by Annett was deliberately adjusted to be near to the subjects' threshold. It is clear that in Wiener's experiment very little learning of the signal characteristics was involved, and the effect of KR was primarily motivational or as an aid in learning the signal distribution.

However, neither of these signals is of the complexity found in a typical inspection task and it remains an open question as to which might be the more relevent to such a task. The experiment reported in a later part of this paper was intended as a preliminary investigation of this question.

3. Training for response strategy

In addition to the objective of enhancing the inspector's sensitivity to defects there is the need to train the inspector to adopt an optimal response strategy in the TSD sense, and to increase his flexibility so that he is able to readily adapt to situations of changing defect density.

Some insights into this problem might come from the results of the many vigilance studies in which the effects of training with signal probabilities which are different from the task probabilities have been compared. Typical studies of this type have been Wiener (1963) and Colquhoun and Baddeley (1964, 1967). However, in these studies the subjects were extensively trained with a particular signal probability and the whole of the test session used a single (different) signal probability. One would expect the subject to be firmly anchored to the criterion established during training and in fact performance typical of an inappropriate criterion was obtained throughout the test sessions. In an inspection situation, where signal probability may change within sessions, the ideal operator is one who is completely flexible in his choice of criterion position.

It seems clear that both KR and cueing might be effective in this context. As already discussed, both techniques seem to enhance performance partly by giving the inspector information about the distribution of defects. The enhanced sensitivity accruing from training would also enable more defects to be detected, giving the inspector a better estimate of the defect density in the real life task, thus enabling him to adjust his criterion to an optimal point. It is of interest to note that this analysis of the situation would suggest that the usual TSD assumption of independence of the criterion and sensitivity measures would not necessarily apply in a situation of changing defect probability. The rate of adaptation to a new signal probability might be expected to be a function of the inspector's sensitivity.

We cannot assume however, that a subject's criterion adjustment will automatically be inferior if he has less evidence available. It may be possible that some subjects are able to accurately infer the parameters of the population of defects and non-defects from a smaller sample than other subjects. A possible method of training inspectors to recognise a particular defect distribution would be to expose them to a range of samples containing different defect probabilities and to give feedback together with a prior knowledge of the actual defect probability used. In this way an inspector could become familiar with the distribution of defects that he might expect to detect in a sample from a population containing a given fault incidence given his particular individual level of sensitivity for the defects. This might be regarded as a cueing technique in which instead of the inspector learning the characteristics of a defect by being given prior warning of its occurrence, he learns the distributional characteristics of a *sample* of defects and non-defects as he would expect to perceive them in the actual task. In order to establish appropriate expectances it would be necessary to ensure that the statistical nature of the defect distribution (i.e. normal, Poisson etc.) corresponds to that found in the real life situation.

As to the relative efficacy of feedback versus cueing in promoting the learning of probability distributions very little information exists concerning situations resembling those found in inspection tasks. However feedback has been used with some success to train subjects to estimate parameters of Bernoulli distributions generated by various random devices (Staël von Holstein 1971). Some of these questions are considered in greater detail in Embrey (1975). It seems possible that the enhanced performance found by Drury and Addison (1973) when KR was given to inspectors in the glass industry could have been due to them gaining insights into the nature of the defect distribution.

4. An experiment on training techniques

There are, then, two main areas of experimental work of particular interest
in the training context. These are the applicability of cueing and feedback techniques in enhancing the inspector's sensitivity for detecting defects, and the
feasibility of training him to use an optimal decision strategy in deciding whether
particular samples of product are to be regarded as acceptable or otherwise.
The former area involves a straightforward comparison between the two methods
of enhancing sensitivity, preferably using stimuli that are of similar complexity
to those found in real life inspection situations. As far as training for an optimal
criterion is concerned however, we lack basic information concerning the
behaviour of subjects in detection situations in which signal probabilities change
within sessions. For experiments of this type it would be reasonable to use
simplified stimuli in order to concentrate on the decision-making aspects of the
task.

An exploratory study has been conducted (Embrey 1975) in these areas.
It involved practised subjects detecting a signal consisting of a slight increment
in brightness of the central disc of a projected display. The effects of a variety
of combinations of signal probability and feedback were used to gain some
insights into the effects of these variables on subjects' response strategy and
sensitivity.

The conditions used in the study were as follows:

1. Constant high probability of signal ($P=0.50$)
   (a) feedback
   (b) no feedback
2. Constant low probability of signal, no feedback ($P=0.10$)
3. Chance in probability of signal during session ($P=0.50, 0.20$)
   (a) no warning, feedback
   (b) warning, no feedback
   (c) warning, feedback

Nine final year undergraduate students served as subjects. They were paid
50p per session with 25p bonus if they reached a target score.

All subjects received condition 1(a) first, and then the remaining conditions
in random order. Where the signal probability changed it did so after the first
two blocks of 100 stimuli. Time-of-day effects were reduced by randomly assigning
subjects to mornings or afternoons. All subjects had received at least 3000 trials
in experiments of a similar nature to this one and in all previous sessions the
defect probability had been 0.50. The last testing in the series prior to this one
had occurred three weeks prior to session 1(a) which was intended as a warm-
up condition and to provide baseline data. If the probability of a signal was to
be 0.50 in a session or if the signal density was to be changed without warning,
subjects were told that they could expect about the same incidence of signals
as in the training sessions. With the 0.10 probability session they were told to
expect a 'low' incidence of signals and with the variable probability schedule
that a 'change' would take place.

Five hundred stimuli were presented under each condition, and in the feedback conditions complete feedback was given every 100 responses. Under
all conditions the subject received a three minute break every 100 stimuli,

in order to reduce the possibility of vigilance effects. The signals were randomised with the constraint that the probabilities were constant within blocks of 100 stimuli.

Subjects responded to the presentation of stimuli by means of a 6 point rating scale. From left to right the ratings were: definitely non signal, probably non signal, possibly non signal, possibly signal, probably signal, definitely signal. A symmetrical pay-off matrix was assigned to the responses in the following manner. Correct positive or negative responses were given 3, 2 or 1 points depending on whether they were made with an extreme intermediate or low level of confidence, incorrect responses gave minus these payoffs. Subjects were given 750 points at the beginning of the session and paid a bonus if they scored a further 750 points from their responses, i.e. if they scored half the total number of possible points.

4.1. *Results*

Table 1 sets out the results for the various conditions in the form of the five blocks of one hundred responses that occurred in each experimental session. The d', β and variance ratios given for each block were obtained using the rating data for each block as input to a maximum likelihood ratio ROC curve fitting program (Grey and Morgan 1972). The means are for the three subjects used under each condition.

4.1.1. *Equiprobable signal and noise conditions*

This condition used an identical signal probability ($P=0\cdot50$) to that with which the subjects had been trained.

Considering the changes in d', there was a slight decline in sensitivity with time on task in the no feedback condition but not in the condition where KR was given. This is consistent with many vigilance studies (Mackworth 1970).

Table 1. Means for d', β and variance ratio for each condition.

Conditions	Variables	Blocks of 100 responses					All
		1	2	3	4	5	
$P=0\cdot50$ feedback	d'	1·549	1·684	1·147	1·131	1·252	1·346
	β	0·622	1·237	1·065	0·700	0·817	0·841
	$\sigma n/\sigma s+n$	0·837	0·731	0·741	0·661	0·579	0·705
$P=0\cdot50$ no feedback	d'	1·226	1·213	0·725	0·867	0·968	0·951
	β	0·710	1·285	1·228	1·274	1·581	1·027
	$\sigma n/\sigma s+n$	0·655	0·856	0·869	0·567	0·522	0·669
$P=0\cdot10$ feedback	d'	1·760	1·795	1·010	1·333	0·204	1·030
	β	1·162	3·148	2·897	1·728	1·321	1·823
	$\sigma n/\sigma s+n$	0·692	0·928	0·852	0·331	0·462	0·573
$P=0\cdot50$, $P=0\cdot20$ no warning, feedback	d'	1·457	0·946	0·632	1·504	0·791	0·990
	β	1·311	1·048	0·594	1·136	0·672	0·913
	$\sigma n/\sigma s+n$	1·128	0·922	0·651	0·796	0·786	0·887
$P=0\cdot50$, $P=0\cdot20$ feedback	d'	1·212	1·409	0·849	1·310	0·957	1·213
	β	1·243	3·004	1·607	4·257	1·831	2·116
	$\sigma n/\sigma s+n$	0·90	1·502	0·455	1·958	0·738	1·057
$P=0\cdot50$, $P=0\cdot20$ no feedback	d'	0·493	1·203	1·109	1·081	0·991	0·975
	β	0·855	1·286	4·163	3·345	4·863	2·902
	$\sigma n/\sigma s+n$	0·796	0·300	0·572	0·314	0·337	0·464

However since this task was self paced and rest pauses were frequently provided the presence of a vigilance decrement would be surprising, and in view of the variability of the data the effect is likely to be statistically non-significant.

The overall criterion adopted in the no-feedback condition was closer to the optimal (Table 2) than when feedback was provided, the *criterion value* (β) in this condition being less than the optimum. This effect could be explained by the tendency of KR to encourage the adoption of a more lax (lower) criterion, as found in the Annett studies discussed earlier. In the no KR condition β gradually increased with time on task, an effect characteristic of vigilance tasks.

Table 2. Comparison of mean criterion used with optimum.

Condition	Actual mean β	Optimal β
$P=0\cdot50$ feedback	0·841	1·0
$P=0\cdot50$ no feedback	1·027	1·0
$P=0\cdot10$ feedback	1·823	9·0
$P=0\cdot50$ / $P=0\cdot20$ no warning, feedback	1·18 / 0·80	1·0 / 4·0
$P=0\cdot50$ / $P=0\cdot20$ feedback	2·12 / 2·57	1·0 / 4·0
$P=0\cdot50$ / $P=0\cdot20$ no feedback	1·071 / 4·12	1·0 / 4·0

4.1.2. *Low probability of signal with KR*

An unexpected finding for this condition was that the sensitivity of the subjects was higher than for the equal probability signal/noise condition where KR was not provided. Most studies of industrial inspection have found that detection probabilities for defects are directly related to their probability of occurrence (Fox and Haslegrave 1969, Drury and Addison 1973), although in some cases the increased detections have been accompanied by increased false alarms, indicating changes in criterion rather than sensitivity.

It seems possible that in the present experiment, the provision of feedback had a more important effect on sensitivity than variations in signal probability.

Considering the block by block changes in criteria it is clear that the subjects did not adopt β values as extreme as the optimal 9·0. This is an example of the conservatism discussed earlier. However a shift of the criterion in the correct direction of greater stringency was apparent during the second block of responses. This is consistent with the idea that the subjects gained insights into the signal distribution during the first block and modified their criteria appropriately.

The fact that β declined in subsequent blocks can be ascribed to tendency of KR to promote a lax criterion as discussed earlier.

4.1.3. *Varying probability conditions*

The most important variable in this set of conditions is β and the accuracy with which the subject can adjust his criterion to the optimum. Table 2 gives the mean

129

β used by the subjects in the blocks before and after the change in defect probability and for comparison the optimal value of this parameter given by the theory of signal detection.

Where the defect probability was changed without the subject's knowledge, the degree of criterial adjustment was slight. Although the mean criterion during the first two blocks was close to the optimal, when the defect density decreased, there was a decrease in β in the opposite direction to that required. In the condition where feedback was provided and the subjects were told that a change in signal probability would occur at some unspecified point, the large fluctuations in β for the different blocks seemed to indicate that some degree of guessing was taking place. The near optimal value of β in block four indicates that the correct conclusions were drawn from the feedback information at the end of the first reduced probability block three. However the lower value of β in block five is difficult to explain, unless it is again the effect of KR in reducing the criterion.

Some evidence for this is to be found in the no-KR condition. In this case the subjects' performance in adopting the optimal β values was highly successful, the criteria being very close to those desired for both the high and low signal probability conditions.

Changes in sensitivity did not appear to fall into any consistent pattern during these conditions.

4.2. Discussion

All the results were fitted well by the theory of signal detection model with unequal variances. The χ^2 statistic output by the Grey and Morgan (1972) program indicated a high degree of fit of the data to a straight line ($p < 0.01$). As is usual with visual experiments, the variance of the signal + noise distribution is greater than the noise distribution, a consequence of the observer having an incomplete knowledge of the signal characteristics. The implications of the results for training are as follows. Provision of KR seems to maintain a higher sensitivity than in non-KR sessions independently of the signal probability. However another way of interpreting the data is to say that KR only maintains high sensitivity during the sessions that it is provided and that when it is removed sensitivity declines. Wiener's experiments suggest however that a true transfer of training takes place.

The finding that the subjects are able to adjust their criterion to the optimal most effectively in the non-feedback condition is somewhat paradoxical, but is explicable in the following terms. During the training preceding the test session it seems possible that the subject, by being given repeated summary KR, is able to learn to modify his response strategy in the appropriate direction for the ongoing defect probability. When the feedback is actually being given, however, the effect of KR in inducing a more lax response strategy means that the criterion adopted by the subject will be less than optimal, During the non feedback conditions the criterion adopted is therefore closer to the optimal.

The effect observed in the $P = 0.10$ condition where the subjects were unable to adopt the extreme criterion demanded for optimal responding, indicates that problems may exist in training subjects to use optimal strategies where a very low incidence of defects exists.

Although results for individual subjects are not quoted here, the data gave no support to the hypothesis that subjects with a higher sensitivity were better able to adjust their response strategy to the optimal. In general it is important to realise that the range of criteria about the optimal that will provide the observer with most of the possible expected value for his decisions is very wide. For this reason it would be pointless to search for training techniques which would lead to inspectors using a single *criterion* value. However it is of interest to note that subjects are able to manipulate their response strategy so precisely in a changing signal probability situation.

5. Summary and conclusions

Given that the training requirements for industrial inspection are related to the problems of enhancing the inspector's ability to identify defects and to modify his response bias to the optimal, two main techniques have been proposed to achieve these aims, feedback or knowledge of results, and cueing. The literature gives no firm conclusions as to which of these techniques is likely to be successful in the context of the complex signals found in the typical inspection task. The results of the recent laboratory study which has been discussed indicated that if the subjects have received training in the form of summary KR they are able to modify their criteria in the optimal direction when a change in ongoing signal probability occurs. The resulting criterion is closer to the optimal in sessions where KR was no longer provided.

The issue as to whether these techniques separately or in combination will enable the proposed training objectives to be met remains an open question: and must be so until considerably more research has been done using signals whose complexity is of a similar order to those found in an industrial environment.

This is a logical step on the path towards the highly desirable goal of validating our theoretically sophisticated ideas in practical applications.

References

ANNETT, J., 1959, *Some Aspects of the Acquisition of Simple Sensori-motor Skills.* (D.PHIL. THESIS, OXFORD UNIVERSITY.)

ANNETT, J., 1961, *The Role of Knowledge of Results in Learning: A Survey.* (NAVTRADEVCEN Tech. Rep. No. 342–3, U.S. Naval Training Device Centre, New York.)

COLQUHOUN, W. P., and BADDELEY, A.D., 1964, The role of retest expectancy in vigilance decrement. *Journal of Applied Psychology,* **68,** 156–160.

COLQUHOUN, W. P., and BADDELEY, A. D., 1967, Influence of signal probability during pre-training on vigilance decrement. *Journal of Experimental Psychology,* **73,** 153–155.

DRURY, C. G., and ADDISON, J. L., 1973, An industrial study of the effects of feedback and fault density on inspection performance. *Ergonomics,* **16,** 159–169.

EDWARDS, W., 1962, Dynamic decision theory and probabilistic information processing. *Human Factors,* **4,** 59–73.

EMBREY, D. E., 1975, *Psychological Methodology in Industrial Inspection.* (PH.D. THESIS, UNIVERSITY OF ASTON IN BIRMINGHAM.)

FOX, J. G., and HASLEGRAVE, CHRISTINE M., 1969, Industrial inspection efficiency and the probability of a defect occurring. *Ergonomics,* **12,** 713–721.

GIBSON, E. G., 1953, Improvement in perceptual judgments as a function of controlled practice or training. *Psychological Bulletin,* **50,** 401–431.

GREY, D. R., and MORGAN, B. J. T., 1972, Some aspects of R.O.C. curve fitting normal and logistic models. *Journal of Mathematical Psychology,* **9,** 128–139.

MACKWORTH, J. F., 1970, *Vigilance and Attention.* (London: PENGUIN.)

STAEL VON HOLSTEIN, C.-A. S., 1971, The effect of learning on the assessment of subjective probability distributions. *Organization Behaviour and Human Performance,* **6,** 304–315.

WIENER, E. L., 1963, Knowledge of results and signal rate in monitoring: a transfer of training approach. *Journal of Applied Psychology,* **47,** 214–222.

WIENER, E. L., 1968, Training for vigilance: repeated sessions with knowledge of results. *Ergonomics,* **11,** 547–556.

Lighting for difficult visual tasks

T. W. Faulkner and T. J. Murphy

1. Introduction

Difficult visual tasks which are often near the limits of human ability have become increasingly common in industry. Greater emphasis on product quality and more extensive use of miniaturized components are two of the reasons for this trend. Two basic approaches to improving task visibility are to change the task or to change the illumination falling upon the task. One common means of changing the task is through the use of magnification. Another important technique is to make some change in the product that is being assembled or inspected. Such changes might include use of different materials or finishes to change the specularity of the reflected light or to introduce additional chromatic contrasts. It is important that the possibility of modifying the visual task to make it easier always be examined because of the many opportunities for improvement which are available.

Unfortunately, constraints introduced by product design requirements or by production deadlines often make this kind of change impossible. When the visual task cannot be changed to make it easier it is necessary to rely on some change in the illumination. By manipulating the illumination it is often possible to vary significantly the ease with which the task can be performed.

2. Changes in light level

The most obvious way in which the illumination can be varied is by changing its intensity. A large body of research exists which has been directed at defining the relationship between task brightness and task performance levels. This field of research has been characterized by controversy. Some authors have reported that visual performance continues to improve as the quantity of light is increased to levels of 1,000 ft.-c. or more, whereas others have indicated that there are no additional improvements at levels higher than 50 ft.-c. Bitterman (1948) reviewed the research that had been conducted during the 1930s and '40s and was broadly critical of the use of measures of performance at threshold levels as a criterion of performance at suprathreshold levels. He also discussed the difficulties that had arisen with attempts to use measures of the cost of visual performance, such as blink rate, heart rate, and muscular tension. A review of the research conducted since 1950 has been provided by Hopkinson and Collins (1970). The more recent research has become increasingly sophisticated and complex but questions continue to be raised about the validity of proposed methods of specifying the optimal levels of illumination needed for various tasks.

Historically, there has been a heavy reliance on the use of increases of light level as a primary method of improving task visibility. As improvements in

This paper appeared in substance in *Human Factors* 1973, **15** (2), 149–162.

K

Figure 1. Recommended levels for visual tasks characteristic of office work.

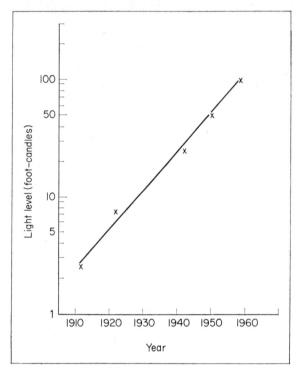

lighting technology have made higher levels possible, these higher levels have generally been quickly adopted in lighting practice. Because of the relative ease with which the quantity of light can be increased there has sometimes been a tendency at the practitioner level to think of increases in quantity as being the only practical means of improving the effectiveness of an illumination system. This trend is illustrated by Figure 1, which shows the levels that have been recommended for the kinds of visual tasks that occur in normal office work. The rate of increase can be plotted as a straight line on log paper. These recommendations were made by the American Illuminating Engineering Society (IES) and other American lighting authorities (see IES 1958, Simonson and Brozek 1952, Tinker 1949). There have been suggestions that further increases in light level should be expected. Referring to the current IES recommendations, Guth (1970, p. 71) noted that they '... are not intended to be final, but as has been done in the past, they will be increased to higher levels as more efficient light sources and improved lighting techniques are developed'. The most recent of the increases in light levels recommended by the IES was based on research by Blackwell (1959). In the discussion section of a paper by Taylor (1962, p. 184), Blackwell observed that the IES had used his data '... to justify increasing luminance levels on the grounds that increases in light always increase visual performance. ... The simple fact is that all sorts of performance data lead to the firm conclusion that the eye performs increasingly better as luminance is increased'.

The idea that increases in light level always result in improved task visibility has been strongly challenged by a number of authors (Hopkinson and Collins 1970,

Figure 2. Effects of changes in task brightness on minimum detectable size and contrast.

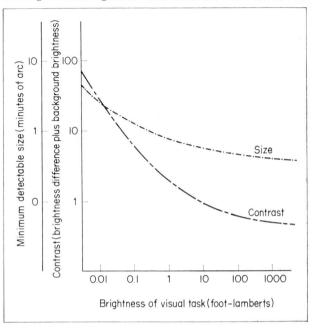

Spencer *et al.* 1959, Weston 1961, Taylor 1962, Tinker 1949, 1959, 1963). Much of this criticism has focused on the experimental procedures used by Blackwell (1959) because of the association of that research programme with the most recent recommendations of the IES. Blackwell has demonstrated that low-contrast visual-detection tasks can be made equal in visibility to high-contrast tasks by increasing the level of illumination. The general form of the relationship is illustrated by Figure 2. As task contrast is reduced, larger and larger increases in illumination are needed to maintain task visibility at a criterion level. Marsden (1964) has observed that this general form of relationship has been reported by a number of different authors for detail discrimination as well as for contrast discrimination.

Since these performance curves tend to flatten out at high levels of task brightness it has been suggested that the very data which are sometimes used to justify higher light levels actually demonstrate that this is an ineffective and inefficient approach. Faulkner and Murphy (1971) reviewed the criticisms that have been directed at the Blackwell (1959) research. They conclude that the most serious objection is related to the nearly flat slope of the standard visual performance curve in the region of task brightness above 10 foot-lamberts (ft.-l.). This indicates that a small decrease in task contrast will require a large increase in illumination level to maintain the level of task visibility. Because of the sensitivity of the method to small changes in task contrast, the relationship between contrast and brightness must be determined with precision. The third and most important consequence of this plateau in the curve is that any small error in the experimental data that tended to translate the performance curve with respect to the contrast axis could produce a large change in recommended task-brightness levels. Blackwell has attempted to overcome some of the objections that have been raised by various authors by expanding his research programme to

135

include additional variables (Blackwell 1969, 1970, Blackwell and Smith 1970).

The recommendations made by the Illuminating Engineering Society (IES 1958) have been accepted by the American National Standards Institute as a standard practice (ANSI 1965, 1970). The levels recommended by the British Illuminating Engineering Society (IES [Brit.] 1961), the Illuminating Engineering Society of Australia (Standards Association of Australia 1965), and the International Labour Office in Geneva (Lowson 1965) are typical of lighting practice in other parts of the world. These standards recommend levels that are substantially below those that are recommended in the United States. A new German standard (Fischer 1969) recommended levels that are somewhat higher but still below those recommended by the American IES.

An important recent development was the adoption by the International Commission on Illumination (CIE) of a basic method of evaluating visual performance (Marsden 1972). This method is based upon the techniques developed by Blackwell. One very significant difference between the new CIE procedure and the procedure (Blackwell 1959) used when the present lighting level standards were adopted by the American Illuminating Engineering Society is the provision of a specific technique for considering other aspects of illumination besides the quantity. The technique for considering these additional factors is based upon the recent research of Blackwell and others. These improvements substantially improve the generality of the method. The CIE report (CIE 1972) does not recommend specific illumination levels for different tasks. Instead, the approach is simply to provide a general method by which the quality of illumination can be related to task performance.

While the evidence on the effectiveness of increases in illumination as a technique for improving task visibility appears to be contradictory, closer examination suggests that there is some consistency when the nature of the task being studied is taken into consideration. High-contrast tasks, such as reading the print on this journal page, seldom show any performance improvement at light levels above 10 to 20 ft.-c. Low-contrast tasks, such as reading from a poor second- or third-generation copy of this journal page may continue to show improvements in performance as levels are increased to 50 or 100 ft.-c. A few specific tasks, which are so difficult as to be at threshold levels will continue to show some degree of improvement as task brightnesses are increased to very high levels. These tasks include the detection of very small or very low-contrast targets. In experimental evaluations these tasks have generally been presented to the observers in a two-dimensional form illuminated by evenly distributed diffuse light. Examples include the reading of very low-contrast print, scanning printed arrays of visual-acuity targets, and observing a rear projection screen to detect occasionally appearing targets. In actual practice in industry, most of the visual tasks that are considered difficult or very difficult are not two-dimensional. The presence of three-dimensional characteristics in a visual task greatly expands the opportunities for effective manipulation of light falling upon that task. In this sense, even a fine line scribed onto a smooth metal surface cannot be considered as two-dimensional. The act of scribing deforms the metal surface to some degree. By using special techniques of lighting it is possible to take advantage of this deformation to improve the visibility of the line. In actual practice the improvements in task visibility that can be achieved by using special purpose lighting are usually substantially greater than the improvements that can be achieved through increases in light level.

3. Special-purpose lighting

The importance of selecting the right light source for visual tasks where colour discrimination is important has been recognized for many years (Taylor 1942, Tiffin and Kuhn 1942). The differences in the spectral characteristics of daylight, tungsten lamps, fluorescent lamps, mercury vapour lamps, etc., can have a substantial effect on the appearance of various colours. The techniques of providing correct colour rendering are well understood and have been adequately described (Hopkinson and Collins 1970, Kaufman 1966).

A few other specialized lighting techniques have also been adequately described in the literature. Polarization of light has been used in the control of glare and in the detection of internal strains in transparent products (Kaufman 1966, Makas and Bird 1965). Frier (1967) has described several ways of manipulating both the illumination and the visual task itself for several different inspection operations. The inspection of specular metal surfaces, glassware, and textiles is covered.

Other, more general, aspects of special-purpose lighting have received less attention in the literature. Hopkinson and Longmore (1959) noted that phototropism (the natural tendency to turn the eye toward the light) made it desirable to have the visual task contrast strongly with its background by means of brightness, colour, texture, or form. Eye movements were recorded in a task where specialized local illumination was compared with general illumination. The authors concluded that 'attention remained on the work more effectively if it was locally lit than if it was seen only in general illumination'. In a discussion of lighting techniques Longmore illustrated twelve different ways of illuminating a cylinder. Four of these ways provided optimum lighting conditions for four different visual tasks: (1) separating the cylinder from its background, (2) revealing the cylindrical shape, (3) highlighting the surface texture, and (4) maximizing the visibility of surface markings such as printing. Lion (1964) showed that fluorescent light provided higher levels of performance than tungsten light on a battery of inspection and manipulative tasks. In a later experiment the relative effects of tungsten and fluorescent lamps on performance of conveyor-belt inspection tasks were compared (Lion *et al.* 1968). The fluorescent lighting was better for detecting breaks in spirals that had been engraved in plastic discs. But for detecting off-centre holes in buttons there was no difference between tungsten and fluorescent. The authors explain this in terms of the different visual demands posed by the two tasks. Rey and Rey (1963) compared two types of fluorescent lighting. Lamps excited by 100,000-Hz. current resulted in better performance than lamps excited by 50-Hz. current. Special-purpose lighting has not been neglected by the lighting industry. At least one firm (General Electric 1964) has described several useful approaches to special lighting problems. Kaufman (1966) also provides an extensive discussion of the techniques of special-purpose illumination.

Inspection lighting is one of the commonest forms of specialized illumination. Before discussing the applications of special lighting techniques to inspection tasks it is necessary to understand some of the factors that affect this kind of work. Inspection is frequently a very difficult visual task. Because of the heavy

137

Figure 3. Loose thread on cloth as seen under 650 ft.-c. of general (diffuse) illumination.

perceptual load present some inspection jobs rank among the most difficult of all industrial jobs. It is essential that the inspector be provided with the best quality of light. During the last eight years the Eastman Kodak Human Factors Group has worked with more than 50 special-purpose lighting systems for different inspection situations. In some cases inspection problems that appear to be very similar to one another can require completely different approaches for their solution. Very small differences in the physical characteristics of the product being inspected can have a large effect on the choice of an optimal lighting situation. The experience gained through the design of these 50 inspection stations clearly indicates that general illumination is seldom, if ever, the best choice for inspection lighting. Figures 3 and 4 show how the results obtained with special-purpose lighting can be completely different from the results obtained with general illumination. The diffuse nature of the general illumination tends to wash out shadows while the surface-grazing light relies upon strong shadows to emphasize objects that project above the surface. Task visibility is distinctly better with the grazing light even though a much lower level of illumination is being used.

A single special-purpose light source is often inadequate. Some inspection jobs require as many as five different kinds of lighting, each being used to optimize conditions for a different class of defects. The use of special lighting systems which make each class of defects most visible has one major drawback. It usually means that a product must be examined for each class of defects sequentially, rather than for all defects simultaneously, and this involves time and

138

Figure 4. Loose thread on cloth as seen by 75 ft.-c. of surface grazing lighting.

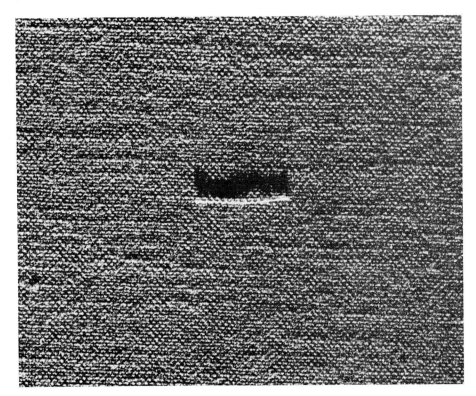

expense. Whether the resultant increase in quality is worth the expense must be determined on an individual basis. In some inspection operations feedback from the inspectors is used as a basis for making changes in the production process. In this situation accurate inspection results are extremely important to ensure that the manufacturing process is kept at the 'aim point' and that waste due to poor quality is therefore kept at a minimum. This is especially vital in a continuous-process industry. These conditions usually justify a considerable expenditure to optimize the inspection operation.

The Eastman Kodak Human Factors Group has attempted to develop a 'lighting library' which contains examples of all of the basically different types of special-purpose lighting. This has been accomplished by reviewing the literature of inspection lighting (and other areas in which special-purpose lighting is used) and by reviewing the product catalogues of the major lamp manufacturers. Light sources that appear to have unique characteristics are obtained and evaluated. In addition, the Human Factors Laboratory has combined elements of existing lighting systems.

At the present time this lighting library contains examples of more than 20 types of lighting systems. The following list describes 17 of these. It includes some of the special-purpose lights mentioned earlier in this paper. This list illustrates the wide variety of visual effects that can be produced by specialized illumination. Although the lighting techniques described here have been called 'supplementary lighting' in other publications (General Electric 1964, Kaufman 1966) this term is misleading. Where they are typically used they are the essential forms of lighting, and general room illumination is subordinate to them. The term 'special-purpose lighting' is preferable. Secondly, the luminaire should not be emphasized so strongly as the differentiating quality of special-purpose lighting. Every reflection of a beam of light creates a new light source with different physical properties than the previous source so that the entire room is reflecting surfaces, and the human observer within it becomes an important part of the lighting system to be reckoned with. Finally, the techniques are not concerned solely with physical properties of light. The important effects as sensed by humans are sometimes psychological and are not photographically reproducible. These would include the 'streaming' or focusing of type-13 lighting; peculiar after-images as a result of exposure to some brightness patterns of type-7 lighting (particularly narrow, high-contrast line patterns); the well-known hypnotic, vertigo, colour-induction, and brightness-enhancement effects of the low-frequency stroboscopic illumination of type-12 lighting; and the illusory surface depth effects of type-11 lighting.

3.1. *Colour*

It has already been noted that the choice of lamp is critical for tasks where colour discrimination is important. The characteristic colour of a light source can also be used in less obvious ways. Kaufman (1966) mentions that the bluish light provided by a 'daylight' type of fluorescent lamp is useful for finding imperfections where chrome has been plated over nickel.

3.2. *Transillumination*

This is the directing of light from a large diffuse source through a transparent or translucent product. The inspector looks directly at the transilluminator, the product being between the eye and light source, and searches for defects causing changes in opacity. The defects then appear as light or dark streaks or spots. The placement of the source in the light fixture is important. It must be a sufficient distance away from the diffusing face of the illuminator so as not to cause a 'hot spot'. The source must also be long enough to include the visual angle subtended by the eye and two outer edges of the product. In other words, it should be wider than the product, or a noticeable fall-off in brightness will occur at the edges which may be confused with a defect in that area. Fluorescent lamps, tubular incandescent lamps, or cold cathode lamps are suitable for this application. It must be remembered that an aged fluorescent lamp is not luminous over its entire length. A typical 48-in. fluorescent is luminous for only 40 in. of its length. Frosted glass is a poor diffuser, whereas opalized glass is a good diffuser for such fixtures but passes a relatively small portion of light. The distance a product should be mounted from the diffusing face of the viewer is a function of the diffusibility of the material being reflected.

Where intensity is not a problem, but depth of the fixture is, one solution has been to use a single side-recessed fluorescent or lumiline incandescent reflected off a curved white surface onto a diffuser. When the viewed objects are uniform in hue, a highly successful technique is to equip the transilluminator with or to view it through a 'negative' filter (one of the opposite hue).

3.3. *Crossed polarization*

A different form of transillumination is the crossed polarizer which uses two sheets of linear polarizer at 90° angles to one another, one on each side of the transparent product being inspected. Certain types of defects cause changes in the polarization of light passing through the product and these will be detected as changes in pattern or colour. This system has also been commonly used for the detection of internal stresses and strains. It has also been used with dichroic materials to monitor variations in thickness which produce varying degrees of light rotation.

3.4. *Polarized light*

Polarizing filters can be used to control glare and to remove unwanted reflections from a light source by eliminating the horizontal component. Another application is to polarize the beam of a spotlight horizontally and direct it at a near-zero angle onto a flat specular product. The specular surface is a natural horizontal polarizer and will reflect the polarized light at a low angle but any non-specular defect will depolarize the light. When viewed from above this defect will appear as a bright spot in a dark surround.

Another application of horizontally polarized light is in the inspection of transparent-glass products by a spotlight for top-surface defects. When the plates are inspected on a conveyor belt, elimination of the vertical component prevents it from being depolarized by the belt beneath and then being trans-mitted back through the plate. This maintains a darker background against which to see various defects.

3.5. *Shadow-graphing*

This consists of projecting a small source of light through a transparent material for the detection of defects which cause changes in refraction, and thereby produce light and dark spots or lines in the projected image of the material.

3.6. *Spotlighting*

Spotlighting is useful in observing very small defects on a surface which result in small projections or indentations. In some products the small defects act like tiny mirrors and project images of the light source at the eye, like small points of light. The placement of the light is important since the defects cannot be seen in the large reflected image of the light source in a specular or polished surface. Where the defect is seen depends on its orientation and the placement of the eye. Scratches, for instance, are best seen when the light is not aligned in the direction of the scratch, but rather off to the side. Where all scratch-type defects tend to occur in one direction, spotlights can be placed to highlight them quite easily. The design of inspection situations using spotlights should include attempts to prevent the direct light from the fixture from becoming a glare source for the inspector. This can be accomplished by placing a mask or louver-like diaphragms in front of the light or by reflecting the source first into a mirror.

3.7. *Brightness patterns*

Some defects on highly polished or specular surfaces can best be seen by observing the reflection of a high-contrast symmetrical image on the surface. Defects causing broad undulations in the surface resulting in hills or valleys will cause a distortion of the pattern and betray their presence. The critical points in the design of such an inspection fixture are the contrast of the pattern, the size of the reflected patterns with respect to the size of the defect, and the orientation of the pattern with respect to the orientation of the defect. Such a pattern can consist of stripes or a grid pasted on the face of an illuminator. The pattern can be reflected off the surface or shown through the product. A high-contrast reflection can be achieved off a transparent surface if a flat-black surface is provided beneath the surface to be inspected.

3.8. *Diffuse reflection*

A lack of any contrast in the brightness pattern is sometimes necessary to see some defects. The reflections of a white diffuse surface on a flat specular product will reveal changes in thickness of various transparent layers. These will appear as an irridescent rainbow of colours, much like the appearance of oil film on water. This same technique is also used to examine chrome-plated surfaces for discolouration, imperfect plating, and other surface defects.

3.9. *Edge lighting*

The internal reflection of light beams in a transparent product can help to reveal internal imperfections or surface scratches by lighting an edge with a fairly high-intensity light source, such as a fluorescent or tubular quartz lamp. This is a common method for inspecting glass plates and similar products.

3.10. *Dark-field illumination*

Scratches on a transparent product or on a specular surface can be detected by using a light system reflected off of or projected through the product and focused to a point just beside the eye. The eye observes a dark field except for scratches which diffract light to the side and are seen as bright lines or specks.

3.11. *Convergent light*

If, in the above system, the focus is at the eye itself, various defects in products having a semispecular surface can be observed as lighter or darker areas due to changes in the sheen of the surface. When inspecting a broad area several feet in width, this necessitates using a spherical mirror larger than the area to be inspected.

3.12. *Stroboscopic lighting*

As was previously mentioned, this is a useful technique for finding repetitive defects where the period of possible recurrence is known.

3.13. *Moving light images*

A major problem in observing a fairly formless moving product is the inability to follow the surface and focus on it. This results in 'streaming', or a blurring of the image similar in appearance to the surface of a flowing stream. This can be alleviated by providing projected images which are observed on the surface to be inspected and move in synchrony with it, thus providing fixation points for the eye. This method has been shown to be especially effective in enabling an inspector to see surface texture in a moving product. How this projection is accomplished will depend on the type of lighting chosen, which, of course, depends on the defects that are present in the product being inspected. If it involves the use of a reflected brightness pattern, the pattern might roll past and under the light source. If it involves spotlighting, the light sources themselves have to move or be reflected off rotating mirrors.

3.14. *Surface grazing or shadowing*

Some defects which result in small raises in the surface, in the order of several hundred microns in diameter, can be highlighted by a collimated source of light with an oval beam directed at the surface at a very low angle. The effect is to create high-contrast shadows and highlights off virtually any such surface irregularity.

3.15. *Black light*

Many materials fluoresce in the presence of near ultraviolet light. This includes some lubricating and cutting oils and other impurities. If certain classes of defects glow under ultraviolet light then this can be an effective inspection technique. It is also possible to introduce fluorescing dyes into the product at critical points in production processes. One example would be dyeing a solvent so that the completeness of a seal could be checked at final inspection under ultraviolet light. If it proves necessary to use intense sources of ultraviolet radiation then special precautions must be taken to protect against conjunctival burns.

3.16. *Moiré patterns*

Patterns of parallel lines can be used to magnify certain surface characteristics so they can be directly observed without resorting to expensive electro-optical devices.

Surface flatness of diffuse light-coloured surfaces can be observed and measured by projecting a bright collimated beam through parallel lines a short distance away from the surface. The inspector observes the interference pattern produced by the original lines and their shadows on the reflecting surface. Irregularities in the pattern will be produced by dents, nicks, or protrusions.

Minute unsteadiness or jitter can be observed and measured by attaching a set of parallel lines to the moving surface and observing them through another similar set of stationary lines set at a small angle (3° to 5°) to the first. A magnification of the jitter of 10–40 × can easily be achieved in the resulting *moiré*. Vertical movement in the object results in magnified horizontal movement in the *moiré*. A second or third pair of line sets is necessary to observe movement in other directions. Using Edmund Scientific Co. Pattern No. 8, all movement directions are independent of one another. The resulting *moiré* is a converging set of lines which can be used to point at a ruler imprinted above the stationary set of parallel lines.

3.17. 'Combination' lights

Light fixtures can be devised to provide, simultaneously, several qualities of illumination where the situation demands a single-pass 100% inspection for several defect classes, as is true for most acceptance inspection tasks. The combination of qualities can be tailored to the importance and relative visibility of the defect classes expected to occur. Since most of the qualities interfere with one another, this necessitates acceptance of the philosophy that this type of light fixture is a compromise favouring speed and results in less than optimal illumination for all defect classes. Since combination lights represent a mix of some of the 16 previously described types of light, this is not a unique type of light itself. It does serve to suggest the complexity and elegance of the lighting system that may be needed for those inspection situations where it is essential that viewing conditions be optimal.

This list of different lighting systems is not all inclusive. New types are continually being developed and added to the 'lighting library' maintained by the Eastman Kodak Human Factors Group. There are no firm guidelines that can be followed in selecting the best type of lighting for a particular situation. One workable approach is to select two promising types from the 'lighting library' and make a comparison. The better type is then compared with another alternative drawn from the library. This continues until all of the reasonable alternatives have been examined. If several of the different types seem to offer

Figure 5. Three scratches in acrylic plastic sheeting viewed from directly above and lit by 650 ft.-c. of general illumination.

Figure 6. Same scratches and illumination, but viewed from a low angle.

Figure 7. Same scratches but with low-angle view in 75 ft.-c. spotlighting.

important and independent advantages then it may be desirable to develop a combination light.

Figures 5, 6 and 7 show how improvements in task visibility can be achieved by using special-purpose lighting and by having the proper geometric relationship between light, task, and observer. When the light is diffuse and when the task is viewed from directly above (see Figure 5) even a high level of illumination does not clearly reveal the scratches. By moving the observer so that the task is viewed from a low angle (see Figure 6) the visibility of the scratches is improved. When the general illumination is replaced by spotlighting a substantial additional improvement is achieved. The detection of fine scratches is a typical difficult visual task in terms of the dependence of task visibility upon the type of illumination being used. The degree of improvement illustrated by this series of figures frequently results when an inappropriate type of illumination is replaced with a type which has optimal characteristics for the specific visual task being performed.

4. Conclusions

Experience with designing lighting systems for inspection work has provided persuasive evidence that the quantity of light directed upon a difficult visual task is less important than the type of light selected. Visual tasks differ significantly from one another in their physical characteristics. The specific characteristics of a task must be taken into account if optimal lighting is to be provided on that task. The wide variance in the quality and characteristics of different forms of light can be appreciated by examining the descriptions of the 17 different types of light used in inspection systems. This wide choice provides the designer with the flexibility that is needed to meet the varying demands of different inspection tasks.

General illumination is not merely a poor choice for difficult visual tasks; it can actually present a hindrance in some situations. Many of these specialized techniques rely on the directional quality of the light. Any general illumination that is present in addition will tend to dilute this directionality and thus reduce the visibility of the task. For this reason it is often desirable to use only low levels of general illumination in areas where difficult visual work is to be done.

References

AMERICAN NATIONAL STANDARDS INSTITUTE, 1965, *American Standard Practice for Industrial Lighting.* (A11.1–1965, March 31, 1965. Reaffirmed as A11.1–1965, 1970.)

BITTERMAN, M. E., 1948, Lighting and visual efficiency: The present status of research. *Illuminating Engineering,* **43**, 906–931.

BLACKWELL, H. R., 1959, Specification of interior illumination levels. *Illuminating Engineering,* **54**, 317–353.

BLACKWELL, H. R., 1969, A more complete quantitative method for specification of interior illumination levels on the basis of performance data. *Illuminating Engineering,* **64**, 289–295.

BLACKWELL, H. R., 1970, Development of procedures and instruments for visual task evaluation. *Illuminating Engineering,* **65**, 267–291.

BLACKWELL, H. R., and SMITH, S., 1970, Additional visual performance data for use in illumination specification systems. *Illuminating Engineering,* **65**, 389–410.

CIE, 1972, *A United Framework of Methods for Evaluation of Visual Performance Aspects of Lighting.* (CIE Publication No. 19.) (Paris: International Commission on Illumination.)

FAULKNER, T. W., and MURPHY, T. J., 1971, Illumination: A human factors viewpoint. *Paper presented at 15th Annual Meeting of Human Factors Society.*

FISCHER, D., 1969, Zum Entwurf 1969 von DIN 5035: Innenraumbeleuchtung mit kinstlichem Licht. *Lichttechnik,* **21**, 111–122A.

FRIER, J. P., 1967, Difficult industrial tasks and how to light them. *Illuminating Engineering,* **62**, 283–288.

GENERAL ELECTRIC CO., 1964, *Supplementary Lighting* (Pamphlet TP–121–R). (Cleveland, Ohio: Large Lamp Department, Nela Park.)

GUTH, S. K., 1970, Lighting for visual performance and visual comfort. *Journal of American Optometric Association*, **41**, 63–71.

HOPKINSON, R., and COLLINS, J., 1970, *The Ergonomics of Lighting*. (London: McDONALD.)

HOPKINSON, R., and LONGMORE, J., 1959, Attention and distraction in the lighting of workplaces. *Ergonomics*, **2**, 321–334.

ILLUMINATING ENGINEERING SOCIETY, 1958, Report No. 1 of Illuminating Engineering Society Committee on recommendations for quality and quantity of illumination. *Illuminating Engineering*, **53**, 422–432.

ILLUMINATING ENGINEERING SOCIETY (British), 1961, *The Illuminating Engineering Code: Recommendations for Good Interior Lighting*. (London: THE SOCIETY.)

KAUFMAN, J., 1966, *Illuminating Engineering Society Lighting Handbook* (4th ed.). (New York: ILLUMINATING ENGINEERING SOCIETY (American).)

LION J., 1964, The performance of manipulative and inspection tasks under tungsten and fluorescent lighting. *Ergonomics*, **7**, 51.

LION, J., RICHARDSON, E., and BROWN, R. C., 1968, A study of the performance of industrial inspectors under two kinds of lighting. *Ergonomics*, **11**, 23–24.

LOWSON, J., 1965, *Artificial Lighting in Factory and Office. CIS Information Sheet II*. (Geneva: INTERNATIONAL LABOUR OFFICE.)

MAKAS, A., and BIRD, G., 1965, Dichroic and reflective polarizers in lighting applications. *Illuminating Engineering*, **60**, 203–216.

MARSDEN, A. M., 1964, Visibility and illumination levels. *Light and Lighting*, 234–239.

MARSDEN, A. M., 1972, Visual performance—CIE style. *Light and Lighting*, 132–135.

REY, P., and REY, J. P., 1963, Les effets comparés de deux eclairages fluorescents sur une tache visuelle et des tests de fatigue. *Ergonomics*, **6**, 393–401.

SIMONSON, E., and BROZEK, J., 1952, Work, vision, and illumination. *Illuminating Engineering*, **47**, 335–349.

SPENCER, D. E., *et al.*, 1959, Discussion and rebuttal of specifications of interior illumination levels. *Illuminating Engineering*, **56**, 775–777.

STANDARDS ASSOCIATION OF AUSTRALIA, 1965, *Artificial Lighting of Buildings*. (Australia Standards, CA 30–1965. (Sydney, Australia: STANDARDS ASSOCIATION OF AUSTRALIA.)

TAYLOR, A. H., 1942, The nature and causes of small colour differences on industry: Lighting for their detection. *Journal of the Optical Society of America*, **32**, 651–658.

TAYLOR, N., 1962, New light on visual threshold contrast. *Illuminating Engineering*, **57**, 177–186.

TIFFIN, J., and KUHN, H., 1942, Colour discrimination in industry. *Archives of Ophthalmology*, **28**, 851–859.

TINKER, M., 1949, Trends in illumination standards. *Transactions of the American Academy of Ophthalmology and Otolaryngology*, 382–394.

TINKER, M., 1959, Brightness contrast, illumination intensity and visual efficiency. *American Journal and Archives of the Optometric Academy*, **36**, 221–236.

TINKER, M., 1963, *Legibility of Print*. (Ames, Iowa: IOWA STATE UNIVERSITY PRESS.)

WESTON, H., 1961, Rationally recommended illumination levels. *Transactions of the Illuminating Engineering Society* (London), **26**, 1–10.

Inspector performance on microminiature tasks

G. L. Smith, Jr.

1. Introduction

The manufacture of miniature electronic devices presents an interesting challenge in work design. In general, the manufacturing problem centres about the physical size of the units being produced. These items are so minute, or they possess characteristics so minute, that it is impractical to view them with the unaided eye. The term microminiature has been adopted to describe this class of minute objects, indicative of the fact that the microscope has received general acceptance as the solution to the visual problem posed therein.

Guidelines for the design of microminiature work are few in number. For example, level of magnification for a given task is rarely specified. In those cases in which level of magnification is specified, there appears to be no factual or rational basis by which the levels were chosen. In addition, there is a dearth of published experimental information available. Notable exceptions to this are studies by Simon (1964) and Simon and Naygar (1963) in which subjects used tweezers to manipulate tiny components viewed through a microscope. Simon's findings that an apparent optimum level of magnification exists for certain aspects of the task suggested that more detailed study could be rewarding.

2. The nature of the study

In selecting the type of microminiature operation to be used in such a study, a conscious effort was made to secure a task which isolated the basic problem: visual performance. It should be emphasized that the sole function of the microscope is the extension of the visual capabilities of the human operator. The task selected to satisfy this objective was a simple inspection task.

The research was conducted in three experiments. In Experiment I, inspectors were studied as they performed a simple detection task in which no acceptance-rejection decision was required. Performance was studied for subjects inspecting two patterns of different complexity at five different levels of magnification. The objectives were to establish the significance of magnification as a variable and to investigate the possibility that a potential optimum level of magnification exists. Experiment II also involved a simple detection task. Two patterns differing in complexity and different from those in Experiment I were used. Performance was studied at two levels of illumination and over four levels of magnification for both patterns. The objectives were to compare the effect of magnification with the results observed in Experiment I, and to observe the effect of level of illumination on inspector performance. Experiment III used a subset of conditions from Experiment II and applied the theory of signal detection as a model of inspector performance.

L   149

2.1. *The variables*

The independent variables which were manipulated in these experiments are, in many cases, unique to the microminiature task. Magnification is the variable which is of prime interest in microscope applications. In actual practice, the absolute level of magnification is irrelevant. The defect size and magnification level combine to determine the visual angle subtended by the image of the defect. The visual angle is the critical parameter. In order to simplify the discussion of methodology, however, reference is made to the levels of magnification used in each experiment. In generalizing the results, visual angle is included. Graphs are plotted to show both the absolute level of magnification and the visual angle.

The second variable of interest is pattern complexity. In discussing this variable, it is necessary to describe the test objects which were inspected by the subjects. For Experiment I, the test object consisted of a square matrix of letters O and C, and C being defined as a 'defective' O. An example of this pattern appears in Figure 1a. The patterns were typewritten and all defects

Figure 1. Test subjects in the experiments.

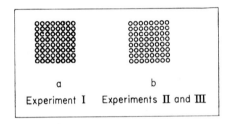

a   b

Experiment I   Experiments II and III

were oriented to the right. For Experiment II, the test object was of the same general form as for Experiment I. However, the master pattern was prepared by a draftsman, permitting accurate control of the size of the gap in the C and variation of its orientation. The pattern for Experiments II and III is illustrated in Figure 1b.

The term pattern complexity is qualitative in this particular application and has been adopted because it seems to best describe the visual effect produced by viewing 6×6 and 8×8 patterns in Experiment I and 7×7 and 8×8 patterns in Experiments II and III.

The third variable manipulated was level of illumination. In Experiment I the level of illumination was above threshold for detection of the defect but unanimously judged 'insufficient' by the subjects. In Experiments II and III the low level of illumination was comparable to that in Experiment I, in that all subjects judged it 'insufficient'. The high level was unanimously judged comfortable and was below the level at which subjects began to report glare. A quantitative measure of the levels was not attempted because of the problems associated with scaling the differences in apparent brightness and proportion of the field illuminated when magnification was changed. When necessary, the amount of illumination was varied to compensate for the difference in the amount of light transmitted by the lens systems at different levels of magnification. In this manner, it was possible to obtain subjective reports of equal brightness for a given pattern at different levels of magnification. These levels were determined for the subjects prior to the commencement of the experiments.

The dependent variable which was utilized in these studies combined speed and accuracy. Accuracy, as an independent measure of inspector performance has been discussed in detail by Wallack (1967). In most industrial situations, however, accuracy is not the sole criterion in the measurement of productivity. Speed is also a significant factor. Even in the absence of incentive systems to stimulate productivity, employees are made aware of the importance of time in their activity. In an investigation of the performance of mail sorters, Bertelson *et al.* (1965) compared self-paced conditions with forced-pace at the mean of the self-paced operation. In transition from self-paced to forced-pace operation, the sorters suffered a 20% reduction in the number of letters sorted in the same period of time. Concomitantly, an increase in sorting errors from 2% during self-paced conditions to 10% in the forced-pace condition was observed.

Recognizing this reciprocal relationship between speed and accuracy, it was decided to use a measure of inspector performance (P) which is given by:

$$P = \frac{T}{N-e}$$

where T is the total inspection time, N is the number of patterns inspected, and e is the number of errors committed or incorrect inspections. Thus, the performance index is an average over a given trial, expressed in units of minutes per correct inspection.

In an effort to provide some homogeneity in the performances, all subjects were instructed that speed and accuracy were both included in the score they would receive. They were asked to operate on the basis that speed and accuracy were *equally* important.

Experiment III introduced the signal detection model and the independent variable d' (*index of discriminability*). The parameter d' as a measure of signal detectability has intuitive appeal in the context of industrial inspection. The more nearly the defective product resembles the acceptable product, the weaker the signal strength, and the smaller the theoretical value of d'.

3. Experiment I

This experiment was performed by 10 female employees of the Western Electric Co. plant in Allentown, Pennsylvania. All subjects had received pre-employment vision checks and were subsequently re-examined as a requirement of their job classifications as inspectors and workers on jobs requiring the use of microscopes. The subjects were all currently working at jobs which required the use of a microscope most of the working day. They ranged in age from 20 to 40 years. For the purpose of administering experimental trials, the 10 subjects were divided into 5 groups of 2 inspectors each.

In order to simplify the task, the subjects were only required to detect the opening in the letter C to distinguish it from the O. Verbally, the response simply involved counting the number of C's aloud.

The defects (C's) were distributed randomly throughout the patterns, the only restriction being that no more than one C could appear in any row or column. A total of 30 patterns were inspected in a single experimental trial.

The patterns were reduced photographically onto 35 mm positive slides. The size of the actual test pattern was 0·06 × 0·06 inches for the 6 × 6 pattern

151

and 0.073×0.073 inches for the 8×8 pattern. In both cases, the letters were 0·0085 inches high and the gap in the C was 0·0012 inches. Based on a standardized viewing distance of 10 inches, the unmagnified gap in the C subtended a visual angle of less than 0·5 minutes at the eye.

The microscope utilized in Experiment I was an *American Optical Company* binocular stereoscopic microscope, equipped with a magni-changer. By utilizing $10 \times$ and $15 \times$ eyepieces, it was possible to obtain a range of magnification of from $7 \times$ to $40 \times$. The maximum magnification used in the study was limited to $40 \times$ in order that the entire pattern would remain within the field of the microscope.

Slides were presented to the field of the microscope using a modified *Kodak Supermatic* slide-changer mechanism. The changer was actuated by a micro-switch which was held by the subject.

Each experimental session was approximately fifteen minutes in length. The subjects began each session by focusing the microscope on a test pattern similar to the patterns to be inspected that day. A practice period inspecting ten slides preceded the actual experimental trial of thirty slides.

Between the practice and the experimental trial, the subjects received instructions which were designed to establish common objectives among the subjects.

Experiment I was conducted over a four-week period. Each subject performed one experimental trial per session. Sessions were limited to one per day, except for the last week.

Table 1. Experimental design for Experiment I. Block 1—8×8 pattern; Block 2—6×6 pattern (see text); Block 3—6×6 and 8×8 patterns.

Ss Mag	1 and 2	3 and 4	5 and 6	7 and 8	9 and 10
$7 \times$	Mon	Wed	Tues	Thur	Fri
$10 \times$	Wed	Thur	Mon	Fri	Tues
$20 \times$	Tues	Fri	Thur	Mon	Wed
$30 \times$	Thur	Tues	Fri	Wed	Mon
$40 \times$	Fri	Mon	Wed	Tues	Thur

(two trials each session).

In the design of the experiment, which is shown in Table 1, the pattern complexity remained constant for an entire week while magnification was randomized among groups in a factorial design. The replication schedule, also in Table 1, shows that the 8×8 pattern was inspected during weeks 1 and 4, and the 6×6 pattern was inspected during weeks 2 and 4.

During week 3, subjects inspected a third pattern of intermediate complexity. The data are not presented because the trials could not be replicated.

Figure 2. Inspectors' performance in Experiment I.

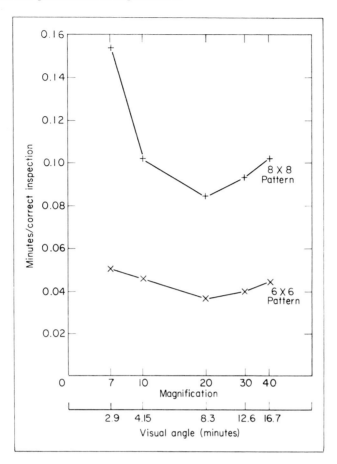

3.1. *Analysis of results*
The performance of inspectors in Experiment I is summarized graphically in Figure 2. The results of an analysis of variance performed on the data are summarized in Table 2.

Table 2. Analysis of variance for Experiment I.

Source	df	MS	F	Approximate p level
Magnification (A)	4	9791	8·6	0·005
Complexity (B)	1	210282	185·1	0·001
Replications (C)	1	23438	20·6	0·001
Groups (D)	4	10701	1·7	0·250
A × B	4	4541	3·9	0·005
B × C	4	3373	2·9	0·025
Subjects (without groups)	1	6248	5·5	0·001
Error	183	1136		
Total	199			

Reference to Figure 2 reveals that inspector performance is clearly affected by the complexity of the pattern. The effect is as would be anticipated with performance on the 8×8 pattern substantially poorer than on the 6×6 pattern. It is also evident that, for a given pattern, performance varies with the level of magnification used in viewing it. The shape of the curve is concave upwards. Deterioration of performance at both extremes of magnification indicates the presence of an optimum point resulting in minimum time per correct inspection. In this case the optimum appears to be in the region of $20 \times$ magnification for both patterns. It is also clear that the effect of magnification is more pronounced for the 8×8 pattern than for the 6×6 pattern.

A review of the results of the analysis of variance provides substantial verification for the qualitative observations. The F ratios computed in Table 2 indicate that the following main effects are significant sources of variation: replications, magnification, task complexity, and groups. In addition, the interaction between magnification and pattern complexity, and between subjects and groups, is also significant. In this case, significance is established at beyond the 99·9% confidence level.

3.2. *Discussion of results*

The significance of the effect due to replications is an affirmation of the presence of learning on the part of the subjects. As was pointed out earlier, recognition of this trend led to the decision to replicate the experiment. The balanced design permits comparison of sample means, compensating for the trend effect.

Magnification is shown to have a significant effect on operator performance. This fact was readily observable from the graphical presentation and is verified by the analysis of variance.

The statistical significance of the effect of complexity on inspector performance was as anticipated. Of considerable interest, however, is the significant interaction between task complexity and magnification, apparent in Figure 2. The critical factor to observe is the basic nature of the interaction. Judging from the two curves, the decrement in performance at the extremes ($7 \times$ and $40 \times$) becomes greater as pattern complexity increases. A possible explanation is that subjects may have approached their maximum performance level for the conditions of Experiment I in viewing the 6×6 pattern. If this were the case, then the classical 'ceiling effect' would be observed. At performance levels approaching maximum, changes in magnification would not have as marked an effect as they would at submaximum performance levels. The behaviour of the subjects during the experimental trials suggested that they had approached maximum productivity.

The significance of the variability due to groups was not anticipated in this study since subjects were randomly assigned into groups. Two other factors have bearing on this particular observation: the *subject × group* interaction and the fact that groups were confounded with time of day.

The confounding was due to the procedure used in the experiment. Due to work planning requirements, management requested that subjects be assigned to participate in the experiment at the same time each day. The subjects volunteered for pre-determined times and were then assigned to groups sequentially. As a result, the differences in productivity across hours of the day were minimized without groups and maximized between groups. The fact that there is no statistical difference between subjects, within groups, confirms this contention.

The *subjects × group* interaction, while significant, has no real meaning in this study. Due to the random assignment of subjects to the experiment, the designation of Subject 1 and Subject 2 within a group is arbitrary. Even though the term is meaningless, there is assignable cause for the observed statistical significance. Reference to the raw data for individual subjects showed that one subject performed very poorly in comparison to other subjects at low levels of magnification. There is no apparent reason for substandard performance by this particular subject, as her vision was normal and her foreman indicated that she was a productive and cooperative employee. The subject did, during the course of the study, express to the experimenter her displeasure at having to inspect 'those little patterns'. There is a possibility that some negative transfer from the normal work activity may have taken place in this instance. Although these observations do not completely explain the statistical significance, they do help to account for it.

In closing the discussion of Experiment I, it should be pointed out that, in giving due consideration to the significance of the main effects, the magnitude of the F ratios is important. Although the level of significance may be somewhat diminished by the presence of statistically significant interactions, the effect of the main effects in the subjects' performance is undeniable.

4. Experiment II

Experiment II was performed by seven female secretaries from the College of Engineering at Oklahoma State University. They ranged in age from 19 to 50 years. All subjects either had normal vision or vision correctable to normal. None had astigmatism.

The decision to use untrained subjects was, in part, made to compare their performance with that of experienced industrial subjects. Since the subjects were untrained, an initial orientation period was utilized to familiarize each subject with the task and to train them in the technique of focusing the binocular microscope. In addition, two days of practice trials were conducted in the week immediately preceding the actual data collection.

In this experiment, as in Experiment I, the task was limited to a simple detection problem for the subjects. No acceptance-rejection decision was required.

Since Landolt rings were utilized as the defects (C's) in the pattern, precise determination of the visual angle subtended by the defect was possible. In construction of the individual patterns, it was also possible to vary the orientation of the gap in the C. For this experiment, the gaps were randomly oriented up, down, left, and right. A total of 112 patterns were inspected by the subjects on each experimental trial.

The number of C's on the individual patterns ranged from 0 to 3, the frequency distribution being uniform. The patterns were arranged in a manner which maintained a constant uniform distribution of the number of C's over 25%, 50%, 75% and 100% of the series of patterns.

In preparing the actual test objects, the patterns were reduced photographically on 16 mm film. The actual size of the resulting pattern was 0.187×0.187 inches for the 8×8 pattern and 0.156×0.156 inches for the 7×7 pattern. The letters were 0.107 inches high and the gap size was 0.0034 inches for both patterns. The visual angle subtended by the unmagnified gap was 1.2 minutes and the visual angles subtended by the patterns were 54.0 minutes for the 8×8 pattern and 64.0 minutes for the 7×7 pattern.

The microscope used in Experiment II was a *Bausch and Lomb Stereo-zoom* binocular microscope. Fitting the microscope with $10 \times$ eyepieces and using an auxiliary $0.5 \times$ objective lens, a continuous range of magnifications from $5 \times$ to $26 \times$ was obtained. As in Experiment I, the upper limit was chosen so that the pattern image did not exceed the field of the microscope.

The film strip was presented to the field of the microscope using a specially constructed adaptation of a film editor. Rotation of a small crank by the subject's right hand advanced the film one frame per revolution.

As the subjects counted the number of C's aloud, the total was recorded by the experimenter. Simultaneous with the recording of the subject's reports, continuous readings from a stopwatch were recorded at 25%, 50%, 75% and 100% completion of the trial.

Each experimental session was approximately 40 minutes in length. After focusing the microscope, subjects began each session with a practice inspection of 56 patterns. During each session, subjects inspected four trials of 112 patterns each. Between each experimental trial, approximately five minutes of rest was provided. During this time, the experimenter changed the experimental conditions and reread the instructions to the subjects.

Experiment II was conducted over a one-week period. The subjects met for their experimental sessions at the same time each day.

Each day the sequence of presentations of experimental conditions was the same. The subjects viewed the 7×7 then the 8×8 patterns at low illumination, then both were viewed at high illumination. This procedure was followed to avoid requiring the subject to accommodate to low illumination following inspection at high illumination. The complete design of the experiment is illustrated in Table 3.

Table 3. Experimental design for Experiment II.

Day	M				T			
Magnification	$26 \times$				$14 \times$			
Illumination	Low		High		Low		High	
Pattern	8×8	7×7	8×8	7×7	8×8	7×7	8×8	7×7
Day	W				Th			
Magnification	$8 \times$				$5 \times$			
Illumination	Low		High		Low		High	
Pattern	8×8	7×7	8×8	7×7	8×8	7×7	8×8	7×7

4.1. *Analysis of results*

The graphical presentation of results from Experiment II appears in Figure 3. The analysis of variance is summarized in Table 4.

Figure 3. Subjects' performance in Experiment II.

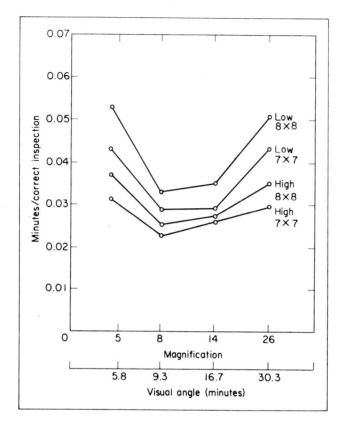

Table 4. Analysis of variance for Experiment II.

Source	df	MS	F	Approximate p level
Magnification (A)	3	133517	17·2	0·001
Complexity (B)	1	75504	32·4	0·005
Illumination (C)	1	290904	124·7	0·001
A × B	3	2843	1·2	0·200
A × C	3	16086	6·1	0·001
B × C	1	6300	2·7	0·100
Subjects (D)	6	106453	45·6	0·001
A × D	18	7765	3·4	0·001
Error	75	2333		
Total	111			

Figure 3 illustrates that combinations of task complexity and illumination produce a scale of performance levels. It is most important to note that the level of magnification which produces best performance is independent of the effects of the other two variables.

157

The analysis of variance (Table 4) provides substantial verification for the observations made from the graphical presentation. The effects which are significant include: magnification, illumination, and pattern complexity—all significant at beyond the 99·9% level; and the interaction between level of magnification and illumination—significant at the 99·5% level.

4.2. *Discussion of results*

The observed results for Experiment II generally achieve the objectives of the study. Magnification is confirmed as a significant variable and the presence of an optimum performance point is also verified.

In observing the effect of illumination, the interaction between illumination and magnification is critical. The nature of this interaction, as apparent in Figure 3, is a reduced sensitivity to the effect of magnification at higher illumination.

As was the case in Experiment I, the presence of a statistically significant interaction effect does not provide grounds for completely rejecting the effect of the main variables on performance.

5. Experiment III

The experimental conditions investigated in Experiment III were a subset of the conditions in Experiment II.

Each experimental session was approximately 40 minutes in length. After focusing the microscope, subjects began each session with a practise inspection of 56 patterns. During each session, subjects inspected four trials of 112 patterns each. Between each experimental trial, approximately five minutes of rest was provided. During this time, the experimenter changed the experimental conditions and reread the instructions to the subjects.

The subjects simply responded 'good' or 'bad' after inspecting the pattern, and the response was recorded by the experimenter. Using the rule that 0 or 1 defects were acceptable and 2 or more unacceptable, the uniform distribution of the number of C's converted directly into a uniform distribution of acceptable and unacceptable patterns, with the probability of a pattern being defective equal to 0·50.

As an additional feature of this experiment, alternative instructions to the subjects were used to test the concept of a moveable *criterion* point (β) for the acceptance-rejection decision.

On the first day of service in the experiment the subjects were instructed that the patterns represented items which were expensive to make, but not critical in terms of customer safety. Under these conditions, it was imperative that good patterns not be rejected. In order to assure this, the subjects were instructed that if they had any doubt as to the actual number of C's in the pattern, they were to accept it. This instruction was designed to avoid false alarms. On the second day, subjects were instructed that the parts were critical and that human life depended on them. Under no circumstances were they to pass any defective patterns. They were instructed that if they had any doubt as to the acceptability of a pattern they were to reject it. This instruction was designed to reduce the probability of a missed defect.

Figure 4. Subjects' performance in Experiment III.

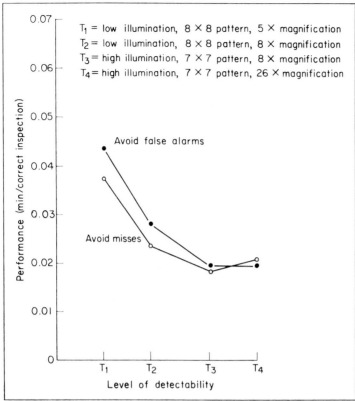

T_1 = low illumination, 8 × 8 pattern, 5 × magnification
T_2 = low illumination, 8 × 8 pattern, 8 × magnification
T_3 = high illumination, 7 × 7 pattern, 8 × magnification
T_4 = high illumination, 7 × 7 pattern, 26 × magnification

Avoid false alarms

Avoid misses

Performance (min/correct inspection)

Level of detectability

5.1. *Analysis of results*

The average performance of the subjects under the four treatment conditions are displayed graphically in Figure 4.

Table 5. Analysis of variance for Experiment III

Source	df	MS	F	p
Subject(s)	6	8·57	117	≪0·001
Instructions (I)	1	0·83	4·15	<0·10
Treatments (T)	3	12·66	1708	≪0·001
S × I	6	0·21	2·82	>0·10
S × T	18	1·42	19·20	<0·001
I × T	3	0·22	2·97	<0·10
Error	18	0·07		
Total	55			

Table 5 is the summary of the analysis of variance. Since the order of the sets of instructions to the subjects was not randomized, the performances were plotted separately and the effect of instructions was included as a separate term in the analysis of variance. Had either learning, or differences in performance due to instructions taken place from one week to the next, any statement about the source of the effect would have been impossible. However, as is indicated by the analysis of variance, there is no significant effect due to instructions, making it possible to disregard differences due to instructions or learning in explaining the remainder of the results.

High levels of significance are observed for the effects due to subject differences, levels of detectability (treatments) and the *subject × treatment* interaction. The interaction had been anticipated, especially since one older subject experienced difficulty at the lowest level of detectability and was extremely slow in performing the inspection task at this level.

5.2. *Discussion of results*

The results of Experiment II would indicate that Treatment 3 would yield best performance. Figure 4 suggests that this is the case although no significant difference between T_3 and T_4 was observed.

The experiment produced estimates of d' for seven subjects under four different visual conditions and two sets of instructions. If the value thus estimated is in fact an index of signal detectability, then it should be a function of the physical parameters of the detection task and be independent of the subject. As has been pointed out, however, the sensory excitation upon which the subject operates is partially a function of his receptor and processing systems and is subject to variability. For example, Sheehan and Drury (1971) found an estimated decrease in d' of 0·2 for each 10 years of age in 5 inspectors ranging from ages 30 to 60. As a result, it was decided to use the mean estimate of d' taken from the performance of all subjects as the best estimate of signal detectability. The inspection of mean d' values reduces to a determination of whether or not d' has any value as an index of detectability. The major potential value lies

Figure 5. Estimates of d' for the instructions 'avoid false alarms' and 'avoid misses'.

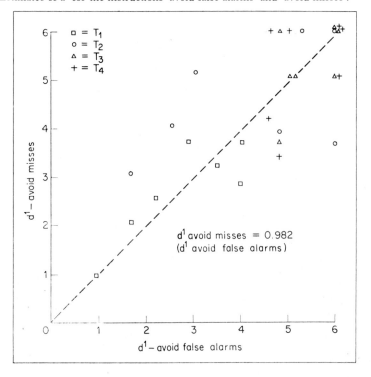

Figure 6. Inspection times *v.* values of *d'* in Experiment III.

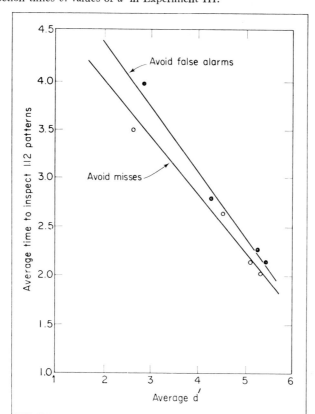

in the fact that *d'* is a characteristic of the properties of the signal and is independent of the *criterion* level selected by the subject. As such, *d'* could serve as a means of comparing alternative designs for inspection of the same components.

The question of consistency of *d'* in the face of shifting criteria can be approached by comparing the estimates of *d'* from each instructional set. Figure 5 is a graph of *d'* estimates (avoid false alarms) vs. *d'* estimates (avoid misses). If the curve is forced through the origin, the slope is 0·9823, a slope of 1·0, of course, being theoretically correct. It is felt that this stable pattern or relationship for *d'* estimates, despite the subject's shifting *criterion* adds significantly to its validity as an index of signal detectability.

Given that *d'* can be estimated, independent of the subject's personal weighting of the importance of misses and false alarms, its relationship to total system performance becomes of interest. For example, the tendency of subjects to trade off between speed and accuracy was mentioned previously. If *d'* does measure detectability, one would anticipate that inspection time might be inversely proportional to *d'*. Figure 6 illustrates the relationship again using separate plots for each set of instructions. Note that the relationship between the estimated value of *d'* and the time to inspect is a linear one and that the two curves are not significantly different. The important fact is that at optimum, the viewing time is one-half the viewing time at the extremely poor point. This makes the improvement one of practical as well as statistical significance.

6. Summary and conclusion

The combined results of these experiments provide some cf the basic information which will be needed if the goal of prior specification of optimal conditions for microminiature work is to be realized. In Experiment I, the effect of magnification on inspector performance was demonstrated and an optimum performance point was noted. Reference to Figure 2 reveals that at this optimum point, the visual angle subtended by the specified defect is 8·3 minutes. However, close inspection of the actual character used in the task (see Figure 1) reveals that the type written 'C' can be identified by a visual cue in addition to the gap in the letter. This cue is the 'knob' at the top of the gap. Consequently, the defect might, in effect, be as large as 0·0018 inches. At $20 \times$, then, the optimal visual angle appears to be in the vicinity of 8·0 to 12·0 minutes of arc.

In Experiment II the effect of magnification was again noted. Under new conditions of complexity and illumination, and given a new defect size, an optimum point was again seen. In this case, the defect size was specified precisely, however, the curves were flatter and the optimum point was not as well defined. Nevertheless, optimum performance appears to have been reached at a visual angle of between 9·3 and 14·0 minutes of arc.

Based on these studies, which utilized trained and untrained subjects, patterns with substantially different defect sizes, different complexities of visual task, and different levels of illumination, *optimum performance can be expected when the visual angle subtended by the defect is between 9.0 and 12.0 minutes of arc.*

Experiment III showed the possibility of transforming accuracy of performance by inspectors into an index of detectability which may in turn be lineararly related to the speed of inspection in a self-paced task. Manipulation of the viewing conditions based on the guidelines given above can be expected to improve the pace of the inspectors. In addition, the confirmation of the existence of a moveable *criterion* point should caution the manager from resorting to 'instructions' in an effort to improve performance. There is a distinct possibility that such action would simply cause a shift in the relative proportion of misses and false alarms. The exception to this case, of course, occurs when there is confusion by the inspector as to what constitutes a defect. In that case, instruction can result in a significant improvement in detectability as estimated by d'.

In considering the speed of performance, the average inspection time in Experiment III was reduced by approximately 50% with maximum detectability. The difference in time per correct inspection in Experiments I and II indicate performance improvements of the same magnitude.

This series of experiments demonstrates the significant effect that engineering design considerations can make in microminiature inspection.

The true improvement in performance and productivity of the inspector which is the goal of our efforts can only be found in the ergonomic design of the man-machine interface.

The author wishes to thank the Western Electric Company, Allentown Works for their continued interest in human factors problems and support of Experiment I.

162

References

BERTELSON, P., BOONS, J.-P., and RENKIN, A., 1965, Free and imposed speed in a task simulating a letter sorting machine. *Ergonomics*, **8**, 3–32.

SHEEHAN, J. J., and DRURY, C. G., 1971, The analysis of industrial inspection. *Applied Ergonomics*, **2**, 74–78.

SIMON, J. R., 1964, Magnification as a variable in subminiature work. *Journal of Applied Psychology*, **48**, 20–24.

SIMON, J. R., and NAYGAR, R. M., 1963, Effects of magnification on a subminiature assembly operation. *Journal of Applied Psychology*, **47**, 190–195.

WALLACK, P. M., 1967, *An Experimental Investigation of Industrial Inspector Accuracy Under Varying Levels of Product Defectiveness*. (Unpublished Doctoral Dissertation, Oklahoma State University, Stillwater, Oklahoma.)

Dynamic visual inspection:
task factors, theory and economics

J. R. Buck

1. Introduction

Dynamic visual inspection (DVI) is that special case of paced visual inspection where the objects being inspected are always in motion. Although this definition includes both inspector-controlled and externally-controlled motion, the latter case is far more typical in contemporary industry and the sole focus here.

A typical industrial configuration consists of a series of production, assembly, and inspection stations linked by a common conveyor. The nature of the product being manufactured often dictates or highly constrains the sequence of the production and assembly stations. Designers of these manufacturing operations typically start at the output end of the operation with information on the desired output quantity. As these designers work toward the input end they determine the individual station production rates with regard to expected losses. These designers must also determine the number and locations of the inspection stations during this planning phase. It is at this point in the planning phase that design problems occur because inspection stations serve the purpose of screening out defectives from downstream operations. Errors made at these inspection stations result in passing on defectives as well as withholding nondefectives; impacting downstream operations. The rate of inspection errors varies with the nature of the upstream operations which determines the presentation rate to inspection, the design of the inspection station, and other factors which receive attention in this volume.

Unless there is some reasonable means for predicting the expected inspection errors, arbitrary design decisions result and the inspection station design must be retrofitted; often with costly redesign or creating ineffective system operations. Accordingly designers need information which will aid them in estimating the inspection accuracy under various operating conditions and they need techniques that serve to guide them toward the more economical system operations. After the design is complete managers must select and train competent persons who will be the inspectors and then man the inspection operations in an economical manner. Consequently inspection management requires this information and these techniques as well. This paper serves to provide some of this needed design and management information and it suggests some analytical techniques for using this information.

The organization of the paper consists of five sections: the general nature of DVI, some experimental evidence, relevant theory and DVI, economics of DVI, and a summary and closing remarks. Task factors and details are given in the second section. In the third section empirical results from several experiments are examined over changes in these factors. These results serve some

M

of the informational needs of designers and managers but the lack of generality limits their applicability. Generality is provided by a proven theory. So in section four attention is focused upon the application of some relevant theories to DVI and the adequacy of these theoretical applications. Whether one uses a theoretical or an empirical basis, analytical techniques are needed for economic analysis and this aspect is addressed in section five. An earlier paper in this volume by Bennett covers the implication of inspection errors in sampling inspection and the effect on quality control. Accordingly the remarks in section five are restricted to one-hundred per cent inspection.

2. The general nature of DVI

Typically in the DVI task a conveyor or a similar device is employed to carry the objects past the inspector. A less typical case is where a sheet of some material flows continuously in front of the inspector. Although many features may be common to these two task variations, the remarks below are focused on the more typical case with discrete objects.

Some of the presentational factors of DVI include: (1) the direction of movement, (2) speed of the conveyor, (3) object interspacing distance and variability, and (4) lateral variability of the object on the belt. Effects from these factors are further modified by fault factors relative to the inspector's viewing position, environmental factors, particularly those which constrain vision, and the visual abilities of the inspector.

Elemental tasks of a single cycle of a DVI situation include: (1) observing the presence of an oncoming object, (2) visual acquisition of the object, (3) visual search within the objects for faults, and (4) decision making and a cycle restart. These elements are strictly sequential. Consequently some factors which affect the first of these elemental tasks cause an impact on the entire cycle sequence. Also if the cycles are temporarily packed tightly together, then effects on one cycle will often cascade over subsequent cycles.

One of the task factors which affects the beginning elements of a DVI cycle is viewing constraints. Figure 1 shows a typical DVI situation with objects of some interspacing distance being carried by the inspection station at some belt velocity. The two viewing constraints shown in this figure are the leftward and rightward shields which are opaque or of some degree of translucency. A fundamental feature of these two constraints is the viewing window between the two shields. When the two shields are opaque, the maximum possible viewing time for an object is the time period of object exposure and that time period depends upon the belt velocity and the size of the viewing window. Accordingly all four of the elemental tasks of the DVI cycle must be performed strictly within this time interval. Now consider changing the opaque shield in the direction of the oncoming object to a translucent shield which only permits the inspector to distinguish between the moving object and the conveyor belt background. This change from opaque to a translucent shield no longer restricts elemental tasks (1) and (2) when the object is left of the viewing window but it precludes elemental tasks (3) and (4). Hence the nature of the visual constraints affects the imposed visual inspection task.

Belt speeds affect viewing dynamics which in turn affect the elemental DVI tasks. Research on visual tracking by Crawford (1960) and others shows that the eyes can move quickly to moving objects in a single saccade when the angular velocity is about 25°–30°/second or less. At higher rotational velocities the eyes always make a first saccadic move toward the object and then added saccades for position and/or velocity correction. Accordingly greater belt velocities entail more time spent in making visual corrections before there is visual acquisition of the object and less time is available for the visual search within the object. The angular eye velocities depend upon the viewing distance and other considerations.

Figure 1. Typical DVI situation.

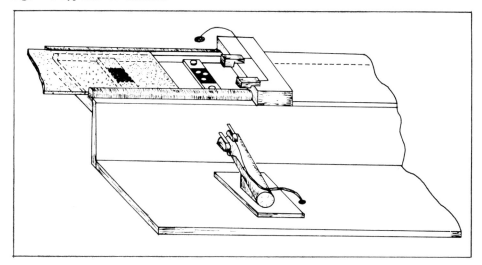

In a typical DVI (Figure 1) situation the inspector sits facing a straight-line conveyor belt with objects moving from left to right at a constant belt velocity. When the inspector is visually tracking an object located to his far left, the movement of the object results in only a small angular rotation of the eyes. As the object approaches the inspector there is an increase in the eye rotation for the same object movement. Since the visual geometry is symmetrical, angular velocities of the eyes in tracking decrease as the object passes farther to the right. Visual tracking requires first an increase in eye movement velocities, then a decrease as the object traverses its left-to-right path. At the same time the visual angle required to see a critical size of fault first decreases then increases over this path. These two features of the visual dynamics are to some degree compensatory. Tests on dynamic visual acuity by Ludvigh and Miller (1958), Burg (1966) and Elkin (1962) show changes in the critical visual angles as a function of the angular velocity of the eyes. However these tests maintained constant viewing distances and angular velocities over the object's path. Results from the dynamic visual acuity tests show that: the minimum visual angle which the observer can resolve increases with greater angular velocities of object (and eye) rotation; this minimum visual angle decreases with greater exposure time in tracking the object; the longer the eyes track a pointer moving with the unexposed object before exposure, the smaller this minimum visual angle; and the correlation within people between the size of this minimum visual angle with and without movement is usually less than 0·20. Figure 2 shows the first three of these effects.

Dynamic visual inspection

When these dynamic visual acuity test results are inferred relative to this typical DVI situation, it is suggested that belt velocities and viewing constraints affect the visual requirements of the elemental DVI tasks in several ways. If the overall size of the object under inspection is relatively large, then visual acquisition is not affected greatly by the angular velocities of the object. The less the visual constraints on viewing oncoming objects, the easier the visual acquisition. Greater exposure time reduces the visual requirements as an aid to visual search within the object. However the visual search task is affected by the object location over the path of travel. Two antagonistic factors change between central and more rightward viewing; central viewing has higher angular velocities which reduce the minimum resolvable angle but the closer object has larger visual angles associated with faults within the object. Hence the belt velocity plays a complex role in DVI both through the angular velocities and the effects on the available visual acquisition and exposure time for visual search. Also there are widely differing individual differences in abilities to cope with these dynamic visual requirements.

Figure 2. Dynamic visual acuity for various anticipatory tracking and exposure times as a function of the angular target velocity (adapted from Elkin).

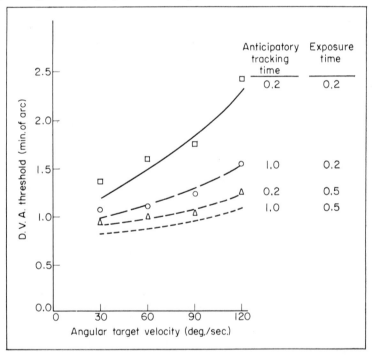

Static visual search is discussed in detail by Bloomfield elsewhere in this current collection of papers. Generally he shows that the probability of detecting a target within some field varies with viewing time and an aggregation of field factors. Part of these field factors includes the size of the target relative to the size of the field being visually searched. Also he denotes the effect of various search strategies. Once visual acquisition of a moving target is achieved, then one would

168

expect the visual search of moving objects to follow similar features to the visual search of static objects. Major exceptions are the expected position and velocity errors and retinal blur which result with dynamic vision. However these exceptions are not expected to change the typical nature of the static visual search effects when applied to DVI but only the magnitudes of these effects.

Wide varieties of DVI situations exist and several versions are shown in subsequent papers by Chapman and Sinclair and Moraal. Extremes in DVI situation are high time-densities of simple objects with relatively little visual search within each through to situations with sparse time-densities with a relatively complex search required for each. Also the presentational discipline varies from the one-at-a-time presentation in strict position and orientation to the many-at-a-time presentation with random orientation. Clearly these variations create considerably different emphasis on the elemental tasks of DVI.

3. Some experimental evidence

Theoretical implications and some of the variations of DVI, as discussed above, are shown in several studies on DVI described in this section. Also these studies show that there are other factors involved which are not adequately described by the theoretical formulations.

A study by Nelson and Barany (1969) involved two principally different types of items under inspection: black Landolt rings of 3/32 and 5/32 inch sizes; and black 1½ inch square targets with three to five 1/8 inch white 'squares' randomly positioned over a 10 by 10 central matrix. In the case of the Landolt rings, conforming targets had a gap at 315 degrees and non-conforming ones at 45, 135 and 225 degrees. Two situations of viewing were employed with the matrix targets: (1) conforming targets contained five squares and targets with only four squares were missing a component and thereby non-conforming; and (2) conforming targets with three squares and targets with four squares containing too many surface defects and thereby non-conforming. These targets were spaced 6, 9 or 12 inches apart and attached to white fibre belts. Dynamic visual inspection was performed at various belt speeds as the belts moved from left to right in front of the inspector. Since the targets were attached to the belts, there was no variation in interspacing or orientation. There was no shield on the inspector's left to obstruct viewing but these targets disappeared under an opaque shield on the right. This experiment examined these types of inspection with fixed factors of viewing time per item and fixed distances between successive targets. Statistical tests on the Landolt ring inspection revealed that both the target interspacing distance and the viewing time per target were significant factors. Average errors by a subject found in this study are reported in Figures 3 and 4 as respective functions of the interspacing distance and viewing time. Although the mean errors were always greater for the 3/32 inch rings over the 5/32 inch rings, the small size difference did not prove to be significant. Similar statistical tests were made on the matrix targets where the missing component case (i.e. 5 *v* 4 squares) was found to create significantly more inspection errors than the excessive surface defects case (i.e., 3 *v* 4 squares). No other effects proved to be statistically significant. Figure 5 shows the results of the matrix target viewing where the trend from the combined results indicates increased errors with greater target interspacing, as does the trend effect with Landolt rings. However increases in the interspacing distance at constant viewing time necessitated faster

Figure 3. Percentage inspection errors for two sizes of Landolt rings as a function of target inter-spacing (adapted from Nelson and Barany).

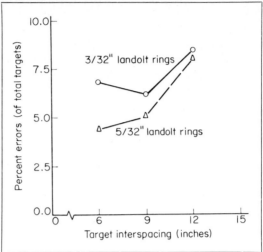

belt speeds and so the interspacing distance factor was confounded with the belt speed factor. Both Foley (1957) and Lippert (1963, 1965) found the opposite effect with interspacing distance. Also no leftward viewing constraints were used in this study so that between four and eight targets were exposed to view at any time; more with the smaller interspacing.

In the study by Smith and Barany (1972) the objects inspected were one-inch diameter metallic discs of a copper colour riding loosely atop a white fibre belt. These discs were viewed by an inspector during the time interval for which the disc was exposed. Two opaque shields blocked disc viewing at either end of the viewing window. Generally the discs were 10 inches apart, as was the open

Figure 4. Percentage inspection errors for two sizes of Landolt rings as a function of the average viewing time (adapted from Nelson and Barany).

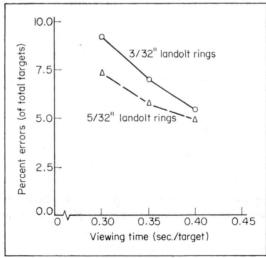

170

viewing window. Since the discs were loose on the belt, there was some variation in the disc interspacing and orientation. Nonconforming discs contained three 1/16 inch diameter holes equally spaced about the disc centre whereas conforming discs had four such holes. Inspectors were instructed to depress a microswitch when they determined that a nonconforming unit was presented. Three factors were examined in this study: (1) discs presented per minute (task pace from 120 to 160 parts per minute or 0·375 to 0·500 seconds viewing time per disc); (2) percentage of nonconforming discs present from 2 to 26%; and (3) instructions on the cost of each type of inspection error.

Figure 5. Percentage inspection errors for matrix targets at three average viewing times and three interspacing distances (adapted from Nelson and Barany).

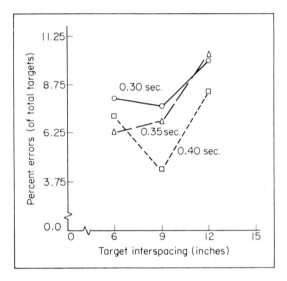

During the laboratory testing it became obvious to the experimenters that the inspectors would, at times, simply look away from the belt and discs. This 'nonobserving' behaviour clearly boosted the Type 2 errors from an estimated $\frac{1}{2}$% nonobserving to about 15%, primarily as a function of task pace. If an item is not observed, then it is automatically accepted and it adds to the Type 2 errors in proportion to the percentage of nonconforming items. Analysis was made on the Type 1 errors separately from Type 2 errors. Type 1 errors were found to increase significantly with the task pace and the percentage of nonconforming items. Type 2 errors were also affected by the task pace. Also some interactions between these factors were found to be statistically significant. Figures 6 and 7 illustrate inspection errors found in this study respectively as a function of the task pace and the percentage of nonconforming items. These error percentages are given relative to the number of conforming and nonconforming items. The effect of incoming quality and pace confirmed the relative nature of results reported by Sosnowy (1967). Smith and Barany (1971) also found that the male subjects made more errors than the female subjects. It should be noted here that the target interspacing was not experimentally manipulated and the viewing

Figure 6. Percentage of errors of each type in disc inspection as a function of the pace and exposure time (adapted from Smith and Barany).

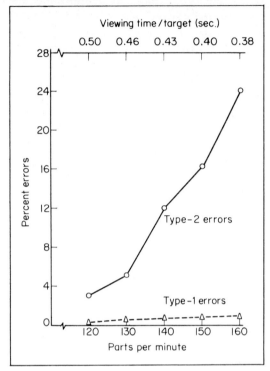

Figure 7. Percentage of errors of each type in disc inspection as a function of incoming quality (adapted from Smith and Barany).

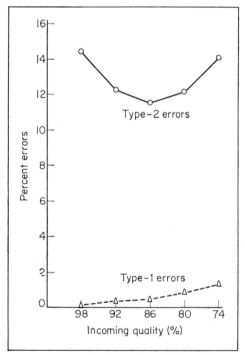

window was held constant so that the task pace was changed by a belt speed change. Unlike the Nelson and Barany (1969) study where downstream targets were open to view, in the Smith and Barany (1971) study only a single target was in view at any time.

A more recent study by Rizzi *et al.* (1974) was performed using targets similar to those used by Nelson and Barany (1969) but with 3/16 inch circular white dots instead of 1/8 inch squares. Three dots were designated as conforming targets and four as nonconforming. These targets were rigidly mounted on a fibre belt 24 inches apart with 40% of them nonconforming. Targets moved from left to right in front of the inspector. A translucent left shield was used to allow the inspectors to see an oncoming target but not to be able to determine if it were conforming or nonconforming until the target was within the viewing window. The size of this viewing window was experimentally manipulated in order to regulate the maximum viewing time available. However no more than a single target was within the viewing window at a time; that target disappeared under an opaque right shield before the next target emerged. Available viewing times ranged from approximately 0·12 to 0·27 seconds (about 0·05 to 0·20 seconds of full target exposure) in four equal increases in the size of the viewing window. Also manipulated experimentally were: (1) belt velocities from 100 to 133 feet per minute; and (2) the position of the inspector as the centre of the viewing window and 6 inches left and right of centre. Three sources of variation were found to be statistically significant: (1) the viewing time, (2) belt velocities, and (3) the interaction of viewing time and viewing position. Figures 8 and 9 show the percentage of inspection errors (based on total targets) as a function of the viewing time respectively showing differential belt velocity and viewing position effects. A quantitative model of the probability of correct target identification (Y) was found for the viewing time T (seconds of full exposure), belt velocity V in feet per second, and inspector position P in feet displacement from the viewing window centre. The resulting equation was:

$$Y = 1 - 2·58 \exp\left[-10·58T + 4·5/V + 0·012/(T + P^2)\right]$$

and the squared correlation coefficient with the data was $R^2 = 0·88$. This equation approximates the classical model for visual search.

Some auxiliary tests reported by Rizzi *et al.* (1974) show that target spacings down to 9 inches with an opaque leftward shield may produce considerably more inspection errors; especially at high belt velocities. These results led to the conjecture that one of the difficulties in DVI may be a 'visual methods' problem. A preliminary test by R. Wentworth using an eye-motion camera led to some confirmation of this effect. It appeared from this test that inspectors would continue to track targets after they went out of view under the opaque rightward shield. This waste of effective inspection time and effort was also indicated from eye-motion recording by electroculography used in the previously reported study. Also the variability in time allocation between successive targets was indicated. Accordingly a directed viewing strategy appeared to have some merit and an elementary methods study was made on target viewing. An experiment was performed, which is reported by Buck and Rizzi (1974), which essentially duplicated the auxiliary test in the previously reported study. In this experiment either a 9 or an 18 inch viewing window was employed for a 9 inch spacing between successive targets. This experimental setup gave only a single target

Figure 8. Percentage of inspection errors for three belt velocities as a function of the full matrix-target exposure time (from Rizzi *et al.*).

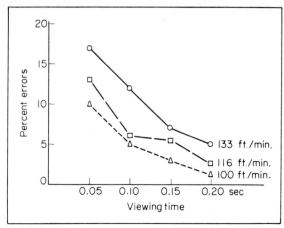

in view at a time (9 inch window) or two targets in view (18 inch window). Data were taken of the subjects' inspection using whatever methods of viewing they themselves devised. Then the subjects were instructed to use a simple viewing strategy which the authors devised. This 'directed viewing strategy' consisted of looking back and forth between a fixed and marked point in the left of the viewing window to the right shield. The left point occurred about where the eyes would normally pick up the next target. Figure 10 shows the concept of this viewing strategy and Figure 11 shows the effects of the viewing windows and strategies on the percentage of inspection errors. It is hypothesized that the wider viewing window allowed for behavioural improvements in observing the presence of new targets and the visual acquisition of these new targets. Whereas the directed viewing strategy helped in reducing inefficient behaviours associated with the tracking of targets and the acquisition of new targets. Indications from eye-motion recordings supported this conjecture.

Figure 9. Percentage of inspection errors for three viewing positions as a function of the full matrix-target viewing time (from Rizzi *et al.*).

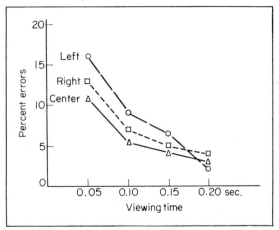

Figure 10. Directed viewing strategy used in the study by Buck and Rizzi.

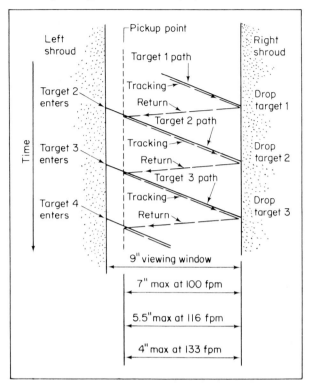

Figure 11. Percentage inspection errors for two viewing windows, self-directed and directed viewing strategies as a function of belt velocities (from Buck and Rizzi).

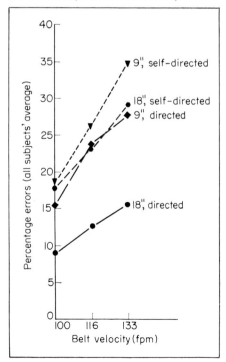

A study in process by Wentworth and Buck (1974) used targets and an experimental situation similar to those reported by Buck and Rizzi (1974) but with higher contrast targets and responses were required for both acceptance and rejection of each target. In this study the belt velocities were experimentally manipulated for 20, $26\frac{1}{3}$ and 40 inches per second (100, $133\frac{1}{3}$, and 200 feet per minute) as were target interspacings at 12, 18, and 24 inches. This test allowed for an untangling of these presentation factors of dynamic inspection which previously has been indicated but not clearly demonstrated. Preliminary results shown in Figure 12 disclosed that the maximum available exposure time was a most important factor but that belt velocities impart additional effects not accounted for by exposure time alone. This result confirmed other studies reported here and elsewhere. Further, some of the Nelson and Barany (1969) study data were superimposed on Figure 12 to demonstrate that the fundamental trend of these two studies follows the effect described by the traditional visual search model reported earlier in this volume by Bloomfield.

Figure 12. Percentage inspection errors at various target interspacings and belt velocities as a function of target exposure times (from Wentworth and Buck with superimposed data from Nelson and Barany).

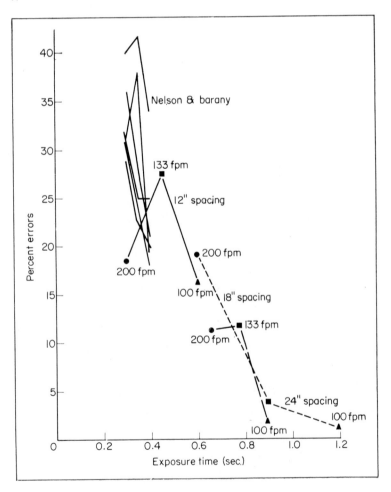

A preliminary test performed by Whitehead *et al.* (1974) on dynamic inspection showed some results with this task interspersed with rest periods. Essentially the task follows that of Wentworth and Buck (1974) using the belt velocity of $133\frac{1}{3}$ feet per minute with 12 inches between successive targets. This task was operated at: (1) 6 minutes continuously, (2) 2 minute intervals with 30 second rest periods, and (3) 1·5 minutes duration for the first and fourth successive trials, 1 minute intervening trials, and 30 second rest periods between all trials. Results in this preliminary test showed that situations 2 and 3 increased the accuracy of the average subject by 12·9% and 16·6% over situation 1. Tests verified that these results were statistically significant at the 95% level of confidence.

The studies shown above demonstrated differences in factors related to faults, presentation, organization, and individuals. Additionally Murrell (1971) and others have summarized studies on environmental factors affecting inspection accuracy. Although not strongly highlighted here, individual factors were identified as very significant; particularly in the dynamic inspection tasks. Presentation factors proved to affect dynamic inspection performance strongly; particularly the exposure time and belt velocities.

Drury (1974) has shown the time or speed effect on paced (static) visual inspection. A few studies shown above have demonstrated that the time and speed effect is even more important in dynamic visual inspection. These studies also show that time and speed are also related to interspacing distances. Designers and managers can clearly improve dynamic inspection accuracy by increasing the viewing time or interspacing distance or reducing the belt velocities but at the cost of less throughput of product or through the use of more inspectors and greater inspection costs. However these studies also show that improvements can be made in the dynamic inspection task if inspectors use more efficient methods of viewing. Improvements were further indicated with shorter continuous work periods followed by short rest periods; confirming results reported by Colquhoun (1959).

4. Some relevant theory and DVI

Preceding papers discuss the theory of signal detection (TSD) in conjunction with inspection. As these papers show, TSD uses decision theory as a basis and it partitions the errors of detection into attributes of detectability (d') and criterion (β) measurements. Criterion measurements are conventionally given as the ratio of conditional probability ordinates. Although there are theoretical reasons for this form of criterion measurements, β is difficult to conceptualize and relate to actual inspection results. An alternative measurement of criterion which avoids these difficulties and relates directly to β is the ratio of Type 2 to Type 1 inspection errors (R) or:

$$R = \frac{p(H_1|h_2)p(h_2)}{p(H_2|h_1)p(h_1)}$$

Figure 13 shows R as a function of incoming quality $p(h_1)$ for selected values of β, d', and X_c which are described earlier in detail. Some of the DVI studies described in the previous section are described below in terms of TSD. In these discussions the criterion measure R is used and Figure 13 may be used to approximate a corresponding value of β.

177

Figure 13. Ratios of Type 2 to Type 1 errors as a function of incoming quality for selected values of β, d′ and X_c from the theory of signal detection.

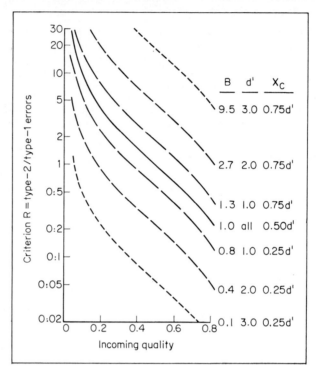

In experimental work with TSD the relative frequencies of Type 1 and Type 2 errors are used as probability estimates along with the incoming quality to find standard normal deviates. The sum of these standardized deviates is d′ whereas the ratio of ordinates at these deviates is β. Since the two principal measures of TSD depend only on the relative frequencies of defectives and the two types of errors used, these TSD measures serve only as a translation of terms unless d′ can be functionally related to the task factors. Even then, the usefulness of this model depends upon such model assumptions as: steady state conditions, perceptive constancy, and the independence between noise and signal. Although TSD adds the criterial richness which is not contained in many models, TSD does not relate physical factors of the inspection task to behavioural difficulties except for the composite measure of d′ and this measure is a consequence of the relative frequency of Type 1 and Type 2 inspection errors. One can argue from this standpoint that use of TSD in inspection offers nothing not already known from empirical evidence. However this model does provide a consistent framework for comparing diverse experiments.

Several investigators show that detectability decreases with factors which obviously increase the difficulty of the inspection task. Of these only the study by Smith and Barany (1971) appears to be a test on the adequacy of this model. Their conclusions are that there is sufficient agreement between TSD and their empirical data to merit further investigation. However these investigators found that the TSD implications did not accurately predict changes in Type 2 error with changes in the incoming quality and that the *implied* value system for error types was not reflected in corresponding shifts in inspection errors.

Data from the Nelson and Barany (1969) study are reduced to discriminability measurements and are shown in Figure 14 along with data from the Smith and Barany (1971) study. These results show that d' tends to increase with greater object exposure time, as the visual search model also predicts. However differences in the wide variety of fault and presentation factors in the Nelson and Barany (1969) study are not discriminated by d'. Figure 15 shows within-subject measurements of d' between the two types of targets from the Nelson and Barany (1969) study to have a relatively low correlation. Additional data from the Rizzi *et al.* (1974) study are reduced to d' measurements and the mean results are shown in Figure 16. The results here show a proper downward trend in d' with belt speed increases, but the effects of changes in the full target exposure time is not as one ought to expect. With two of the subjects in this study whose errors with exposure time correspond to expectations from d', criterial R data indicated radical shifts with changes in presentation factors. Figure 17 shows changes in the inspection performance of subjects reported from the Buck and Rizzi (1974) study which shows changes in presentation factors and in the visual strategy; supporting the criterial shifts observed by Smith and Barany (1971) and Rizzi *et al.* (1974). A contrast to these dynamic inspection studies is provided by the paced (static) inspection data reported by Drury (1974) in his study. These data are shown in TSD measurements of d' and R as a function of the average viewing time per item in Figure 18. Here again are nonlinear d' changes and criterial shifts with changes in task factors.

Figure 14. Discriminability (d') for various types of targets and interspacings as a function of target exposure time (adapted from Nelson and Barany (on left), and from Smith and Barany (on right)).

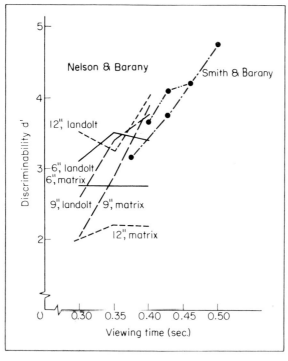

Figure 15. A scatterplot of each subject's discriminability (*d'*) on both the matrix and Landolt ring targets (adapted from Nelson and Barany).

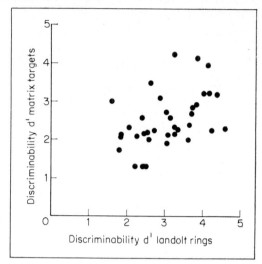

Figure 16. Discriminability (*d'*) for four exposure times (full targets) as a function of belt velocities (adapted from Rizzi *et al.*).

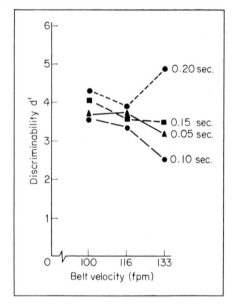

    The empirical tests shown here on the TSD model for the visual inspection task proved disappointing. However this result should not be too surprising because none of these studies provided a precise study of the inspection behaviour. Gross behavioural differences by different inspectors affects the time available for the visual search and, hence, performance. Results from the Smith and Barany (1971) study demonstrate a need for precise behavioural measurement.

Except for the static vision test of 'resistance to visual blurring' performed by Nelson and Barany (1969), none of the reported studies examined visual abilities beyond the most typical static tests. Resistance to visual blurring is a visual ability which is necessary during the dynamic visual search subtask. Visual-motor control abilities are additionally necessary. Since the blurring-resistance test provided remarkably good prediction of DVI performance, further improvements

Figure 17. Conditional probability changes with different belt velocities, viewing windows, and viewing strategies (from Buck and Rizzi).

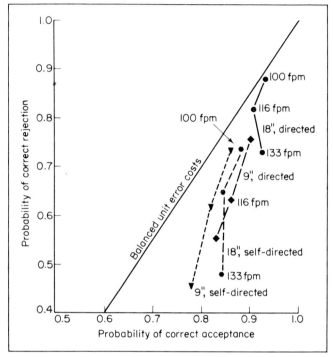

Figure 18. Discriminability (d') and criterion (R) changes as a function of the average viewing time (adapted from Drury).

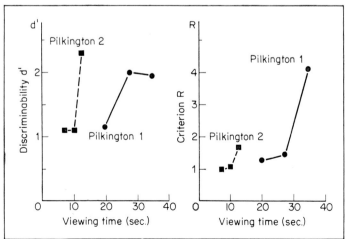

in predicting dynamic inspection accuracy appear to be possible with additional dynamic ability measurements. It also seems possible to relate changes in d' for individuals of different visual abilities and bring individual factors into the TSD model.

In all fairness to TSD, it should be pointed out that only the most elementary model aspects are investigated here. Many variations of TSD and concepts from this theory are not considered. Further it should be noted that general trends are typically indicated by TSD and that this theory does provide a vehicle for contrasting diverse laboratory and site studies on inspection. However these contrasts are restricted to performance alone; not behaviour and not abilities. In this author's opinion TSD can provide a useful vehicle for analysis by designers and managers if strong relationships can be established between the various factors in the inspection task and behavioural relationships can verify the causes of these relationships.

Examination of the empirical evidence in the previous section shows the general trend of decreasing DVI errors with increased exposure time. Figure 12 gives a particularly good illustration of this general trend. This trend is predictable from visual search theory (see Bloomfield's paper in this volume). However belt velocity effects are not and presentation density effects are a bit abstract in this theoretical translation. Criterial effects of detection errors are not typically part of visual search and so no translation is possible. It should also be noted that the evidence cited in the previous section used very elementary targets but target difference effects appear to exist, as visual search theory would predict. Although visual search theory appears to fit empirical results from DVI experiments, there are several important but missing elements between DVI and this theory.

Vigilance theory is another relevant theoretical approach for inspection as Fox has shown in his case study in this work. However most of the laboratory work cited above dealt with relatively short inspection runs. Hence little can be said here on the correspondence between vigilance theory and DVI.

5. Economics of DVI

When the current inspection operations are not significantly impacting production or other operations, then the economic considerations are primarily a case of 'cost savings'. Drury (1974) describes this aspect of inspection economics. This approach is summarized below:

$p(h_1)$ = The probability that an incoming item is conforming to specifications,

$p(H_2|h_1)$ = The probability of rejecting a conforming item,

$p(H_1|h_2)$ = The probability of accepting a nonconforming item,

C_1 = The unit cost of rejecting a conforming item,

C_2 = The unit cost of accepting a nonconforming item.

Minimize

$$C_1 p(H_2|h_1)p(h_1) + C_2 p(H_1|h_2)[1 - p(h_1)].$$

In the cost minimizing approach, shown above, the expected costs of Type 1 and Type 2 errors are assumed to be linear with the number of such errors. Although this assumption conforms with most industrial situations, there are a number of cost reduction situations where this assumption is inappropriate. A case in point is when a critical number of errors at a station necessitates an additional production run for work preceding that inspection station.

As the theory of signal detection clearly demonstrates with the criterion measurement β, inspectors operate with some implicit value scale between these costs of Type 1 and Type 2 errors. In the application of this theory to inspection one assumes that inspectors have some concept of C_1 and C_2 and that they modify $p(H_2|h_1)$ and $p(H_1|h_2)$ in some manner which balances the expected costs of these two error types. If both types of errors are equally important, then:

$$C_1 p(H_2|h_1)p(h_1) = C_2 p(H_1|h_2)[1 - p(h_1)]$$

From the equation above, it readily follows that:

$$\frac{C_2}{C_1} = \frac{p(H_2|h_1)p(h_1)}{p(H_1|h_2)[1 - p(h_1)]} = R$$

When the incoming quality is constant, then one would assume that R and β would remain relatively fixed for a given inspector. However the experimental evidence cited above shows that the implicit concept of costs by inspectors shifts with task factors other than incoming quality. Buck and Rizzi (1974) show the shifting nature of these implicit cost concepts in Figure 17 with changes in belt velocities, viewing windows, and viewing strategies. Table 1 describes the twelve average R values found with changes in these task factors. Behavioural shifts under task changes pose a vexing problem to engineers and managers who must design and manage inspection operations. Unless the inspectors' concepts of error costs can be made to conform to those of management, corrections to the task factors are likely to produce unanticipated behavioural shifts away from the economic objectives of management.

Table 1. Criterion R values of the average subject under each of twelve experimental conditions (adapted from Buck and Rizzi).

| Viewing window | Viewing strategy | Belt velocities (fpm) | | |
		100	116	133
9″	Self-directed	0·76	0·72	0·60
18″	Self-directed	0·67	0·65	0·45
9″	Directed	0·67	0·60	0·60
18″	Directed	0·89	0·81	0·44

Inspection operations almost always impact other industrial operations in some direct or indirect nature. Expected Type 1 errors at an inspection station requires increased production quantities in the upstream operations. Accordingly the failure to account for the value of the throughput of conforming items can lead to fallacious economic results. If the unit value of a correctly identified conforming item is valued at one economic unit (i.e. $v_1 = 1$), then the unit costs of the two types of errors scaled accordingly to C_1' and C_2' which are defined as:

$$C_1' = C_1/v_1 \text{ and } C_2' = C_2/v_1$$

Here one notes that $C_1'/C_2' = C_1/C_2$. The expected net worth under this scaling is:

$$E(\text{net worth}) = E(\text{correct acceptances}) - C_1'E(\text{Type 1 errors}) - C_2'E(\text{Type 2 errors})$$

183

and the economic objective is to maximize the expected net worth. If these three expectations on the right-hand side of the above equation can be estimated under each of alternative task conditions, then the greater expected net worths can be found as a function of C_1' and C_2' by break-even analysis. Figure 19 shows the break-even analysis for alternative belt velocities using both the 9 and 18 inch viewing windows and both viewing strategies described by Buck and Rizzi (1974). Empirical estimates of the error probabilities $p(H_2|h_1)$ and $p(H_1|h_2)$ under a given set of task conditions formed the expected net worth as a function of C_1' and C_2'. Two expected net worth functions, at two different belt velocities, were equated and solved. This analysis denotes those combinations of C_1' and C_2' where the expected net worths of two belt velocities are equal; at other combinations one of the two belt velocities has a worth which is greater. Shaded areas in this figure denote the belt velocity of the three examined which yields the greatest expected net worth. Naturally the lower error costs will favour higher belt velocities and the shaded region nearest the origin in Figure 19 favours the belt velocity of 133 feet per minute. This figure also shows a cross-hatched region where the 116 feet per minute belt velocity gives the greatest expected net worth and a white region where 100 feet per minute is optimum.

Figure 19. Break-even net worths between belt velocities as relative Type 2 and Type 1 error unit costs and cost ratios for both viewing windows and both viewing strategies (from Buck and Rizzi).

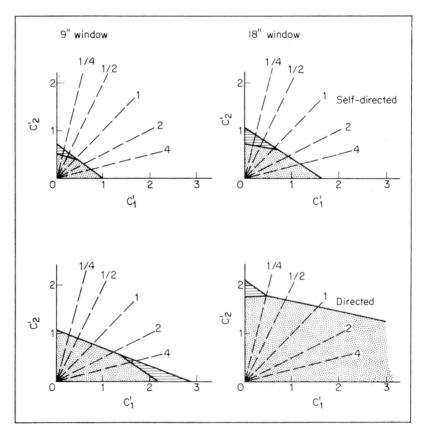

The figure also shows contours of constant ratios of C_2'/C_1' where the criteria remain unchanged relative to inspection errors. The distance from the origin along one of these C_2'/C_1' contours simply specifies the importance of correct throughput to an inspection error. At least three measurements are required to fully state the inspection criteria.

Another aspect of inspection-system design problem lies in locating inspection stations for greater economy. Wiebe and Byers (1974) show how computer simulation might be employed advantageously for solving this problem. A recent classroom project at Purdue University was performed by Mr. Mitchell Berman who addressed the question of comparing four schemes in locating a second inspection station (A) as shown in Figure 20. The GASP IV simulation technique which embeds cost considerations, was employed by Berman. Annual cost results from this analysis were generated as a function of Type 1 inspection errors. Incoming quality in this simulation was arbitrarily set at 95% with defectives of minor or major types. Arbitrary error costs and detectabilities (d') were also assumed. Scheme 3 turned out to have the best annual cost for any Type 1 error probability. In spite of these arbitrary values, this simulation example shows that the simulation approach is capable of handling the complexities which approach those that exist in current industry.

Figure 20. Four schemes of locating a second inspection station in a manufacturing operation (from the Berman Report).

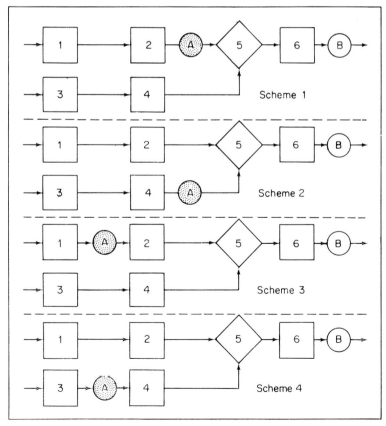

6. Summary and closing remarks

In DVI the object being inspected is in externally-controlled motion. Characteristics of this motion and other presentation factors affect the ability of people performing this task; resulting in inspection errors. To perform this task inspectors must detect the oncoming object, obtain visual acquisition of this object, visually search the object for faults, make the accept–reject decision, and start again. This task sequence is fixed. Difficulties in performing earlier elemental tasks cascade to later ones. Empirical results from experiments show that there are very large individual differences in the effects of presentation factors on DVI accuracy. Parts of these individual differences are due to visual and visual-motor abilities. As the presentation factors are changed, these visual and visual-motor abilities must keep pace or DVI errors result. Factor changes which improve DVI accuracy include: (1) greater exposure time of an object, (2) lower belt velocities, (3) greater interspacing distances between successive objects, and (4) more open exposure of oncoming objects. The first three of these factors affect the throughput rate of accepted and conforming objects. Accordingly the control of these presentation factors impacts production operations and the economics of quality control. These implications are also considered here.

Presentation factors also play a role in affecting visual behaviour and the inspectors' error-type criteria. Smoother, more regular, and more effective visual behaviour appears to improve DVI accuracy. Differences in the visual constraints between several studies and the corresponding results suggests that peripheral vision plays an important role in DVI accuracy. Better peripheral vision appears to reduce the time required for visual acquisition of the objects. One could theorize that better peripheral vision reduces velocity and position errors in the visual-motor process which require saccadic correction. With fewer corrections, the visual behaviour is smoother and more regular. Experimental evidence supports this theory but no critical test has yet been made. An effect from presentation factors which is perplexing is the criterion changes between the two error types. Ratios of Type 2 to Type 1 errors change with changes in incoming quality, visual strategies, belt velocities, and viewing windows. These perplexing effects create obstacles in theoretical developments for the DVI task.

Visual search theory and the theory of signal detection have been proposed for adaptation to the DVI task. Both theories appear quite plausible in light of the elemental tasks. However the direct application of one theory or the other, rather than both, appears to be a selective emphasis between the elemental tasks. Visual search theory, in its most simplistic form, shows a relationship between the probability of a correct detection and the viewing time and a composite of viewing-field factors. Although the empirical data appear to support the application of this theory to DVI, many task factors of DVI are directly converted to this composite field factor and visual search theory does not include a means for giving a criterial relationship between error types when the detection is incorrect or the detection is missed. On the other hand, the theory of signal detection (TSD) provides this criterial relationship. Unfortunately TSD has proved to be disappointing when applied to DVI primarily because of the assumption of within-person constancy on the criterial relationship. Both theories have good features and voids relative to their use in DVI. A common void between them is a lack of a connection between performance and such features as: presentation factors, visual and visual-motor abilities, and behaviour in light of these abilities.

Although the lack of a substantial background theory may disturb experimenters in this field, designers and managers of DVI operations do not have an adequate mechanism for predicting economic implications of various designs or modes of operation. Some analytical approaches are shown above based upon empirical data. However the missing links between abilities, behaviour, and criterion preclude a general application of these approaches. Research is needed to complete this linkage for a theoretical model and a general basis aiding engineers in design and managers in the operations of these designs.

References

BUCK, J. R., and RIZZI, A. M., 1974, Viewing strategy and window effects on dynamic visual-inspection accuracy. *AIIE Transactions*, **6**, 196–205.

BURG, A., 1966, Visual acuity as measured by dynamic and static tests: A comparative evaluation. *Journal of Applied Psychology*, **50**, 460–466.

COLQUHOUN, W. P., 1959, The effect of a short rest-pause on inspection efficiency. *Ergonomics*, **2**, 367–372.

CRAWFORD, W. A., 1960, *The Perception of Moving Objects, Parts I to IV*. (Air Ministry Flying Personnel Research Committee, FPRC/Memo, London, England.)

DRURY, C. G., 1974, The effect of speed of working on industrial inspection accuracy. *Applied Ergonomics*, **4**, 2–7.

ELKIN, E. H., 1962, Target velocity, exposure time and anticipatory tracking time as determinants of dynamic visual acuity (DVA). *Journal of Engineering Psychology*, **1**, 26–33.

FOLEY, P. J., 1957, *Legibility of Moving Digits as a Function of their Separation and Direction of Movement*. (Defense Research Board of Canada, DRML Report No. 76–4.)

HOWARTH, M. A., and BLOOMFIELD, J. R., 1971, Search and selective attention. *British Medical Bulletin*, **27**, 253–258.

LIPPERT, S., 1963, Dynamic vision—The legibility of equally spaced alphanumeric symbols. *Human Factors*, **5**, 129–138.

LIPPERT, S., and LEE, D. M., 1965, Dynamic vision: The legibility of moderately spaced alphanumeric symbols. *Human Factors*, **7**, 555–560.

LUDVIGH, E. J., and MILLER, J. W., 1958, Study of visual acuity during the ocular pursuit of moving test objects. *Journal of the Optical Society of America*, **48**, 799–802.

MURRELL, K. F. H., 1971, Ergonomics. (London: CHAPMAN and HALL.)

NELSON, J. B., and BARANY, J. W., 1969, A dynamic visual recognition test. *AIIE Transactions*, **1**, 327–332.

RIZZI, A. M., BUCK, J. R., and ANDERSON, V. L., 1974, *Effects of Some Task Variables on Conveyor-Paced Visual Inspection Accuracy*. (Working Paper, School of Industrial Engineering, Purdue University.)

SHEEHAN, J. J., and DRURY, C. G., 1971, The analysis of industrial inspection. *Applied Ergonomics*, **2**, 74–78.

SMITH, G. L., 1972, Signal detection and industrial inspection. *Proceedings of the Sixteenth Annual Meeting of the Human Factors Society*. Pp. 284–290.

SMITH, L. A., and BARANY, J. W., 1971, An elementary model of human performance on paced visual inspection. *AIIE Transactions*, **4**, 298–308.

SOSNOWY, J. K., 1967, *An Investigation of the Effects of Incoming Quality and Inspection Rate on Inspector Accuracy*. (M.S.I.E. Thesis, Texas Technological College.)

WENTWORTH, R., and BUCK, J. R., 1974, *Dynamic Visual Inspection and Eye Movements*. (Working Paper, School of Industrial Engineering, Purdue University.)

WHITEHEAD, D., BISSEY, J., MARTIN, J., and LINEGAR, D., 1974, *Fatigue in Relation to Visual Acuity*. (Project Report to Professor J. Buck, School of Industrial Engineering, Purdue University.)

WIEBE, H. A., and BYERS, J. K., 1974, Simulation 2 (Quality Control). *Industrial Engineering*, **6**, 18–24.

Effects of information on industrial inspection performance

X. K. Zunzanyika and C. G. Drury

1. Introduction

The information environment in which the inspector operates has been found to be an important determinant of performance. One industrial study by Drury and Addison (1973) confirmed the many laboratory results (e.g., Wiener 1968, Hardesty *et al.* 1963) that feedback or knowledge of results improved inspection performance markedly. Similarly Drury and Sheehan (1969) have shown that prior knowledge of probable fault types (feed forward of information) improves performance on another industrial inspection task.

The experiment reported here is an attempt to assess the value of combining feedback and feedforward information in an on-going industrial inspection task. It is also an extension of the studies of inspection as a signal detection task (e.g., Drury and Addison 1973, Sheehan and Drury 1971, Wallack and Adams 1969). These and other studies have used a simple Accept/Reject decision by the inspectors, analogous to the 'Fundamental Detection Problem' described by Green and Swets (1966). The current study allows the inspector to use four response categories; 'definitely good', 'probably good', 'probably faulty' and 'definitely faulty' analogous to the rating procedure reported by Egan *et al.* (1961); who showed that in a laboratory situation in psychoacoustics the subjects were able to maintain the same discriminability (d') despite using multiple criteria. The advantage of this method is that the same reliability in estimates of d' is obtained with one-third the data: it precludes the collection of data on the subject's normal *criterion* value, β, and its variation with experimental conditions, without the assumption that β can be identified with the division between 'probably good' and 'probably faulty'. In this study the main interest was in the variation of d' with experimental conditions so that this was not a significant problem.

2. Method

2.1. *The product*

The product used for this study was a semi-conductor used as one of a three-component Gas Dryer Ignition System. The quality requirements for this product are very tight and field failures must be held to a minimum level. All the possible causes of field failures attributable to this product had been clearly identified and the inspection group studied was charged with the responsibility of finding items with these defects and eliminating the items from the batches before final inspection for electrical properties is conducted on a sampling basis. There are a total of 14 possible defects for which an item can be rejected and these are classified into four major groups. It is also known, approximately, what percentage of each of the four major categories of defects the process produces. Thus in this experiment batches with a known number of defects were prepared and the composition of each batch was such that it included defects from each of the four categories. Three batches of 50 items each were prepared. The three batches contained 10%, 20% and 30% defective items respectively. The experiment lasted four weeks and except for the first week the inspectors examined the same batches. All the items were identified and the identification system was changed at the beginning of each week. Each inspector examined each batch once every week so that by the end of the experiment each inspector had examined each batch three times.

2.2. *The inspectors*

There were six inspectors at the inspection station studied. Their average service with the company was over six years but their range of time at this inspection station was four to eight months. Prior to the experiment they separated the batches into the usual good and bad categories. There was also a special examiner whose responsibility was to check all the rejected items for possible good ones. In this experiment this special inspector was also used. In an attempt to match the control group and experimental group three samples were prepared (10%, 20% and 30% defective respectively) and a pre-test conducted during the first week. The pre-test served two purposes, namely to match the experimental group with the control group and to familiarize the inspectors with the four response categories. After the pre-test week the inspectors were divided into two groups of three each with one group serving as the experimental group and the other the control group. The number of inspectors used in each group was rather limited for conclusive results, but these were the only inspectors available.

2.3. *Experimental design*

The variables considered for the experimental design were the *Inspector (I)*, *Batch (B)*, and *Week (W)* each at three levels. For the experimental group the batch levels were 10%, 20% and 30% defective, and the three-week levels were feedback, feedforward, and feedback-feedforward. The control group received no information so that the three-week levels were just the weeks 2, 3 and 4 of the experiment with the same batches as for the experimental group. For the experimental group the order of batch presentation was determined by a Graeco-Latin Square design. The experiment was self-paced and took between 45 and 60 minutes for each batch, the normal working pace for inspection of this product.

2.4. *Data collection*

For each batch examined there were four small empty boxes which were marked 'Definitely Accept', 'Probably Accept', 'Probably Reject', and 'Definitely Reject' respectively. The inspectors examined the items and placed them in one of these four boxes depending on their decision as to which of the four categories the item(s) belonged. In the pre-test week emphasis was put on explaining the meaning of these four categories particularly the two middle ones. Thus the inspector was to place an item into the 'Probably Accept' box if she was not quite sure that the fault she had observed was rejectable but would have accepted it under the Accept/Reject categories and similarly she was to place an item into the 'Probably Reject' box if she was not quite sure the fault she had observed was rejectable but would have rejected it under the Accept/Reject criterion.

The experimenter and the special examiner went over the items in each of the small boxes and recorded the results on a pre-designed form from which a number of calculations were made.

2.5. *Performance measures*

Following Egan *et al.* (1959) the dividing line between adjacent pairs of response categories was used to define the probability of correct acceptance (P_1), and the probability of correct rejection (P_2). The detectability, d', was determined using the normal deviates of P_1 and P_2, i.e.

$$d' = Z(P_1) + Z(P_2). \tag{1}$$

The *criterion* (β) was calculated from the P_1 and P_2 values, i.e.

$$\beta = \frac{\text{Normal ordinate corresponding to } P_2}{\text{Normal ordinate corresponding to } (1 - P_1)}. \tag{2}$$

In cases where P_1 or P_2 was 1·0 or 0·0 because of the small number of faults, an effective P_1 or P_2, equivalent to half of an error, was used to avoid infinite Z values (Wallack and Adams 1969).

3. Analysis

3.1. *Analysis of d'*

For each condition of *Inspector* (I), *Batch* (B) and *Week* (W) there were three values of d' for the three criteria, defined between adjacent response categories. If the theory of signal detection is applicable to this situation, then the d' values should show no effect of criterion level, either as a main effect or in interactions. To test this, the analysis of variance of d' was treated as a four factor factorial with *Criterion* (C) as the fourth factor.

The analyses of variance for both experimental and control groups are summarized in Table 1. All factors are treated as fixed, including *Inspectors* where the whole population was used in the experiment.

Table 1. Summary analysis of variance of d'

Source of variance	df	Experimental group mss	F	Signif	Control group mss	F	Signif
B	2	0·20707	3·59	*	1·87221	11·97	***
W	2	2·04203	35·43	***	3·08107	19·69	***
$B \times W$	4	0·68183	11·83	***	0·40518	2·54	
I	2	0·75953	13·18	***	4·32321	27·63	***
$B \times I$	4	0·21910	3·80	*	0·58879	3·76	*
$W \times I$	4	0·15615	2·71	*	0·30915	1·98	
$B \times W \times I$	8	0·31025	5·38	***	0·38173	2·44	*
C	2	0·15578	2·70		0·26285	1·68	
$B \times C$	4	0·16507	2·86	*	0·15277	0·98	
$W \times C$	4	0·17539	3·04	*	0·05379	0·34	
$B \times W \times C$	8	0·09760			0·12088		
$I \times C$	4	0·04369	0·76		0·46366	2·96	*
$B \times I \times C$	8	0·04612			0·21867		
$W \times I \times C$	8	0·06804			0·08519		
$B \times W \times I \times C$	16	0·03825			0·17879		
Total	80						

*** indicates $p < 0.001$ * indicates $p < 0.05$

Effects of information

An initial test of the second order interaction involving C against the third order interaction $(B \times W \times I \times C)$ showed no significant effects at $p < 0.05$ so these were pooled with $(B \times W \times I \times C)$ for each group to give 40 df for a measure of residual variance, rather than the 16 df for $(B \times W \times I \times C)$.

There was no significant main effect of C for either group but three first order interactions with C reached significance at $p < 0.05$. Overall, of the 16 possible effects involving C, only three were significant at $p < 0.05$. This is somewhat equivocal evidence as regards the applicability of the theory of signal detection: d' is not entirely independent of criterion but the dependence is small.

Inspectors and *Weeks* are both highly significant effects $(p < 0.001)$ for experimental and control groups. Inspector differences are always expected but in this experiment the small number of inspectors precludes meaningful *post-hoc* correlations of performance with inspector variables such as age, experience, etc. There is a significant *Weeks* effect for both groups, which is shown in Figure 1.

Figure 1. Change in d' over the last 3 weeks of study.

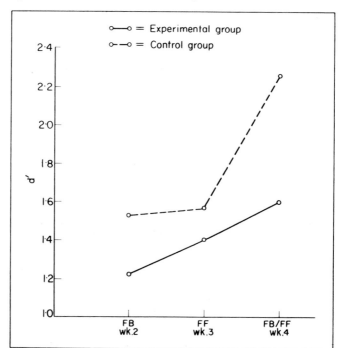

Both groups improve over weeks by approximately the same amount with the control group having a higher d' than the experimental group. Provision of information was no more useful in improving performance than was merely running the experiment.

For the control group the *Batch* effect was highly significant but for the experimental group *Batches* and *Weeks* interacted significantly. Figure 2 shows these two effects. There is no consistent change of d' with *Batch* between groups or between weeks within the experimental group. Indeed, Table 1 shows that the effects of *Batch* and *Week* depend upon the inspector for the experimental group ($B \times W \times I$ interaction). A graph of this interaction provides no ready interpretation. The other significant effects are quite small.

Figure 2. *Batch* × *Week* interaction.

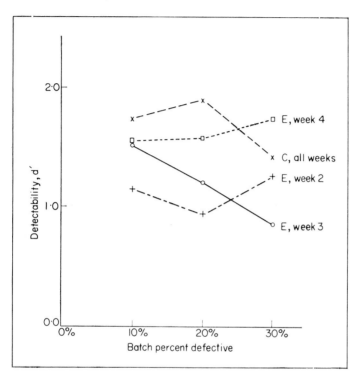

3.2. *Analysis of criterion β*

Because of the fact that the actual *criterion* information is lost with a multi-category rating, the only tests possible were of internal consistency. One prediction of TSD is that if the cost structure of decisions remains constant, the *criterion* should vary with input quality level thus:

$$\text{optimum } \beta = k \cdot \frac{P}{1-P}. \tag{3}$$

Drury and Addison (1973) showed that this was approximately true for an inspection group as a whole. Hence, the only variation of P was by batch, giving only three points to check equation (3) for each group at the middle *criterion* level. A linear regression gave the following results:

$$\text{control group } \beta = 0.24 \; \frac{P}{1-P} + 6.12$$

$$\text{experimental group } \beta = 0.16 \; \frac{P}{1-P} + 3.36.$$

These results are plotted in Figure 3. The correlation coefficients were $r = 0.390$ and 0.995 respectively. The value for the experimental group was

193

significant ($t_1 = 9.96$, $p < 0.05$) whilst that for the control group was not significant. The experimental group was apparently able to use the batch quality
information to adjust its criterion in the appropriate direction. Neither line
passes through the origin showing that neither group made full use of batch
quality information.

Figure 3. Change in *criterion* with input quality.

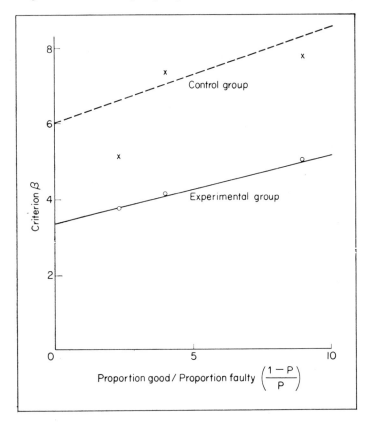

4. Discussion of results and conclusions

In an experiment with so few subjects in the population, any matching of groups
must be crude. Here they were matched by mean d' on the pre-test but inspector
variation within groups was still large. Also with a small group of inspectors
independence cannot be assumed over a period of weeks because of social and
technical interaction between the inspectors. This is one possible interpretation
of the significant effect of *Weeks* whether or not information was given to the
inspectors. It could also be a manifestation of the classic 'Hawthorne' effect of
merely taking part in an experiment. It may be noted parenthetically that after
the experiment the inspectors and management realized that standards could be
inconsistent between inspectors and a re-calibration exercise was undertaken.
Yet another explanation would be the inability of the inspectors to make use of
the information given to them without detailed training. A similar effect was
found when inspectors were given comparison standards for the first time in an
earlier industrial study (Drury 1973).

194

These alternatives can only be differentiated by experimentation in a more controlled setting.

Input batch quality had a significant but idiosyncratic effect on *detectability* and a more obvious effect on *criterion*. The latter showed that only the experimental group who were given reliable prior quality information in two out of the three weeks were able to use this effectively and even they did not use it as effectively as they should if they were perfect signal detectors. Again, lack of detailed training may be the cause.

Does the theory of signal detection apply to this situation? The two internal checks gave equivocal results. The check on criterion discussed above can be interpreted as at least qualitative support but the dependence of *detectability* on *criterion* in three out of 16 tests is open to either interpretation. The chance probability of three or more out of 16 tests being significant at $p = 0.05$ is 0.042. This is a low enough probability to reject the hypothesis of chance effects at the conventional $p = 0.05$ level. It appears that there are significant departures from the theory of signal detection applied to individual inspectors in an on-line experiment.

The authors would like to thank the Carborundum Company for permission to carry out this study and publish the results, the individual inspectors for their time and trouble and the Department of Industrial Engineering at State University of New York at Buffalo for guidance and analysis facilities.

References

DRURY, C. G., 1973, The inspection of sheet materials—model and data. *Proceedings of 17th Annual Meeting of the Human Factors Society*, Pp. 457–464.

DRURY, C. G., and ADDISON, J. L., 1973, An industrial study of the effects of feedback and fault density on inspection performance. *Ergonomics*, **16**, 159–169.

DRURY, C. G., and SHEEHAN, J. J., 1969, Ergonomics and economic factors in an industrial inspection task. *International Journal of Production Research*, **7**, 333–340.

EGAN, J. P., GREENBERG, G. Z., and SCHULMAN, A. I., 1961, Operating characteristics, signal detectability and the method of free response. *Journal of the Acoustical Society of America*, **33**, 993–1007.

GREEN, D. M., and SWETS, J. A., 1966, *Signal Detection Theory and Psychophysics*. (New York: WILEY.)

HARDESTY, D., TRUMBO, D., and BEVAN, W., 1963, Influence of knowledge of results of performance in a monitoring task. *Perceptual and Motor Skills*, **16**, 629–634.

SHEEHAN, J. J., and DRURY, C. G., 1971, The analysis of industrial inspection. *Applied Ergonomics*, **2**, 74–78.

WALLACK, P. M., and ADAMS, S. K., 1969, The utility of signal detection theory in the analysis of industrial inspector accuracy. *AIIE Transactions*, **1**, 33–44.

WIENER, E. L., 1968, Training for vigilance—repeated sessions with knowledge of the results. *Ergonomics*, **11**, 547–556.

Factors affecting inspection performance

The list of factors which it may be relevant to control for optimum inspector performance appears formidable. Eight major points have been noted and some of these have further aspects so that some thirty questions might be posed in a checklist to evaluate the human factors requirements for inspection.

Checklists have, of course, little value unless criteria are available. However, the claim that research has produced these criteria in many respects can be sustained. Especially, it would seem, on questions of illumination, magnification and pacing.

It would be foolish to minimize the practical difficulties of making an attack on the inspector's efficiency in such depth and on such a broad front. The comprehensive approach to illumination described by Faulkner and Murphy is sustained by a very large Corporation. Provision of the feedforward of production quality information and the feedback of performance results to inspectors can be difficult in a complex production plant. Social and motivational factors in the inspection group as often as not are closely linked with the industrial relations climate of the whole Corporation. Similarly with training: and certainly the exciting possibilities discussed by Wiener and by Embrey for training with computer based systems would demand much management skill to implement and use effectively. Dealing with the questions of magnification and pacing may be less complex: armed with the data from Smith and from Buck the former may perhaps be simply a question of purchasing, the latter a matter of enlightened engineering. But in any event, to carry through the human factors refinement of a quality control system a considerable range of expertise is required.

It thus seems self evident that obtaining the optimum conditions for inspector efficiency and maintaining it is a considerable exercise in the management of people and resources. The identification and the partial solution of a large number of human factors has in its turn produced a significant management activity giving a new dimension to the role of the quality control manager or engineer. It was no part of the plan for the present volume, perhaps fortunately, to explore this new dimension. This was not an avoidance of the issues but simply that the management of inspection resources in the human factors context deserves an individual volume. The final section of this volume, however, shows that in part, at least, the various human factors contributing to an inspector's efficiency have been tackled in many industries. It will be seen that even with a limited approach the benefits have been not insignificant.

Wiener's mention of the study of radiologists recalls the point that the human factor concepts in quality control extend beyond the narrower definition of industry and have relevance for more effective performance in aspects of many of the systems created by our Society.

o

3. Industrial applications

Some human-factor applications to quality control in a high technology industry

L. V. Rigby and A. D. Swain

1. Introduction

Sandia Laboratories, a prime contractor to the U.S. Atomic Energy Commission, is a high technology research and development organization. Its main job is the design and development of nuclear weapon fuzing and firing systems. Other R & D efforts have included the development of SNAP (System for Nuclear Auxiliary Power) for satellite systems; laminar flow clean rooms for extremely clean assembly or biomedical research; unattended seismological observatories; and rolamite, with its manifold applications. In such research, considerable use is made of new and exotic materials, some of the most advanced equipment that our society is capable of supplying, and the most advanced knowledge in many fields. This, of course, pushes the state-of-the-art with respect to assembly, testing, and quality assurance.

For example, recent production jobs involved lengthwise welding of 3-inch tubes of rhenium 1·2 mils thick and 0·020 inch in diameter; winding 140 turns of No. 55 wire (0·00025 inch in diameter) onto a core roughly the width of a single ridge in a person's fingerprint; and attaching thermocouple wires to kitchen variety aluminium foil. Each of these involved many new and delicate operations that required new specifications and new methods, especially in assembly, inspection, and testing.

This paper describes some of the things that Sandia's human factors specialists have done and recommended to improve quality assurance in such development efforts. We mention these things, not because they have not been talked about or done before, but because they are not known or done nearly so widely as we believe they should be, and we think that they deserve discussion. Moreover, these are areas in which quality control and human factors (ergonomics) people, working together, could accomplish a great deal that neither discipline seems likely to accomplish alone.

2. The need for quality control in development

In high-technology industries, quality control is especially important in the development phases of a new product or component. Inadequate evaluation here can lead to the rejection of a good design on the basis of bad data, or to commitment to a poor design whose faults were simply not recognized early enough. A common fault is inability to define the process controls essential to consistent production. In development, many product lines grow, 'like Topsy', as the product itself is being defined. We may never realize the true cost in alternatives thus prohibited or inefficiencies thus cemented into place.

Despite the obviousness of such matters, there seems to be a tendency to downgrade the need for a formal quality programme on items under development. The reasoning is often that the item does not represent final design and that, since any work will have to be redone, quality work in the development stage would be wasted. We are also told that the development group will use its own 'top notch' engineers to do the necessary tests and inspections, and that this is more efficient than trying to explain the product and its needs to others.

One might suppose that, if the developer does his own testing and inspection, he will be doubly careful because so much hangs on his decision. But as we know from innumerable studies, people are their own worst monitors, especially when they are ego-involved. Experience has shown (Finley *et al.* 1974) that the development engineer tends to give inspection the 'once-over-lightly' treatment. Too many are quick to excuse poor performance and to accept modest success on the grounds that 'It works; now all we have to do is to iron out the bugs'. The most fundamental principle of science, independence of observations, is too often sacrificed with just these words.

Several factors make the quality job difficult in development work. Design changes are frequent and difficult to keep up with. Hard tooling is seldom available and open setups prevent standardization in both production and inspection tasks. And the emphasis on schedules and costs often precludes serious attention to secondary problems. Yet, quality must be designed in as surely as function. The presence or absence of quality control will often prove decisive, as illustrated by the following example.

A small electromechanical timing device was being developed at Sandia Labs, and a rush order was put out for a small quantity of precision piece parts, including pawl and ratchet assemblies and shafts. Two expert machinists were asked to fabricate the parts. Each was furnished only drawings of the parts. In the absence of specified procedures, one machinist oriented the sequence of machining operations from the outer diameter of a particular shaft. The other used a counterbore for orientation. Each turned out several parts. Each inspected his own work, and no other inspection was performed.

The parts were immediately installed in development systems and tested. There were several successes and several failures. Management was unimpressed and the development programme was near cancellation. Fortunately, the development engineer disassembled each system and got others to help determine what went wrong. It turned out that the dimensions of parts in failed systems were materially different from those in successful systems. Once this was discovered, the programme was 'saved', and later became highly successful.

This example illustrates the old adage: 'We never have time to do it right, but we can always find time to do it over'. This is one case in which an excellent product was almost lost because of a lack of quality control during its developmental phase. Incidentally, the cost of a reasonable quality programme here would have been less than the cost of any one of the failures. These are some of the reasons why we try to get the quality control people involved at the very beginning.

3. Communication

The foregoing, like so many things, is largely due to problems in communications. It is entirely to be expected, but continually disappointing, to find that the vast majority of those working in industry—be they managers, engineers, inspectors, or assemblers—are blissfully unaware of the basic principles and methods of either quality control or human factors. In fact, a major problem in our exploding technology is the credibility gap developing between specialists who no longer appreciate each other's problems or contributions. Cooperation is usually proportional to the degree of mutual understanding.

One of the more useful things that we have done at Sandia is to teach two in-house courses: one on human factors in quality assurance and one on human factors engineering. We feel that this has been very beneficial for a number of reasons. It brings us more business of more interesting kinds; it forces us to think more carefully about what we do and believe; and it spreads a little gospel. Scores of people are somewhat more knowledgeable and somewhat more sensitive than they were before. Acquainting others with the elements of our discipline is one of the most valuable things that we can do. As Glenn Frank put it years ago (*c.* 1960):

> "The practical value of every social invention or material discovery depends upon its being adequately interpreted to the masses . . . A dozen fields of thought are today congested with knowledge . . . and the whole tone and temper of American life can be lifted by putting this knowledge into general circulation . . ."

The kinds of things that need to be communicated are fairly elementary. For example, one of us (Rigby 1973) has pointed out that people drop things primarily because those things have no handles or inadequate handles; because they are unnecessarily awkward to move or carry; and because there are inadequate protections on open shelving, and so on. These conditions are not likely to change until those of us who understand such matters communicate this knowledge to those who do not, and yet are responsible for designing or selecting fixtures that contribute to the dropping of things.

What percentage of an intended audience will actually read a given article in a given journal? Certainly less than 50%, probably less than 5%. And we publish in sources that reach only a few thousand at best. If we are going to influence the masses, we must publish where they will see it; we must use language that they will understand; and we must repeat and repeat until those things which should be common knowledge are common knowledge. If the colleges are to teach what we have learned, we must communicate that knowledge to the teachers.

4. Paperwork

Paperwork is one of our basic tools and one of our basic problems. Pound for pound we use more paper than anything else. Most of that paper is wasted, for it is produced as a matter of ritual, rather than as a matter of science; that is, it is done according to custom rather than according to any deliberate system analysis or process control. Try these common techniques on your paperwork system, or any part of it, and you may really improve things.

People do not use instructions largely because the instructions just are not usable. Consider a recent example of instructions intended for use by a soldier to inspect ablative material on a missile:

> The defined widths and depths set the limits at the end points of defects, and intermediate points of depth allowables shall not exceed the depth of any imaginary straight line connecting the end points.

Most instructions violate design principles established by research. And a lot of excellent research has been done in this area, especially for advertising (e.g., see Cornog and Rose 1967). If it helps advertisers to get their message across, it should help us to get our message across. But few of those who write instructions, or the other paperwork items that we use, know anything about that research.

For instance, if there is one thing established by research, it is the fact that all capital letters, especially when typewritten, are the slowest and most difficult type of font to read. Yet we find all caps being used with abandon. If anything is more difficult to read than all caps, it is all numbers; yet our paperwork is filled with numbers that are both unnecessary and unused. Short paragraphs minimize errors and tables are a better way to present factual data; yet, we find long paragraphs sprinkled with bits of data that are hard to find when you need them. Home-made data forms are particularly bad; spacing is terrible, abbreviations and coding are inconsistent, instructions are unclear; and we wonder why people do not use the forms correctly.

Many of the difficulties that people have with paperwork are due to the failure of the author to consider very elemental matters. For instance, Figure 1a is an example of how reference material is commonly presented in engineering and manufacturing materials. The bottom method (Figure 1b) is better than the top for a number of reasons.

> The space between columns is less than one eye fixation, thus helping the reader to avoid the tendency to go to the wrong line. The eye has difficulty in crossing more than one-half inch of white space.
> The elements are grouped in fives. This enables the reader to determine which group to deal with, then which item in that group. Span of attention data show that groups of five are optimum; people can easily find and track the first, middle, or last item in a group.
> The elements are ordered in a sensible way. Like items are grouped together, doing some of the mental processing for the reader.

This sort of spacing, grouping, and ordering takes time and effort, but it certainly helps the reader. A basic problem is the fact that we usually prepare such things by habit or custom without really thinking about the effects on the reader. Or even worse, we prepare things for our own convenience rather than for the convenience of the reader. Of course, the effects on the reader are seldom self-evident. It is a rare reader who is aware of even having any difficulty, let alone the discrete elements which cause difficulty or errors. And few of us are aware of the research literature that explains the likely causes of such difficulty or errors. But these matters can be made clear by example. For instance, Figure 2a shows a common approach to home-made data forms. Again, research suggests that the bottom portion (Figure 2b) will be more effective, because:

> lower case lettering is easier to read than all caps;
> unnecessary lines and distractions have been removed;
> spacing and grouping help the reader keep track of where he is;
> data columns are ordered to keep the decimals in line.

The overall result is a cleaner, neater, smaller, more useable, and less error-likely format. But the preparation of such a format requires a better understanding of how people read and more careful control over the variables that make a difference in reading speed, difficulty, and error. Such control can be exercised

Figure 1. Uses of space and grouping.

```
                                    a. Usual Listing

   DS495011         Operating procedures for XM-7921, April 54
   TR652-354        Development of XM-7921, January 57
   SS01194          Preliminary design of XM-7921, revised
   SS01195          Detail design of XM-7921 Foreward Section
   SS01196          Detail design of XM-7921 Aft Section
   SS01274          Preliminary Operating procedures for XM-7921
   DS495099         Operating Procedures, Aft Section, XM-7921
   DS495100         Operating Procedures, Foreward Section, XM-7921
   DS495101         Operating Procedures, Middle Section, XM-7921
   DS495098         Maintenance Instructions, Foreward Section, XM-7921
   DS495102         Maintenance Instructions, Aft Section, XM-7921
   DS495103         Maintenance Instructions, Middle Section, XM-7921
   SP1198           Supply Program for XM-7921
   SP1199           Supply Procedures, Foreward Section, XM-7921
   SP1200           Supply Procedures, Aft Section, XM-7921
   SP1201           Supply Procedures, Middle Section, XM-7921
   DD649-0          Disposal of XM-7921
   DD649-1          Disposal of Foreward Section, XM-7921
   DD649-2          Disposal of Middle Section, XM-7921
   DD649-3          Disposal of Aft Section, XM-7921


                                    b. Improved Listing

   TR652-354     Development of XM-7921, January 57
   SS01194       Preliminary design of XM-7921 Foreward
   SS01195       Detail design of XM-7921 Foreward Section
   SS01196       Detail design of XM-7921 Aft Section
   SS01274       Preliminary Operating Procedures for XM-7921

   DS495011      Operating procedures for XM-7921, April 54
   DS495099      Operating Procedures, Foreward Section, SM-7921
   DS495100      Operating Procedures, Middle Section, XM-7921
   DS495101      Operating Procedures, Aft Section, XM-7921

   DS495098      Maintenance Instructions, Foreward Section, XM-7921
   DS495102      Maintenance Instructions, Middle Section, XM-7921
   DS495103      Maintenance Instructions, Aft Section, XM-7921

   SP1198        Supply Program for XM-7921
   SP1199        Supply Procedures, Foreward Section, XM-7921
   SP1200        Supply Procedures, Middle Section, XM-7921
   SP1201        Supply Procedures, Aft Section, XM-7921

   DD649-0       Disposal of XM-7921
   DD649-1       Disposal of Foreward Section, XM-7921
   DD649-2       Disposal of Middle Section, XM-7921
   DD649-3       Disposal of Aft Section, XM-7921
```

effectively only by those who design the forms or who prepare written material for publication.

Excellence in forms, like excellence in other things, requires specialized knowledge and attention to details. If you want good paperwork, encourage people to specialize and to familiarize themselves with the experiences and research of others. In many cases, final form design is left to the typist, who probably knows the least about it. Rarely is the form given a tryout by the intended users to see what problems there are before they are required to use it in everyday work. Even more rarely does a tryout consist of a quantitative evaluation. There is a tremendous opportunity here for quality control and human factors people, working together, to improve both production and job satisfaction by the relatively simple means of designing paperwork to better serve its users.

Figure 2. Space and other improvements in data forms.

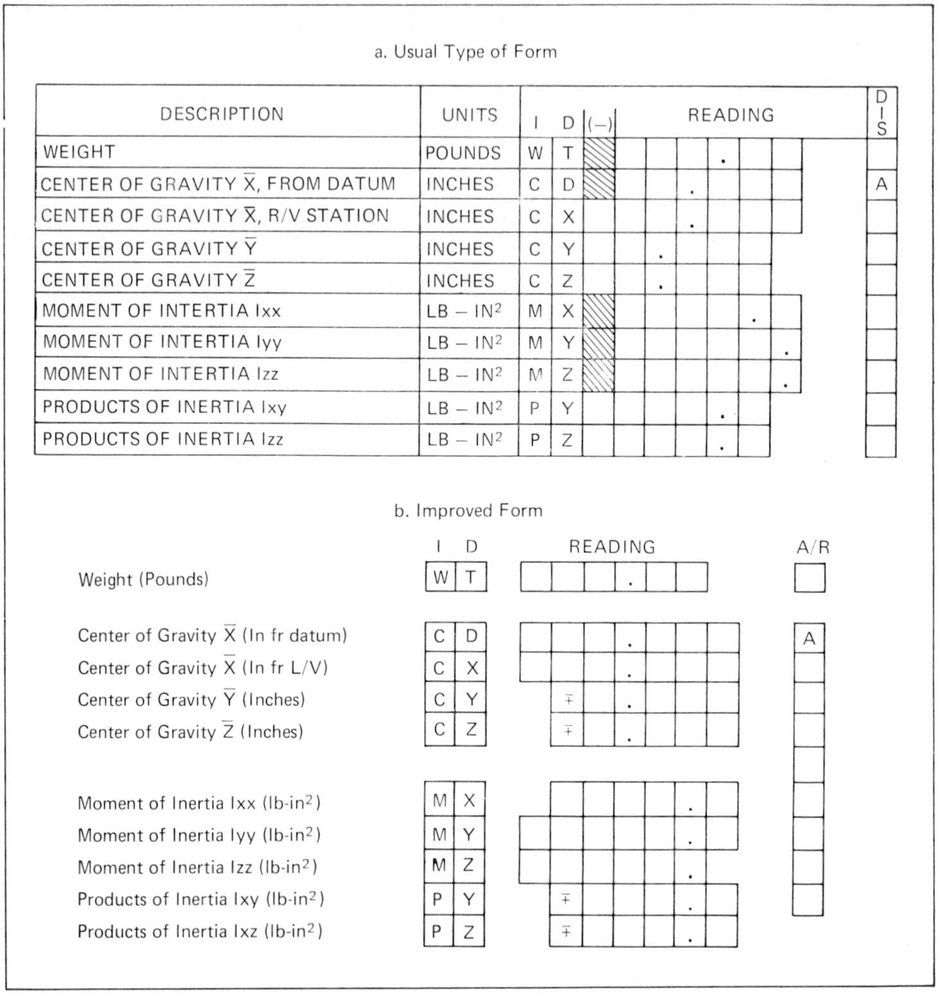

a. Usual Type of Form

DESCRIPTION	UNITS	I	D	(−)	READING	DIS
WEIGHT	POUNDS	W	T		.	
CENTER OF GRAVITY X̄, FROM DATUM	INCHES	C	D		.	A
CENTER OF GRAVITY X̄, R/V STATION	INCHES	C	X		.	
CENTER OF GRAVITY Ȳ	INCHES	C	Y		.	
CENTER OF GRAVITY Z̄	INCHES	C	Z		.	
MOMENT OF INTERTIA Ixx	LB − IN²	M	X		.	
MOMENT OF INTERTIA Iyy	LB − IN²	M	Y		.	
MOMENT OF INTERTIA Izz	LB − IN²	M	Z		.	
PRODUCTS OF INERTIA Ixy	LB − IN²	P	Y		.	
PRODUCTS OF INERTIA Izz	LB − IN²	P	Z		.	

b. Improved Form

Description	I	D	READING	A/R
Weight (Pounds)	W	T	.	
Center of Gravity X̄ (In fr datum)	C	D	.	A
Center of Gravity X̄ (In fr L/V)	C	X	.	
Center of Gravity Ȳ (Inches)	C	Y	∓ .	
Center of Gravity Z̄ (Inches)	C	Z	∓ .	
Moment of Inertia Ixx (lb-in²)	M	X	.	
Moment of Inertia Iyy (lb-in²)	M	Y	.	
Moment of Inertia Izz (lb-in²)	M	Z	.	
Products of Inertia Ixy (lb-in²)	P	Y	∓ .	
Products of Inertia Ixz (lb-in²)	P	Z	∓ .	

5. Human error rates

Our work with human error has been published quite widely, and we will not dwell on it here (see all Swain and Rigby references). But the basic concept is not being accepted or applied as widely as we had hoped. The concept is simple. If you keep records both on errors and on the opportunities for error, you have a fairly stable statistic that we call the Human Error Rate, or $HER = E/0$.

For instance, you can count the number of soldering errors and divide that by the number of joints soldered in producing those errors. In one instance, when this was done on two similar production lines, we found that the HER on one line was 10 times that on the other. Such facts can easily escape notice until they have been reduced to some basis for comparison. Error rates are excellent for comparing methods, conditions, or groups of people. In this case, the comparison led to a rather dramatic improvement in soldering techniques.

One problem in getting people to use error rates is the difficulty in acquiring denominator information. Most data systems used in quality control work that we have been exposed to do not seem to be able to relate defects to the number of units produced. We recommend this as a problem for you to ponder. We also recommend that you try using error rates to reveal differences between products or methods over time.

You can be more successful in identifying, predicting, and preventing product problems if you think of them as 'errors' rather than as 'defects'. The term 'error' tells you something about causes, whereas the term 'defect' tells you mainly about effects. Effects are important, of course, and we should only be concerned with errors that will degrade the product. But consider the differences between compiling a list of defects and compiling a list of error opportunities. The latter can give you a whole new perspective, a much more analytic perspective.

Once you start thinking in terms of human error, it becomes clear that the best approach to many, if not most, quality problems is to eliminate potential production errors by human engineering the contributing factors, e.g., the working environment and its many elements, the tools and test equipment, instructions and forms, and even product design.

One way to help others avoid or detect errors is to be more humble about ourselves as human beings, to be aware of our own limitations and frailties as well as our capabilities and strengths. If you were doing this job, any job, thousands of times, what errors would you be likely to make? Let us not 'kid' ourselves; of course you would make errors, everyone does. When it comes right down to actual measurements, the types and numbers of errors that you would make are very similar to those that anyone else would make. Think in these terms in design reviews, tests and inspections, and you will be much more effective in preventing defects. We recommend to others the routine practice we follow when evaluating a new job for the kinds of human errors to expect: perform the job yourself.

Too many times in our reviews, we base decisions on what people 'can do' rather than on what they 'will do'. We go through the procedures and conclude, 'Sure, they CAN do it with a little practice'. And they will, most of the time; but defects are caused those few times that they do it wrong or not exactly right. To understand human error, we must understand human variability. If a worker does a given task thousands of times, he will make a few errors; but he will make fewer errors under some conditions than under others. What we must do is be aware of the conditions that really make a difference in error rates.

The first and most important step in error analysis is to identify the types of errors which can occur in a given situation. This is often a sufficient step. Most serious problems prove to be cases where it never entered anyone's mind that a given error might occur until after that error had caused some catastrophe. We have, on occasion, even argued that every product design should be accompanied by a list of recognized error opportunities existing in its manufacture, its use, and its repair. This would assure that we are at least aware of these potential problems as we proceed with design acceptance, production, and marketing.

Once the potential error has been identified, our task is to convince others that the error really will occur. This is usually done most effectively by converting what knowledge we have on the subject to reasonable estimates of frequency. In practical analytic work, we are usually satisfied if two knowledgeable analysts can agree on the error rate within an order of magnitude. (Generally they agree within a factor of two, with initial disagreement only occasionally reaching a factor of five.) To repeat the prior message: the value of error analysis often lies, not so much in its accuracy, but in the identification of otherwise inconceivable events. To quote a supporter: 'This is a way of turning the rocks over to see where the worms are'.

6. Inspector accuracy

Inspectors make errors too. According to many studies inspectors detect only 30 to 90% of the existing defects, depending upon many variables (see Harris and Chaney 1969, McCornack 1961, and McKenzie 1958). We mention this because part of the reluctance to deal with human error objectively is the presumption of infallibility on the part of inspectors, supervisors, and engineers. Assemblers are looked down upon by inspectors, in many cases, partly because there is evidence (in the form of defect reports) to prove that the former make errors. We here offer some evidence that the latter make errors as well, and we have an obligation to remind others of this, especially those who seem to believe that 100% inspection means that you catch all of the defects.

One of the stronger influences on inspection accuracy is time at work. Maximum accuracy is maintained for only 15 to 30 minutes at a time under most conditions, and overall accuracy is often markedly increased by frequent rests or changes in the task. An inspector will tire more quickly when looking for fine details, or where movement is restricted, such as in using a microscope. Except where vision is impaired, as it often is with age, older and more experienced inspectors are generally more accurate than the younger and less experienced. Inspectors tend to lose objectivity where they are personally involved with assemblers and know which assembler submitted which products or will do the rework. They tend to 'find' slightly more defects in the work of those they dislike; and they find more defects when reworkers are not busy and fewer when the reworkers are overloaded. Inspectors also tend to 'censor' and 'flinch' on near-acceptable defects. As a result, an unbelievably large number of lots 'just happen' to have the maximum number of allowable defects, or more defects than we would expect statistically are just below the reject limits.

Inspectors will under-report defects where the inspector must do the rework, do a lot of paperwork, or face pressure from assemblers, supervisors, or peers. The inspector who finds more defects than other inspectors faces difficulties regardless of how accurate he is. And inspectors, like the rest of us, tend to vary or 'drift' in their interpretations of what is acceptable unless clear and constant standards are provided (e.g., samples of good and bad product characteristics).

Inspector accuracy varies with the type of defect and the total number of types of defects. In general, the larger the total number of types, the more likely it is that the inspector will concentrate on some limited number of those types and tend to overlook other types. Any human being can pay 'equal attention' to only three to nine things at a time, depending upon the discriminability and frequency of occurrence of those things. We find it difficult to give equal attention to things that are either too much alike or too different in any respect, including frequency of occurrence. Nine very easy defects or three very difficult defects are limits that can be converted into deliberate job structure, so inspectors are encouraged, aided, and forced to deal with a limited number of types of defects at a time.

In an unpublished survey of quality control practices at an industrial plant, we (Rigby) found that inspectors of one complex device were asked to use 41 defect categories in routine inspection tasks. When the defect records were analysed, it was found that of these 41 defect categories,

9 (22%) were not used at all
18 (44%) were rarely used
7 (17%) were used infrequently
7 (17%) accounted for 77% of the defects reported and one of these 7 accounted for 24% of all defects reported.

While not all of the 41 types of defects were equally likely to occur, the above distribution differed markedly from the expected distribution of defects. Data like these reinforce the principle that inspectors can pay equal attention to only a relatively few categories and that if a great many categories are truly important, then different inspectors should be given different sets of inspection criteria to inspect to.

Inspector accuracy also varies with the frequency of defects, but the effects are highly job-specific. Accuracy seems to be best when the defect rate is about 5 to 20%, but in the kinds of assemblies with which we are concerned, most defect rates are less than 0·01% for each type of defect. These rates are very difficult to detect, and inspectors deserve more help in the design phase than we give them.

Each of the above effects can be demonstrated only by carefully kept records of defect occurrence and defect detection. None of these effects is deliberate, and an inspector is seldom, if ever, aware of his biases or of changes in defect-detectability as a function of changes in working conditions or material inspected. Most would heatedly deny any assertion of bias, and this is one of the major reasons why studies of inspector accuracy are so infrequently accomplished and less frequently published. Such studies are difficult to do, and particularly difficult to do well; but if we are going to talk about human factors in quality control, we should hardly overlook this critical area.

Defects are important because they are costly. But the most serious defects are those which go undetected. Thus, the probability of detection is every bit as important as the probability of the error or defect itself. Very little research has been reported in this area of late. The old research seems to be forgotten, and there are many in industry who need to be told some of the facts about inspector accuracy and its whys and wherefores.

7. Human redundancy

One of the most effective ways to reduce the effects of human error is to employ maximum use of 'human redundancy' by having the task repeated by a second person (Swain 1970). For instance, in one study (Rigby and Edelman 1968), we found that even experienced mechanical inspectors were reaching erroneous conclusions about 15% of the time because of errors in their somewhat complicated paper-and-pencil calculations. One answer to the problem seemed obvious. Have someone check the arithmetic before announcing the findings.

In this and many other human tasks, the only way to reduce the effects of human error is to have the task done by two different people. There is nothing new about this technique. We have all used it, and we all know that it works. So why is it so difficult to get it used in daily work situations? The answer, of course, has to do with the frequency of reinforcement. We do not find errors very often, and it doesn't seem economical to do things twice until the risks get pretty high. It is particularly uneconomical if we have deluded ourselves about the risks, especially the risks for someone else. Assembly errors, for instance, pose negligible risk for those doing the assembling.

But there is more to it than that. In order to use human redundancy, we must first accept the fact that everyone makes mistakes. This is very difficult, particularly where this concept is contrary to the common desire to fix responsibility (and blame). The facts, of course, are as follows. First, everyone does make errors; second, the error rates for given actions tend to be fairly consistent; and third, given good human engineering, the error rate tends to be about one error per 1000 opportunities for simple actions like pushing the right button or reading a number correctly (Rigby 1971). Until these fundamental concepts are generally accepted, it is very unlikely that human redundancy will be used either appropriately or effectively.

The above statements imply that we will have errors in anything that people do. We must therefore judge whether the significance of the errors warrants action to detect and correct those errors at the point of occurrence. Even the most innocuous appearing action can sometimes lead to a significant defect. The only sure way is to check everything, but that is not always practical; and we must therefore determine where human redundancy can be applied most effectively. It should certainly be applied wherever errors are critical and there is no other way to detect errors.

Once we have defined a situation in which human redundancy should be used, the basic principles for that use are as follows. (1) Every human action that can be repeated without undoing what has previously been done should be repeated. (2) Every human action that cannot be repeated without undoing what has been done should be verified as it is being done. (3) Every repetition and verification should be as complete as circumstances permit; the goal is exact replication and complete independence of observations. In theory, the implementation of these principles is simple, it requires only management directive and enforcement in appropriate work situations.

8. The 'Do-Check-Do' method

Various forms of human redundancy may become appropriate as modern technology pushes the limits of human capability. For instance, as components become smaller, more numerous, more complex, and more densely packaged with more allowable substitutes, there may be more to learn and remember than one individual can handle.

Feedback and reinforcement are extremely important to human memory and related functions. We tend to forget or misremember that which is not periodically reinforced. The more immediate the reinforcement, the more effective it is, and the less drift there is in perceptual or response patterns.

With such things in mind, when we look at standard assembly procedures, we find that one person often deals with an enormous number of different things with no feedback at all. For instance, an assembler may build a printed circuit board containing 300 or more items. Any defects found in inspection may be referred to a rework group and the original assembler is not even told how many defects were made, let alone of what type or when. The only feedback received is very general, e.g., ' We're getting a lot of reversed diodes'. Such an announcement may be made to 10 or 100 people doing the same work.

An alternative feedback method, called the 'Do-Check-Do' method, was proposed by one of us (Rigby) in 1971 to solve a specific production quality control problem. Using this method, assemblers work in pairs rather than as individuals. Both work on identical assemblies, but they periodically exchange units. That is, they do some assembly; they exchange units, they check each other's work; then do more assembly, continuing where the other left off. It does not matter that one worker has done more or less than the other; in fact, there is a training advantage for the slower worker.

Each worker would have freshly in mind what he had just done, each would be particularly sensitive to any differences in the other's work, and each would continually improve and reinforce the other's understanding of what is good and what is bad. This immediate feedback should allow workers to make more and more accurate discriminations among more varied and more numerous good/bad situations.

This approach would also add another inspection, or perhaps eliminate the need for later inspection. Those who do the work are particularly adept at picking out errors because they know better than anyone else what kinds of errors occur, what to look for, and how to avoid or correct the error. Any re-work required could take place on the spot, and such problems as digging out potting could be avoided. The time required for checking would be compensated by less re-work later on. Finally, the pairing of workers could be varied to ensure standardization of quality judgements, a goal not often achieved on high-technology production lines.

Theoretically, then, the 'Do-Check-Do' method should improve productivity, product quality, and job satisfaction. But in so far as we know, it has yet to be seriously attempted as a production technique, let alone under conditions that would really prove or disprove its relative effectiveness. Of course, this is another method that requires a drastic change in the philosophy of most manufacturing organizations: from individual responsibility to team responsibility.

The team approach to productive work has been described more fully elsewhere (Swain 1972 Ch. IX, 1973a, 1973b, 1974b). We will only say here that it promises potential. The worst part of many assembly jobs is the loneliness of not being able to identify either with one's work or with one's co-workers. The psychological/sociological benefits of team work tend to make work more attractive as well as more efficient.

9. Feedback

If we want people to improve their performance, the first step is to give them clear instructions on what to do; the second step is to tell them how well they are doing it. In most work situations, we do not describe what people are to do very well, and we almost never give them meaningful feedback.

We hope you noticed the recent article by Henry Parsons (1974), in which he argues persuasively that the noted *Hawthorne Effect* was really a feedback effect. Performance kept improving in the famous Hawthorne studies (1924–32), despite variations in working conditions, because the workers knew exactly how many units they were producing. That feedback had the effect that behaviourists tell us it does. It improved performance.

If we are serious about such things as improving performance or improving worker satisfaction, we should be developing ways to provide consistent and reliable feedback. Each worker should know—not only at the end of the day, but as the day progresses—how well he is doing and how much he is producing or contributing. We don't do much of this because it is not an easy thing to do. But this is another of those things that we should be working on, and there is a lot of room for improvement. The fact that feedback is difficult for one job is no excuse for not providing good feedback on other jobs where it is less difficult.

10. Personnel selection

One of the problems in maintaining a good quality control programme is that the tasks of an inspector are often considered by him to be dull and unchallenging. Studies on vigilance (e.g., Broadbent 1971 Ch. II, O'Hanlon and McGrath 1968, and Poulton 1970 Ch. 7) clearly show that reliable monitoring performance by humans is not long sustained in essentially passive tasks where the events to be detected occur infrequently. Yet dull, monotonous inspection tasks continue to be assigned and management continues to complain about defective products getting by inspectors.

There seem to be two basic approaches to this problem. The first is to select the man to fit the job. The other is to design the job to fit the man. The first is seldom used, and could be used both much more frequently and much more effectively (Swain 1972 Ch. IV). The point can be made by an example.

Back in the early 1950's, there was a continuing problem of debris in soft drinks put out by a bottling plant of a well-known firm. This plant, which was highly automated, employed photosensors of various sorts to scan each bottle passing by on a conveyer. If debris was detected, the bottle was automatically rejected. Unfortunately, the automatic system occasionally let a bottle containing debris get by and out to a customer. Because of the nature of the debris (bugs, cigarette butts, etc.), such an occurrence could have terrible effects on public image and sales.

So the plant manager did what seemed the logical thing to do. He hired a person with good eyesight to serve as a backup to the automatic system. Can you really picture this poor person's job? Can you imagine the vigilance effect on most people? Fortunately, the manager concluded that for a dull, stupid job you should hire a dull, stupid person. And he did. Furthermore, realizing the importance of positive reinforcement, he told this person that whenever a defective bottle was found, he, the plant manager, was to be notified immediately. And when he was so notified, this plant manager would come down to personally see the defective product, congratulate the dullard, and carry out the defective bottle.

In case this sounds like a trivial thing for the plant manager to do, keep in mind, first, that the probability of the monitor finding a defective bottle was very, very low. He could go for days, working eight hours a day, without finding a bad bottle. Second, his motivation remained high. Third, his visual monitoring prevented debris from getting by due to occasional failure of the automatic monitors. Fourth, this solution reduced customer complaints practically to zero.

When this example was described by one of us (Swain) in a European seminar he annually conducts on reducing human errors in industry, one of the attendees became more and more agitated. At the finish of the story, he blurted out, 'That's it; that solves my problem'. It turned out that in his chemical plant, employing exotic fuels and materials, there was a requirement for a similar type of visual inspection. Despite the fact that consequences of inspection errors were very costly, and the job was obviously important, no one would stay on this job for very long. This man went away from the seminar convinced that he had a solution for at least one serious quality problem in a high technology industry.

Dullness, of course, is not really an inherent quality of a job. It is defined by a person's perception of the job. So, for jobs that most people might call dull, we should be able to find matching people; or at least, we should be able to select those most likely to do the best work with the fewest errors. Yet, scientific personnel selection is seldom given a sincere trial.

The current emphasis on equal employment and affirmative action, and the court cases growing out of the conflict here, will be extremely beneficial to our nation and its future. In order to prove that we do not discriminate, we are going to have to do a much better job of describing what people do and how well they do it. And we are going to have to develop and use meaningful measurements of job performance and job satisfaction. For an excellent summary of the problems and research in this area see O'Toole (1973).

11. Monitoring people

Many problems of quality arise because we have no way to monitor the state of the individual worker. From motivation research, we know that people do best that which they want to do. It follows that they do not do well on things that they do not want to do; yet, few work situations allow a worker to refuse to do something that he does not feel up to. We must somehow develop the attitude that, first, it is good to pay attention to how people feel and, second, it is all right for people to not work, or to not do certain work, when they do not feel like it. This concept is subject to misinterpretation and abuse, but it deserves consideration, as suggested by the following example.

At a certain plant, the item being produced was a very expensive military item which would be employed only in the case of actual hostilities. Since the item was far too complex for routine testing, periodically a sample was returned to the manufacturer for disassembly and inspection. One such sample revealed production-initiated defects which made the unit inoperable. The defects were so serious that doubt was cast on other units containing the same parts. Yet, physical inspection of all units was virtually impossible.

When one of us (Swain) was called in to work with quality control specialists in the firm which built the units, a thorough search of original inspection records revealed an interesting fact. The known defective parts had all been passed by *one* inspector. Further inquiry revealed that shortly after he had missed these particular defects, this inspector had been reassigned. Of course, no one knew at that time that he had made some errors; he was removed because he had become so despondent over the death of his wife that supervision decided he was in no condition to bear the responsibility of his usual job. This action had just not been taken soon enough.

Given this information, the sample of units to be reinspected was reduced to a more manageable size, namely, those units inspected by this particular inspector during that particular period. This example illustrates one advantage of knowing which inspector inspected which units. But of greater importance is the general principle that we must be alert to human conditions which foster a high degree of error. Once we accept the concept, the critical conditions are fairly apparent, but management policies and administrative mechanisms are necessary to inaugurate the exceptions that must be made. We might also wonder if there are not better ways to record what goes on during the work day so that we will be more sensitive to such problems and more likely to take effective action in appropriate cases.

We spend millions on elaborate systems to check on the status of our machinery, but pay little attention to the status of a worker unless he happens to stay home or faint on the job. Yet, there is growing evidence that a sizable portion of our society may be categorized as the walking wounded. They are ill. The list includes alcoholics and drug addicts and those with ulcers, hypertension, hypoglycaemia, and a long list of chronic ailments. It also includes those who are temporarily disturbed by recent deaths, divorces, hangovers, and the various influenzas, ailments, and traumas imposed by a rapidly changing and fast-moving society and the frailty of mortal form.

On any given day in any given facility, office, or production line it has been estimated that at least 20% of those present are sufficiently below standard operating levels that they should definitely not do some things, and perhaps should not work at all (Rappaport 1974). They should most certainly not be asked to do things where errors can be critical. And it is for such reason that 'human reliability' programmes have focused on aircraft and missile launch crews, whose errors are so obviously critical.

There are problems in monitoring people. If we depend on other people to do the monitoring (e.g., supervisors or company doctor), we may find it very difficult to be thorough. We may also run into 'big brothers' and 'big brother reactions'. The only practical solution is to develop a working atmosphere in which the individual worker can honestly monitor himself, without penalty. (Who is going to tell you he is sick, if you'll send him home without pay?) It has only been in recent years that we have accepted fairly uniform allowances for illness (usually six days a year off without penalty). It is time to consider similar allowances for these similar reasons. It is time, at least, that we begin to amass the data that would define and support those allowances and related work limits, however few or many, large or small, those might be.

12. Task variation

Our society is so accustomed to the eight-hour job that it is difficult for people to recognize the advantages of task variation, that is, of deliberately changing the worker's task periodically so that the individual is not required to perform longer than people can perform that task effectively. The following example illustrates a general principle that has many practical applications.

This example involves another vigilance problem in inspection. The product was a low pass filter to attenuate radio-frequency energy from exterior sources. The inspection process included visual study of X-ray pictures of parts in the finished unit. Twenty-five units appeared on one X-ray picture in one orientation, and another picture showed the same units in a different orientation.

The problem was that the defect rate after inspection varied from 3% to 5%, a variation that was far in excess of what could be tolerated for the explosive item that the filter was to protect. When asked to investigate the problem, the first question we (Swain) asked was: 'How long are the inspectors kept busy evaluating the X-ray pictures? The question was based on the well-known principle that in a passive monitoring task with a low-signal frequency, inspection accuracy begins to fall off rapidly after some 15 to 30 minutes.

The answer to the question was 'We don't produce enough items to keep the inspectors busy all the time, so we save up until we get enough X-ray pictures to keep them busy for a full day. It's more efficient that way'. This is not an uncommon mistake.

After explaining how the vigilance effect might well be responsible for the poor inspection, we recommended that the inspectors should inspect for no more than one-half hour at a time, and then do something else (but not another inspection task) for an hour before returning to the inspection task for another half-hour period. The company representative thought this arrangement was inefficient, but in view of the problem and the pressure to solve it, he promised to implement the recommendation for a trial period.

The company also decided to change the inspection procedure in another way. During the first half-hour, each inspector examined one of the two different views of the same 25 items. When one decided that he had a defect, he would check his decision with the other. After this inspection, both inspectors did other jobs for an hour, then returned to another one-half hour inspection period. This time, they exchanged the pictures they had inspected during the first period.

As expected, the number of uncaught defects was greatly reduced. How much of the reduction was due to shortening the inspection period could not be determined because the inspectors were also working as a team ('Do-Check-Do') and were inspecting each picture twice (human redundancy). Both of these changes would also assist detection. If we want to minimize the effects of human error, it is well to use every trick we can think of, especially when the benefits more than outweigh the costs. In this instance, the new procedure was permanently adopted.

The above was a fairly straightforward application of knowledge regarding the use of a work/rest cycle appropriate for tasks susceptible to the vigilance effect. Much of the boredom, error, and dissatisfaction attending routine work, however, can be alleviated by comparable means. The old saying, 'A change is as good as a rest' contains much truth, and we would do well to develop specific recommendations for implementing task variation in our respective facilities. It would also be well to test such applications with performance data. Again, the most effective measurement to use will probably be the human error rate.

13. A concluding comment

For the most part, these are thoughts and experiences that we have not published elsewhere. We therefore appreciate this opportunity to bring them before our colleagues for whatever interest value they may have. We are sincere in our belief that each topic deserves the joint cooperation of quality control and human factors specialists (ergonomists).

Some human-factor applications to quality control in a high technology industry

This work was supported by the United States Atomic Energy Commision. Elements of this paper were also presented (by Rigby) to a joint conference of the Bay Area sections of the Human Factors Society and the American Society for Quality Control, on 29–30 March 1974, at the Marina Hotel, Burlingame, California.

References

BROADBENT, D. E., 1971, *Decision and Stress*. (London: ACADEMIC PRESS.)

CORNOG, D. Y., and ROSE, F. C., 1967, *Legibility of Alphanumeric Characters and Symbols, II. A Reference Handbook*. (National Bureau of Standards Miscellaneous Publication No. 262–2, Washington D.C.)

FINLEY, B. H., WEBSTER, R. G., and SWAIN, A. D., 1974, Reduction of human errors in field test programs. *Human Factors*, **16**, 215–222.

HARRIS, D. H., and CHANEY, F. B., 1969, *Human Factors in Quality Assurance*. (New York: JOHN WILEY.)

McCORNACK, R. L., 1961, *Inspector Accuracy: A Study of the Literature*. (SCTM–53–61(14), Sandia Laboratories, Albuquerque, New Mexico.)

McKENZIE, R. M., 1958, On the accuracy of inspectors. *Ergonomics*, **1**, 258–272.

O'HANLON, J. F., and McGRATH, J. J., 1968, *Studies of Human Vigilance, an Omnibus of Technical Reports*. (Goleta, California: HUMAN FACTORS RESEARCH INC.).

O'TOOLE, J., *et al*., 1973, *Work in America*. (Cambridge, Mass.: MASSACHUSETTS INSTITUTE OF TECHNOLOGY PRESS.)

PARSONS, H. M., 1974, What happened at Hawthorne. *Science*, **183**, 922–931.

POULTON, E. C., 1970, *Environment and Human Efficiency*. (Springfield, Illinois: CHARLES C. THOMAS.)

RAPPAPORT, M., 1974, Psychological factors in quality interference. *Unpublished paper at Quality Week Conference, 29–30 March, Bay Area sections of Human Factors Society and the American Society for Quality Control, Burlingame, California.*

RIGBY, L. V., 1971, The nature of human error. *Chemical Technology*, 712–718.

RIGBY, L.V., 1973, Why do people drop things. *Quality Progress*, September, 16–19.

RIGBY, L. V., and EDELMAN, D. A., 1968, A predictive scale of aircraft emergencies. *Human Factors*, **10**, 475–482.

RIGBY, L. V., and SWAIN, A. D., 1968, Effects of assembly error on product acceptability and reliability. In *Proceedings of the 7th Annual Reliability and Maintainability Conference*. (New York: AMERICAN SOCIETY OF MECHANICAL ENGINEERS.) Pp. 3–12 to 3–19.

SWAIN, A. D., 1963, *A Method for Performing a Human Factors Reliability Analysis*. (Monograph SCR–685, Sandia Laboratories, Albuquerque, New Mexico.)

SWAIN, A. D., 1970, Development of a human error rate data bank. In *Proceedings of U.S. Navy Human Reliability Workshop*. (Edited by J. P. JENKINS.) (NAVAL SHIP SYSTEMS COMMAND, WASHINGTON D.C.) Pp. 112–148.

SWAIN, A. D., 1972, *Design Techniques for Improving Human Performance in Production*. (London: INDUSTRIAL & COMMERCIAL TECHNIQUES LTD.)

SWAIN, A. D., 1973a, Design of industrial jobs a worker can and will do. *Human Factors*, **15**, 129–136.

SWAIN, A. D., 1973b, An error-cause removal program for industry. *Human Factors*, **15**, 207–221.

SWAIN, A. D., 1974a, Short cuts in human reliability analysis. In *General Techniques in Systems Reliability Assessment*. (Edited by E. J. HENLEY and J. W. LYNN.) (The Netherlands: NOORDHOFF INTERNATIONAL.) Pp. 407–424.

SWAIN, A. D., 1974b, *The Human Element in Systems Safety: A Guide for Modern Management*. (London: INDUSTRIAL & COMMERCIAL TECHNIQUES LTD.)

The analysis of an inspection task in the steel industry

J. Moraal

1. Introduction
This case study relates to an inspection task at the Royal Dutch Steelworks ('Hoogovens') in the Netherlands and was supported financially by the European Coal and Steel Community at Luxembourg. It concerns the visual inspection of the surfaces of sheets of steel. Although automatic *detection* devices for surface defects on steel sheets are being developed, it is certain that automation of the *interpretation* of a number of these defects will be very difficult. The reason is that in addition to the intensity of the defects, the main dimension for automatic detection at this moment, other dimensions may enter into conclusions about the quality level of the product: e.g. size, colour, number, combination of the defect with others, etc. It therefore is expected that in the future visual inspection in the industry will remain an important activity except for more rough or highly routine inspections.

2. The task
The task of the quality controller is to divide the products into two categories: those which meet the specified standards and those which do not. The 'standard' is defined by tolerance limits on deviations and defects in the product, such as deviations in dimensions or weight, damage, surface finish etc. Figure 1 gives an idea of the work station.

Figure 1. Diagram of the sheet inspector's work-place.

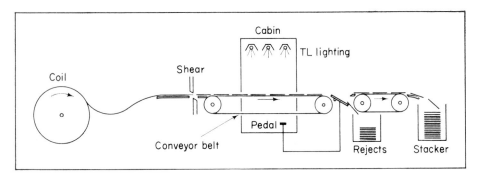

A coil of cold rolled steel is unwound and cut into sheets on a cut-up line. The sheets pass along a conveyor belt. An inspector is situated in a cabin along-side the conveyor belt. He examines the dimensions and surfaces of the sheets. When he detects surface defects such that the sheets are unacceptable to the customer he rejects these sheets by actuating a pedal to open a selection gate in the conveyor belt. The good sheets are conveyed to the end of the conveyor belt where they are piled up. Afterwards they are packed and taken away for dispatch to the customer.

The speed of the conveyor belt during inspection varies from 200 to 400 feet per minute. The speed is controlled not by the inspector but by a line operator who is in contact with the inspector by an intercom. Dimensions of the sheets vary within the following limits: length 0·5 to 4 m; width 0·56 to 2·5 m. The smallest diameter of the defects is about 1 mm². The total number of different defects exceeds fifty; however, about nine defects are responsible for about 75% of the rejections. When a coil has been cut-up and inspected the inspector fills in an inspection report on which he records an approximate breakdown of detected defect types from memory.

3. Methodology used in the study

Figure 2 presents diagrammatically the main types of research methods in the study of man-machine systems.

The several types of research methods vary from observations and measurements on the real world to purely mathematical models. In this order there is an increase in the ease and flexibility of carrying out tests while at the same time a decrease in the fidelity of test conditions.

Figure 2. Research methods in the study of man-machine systems (after Bernotat 1974).

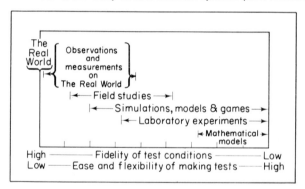

Tasks in the real world situation most of the time are very complex and are influenced by a multitude of social and technical factors, many of them being unpredictable or even unknown. For example, in this study, if one wanted to study systematically fault detection performance as a function of line speed or quality requirements one must know beforehand what types of defects and how many of each type are present on the sheets. This would have been practically impossible because inspection takes place immediately after the sheets are cut from the coil. Re-inspection of the sheets would have been a very costly procedure and would have demanded special arrangements. So observations and measurements in the real world situation are by definition of an explorative nature and can only give indirect performance measures.

Laboratory experiments, on the other hand, are always abstractions because it is impossible to duplicate all real world factors in the laboratory. Although laboratory experiments give more direct performance measures, related to variations in one factor while keeping all others under control, the results sometimes may be of low relevance in predicting actual task performance.

Three methods were used in the study reported here. The first two of these methods may be regarded as observations in the 'real world': an analysis of data from inspection reports filled in by the inspectors themselves, and an analysis of eye movements during actual inspection. The third used the laboratory where two experiments took place, one in which inspection performance of static and dynamic patterns was compared and one in which the effect of sleep deprivation on inspection performance was investigated.

4. Analysis of inspection reports

4.1. *Method*

Inspection reports of ten subjects were analyzed in order to get an impression of the magnitude of individual differences in overall rejection percentages. Data were based on periods of three months for four successive years: the first quarters of 1965 to 1968. Periods of three months allow one to overcome variations in rejection percentages due to an uneven distribution of type of material or required quality levels. Recording of the breakdown of detected defect types on the inspection reports also made it possible to look for individual differences in rejection percentages for several defects separately. It was hypothesized that if rank correlations of rejection percentages between successive years turned out to be significant this would support the evidence for 'inspector-bound' factors in inspection.

4.2. *Results*

Table 1 gives rejection percentages over periods of three months (first quarters of 1966 and 1967) for sheets of first and second quality level. The figures show substantial differences between inspectors.

Table 1. Rejected sheets of first and second quality steel over the first three months of 1966 and 1967. Figures are mean percentages per month and per inspector.

Inspector	Rejection percentage 1st quality		Rejection percentage 2nd quality	
	1966	1967	1966	1967
1	14·2	18·4	5·9	6·5
2	11·2	10·4	5·7	5·0
3	11·2	10·8	4·7	4·2
4	11·1	14·5	4·7	8·3
5	10·3	10·1	6·0	6·0
6	9·5	11·5	4·1	5·0
7	11·5	12·9	4·6	5·3
8	7·4	9·9	3·2	3·6
9	12·4	13·3	8·2	5·7
10	9·6	9·6	5·1	4·8

Rank correlations (Spearman) were computed between rejection percentages for three pairs of successive years (from 1965 to 1968) for the same ten inspectors. For the results see Table 2.

Table 2. Rank correlations between successive years for rejection percentages of first and second quality steel. Figures are based on data of ten inspectors for the first three months of each year.

	Rank correlations		
	1965/1966	1966/1967	1967/1968
Rejection percentage			
—1st quality	0·66	0·71	0·81
—2nd quality	0·80	0·53	0·89

Limits of significance: 0·56 (5%) and 0·74 (1%).

The results of Table 2 show that there is considerable consistency in rejection percentage per inspector over several years. If an inspector tends to reject a large number of sheets, this seems to remain fairly constant from year to year. Both the results of Table 1 and Table 2 support the evidence for inspector-bound, or personal factors, influencing inspection performance. This may be due to factors such as differences in eye sight, or individual differences in working methods or strategy, e.g. in applying quality standards, which in turn may be caused by insufficient knowledge, inadequate training or personality factors such as risk-taking behaviour.

The figures relate only to overall rejection percentages. Table 3, however, shows the results for only three types of defects (F, O and B). For every defect the two out of ten inspectors who showed the highest (H) and the two who showed the lowest (L) rejection percentages are indicated.

Table 3. Inspectors with a high (H) or low (L) rejection percentage for three types of defect.

Inspector	Rejections in 1966 (1st three months)			Rejections in 1967 (1st three months)		
	F	O	B	F	O	B
1						L
2		H				
3		L	H		L	
4	L		H			H
5				L		
6	H		L	H		L
7						
8		L			L	
9	H	H	L	H	H	
10	L			L		H

The results of Table 3 also show a large consistency over the two years. Inspectors 6 and 9 for example show a high rejection percentage for defect F, while inspector 10 shows a low percentage. These results may indicate differences in opinion among inspectors with regard to quality standards to be applied for different defect types.

5. Analysis of eye movements

5.1. *Method*

The analysis of eye movements during the study has been reported by Sanders and Hoogenboom (1969),

To record eye movements they used the method of cornea-reflection: in which a small ray of red light is directed towards the right eye and the quantity of reflected light, determined by the state of the iris, is received by a photo-electric cell. By continuous recording of the quantity of reflected light on a recorder the horizontal eye movements are reproduced. Simultaneously an electro-magnetic detection device under the conveyor belt recorded the passage of the sheets and a photo-electric cell above the reject pile recorded the rejected sheets. Figure 3 gives an example of the recordings obtained by this method.

Figure 3. Horizontal eye movements during on-line inspection of steel sheets (1 × 1 m; 300 f.p.m.); one sheet rejected.

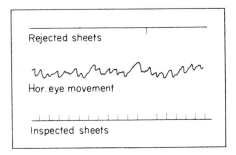

The central graph of Figure 3 represents horizontal eye movements. The lower graph shows the moment of passage of a sheet while the upper graph indicates rejected sheets: one in this case. Figure 4 shows what may happen when a series of six consecutive sheets is rejected.

Figure 4. Horizontal eye movements during on-line inspection of steel sheets (1 × 1 m; 300 f.p.m.); six sheets rejected.

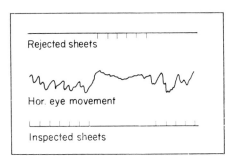

Steel inspection

The eye movements are built up from several components. In Figure 5 these components are presented schematically.

Figure 5. Schematic diagram of components of horizontal eye movements; time criteria based on data in the literature.

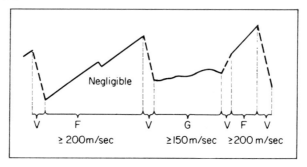

Sanders and Hoogenboom (*op. cit.*) distinguished the following components.

Fixations: resulting from following the sheet by fixating a given point on it; the angle of movement is proportional to the speed of the sheet;

Saccadic movements: rapid movements closely linked with the passage of a new sheet and which may arise from a shift of attention to the next sheet or may take place within the inspection of a sheet;

Sliding movements: in which the eye shows a strong tendency to remain stationary for a certain length of time during which the inspector allows the sheets to 'slide' past him.

In order to neutralize inspectors' head movements as far as possible, the light and photo-electric cell were fixed around the head. In addition, inspectors were instructed to move their head as little as possible during their inspection work and they followed this instruction carefully. Measurements were taken for three conveyor belt speeds, 200, 250 and 300 f.p.m. (about 1, 1·25 and 1·50 metres per second) and for sheets measuring about 1×1 m and 2×1 m. Thus six conditions in all were examined.

Ten inspectors acted as test subjects and the measurements lasted for a period corresponding to the passage of about 150 to 200 sheets.

5.2. *Results*

The rapid saccadic movements which are closely related to the passage of the sheets, gave an impression of the extent to which inspectors make checks of individual sheets. There is some evidence for a possible distinction between two types of strategy: in one of them the inspector attempts to make as many checks as possible on a sheet-by-sheet basis while in the other there is more of a tendency for the inspector to keep his eyes fixed resulting in very few eye movements.

Figure 6 illustrates these two possible strategies.

No significant differences could be found between the two strategies with regard to speed or size of the sheets. This means that inspection on a sheet-by-sheet basis is at least possible for speeds up to 300 f.p.m. However, with this speed the inspectors do not always have optimal time at their disposal for the inspection of every sheet. The inspection times per sheet vary due to the fact

Figure 6. Two patterns of horizontal eye movements during on-line inspection of sheet steel; upper curve many eye movements; lower curve few eye movements.

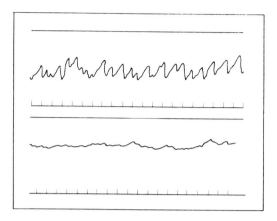

that if an inspector is in doubt he will tend to examine a sheet for a greater length of time at the expense of the time for the next sheet(s). Very often this also happens when the inspector wants to reject a sheet and follows it until the selection gate is reached (see Figures 3 and 4).

In Table 4 the mean and variance of the inspection times for the six test conditions are given. Inspection times are not exactly twice as long for 2 m sheets compared with 1 m sheets because the sheet dimensions are only approximations.

Table 4. Inspection time per sheet; means and standard deviations (in milliseconds).

Sheet length		Speed (in feet/minute)		
		300	250	200
1 m sheets	M	620	770	920
	σ	135	145	175
2 m sheets	M	1190	1420	1730
	σ	175	235	300

The mean values of inspection time per sheet increase linearly with speed. It seems that on the average a sheet is inspected for a slightly shorter period than the theoretical duration with regard to the length of the sheet: about 600 msec at 300 f.p.m. and 900 msec at 200 f.p.m. In general, a simple reaction which is not accompanied by a search procedure takes about 400 msec. This time increases rapidly when difficulty in discrimination and spatial uncertainty increase. Therefore 600 msec must be regarded as a very short inspection time for defects which are difficult to detect. Put another way, a speed of 300 f.p.m. may be too fast for optimal inspection performance. The rapid increase of the variance in inspection times shows that at a lower speed inspectors examine some sheets for a much longer time than other sheets for which a minimum permissible time still remains. However, if inspectors also do this at high speeds the time available for a number of sheets is definitely too short. Only for surface defects which tend to arrive in batches will this cause no serious problems because after the first decision has been made, the time for repeated decisions can be shorter.

No evidence exists as to whether the different strategies are typical for individual inspectors; all inspectors seem to use both strategies alternatively. However, the general tendency seems to be to follow the sheets by fixating them at certain places. For a more detailed analysis of the three types of eye movements, fixations, saccadic movements and 'sliding movements' (stationary eye), Sanders and Hoogenboom (*op. cit.*) took samples of eye movements of all inspectors in which clear transitions (saccadic movements) between successive sheets could be observed. Table 5 shows in mean percentages the time devoted to each of the three types of eye movements.

Table 5. Mean percentages of inspection time per sheet with reference to the different patterns of eye movement.

Pattern of eye movement			Speed (in feet/minute)		
			300	250	200
Fixations	(F)	: 1 m sheets	58	59	48
		2 m sheets	42	45	45
Saccadic movements	(V)	: 1 m sheets	8	11	9
		2 m sheets	13	12	11
Eye stationary	(G)	: 1 m sheets	34	30	43
		2 m sheets	45	43	44

It seems from this data that inspectors keep their eyes stationary for a substantial part of the sheet inspection cycle, about 35–45% of the time. Saccadic movements take only a small percentage of the time which is obviously due to the fact that they only serve in reorientation of the line of sight. There are no significant differences with either speed or length of the sheets. Table 6 shows the mean absolute frequency of the three types of eye movements per sheet.

Table 6. Mean absolute values for the different patterns of eye movement per sheet as a function of the conveyor speed and length of sheets (←→ = significant difference).

Pattern of eye movement		Speed (in feet/minute)		
		300	250	200
Fixations	(F)			
1 m sheets		1·0	1·2	1·3 ↑
2 m sheets		1·3 ←→	1·7 ←→	1·9 ↓
Saccadic movements	(V)			
1 m sheets		↑ 0·4	0·7 ↑	0·7 ↑
2 m sheets		↓ 1·0 ←→	1·3 ↓ ←→	1·8 ↓
Eye stationary	(G)			
1 m sheets		↑ 0·7 ←→	0·9 ←→	1·1
2 m sheets		↓ 1·4	1·2	1·4

The absolute values of Table 6 show a relation between speed and length of the sheets. When speed is reduced one may expect inspection to become easier and this may be reflected by an increase in the number of fixations per sheet. For some inspectors this may go together with a reduction in the mean duration of the fixations.

6. Laboratory experiments

Formerly no systematic training was given to the inspectors. In developing ideas on training procedures it soon became evident that on-line training with moving sheets would be practically impossible because of lack of time when one wants to examine a special defect more carefully. So, acquiring knowledge on surface defects was only possible when presenting sheets statically. In this respect the question arose of how much transfer could be expected from training with statically presented sheets to real inspection of moving sheets. To find an answer the task was simulated in the laboratory (Bosma 1969).

6.1. *Experiment* 1

Subjects were seated in semi-darkness at a distance of about 4 m from a screen on which 'sheets' were projected either by film or slides. Instead of photographs of real sheets random optical noise patterns of black and white dots were used to overcome the problem of dust on the film which might have been seen as defects on the 'sheet' when projected. The patterns measured 1×1 m. Some of them contained a 'defect' while others did not. The 'defect' in this case was a small black triangle merging into the noise pattern and therefore relatively difficult to detect. The position of the triangle on the pattern was randomized throughout. The patterns were presented in two ways: statically and dynamically. In the static presentation one pattern was shown for 0·5 sec. In total 200 patterns were presented consecutively with an interval between successive patterns of 2 sec. In the dynamic presentation the patterns moved in a series of 200 or 500 from right to left across the screen at a constant speed of 200 f.p.m. The space between successive patterns was about 15 cm. About three patterns were visible simultaneously according to the dimensions of the screen. In this way a fairly good analogy of the real task was achieved. In both presentations 20% of the patterns were 'defective', i.e., contained a triangle.

Subjects were asked to respond when they detected a triangle: in the case of static presentation by saying 'yes', in the case of dynamic presentation by reading out a number placed directly above the pattern. Five groups of six subjects each participated in the experiment: four training groups and one control group having no special training. Of the training groups, two were trained statically; they had to judge series of 200 static patterns: one group with defect indication (by an arrow) and the other group without. The other two training groups were trained dynamically by judging a series of 300 patterns; again one group with defect indication and the other group without.

Performance was tested before the first and after each of three training sessions. In these four test sessions subjects had to inspect a series of 200 static and a series of 500 dynamic patterns presented in a balanced order. It therefore became possible to get an impression of transfer of training from static to static and dynamic presentation as well as from dynamic to dynamic and static presentation. In addition, the effects of training *per se* could be evaluated by comparing the results of the training groups with those of the control group.

6.1.1. *Results of Experiment* 1

Results were analyzed by analysis of variance (randomized group design). When the results of all groups were combined, performance improved significantly with test sessions ($p < 0.01$). Improvement of performance on the static test was highly significant for both the two statically trained groups ($p < 0.01$); of the two dynamically trained groups only the group with defect indication during training showed a significant effect ($p < 0.05$). In contrast, improvement of performance on the dynamic test was significant for both of the two dynamically trained groups ($p < 0.01$ for training with defect indication and $p < 0.05$ for training without defect indication); of the two statically trained groups, the group with defect indication during training showed a significant effect ($p < 0.05$). However, the differences in improvement of performance between all five groups turned out not to be significant on the static as well as on the dynamic tests.

With regard to our practical situation the conclusion was that although subjects seem to benefit a great deal from repeated exposure of dynamic test patterns in looking for defects (which is a kind of experience of the task) training with static patterns may still improve performance, be it not significantly.

The overall differences in performance between static and dynamic tests were highly significant ($p < 0.001$). For this result see Figure 7; as a measure of

Figure 7. Performance differences in visual inspection of static and dynamic patterns; mean *d'* values of 30 subjects.

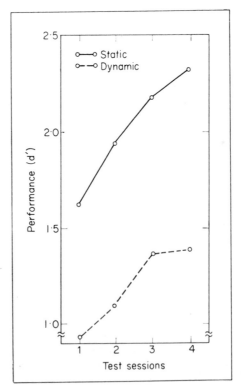

performance d' was used, being a weighted score of correct detections ('hits') and incorrect detections ('false alarms').

6.2. *Experiment 2*

Since inspection tasks often have to be performed at a machine-paced rate and require concentration for long periods, they are often of a monotonous character. The possibility that defects may be overlooked increases as concentration falls off or motivation diminishes. A second experiment investigated how performance in inspecting static or dynamic patterns may become less effective as a result of decreased motivation. A condition of diminished motivation was created by keeping subjects deprived of sleep for 24 hours.

Two groups of eight subjects each (students) took part in the experiment. Performance of the subjects was measured on series of 200 static and 500 dynamic patterns. The first two test trials were given on the afternoon of one day and the following three on the morning of the next day. One group had normal sleep during the night, while the other group was kept awake.

6.2.1. *Results of Experiment 2*

For the results of Experiment 2 see Figure 8. Again, a significant difference between performance on static and dynamic patterns was found ($p < 0.01$) and also an improvement of performance with test sessions ($p < 0.01$). A significant

Figure 8. Results of visual inspection of static and dynamic patterns for groups with and without 24 hours of sleep deprivation. Normal sleep (eight hours) or sleep deprivation took place between test sessions two and three; mean d' values of eight subjects.

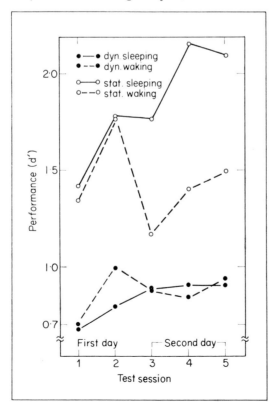

interaction was found between static or dynamic presentation of patterns and sleep deprivation. Inspection of static patterns was greatly impaired after subjects were deprived of sleep while the inspection of dynamic patterns did not seem to be influenced by this factor. The difference in performance between both kinds of inspection remained significant. This result may be of great importance in designing inspection stations.

7. Discussion

The results on individual differences in rejection percentages (overall as well as for individual defects) are in agreement with data in the literature (McKenzie and Pugh 1957, McKenzie 1958, Thomas and Seaborne 1961, Murrell 1965). These differences may be due to several factors. Two are mentioned by Mobbs (1970) in his study of sheet inspection; namely, differences in eyesight and 'drifting standards'. Other factors may be added: a bias of inspectors towards certain defects sometimes due to a misinterpretation of customer requirements, working up to a percentage of rejection which may be classified as a social-psychological factor which together with risk-taking capabilities may result in 'being on the safe side'; faulty identification of defects and classifying two (or more) as one; and last but not least, inadequate training or no training at all. As in Mobbs' study (*op. cit.*) no relation could be found between rejection percentages and customer complaints so that inspectors with a low rejection percentage seem to be more efficient than others. In trying to make these differences smaller several measures could be used. A regular check of relevant eye sight parameters (acuity, accommodation etc.) is recommended. Furthermore, a regular calibration of inspectors is very necessary to overcome the problem of drifting standards. Indexed books of photographs of defects in several grades and the customer requirements available at the inspection stations may be of great help. Training of inspectors is essential, preliminary as well as repeated training. During training sessions attention has to be paid to quality of material, to number and type of defects, how they originate, their possible size, colour etc., and to customer requirements. Training must be evaluated by letting inspectors judge under standardized conditions samples of small sheets (for example 20×30 cm) with and without defects. The results of these inspections will throw light upon the time needed for detection (whether any defect is present or not), the time needed for identifications (what kind of defect), faulty naming or misclassification of the defect, defects which cannot be distinguished from each other, the application of standards and so on. In this way, special problems will emerge and attention can be paid to them.

Finally, in bringing quality control tasks in general more into line with human capabilities the number of quality levels on which absolute quality judgments have to be based must certainly not exceed six or seven, but four or five is to be preferred (Miller 1956).

The question arises as to what types of eye movements really can be distinguished. In two Japanese studies on the analysis of eye movements which included sheet inspection (Shimabukuro *et al.* 1967, Ohtani 1971) only two types of eye movements were distinguished, following and saccadic. The former are smooth movements, occurring when looking at a moving object and during which in the case of following steel sheets any anomalies can be sensed. Saccadic movements are jerky rotations the function of which is to change the fixation point and thus to enlarge the area of inspection. Neither author mentions 'sliding movements' during which inspectors keep their eyes stationary as was found in our study. This may be due to differences in methods of analysis used. Instead of the cornea-reflection method which only records horizontal eye movements, the Japanese authors used electro-oculography (EOG) by which it is also possible to record vertical eye movements. So the 'sliding movements' in the study of Sanders and Hoogenboom (*op. cit.*) may be an artifact of the method used during which vertical eye movements may have taken place. However, the analysis by Shimabukuro is only based on horizontal eye movements which are in fact the most frequent when observing objects moving horizontally in the visual field. Furthermore, the findings of Sanders and Hoogenboom (*op. cit.*) are supported by those of Mobbs (*op. cit.*) who filmed eye movements during inspection, the results of which show that ' either the inspector scans continuously from side to side across the sheets or he looks fixedly at the centre line of the sheets, moving his eyes from this position only when he wishes to look at a blemish on the sheet seen in the periphery of his visual field'. Subjective statements by all the inspectors in Sanders' and Hoogenboom's study also supported this. It would be rather arbitrary to state that there are two entirely different strategies because all inspectors use both methods of inspection, even during the inspection of one sheet. So the most frequently occurring strategy might be one as described in Mobbs' terms. It may be hypothesized that a relation exists between the number of following movements and the total number of blots, lines, colours etc. to be seen on the sheets, only a minority of which have to be classified as defects. So, the more irregular the surface in appearance the more 'anchor points' for inspection and consequently the more following movements. This hypothesis was supported strongly by the results of the laboratory studies using optical noise patterns. These patterns are very irregular by nature and indeed only following and saccadic movements were found when eye movements were recorded. In this respect one may doubt whether the number of following movements (fixations) may serve as a relevant criterion in assessing inspection accuracy as in fact Shimabukuro *et al.* (*op. cit.*) used them. Ohtani (*op. cit.*) used a simulated inspection as a criterion measure, namely searching for incomplete rings (Landolt's rings) from a series of complete rings of the same size, again a very irregular field, which may fall short in relevance to the real task. All studies mentioned are in agreement on the duration of fixations: between about 330 to 450 msec. Both Japanese studies regard a line speed of about 300 f.p.m. as becoming critical for optimal inspection: Shimabukuro *et al.* (*op. cit.*) because the number of following movements decreases in the range of 250 to 300 f.p.m. and Ohtani (*op. cit.*) because this speed is related to missing critical objects (incomplete rings) in the simulated study. Sanders and Hoogenboom (*op. cit.*) also regard 300 f.p.m. as a critical speed because time for inspection given the variability in inspection times, is nearly enough for making at least one fixation (following movement) per sheet (about 300 msec). However, even this will not always be a necessity, for example when defects arrive in batches a peripheral glimpse will suffice. For defects new in appearance, however, a line speed of 300 f.p.m. may be regarded as becoming critical.

The difference between inspection of static and dynamic patterns, the former leading to much better performance, is supported by a study by Williges and Streeter (1971). Normally, sleep deprivation does not have an effect on very

Q

short-duration tasks. Inspection of 200 static patterns in about 8·5 min., however, was greatly impaired by sleep deprivation. As stated earlier one may profit by presenting products for inspection statically but one has to take great care that the task does not become monotonous. Inspection of dynamic patterns allows for a variability in inspection times per pattern. The fall-off in performance on inspection of static patterns may be caused by the temporally rigid manner of presentation: 0·5 sec for inspection of each pattern with intervals of 2 sec between patterns. Even in cases of static presentation inspector-paced inspection is to be preferred as a means of overcoming monotony and decreased motivation.

References

BERNOTAT, R., 1974, Overview of human engineering. *Paper presented at a NATO course on human engineering, held in Wiesbaden, April 3.*

BOSMA, R. P., 1969, *Een Ontwerp van een Simulator voor Kwaliteitsinspectie van Staalplaten.* (Report Nr. IZF 1969–C7, Institute for Perception, Soesterberg, the Netherlands.)

LEPLAT, J., and CHESNAIS, M., 1973, Le contrôle des produits industriels: travaux actuels et perspectives d'études. *Travail Humain,* **36,** 75–94.

McKENZIE, R. M., 1958, On the accuracy of inspectors. *Ergonomics,* **1,** 258–272.

McKENZIE, R. M., and PUGH, D. S., 1957, Some human aspects of inspection. *Journal of the Institute of Production Engineers,* **36,** 378–386.

MILLER, G. A , 1956, The magical number seven, plus or minus two: some limits on our capacity for processing information. *Psychological Review,* **63,** 81–97.

MOBBS, R. F., 1970, *The Visual Inspection of Sheet Steel Surfaces on High-Speed Cut-Up Lines.* (Report Nr. OR/HF/29/70, BISRA, London.)

MURRELL, K. F. H., 1965, *Ergonomics; Man in His Working Environment.* (London: CHAPMAN AND HALL.)

OHTANI, A., 1971, An analysis of eye movements during a visual task. In *Methodology in Human Fatigue Assessment.* (Edited by K. HASHIMOTO, K. KOGI and E. GRANDJEAN.) (London: TAYLOR & FRANCIS.) Pp. 167–174.

SANDERS, A. F., and HOOGENBOOM, W., 1969, *Oogbewegingen bij Controle van Staalplaten.* (Report Nr. IZF 1969–C8, Institute for Perception, Soesterberg, the Netherlands.)

SHIMABUKURO, M., HAYASHI, E., HIRANO, S., and OGAWARA, Y., 1967, Study on line inspection from a human engineering viewpoint. (In Japanese.) *Technical Report of Fuji Steel,* **16,** 29–35.

THOMAS, L. F., and SEABORNE, A. E. M., 1961, The socio-technical context of industrial inspection. *Occupational Psychology,* **35,** 36–44.

WILLIGES, R. C., and STREETER, H., 1971, Display characteristics in inspection tasks. *Journal of Applied Psychology,* **55,** 123–125.

Ergonomics in inspection tasks in the food industry

D. Elizabeth Chapman and M. A. Sinclair

1. Introduction

Over a period of several years a number of studies have been carried out by the Department of Ergonomics and Cybernetics, Loughborough University, on inspection tasks within industry. Two of these studies were concerned with the food industry and are reported here in the hope that they will be of interest in view of their relevance both to recent findings and to the companies involved. The first project was carried out in the baking industry, and was concerned with the inspection of mass-produced jam tarts. The second project was concerned with the inspection of chicken carcasses in a poultry packing station.

For reasons of brevity, and because this paper is concerned with applications, much of the experimental detail has been omitted.

2. Inspection of jam tarts

2.1. *The job and its analysis*

Given the nature of the product, it is obvious that quality control is of prime importance to the company concerned. Investigations on the jam tart production line had shown that at a particular point on the production line, just after the tarts had been formed from dough and prior to baking, 4% of the tarts were defective. An inspection site had been installed at this point, which resulted in the detection of 77% of the faulty tarts, equivalent to 3% of production. These defects could be recycled into the production line. The remaining 1% of production which was defective represented true wastage. The company was keen to reduce this percentage, as it represented a loss of approximately one million tarts per annum.

The inspection site was at the output side of two forming machines at the beginning of the main conveyor belts (see Figure 1). The machines produced tarts positioned six abreast on a linen conveyor belt. These were transferred to wire mesh frames on another conveyor belt. The tarts were arranged on each frame in six rows of eight tarts, and the frames were 2·5 cms apart. At each inspection site there were three operators, each of whom, at any one time, performed one of the following tasks:

inspecting the products, and removing defects from wire frames on the production line;

replacing the defects with good products, and carrying out general maintenance at the site;

feeding wire frames, on which the tarts were arrayed, into the forming machine.

Figure 1. Showing a plan to the production line for jam tarts.

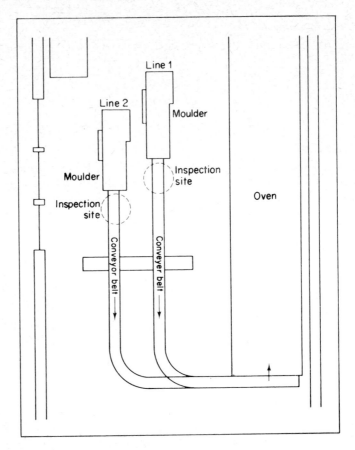

The tasks were rotated among the three operators at half-hour intervals. This was because the third task was tiring to the inspectors since the design of the work station imposed considerable static loading on the muscles of arm and shoulder girdle, as the wire frames had to be loaded above shoulder height. This however had the fortunate side-effect that the operator who was inspecting the tarts was not exposed to a perceptually demanding task for very long.

The defects for which the operators were inspecting were as follows.

(1) 'Crimp' defects. The crimp is the crenellated edge to the tart. A crimp defect is defined as occurring when one or more of the crenellations is missing.

(2) Loss-of-edge defects. These occur when part of the wall of the tart is detached, or split sufficiently to allow a jam filling to leak out.

(3) Base defects. These occur when there is a split or hole in the base of the tart.

(4) Contamination defects. These are caused by detritus associated with production lines, such as oil, grease spots, burnt crumbs, metal fragments, etc., getting into the product.

(5) Transference defects. These occur as tarts are passed from the forming conveyor belt to the wire frames on the transfer conveyor belt, and were caused by the join in the forming conveyor belt buckling the tarts.

In the experiments described later only two classes of defects were used, for the following reasons. Transference defects were entirely cyclic in their occurrence, and hence predictable, and therefore required minimal inspection for detection. Contamination defects were extremely rare in occurrence and could therefore be ignored. In the period of time over which the experiments were conducted the number of such contamination defects occurring was approximately three in one million tarts.

It was decided that the first two categories of faults should be combined, as there was no clear operational distinction between them, and thus only two categories of defects remained, (*a*) loss of edge/crimp defects, and (*b*) base defects.

A study of the inspection site revealed the following. If it is accepted that the visual angle for maximum acuity is 1–1·5° from the central line of sight and acuity falls off to 50% at a visual angle of 5° (e.g. Weymouth 1958) then this inspection task may be classified as one which is quite difficult for the following reasons. As the tarts reach the inspection zone each subtended a visual angle of between 3° and 5°, depending upon its position on the wire frame. Owing to problems of contrast, it may be assumed that it was difficult to detect faults by peripheral vision outside the central 5° cone. Consequently, it can be assumed that in order to detect a fault on a tart it was necessary for the inspector to look directly at it. If it is accepted that the mean fixation time is 0·3 seconds (e.g. Gould and Schaffer 1965), then to inspect one frame of 48 tarts, using one fixation per tart, would have required 15 seconds, including saccades, from tart to tart. This excludes the time necessary to reject a defective tart. The speed of the production line was such that one frame of tarts passed the inspection zone every 7·5 seconds, which was half the time required according to the above considerations.

Furthermore, the speed of the production line was such that the tarts were moving past at a mean angular speed of 7° per second, relative to the inspectors' eyes. If it is assumed that for faults to be detected the eyes must be fixated on the tarts, then the eyes had to perform pursuit tracking at this speed. According to the literature (Williams and Borow 1963) the eyes can only pursue targets and remain fixated on them up to angular velocities of about 8° per second. In other words, the inspection task was near the limits of human ability in respect of visual pursuit.

It seemed likely from the above considerations that inspection performance would be impaired. This view was reinforced when the physical environment of the inspection site was examined. Conditions were less than ideal as reference to Table 1 shows.

It will be seen from this table that the inspectors were subject to heat stress, that they were working in very poor illumination conditions, and that the noise levels were close to damage risk criteria (Glorig *et al.* 1962).

The questions the research set out to answer were as follows.

Is the inspectors' task possible?

If so, what is the effect of time available for inspection upon inspection performance?

What is the effect upon inspection performance of movement of the tarts?

It was impossible to carry out investigations on the production line itself, as the company quite reasonably would not accept the loss of production involved. A simulation of the task was created in another part of the bakery, using a variable-speed conveyor belt situated by an oven, as in the on-line site. However, neither the physical environment nor the visual environment was as close a match to the on-line site as might be desired, as can be seen from Table 1.

Table 1. Environmental conditions of experimental site and on-line site.

Factor	Experimental site	On-line site	
		1st Line	*2nd Line*
Environment	73–80° C.E.T.	75–82° C.E.T.	
Illumination:			
Vertical	527 Lux	86 Lux	161 Lux
Horizontal	581 Lux	226 Lux	560 Lux
Noise:			
A scale	76–78 db.	86–88 db.	
B scale	78–81 db.	86–88 db.	
C scale	77–81 db.	87–90 db.	
Peaks	94 db.	94 db.	
Conveyor:	Canvas	Link chain	
Height	0·91 metres	0·92 metres	0·76 metres
Width	0·71 metres	0·64 metres	0·64 metres
Speed	0·045–0·135 metres/sec	0·09 metres/sec	
Viewing distances	0·68–0·96 metres	0·68–0·94 metres	

A test batch of frames of tarts containing a known number of defects were created, to provide the simulated task. It was arranged that the six inspectors working on the production line would be released one at a time to perform the task at the experimental site. Two quality control inspectors who had had much experience on the line were also used as subjects, making a total of eight subjects in all. These subjects were used for all the experiments discussed below.

Three experiments were carried out to investigate the above questions. Experiment I tested the hypothesis that the inspectors could detect faults on tarts to a high level of accuracy consistently (i.e. on two occasions) under conditions where (*a*) there was almost no visual search element in the inspection task, and (*b*) where unlimited time was available. This experiment was designed to determine if, under the most favourable conditions of 'no search' and 'unlimited time', the inspection task was within the capability of the operators. Experiment II tested the same hypothesis as Experiment I, except that a significant search element was added to the inspection task. The analysis of the results of these two experiments showed that the inspectors could perform the task to a high level of accuracy, that they were consistent in detection rates for defective tarts on two separate occasions, and that the introduction of the visual search element did not produce any significant alteration to performance levels. Tables 2 and 3 show the results of Experiments I and II. For brevity, the detailed analysis has been omitted.

Table 2. Hit rates (%), correlation coefficients (Kendall's τ) and related normal deviates for all subjects against the standard for Experiment I (no search) for the detection of faults.

	1st sessions			2nd session			Between sessions	
	H.R.	τ	Z	H.R.	τ	Z	τ	Z
A	97	0·95	9·3	94	0·86	8·3	0·81	7·9
B	87	0·88	8·6	90	0·90	8·6	0·88	8·5
C	84	0·84	8·2	77	0·84	8·2	0·92	8·9
D	84	0·83	8·0	77	0·77	7·4	0·82	8·0
E	87	0·88	8·5	81	0·72	6·9	0·69	6·7
F	87	0·86	8·6	65	0·72	6·9	0·75	7·3
G	94	0·72	7·9	90	0·90	8·6	0·70	6·8
H	97	0·91	8·6	94	0·86	8·3	0·82	8·0

Table 3. Hit rates (%) correlation coefficients (Kendall's τ), and related normal deviates for all subjects against the standard for Experiment II (search) for the detection of faults.

	1st session			2nd session			Between sessions	
	H.R.	τ	Z	H.R.	τ	Z	τ	Z
A	93	0·95	9·0	96	0·92	8·8	0·90	8·6
B	93	0·95	9·0	93	0·92	8·7	0·86	8·1
C	89	0·92	8·7	79	0·79	7·5	0·83	7·9
D	96	0·98	9·2	86	0·87	8·2	0·92	8·8
E	93	0·85	8·0	86	0·73	6·9	0·63	5·9
F	89	0·92	8·7	79	0·85	8·1	0·83	7·9
G	93	0·92	8·7	82	0·63	5·9	0·52	4·8
H	100	0·86	8·1	89	0·72	6·8	0·72	6·8

Experiment III tested the hypothesis that speed of movement of the tarts, and changing the presentation time for the tarts, had no effect either individually or conjointly upon the performance of the inspectors.

It was decided that in view of restrictions in the time available within which to carry out the experiment only two movement conditions and three presentation times should be considered, and that only two test sessions per subject should be used.

The conditions chosen were:

tarts moving, and tarts stationary;

long presentation time—22·5 secs. per frame;

medium presentation time—15 secs. per frame;

short presentation time—7·5 secs. per frame.

When the tarts were moving the above presentation times involved the frames passing inspectors at angular velocities of 3°, 5·5° and 8° per second respectively. The particular presentation times given above were chosen because:

the conveyor belt at the experiment site would run no slower than 25 secs. per frame,

15 secs. represents the minimum 'required' calculated inspection time,

7·5 secs. was the available time for inspection on the actual production line.

Each subject therefore performed twelve inspections, divided into two test sessions of six inspection conditions each, as shown below:

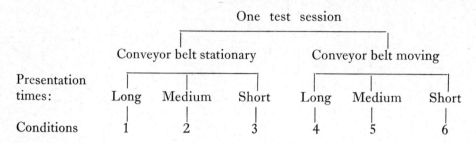

A total of 12 frames of tarts were used for each condition. The first and last frames of tarts were used as 'lead-in' and 'lead-out' frames respectively, and only the 10 frames in the middle were used for the actual test. This meant that for each condition 480 tarts were inspected. Seventy-three tarts were defective, equivalent to 15·2%; three times as many as on the production line. This was necessary to give an adequate measure of the number of correct detections of faults. The number of faults was varied from frame to frame. Care was taken to exclude 'borderline faults', so that all faults, once detected, were obvious as such.

It was thought that an analysis based on the theory of signal detection (TSD) would be advantageous, following the work of Swets (1964), Wallack and Adams (1969), Sheehan and Drury (1970), and Drury and Addison (1973). As these authors have pointed out, however, there are fairly strict assumptions underlying TSD which are not known to be followed in industrial situations such as the one described. Nevertheless, when checks are made on the results, they seem to be in basic agreement with predictions from the theory (see, for example, Drury and Addison 1973).

For the purposes of this analysis the data were summarized to show the following.

(*a*) The number of faults detected by each subject on each frame for each condition for each session.

(*b*) The number of false detections made by each subject on each frame for each condition for each session.

(*c*) The proportion of correct rejections (hit rate), the proportion of false detections (false alarm rate), the *discriminability* of the defects (d') and the subjective *criterion* adopted (β) according to the theory of signal detection. These values were calculated from (*a*) and (*b*) and were aggregated over the frames presented, for each condition for each subject for each session, since the data were considered to be too sparse to allow a frame-by-frame analysis.

Four analyses of variance were carried out examining the effects of subjects (8), sessions (2), movement (2), and presentation time (3) upon:

the hit rate (HR);

the false alarm rate (FAR);

d';

β.

These analyses are presented in Tables 4, 6, 9 and 11. In all cases the analysis of variance is assumed to be Model I. This is because the eight subjects were the entire population of inspectors, the two sessions used were thought to be representative of all sessions in view of the overlearned nature of the task, there are only two movement conditions available, and the presentation times used were the three levels of this factor thought to be of interest. Consequently all main factor and interaction mean squares are evaluated against the 'residual' mean square.

2.2. *Discussion*

Considering each table in turn, the following points can be made:

Table 4. Analysis of variance for hit rate.

Source	SSQ	dF	MSQ	F	Significance
Between subjects	0·2255	7	0·0322	4·7660	$p<0·001$
Within subjects	1·3687	88	0·0155		
Movement (M)	0·0000	1	0·0000	0·0013	NS
Presentation time (T)	0·7918	2	0·3959	58·5556	$p<0·001$
Session (S)	0·0052	1	0·0052	0·7765	NS
M×T	0·0008	2	0·0004	0·0615	NS
M×S	0·0012	1	0·0012	0·1887	NS
T×S	0·0234	2	0·0117	1·7341	NS
M×T×S	0·0253	2	0·0126	1·8746	NS
Residual	0·5206	77	0·0067		
Total	1·5942	95			

Table 5. Effect of presentation time on the hit rate, expressed as the fraction of defective tarts detected. (No. of readings=32.)

Presentation time	22·5 secs	15 secs	7·5 secs
Mean hit rate	0·85	0·77	0·63
S.E. mean	0·014	0·014	0·014

Hit rate

Considering Tables 4 and 5, as might be expected, the hit rate drops as presentation time decreases, in a linear fashion. It is worth noting that the hit rate at the on-line presentation time of 7·5 seconds was 63%; somewhat lower than that on the production line. This may have been due to the comparatively high proportion of defective tarts in the test batch, coupled with the supposed inability of the inspectors to search the entire frame adequately in the time available.

False alarm rate

Turning to Tables 6, 7 and 8 it will be seen that the false alarm rate increased as movement was introduced, but decreased as presentation time was reduced. The latter effect appears to be linear. An interesting point that emerges is that given that the pay-off matrix is the same for the experimental and on-line sites,

Table 6. Analysis of variance for false alarm rate.

Source	SSQ	dF	MSQ	F	Significance
Between subjects	0·0037	7	0·0005	4·651	$p<0·001$
Within subjects	0·0119	88	0·0001		
Movement (M)	0·0004	1	0·0004	4·026	$0·01<p<0·05$
Presentation time (T)	0·0018	2	0·0009	7·930	$0·001<p<0·01$
Session (S)	0·0001	1	0·0001	0·447	NS
M × T	0·0003	2	0·0002	1·421	NS
M × S	0·0001	1	0·0001	0·447	NS
T × S	0·0001	2	0·0001	0·947	NS
M × T × S	0·0003	2	0·0001	1·351	NS
Residual	0·0088	77	0·0001		
Total	0·0156	95			

Table 7. Effect of presentation time on the false alarm rate, expressed as the fraction of good tarts rejected. (No. of readings=32.)

Presentation time	22·5 secs	15 secs	7·5 secs
Mean false alarm rate	0·025	0·020	0·015
S.E. mean	0·0018	0·0018	0·0018

Table 8. Effect of movement on the false alarm rate, expressed as the fraction of good tarts rejected. (No. of readings=48.)

Movement conditions	Moving	Stationary
Mean false alarm rate	0·022	0·018
S.E. mean	0·0045	0·0045

the false alarm rate of 1·5% for the on-line presentation time of 7·5 seconds indicates that on the production line more good tarts are rejected by the inspectors than defective tarts are missed; this effect becomes even more pronounced as presentation time increases. If the above assumption is true, it was fortunate for the company that the rejects at this stage could be reprocessed, thus minimising the financial cost. It indicates the necessity of inspection at a point where remedial action can be taken (if inspection is considered to be important), and also the need to pay particular attention to the position of β, the *criterion* measure and its precursors, namely the training of inspectors in what constitutes a defect, the reward structure created for the inspectors, and the feedback of performance to the inspectors. This is also discussed in the paper by Sheehan and Drury (1971).

The value of d'

It will be seen from Tables 9 and 10 that reducing the presentation time caused a reduction in d'. Inspection of Table 11 reveals that the reduction followed a curvilinear form. The mean d' of 3·09 for a presentation time of 22·5 seconds is worthy of comment. This value of d' means that there was still a considerable

Table 9. Analysis of variance for d'.

Source	SSQ	dF	MSQ	F	Significance
Between subjects	4·5969	7	0·6567	5·9340	$p < 0·001$
Within subjects	13·8092	88	0·1569		
Movement (M)	0·0675	1	0·0675	0·6106	NS
Presentation time (T)	4·7959	2	2·3979	21·6680	$p < 0·001$
Session (S)	0·1738	1	0·1738	1·5706	NS
M × T	0·0607	2	0·0303	0·2746	NS
M × S	0·0144	1	0·0144	0·1304	NS
T × S	0·1193	2	0·0596	0·5394	NS
M × T × S	0·0559	2	0·0279	0·2527	NS
Residual	8·5214	77	0·1106		
Total	18·4061				

Table 10. Effect of presentation time on d'. (No. of readings = 32.)

Presentation time	22·5 secs	15 secs	7·5 secs
Mean d'	3·09	2·91	2·56
S.E. mean	0·059	0·059	0·059

overlap of the noise, and a signal-plus-noise distributions (if, for example, β is positioned centrally, 6% of each distribution is cut off). This has considerable implications for the production line; if a reduction in the overlap is desired, then a fairly large increase in d' is indicated, which would appear to be achieved only at the cost of a large increase in presentation time, and consequent slowing of the production line. Alternatively the inspection task could be redesigned. The paper by Drury (1973a) expands this point.

Table 11. Analysis of variance for β.

Source	SSQ	dF	MSQ	F	Significance
Between subjects	157·7799	7	22·5399	2·2960	$0·01 < p < 0·05$
Within subjects	1487·4361	88	16·9026		
Movement (M)	28·2837	1	28·2837	2·8813	NS
Presentation time (T)	598·5489	2	299·2744	30·4874	$p < 0·001$
Session (S)	1·5708	1	1·5708	0·1600	NS
M × T	56·9888	2	28·4944	2·9028	NS
M × S	6·1448	1	6·1448	0·6260	NS
T × S	4·1457	2	2·0723	0·2111	NS
M × T × S	35·8965	2	17·9482	1·8284	NS
Residual	755·8565	77	9·8163		
Total	1645·2161				

Table 12. Effect of presentation time on β. (No. of readings = 32.)

Presentation time	22·5 secs	15 secs.	7·5 secs
Mean β	5·25	7·44	11·29
S.E. mean	0·55	0·55	0·55

The value of β

Once again, presentation time is significant in its effects (see Tables 11 and 12); in this case a reduction of presentation time produced a more conservative effect (in other words, the inspectors were less likely to reject defective tarts as presentation time was reduced). The consequences of shifts in β have been indicated in the discussion of the false alarm rate earlier.

The overall conclusions from analyses of variance may be summarised as follows:

For all four tables, there are significant differences between inspectors, a standard finding in human factors experiments. It is interesting to compare this result to that of Drury and Addison (1973), in that it indicates the importance of feedback of performance to inspectors in minimising the variability within the group.

Secondly, movement exerts no significant effect upon performance (except when considered in terms of FAR). The relative unimportance of the speeds used in this experiment concur with the findings of Williams and Borow (1963).

Thirdly, it is evident that presentation time exerts a significant effect upon performance whether measured in terms of HR, FAR, d' or $β$. This factor has been discussed in detail by Drury (1973a) and therefore will not be elaborated further here.

Fourthly, all four analyses indicate that performance in session 1 is effectively the same as in session 2. This means that for each performance measure there is no evidence of learning or decrement between sessions. In addition it indirectly supports the application of the TSD model to such an industrial situation; one of the consequences of the TSD model is that under comparable inspection conditions and the same pay-off matrix, d' and $β$ should be constant; the results agree with this.

2.3. Recommendations

The recommendations made to the company included the following.

(a) The characteristics of the environment should be altered, to improve the working conditions.

(b) In particular, the lighting conditions should be improved. The improvements should be directional lighting, to improve contrast, and considerably increased illuminance, to comply with the I.E.S. Code. The intention here would be to increase the signal strength, and consequently improve d'.

(c) Since slowing down the production line was not considered possible, it was suggested that the number of inspectors should be doubled, so that each inspector inspected only half the frame of tarts, thus doubling the presentation time.

These recommendations were accepted by the company. However, during the course of the study it had been discovered that the building in which the production line was situated was in a state of near collapse. The company therefore decided that in the interim period before the line was moved, only temporary solutions should be adopted. These entailed fitting fluorescent tubes above the inspection site, and doubling the number of inspectors. It is understood that the effect of these improvements was to increase the detection rate by approximately 5%.

2.4. *Conclusion*

Perhaps the most important thing to emerge from this study is the usefulness of the theory of signal detection in industrial inspection situations both from a theoretical and a practical point of view. The theoretical value lies in the insights it provides into an inspection task, and the practical value arises from the fact that it allows economic justification for the application of ergonomics to inspection, and the relative ease with which recommendations for improvement can be derived.

3. Inspection of chicken carcasses

3.1. *The job and its analysis*

The management of the company concerned were well aware of the inspection problems with which they were faced, in that about 15% of birds on the production line studied were rejects. They were also aware that a number of these rejects found their way on to the market. The company was concerned to improve inspection performance, to prevent such occurrences. During preliminary studies, it appeared likely that two factors in particular might be contributing to lowered inspection performance; the rate at which the birds passed the inspection point, and the duration of shifts for the inspectors. Accordingly, these factors were investigated.

Of the poultry handled at the packing station, 30% is eviscerated and blast-frozen as 'oven-ready' poultry, while the remainder is packed for the 'fresh' market. This project was concerned solely with the inspection of the 'fresh' poultry. These birds, after being killed, plucked, cooled and trussed are received into the packing shed (see Figure 2). The birds are then placed on a conveyor belt in individual trays and pass in front of an inspection site before falling into weighing pans on a rotary belt. It is this inspection site, occupied by a single inspector, with which the study was concerned.

The birds are then tipped into bins according to their weights and from there are packed in boxes. These boxes are sent to a final grader whose responsibility it is to ensure that no sub-standard birds are allowed to reach the customer, before being lidded and stored in a refrigerator until required for despatch.

The speed of the process in the packing shed is controlled by a switch placed slightly above the inspector's head. It can be set at any one of twelve positions so that the birds can pass the inspector at rates ranging from 1,080 units per hour to 4,680 units per hour. However, this is usually fixed by the foreman at a rate dictated by the speed of processing in the killing shed, which can reach 6,000 birds per hour.

The operatives in the packing shed are able to perform most of the different tasks involved in the whole process and are interchanged in an attempt to alleviate the boredom which most of them seem to experience. Only four of the employees however had been trained to perform the inspection task, of which two were experienced. Apart from meal breaks, at infrequent intervals throughout the day the inspector is relieved and given alternative work, but at present this is only when he or she asks to be taken off or when required to perform another task.

241

Figure 2. Production processes in the poultry packing station.

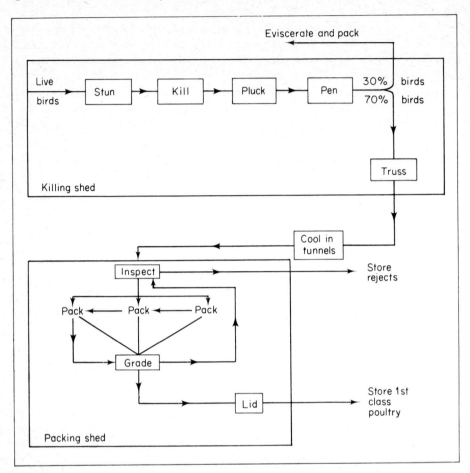

The job entails removing from the belt any sub-standard bird. The defects for which the operatives are inspecting are largely marks incurred during processing, bruising and broken limbs. These down-graded birds are subsumed into three classes according to the extent of bruising, etc. The inspector lays the second-class birds on a line moving in front of him at eye-level. The other two grades he places in separate bins behind him. These rejected birds are packed separately. The rejects the inspector misses are picked up by the packers and the grader further down the packing line. These birds are all sent back to the inspector by the grader who puts them back on the line going past the inspector between the trays. These the inspector disposes of as he did the other rejects.

The task is made increasingly difficult for the inspector since the inspection standards are not rigidly defined. They are determined to some extent by the state of the market. Birds which may well be down-graded on a day when poultry is not selling well could conceivably be allowed through as first class when there is a good market. Consequently, the foreman has to define the standards for the inspectors daily.

Two conclusions were immediately drawn concerning the inspection task; firstly that the speed at which the conveyor belt was moving was likely to overload the inspector, and secondly that it was unlikely that the inspector would maintain efficiency for any great length of time—certainly not for the eight-hour period that was then expected.

Accordingly, the investigation was designed in two parts; an initial investigation to discover whether the task was in fact possible, and a second experiment to investigate the importance of presentation time and shift duration on performance.

Originally it had been intended that the four inspectors (the entire population) should be used in this experiment. However, two of these were not available at the time, and the investigation had to proceed with the remaining two, who as it happens were the most experienced inspectors. The small number of subjects is regrettable, as it constrains the generality of the findings.

The preliminary investigation was carried out to ascertain whether or not the inspectors could perform the task in the normal environment of the packing shed, but with unlimited time for the inspection of each carcass. The results of the experiment are shown in Table 13. The investigation established that under the condition of 'no time stress' the job was in fact possible.

Table 13. Subject's classification of birds against the quality control standards, with correlation coefficients.

		Subject 1 Standards			
		Perfect		Reject Grades	
		1	2	3	4
Perfect	1	10	4		
Judgement of Subject 1	2		6		
	3			10	
Reject grades	4				10

Spearman Rank Correlation Coefficient $r_s = 0.99$ significant at the 0.001 level.

		Subject 2 Standards			
		Perfect		Reject grades	
		1	2	3	4
Perfect	1	10	5		
Judgement of Subject 2	2		5		
	3			10	
Reject grades	4				10

Spearman Rank Correlation Coefficient $r_s = 0.99$ significant at the 0.001 level.

243

Since the only errors in classification occurred between first- and second-grade birds, it was decided that the three sub-standard grades should be grouped into the one class of 'reject' birds to simplify the analysis.

Having established that the task was possible, the second phase of the investigation was begun. This was carried out on the production line during normal working hours, to obtain as close a match as possible with operational conditions.

The object of this investigation was to assess the effects of speed of working, and time since commencing work, on inspection performance. Initially, it was hoped that the theory of signal detection could be used to analyse the data, as in the previous study. If this were to be the case, then four sets of figures would be required:

number of good items accepted;

number of good items rejected;

number of faulty items accepted;

number of faulty items rejected.

However, when attempts were made to collect the data it became apparent that no good items were rejected. This was totally unexpected in the light of other research carried out in this field. It would appear though, from the results of the preliminary investigation, that the inspectors tend to be conservative in their attitude and let a bad bird through as good rather than reject a good bird. In addition, there may have been some social pressures operating in that the day-to-day variation in the quality standards removed the notion of absolute, immutable standards, and consequently border-line decisions might be seen as one person's judgement against another on a single day's standards, and in such circumstances it is quite understandable that no-one would be prepared to argue with the inspector's decision. Because of this absence of good items rejected, TSD could not be used, and it was decided that the percentage of sub-standard birds correctly rejected by the inspectors (the hit rate) would be taken as a measure of their performance. The data was obtained by re-inspection, by doubling up the graders at the end of the packing line and by random checks on boxes of birds in the warehouse.

The experiment was carried out in the normal working environment of the inspection situation in the packing shed. An environmental survey was carried out revealing an air temperature of 14·4°C. The noise level was 79 dbA. The level of illuminance at the inspection surface was 705 lux, which is the level recommended for inspection of meat (I.E.S. Code 1973).

The same two inspectors who had participated in the preliminary investigation were assessed in this major study. Each subject carried out the task as explained above, taking the sub-standard birds from the line, grading them, and disposing of them according to grade. All missed rejects were sent back to the inspector between the trays on the inspection line, of which he disposed as he had the other rejects.

After some initial investigation, it was found that it took approximately five minutes for a bird to pass the inspector and reach the grader. Consequently for five minutes the number of rejects taken out by the inspector could be counted as well, as the grader sent them back. This also enabled a check to be made on the variability of the hourly and daily defect rate; this was found to average 15%, the range being 13–15%.

The performance of the inspector was assessed for nine periods of five minutes at five minute intervals. This procedure was carried out twice for each inspector at seven different speeds for periods of 1·5 hours. The speeds ranged from 2,700 birds per hour to 4,680 per hour. These speeds were within the range commonly encountered on the production line. Most of the time, however, the line was run at full speed.

It was noticed that when the inspector first knew his performance was being assessed he redoubled his efforts. One inspector remarked that he would be glad when the assessment was over because he did not like having to work so hard—an explicit statement of the problem also discussed by Fraser (1950), Bergum and Lehr (1963) and Ware *et al.* (1964). Since it was impossible to appraise performance without the inspector's knowledge, in an attempt to alleviate this it became necessary to measure performance continuously throughout the day over a period of six weeks. The results used in the analysis are for the last two weeks, and are the figures obtained only between 10 a.m. and 1 p.m. The time of day was kept constant to eliminate any effects circadian variation might have on performance under the various experimental conditions. It was also ensured that the period over which each subject was monitored was his first spell of inspection for the day.

The results were analysed by analysis of variance as shown in Table 14. Model 1 was assumed, since the subjects were the entire population of subjects, and all other factors were fixed. Consequently all main factor and interaction mean squares were tested against the residual mean square.

Graphs of the two significant terms are shown in Figures 3 and 4. In Figure 4 'speed' has been transformed into presentation time per bird. Thus 0·77 seconds represents a speed of 4,680 birds per hour, etc.

Table 14. Analyses of variance for hit rate for the inspection of chicken carcasses.

Source	SSQ	dF	MSQ	F	Significance
Between subjects	2·3	1	2·3	0·01	NS
Trials (T)	117·5	1	117·5	0·71	NS
Speeds (S)	6043·5	6	1007·2	6·05	$P<0·01$
Periods (P)	4992·2	8	631·5	3·79	$P<0·01$
T×S	762·8	6	127·1	0·76	NS
T×P	1416·3	8	177·0	1·06	NS
S×P	5104·4	48	106·3	0·64	NS
T×S×P	2243·3	48	46·7	0·28	NS
Residual	20829·1	125	166·6		
Total	41511·4	252			

3.2. Discussion and conclusions

From the analysis of variance (Table 14) it can be seen that there is no significant difference between the two inspectors, and similarly, performance in the first trial was ostensibly the same as in the second. This would suggest that the two inspectors have reached such a level of training that their performance is consistent. This supports Drury and Addison's suggestion (1973) that knowledge of

Figure 3. Graph showing the mean change in performance over the length of the shift.

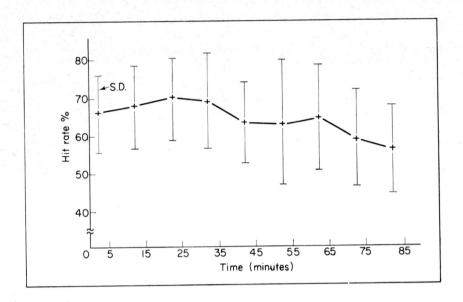

Figure 4. Graph showing the mean change in performance with change in presentation time.

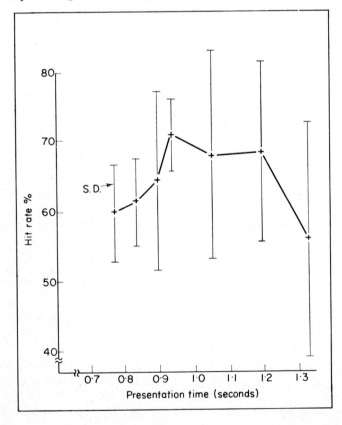

results in an inspection situation would enable the inspectors correctly to adjust their criteria, thus minimising variability. In this study, the inspectors received feedback continually and so this result seems to add weight to their theory. However, since only two subjects were involved in the experiment, perhaps the findings should not be interpreted too rigidly.

It was found that performance was significantly affected by the length of time the inspectors had spent at the task during a shift. Figure 3 shows that their performance steadily improved over the first 25 minutes and then began to deteriorate. Following Mackworth (1950), it is suggested that this corresponds to a brief 'warm-up' period at the beginning of a shift.

The analysis reveals a steady decrease in performance after the first 25 minutes for the rest of the 1·5 hour period. Closer examination of the hit rates by means of orthogonal contrasts reveals a substantial quadratic trend in the results, indicating that an inverted 'U' shaped curve is the best explanation of performance. This result seems to be of importance in view of some of the conflicting viewpoints on the authenticity of the 'vigilance decrement' in non-laboratory situations (see for example Elliott 1960, Smith and Lucaccini 1969). It is unlikely that circadian rhythm could be an explanation of the results, despite its presence as a confounding factor, since research in this field indicates that performance should improve over the time period used in this experiment (Colquhoun *et al.* 1968a, b).

The most interesting results are those concerned with the speed of the conveyor belt. It was found that the speed of working had a considerable effect on the inspectors' performance. As illustrated in Figure 4, performance as measured by the proportion of birds correctly rejected increased as the length of time allowed for the scrutiny of each bird increased. This reached a maximum hit rate of 71·3% when the birds were moving at the rate of 3,840 per hour, equivalent to an exposure time of 0·94 seconds per bird. However, further increases in exposure time yielded a deterioration in performance; as the viewing time increased to 1·2 seconds per bird (3,000 per hour) performance fell slightly to 68% and at 1·33 seconds per bird (2,700 per hour) performance deteriorated to 56%. The deterioration is statistically significant ($p < 0.05$). It appears that the most likely explanation of these results is that there are two main processes at work, and that the curve must be split into two components; the ascending part, from a presentation time of 0·76 seconds to 0·94 seconds, and the descending part, from 0·94 seconds to 1·33 seconds presentation time.

Considering the ascending part first; it appears that a partial explanation of this section of the curve is purely mechanical, in that the operations necessary when an inspector detects a defective carcass and decides to remove it require that he must spend a portion of time looking away from the conveyor belt. During this time, the speed of the line is such that several birds may pass by and consequently escape detection. Some calculations have been made based on this explanation, using the data of Wargo (1967) and a simplified version of MTM. The results are shown in Figure 5. In this figure are plotted the actual curve obtained, and three calculated curves; one for a 'quick' inspector (a highly experienced, fast reacting, skilled inspector i.e. using minimum times in the calculations), and 'average' inspector (using median times) and a 'slow' inspector (who reacts slowly, moves slowly, and spends longest looking away from the display). As can be seen, these three curves comfortably bracket the range found

Figure 5. Graph comparing calculated performance of a 90% efficient inspector with the experimental results, assuming that the inspector is 'fast', 'average', or 'slow', in removing defects from the conveyor belt.

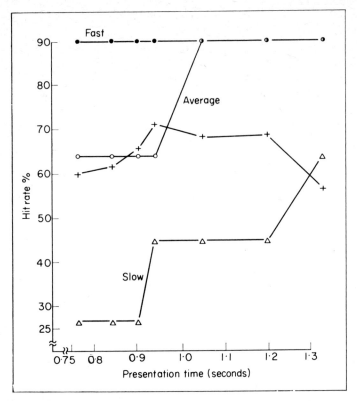

over the initial part of the actual curve. What is thought to be of interest is that the 'average' curve is of the correct shape to explain the results.

Undoubtedly another important determinant of the curve is the effect of the speed of working on the psychological inspection process itself, explained cogently by Drury (1973a, b). The model he proposes was also fitted to the data, and produced the graph shown in Figure 6. It is thought that a combination of these two explanations would be sufficient to explain the actual curve obtained. The attempt was not made mathematically; there are enough inherent assumptions already in these two partial explanations.

It is more difficult to explain the second part of the curve. Three explanations might be advanced. Firstly, it could be argued that as the event rate (birds passing the inspection point) drops, so will the hit rate. However, much of the available evidence is against this explanation, as the signal rate remains constant (e.g. Colquhoun 1961, 1966, Harris 1968, Loeb and Binford 1968, Fox and Haslegrave 1969). What evidence there is as to the effects of event rates predicts the opposite of what was found (Jerison 1967b). It should be pointed out however that both the signal probabilities and the event rates used in these studies are less than the equivalent values in this study.

Secondly, the results could be explained in terms of Poulton's 'range effect'; an artefact of the particular experimental design used (Poulton 1973). According

248

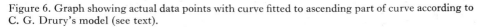

Figure 6. Graph showing actual data points with curve fitted to ascending part of curve according to C. G. Drury's model (see text).

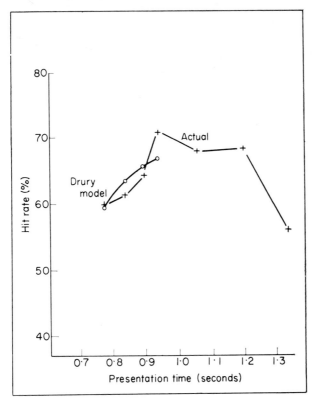

to this, one would expect a performance peak at the most common presentation time, (i.e. 0·76 seconds) decreasing towards the least common presentation time (1·33 seconds). However, one of the effects of increasing presentation time should be to improve inspection efficiency, and furthermore, the least common speed was used on the production line under normal conditions at least once every other week. It is thought that the decrement is too great to be explained by this theory.

The third explanation arises from the discovery that at the lower speeds there appeared to be greater variability in performance between the five-minute intervals during the sessions—both the best and worst performances of the entire experiment occurred at the lower speeds. The differences are not significant, but they do suggest an alternative hypothesis, that during the course of such a task periods of inattention occur (Jerison *et al.* 1965, Jerison 1966, Kogi 1972) which become more frequent or prolonged as presentation time increases. This coincides with observation of the inspectors, and the experience of one of the experimenters. It remains to explain why these periods of inattention should become more frequent or prolonged. It appears that the literature is of no help in this matter. A possible answer may be that the human organism maintains an homeostatic level of arousal, and if this is dependent on incoming stimuli, it could be argued that at the lower speeds additional stimuli are required which are obtained during the extended periods of inattention to the task.

249

3.3. *Recommendations*

While the academic aspects of the study are perhaps interesting, the practical recommendations were as follows.

(*a*) The inspector should be changed every 40 minutes during the day.

(*b*) A number of other operators should be trained to become inspectors.

(*c*) The speed of the conveyor belt should be reduced whenever production scheduling allowed to 3,840 birds per hour.

At present these recommendations are being implemented, so, as yet, no follow-up study has been made to evaluate their effectiveness.

References

BERGUM, B. O., and LEHR, D. J., 1963, Effects of authoritarianism on vigilance performance. *Journal of Applied Psychology*, **47**, 75–77.

COLQUHOUN, W. P., 1961, The effects of 'unwanted' signals on performance in a vigilance task. *Ergonomics*, **4**, 41–51.

COLQUHOUN, W. P., 1966, The effect of 'unwanted' signals on performance in a vigilance task: a reply to Jerison. *Ergonomics*, **9**, 417–419.

COLQUHOUN, W. P., BLAKE, M. J. F., and EDWARDS, R. S., 1968a, Experimental studies of shiftwork I: comparison of 'rotating' and 'stabilised' 4-hour shift systems. *Ergonomics*, **11**, 437–453.

COLQUHOUN, W. P., BLAKE, M. J. F., and EDWARDS, R. S., 1968b, Experimental studies of shiftwork II: stabilised 8-hour shift systems. *Ergonomics*, **11**, 527–546.

DRURY, C. G., 1973a, The effect of speed of working on industrial inspection accuracy. *Applied Ergonomics*, **4**, 2–7.

DRURY, C. G., 1973b, The inspection of sheet materials—model and data. *In Proceedings of the 17th Annual Conference, Human Factors Society*. Pp. 457–464.

DRURY, C. G., and ADDISON, J. L., 1973, An industrial study of the effects of feedback and fault density on inspection performance. *Ergonomics*, **16**, 159–170.

ELLIOTT, E., 1960, Perception and alertness. *Ergonomics*, **3**, 357–364.

FRASER, D. C., 1950, The relationship between angle of display and performance in a prolonged visual task. *Quarterly Journal of Experimental Psychology*, **2**, 176–181.

FOX, J. G., and HASLEGRAVE, C. M., 1969, Industrial inspection efficiency and the probability of a defect occurring. *Ergonomics*, **12**, 713–722.

GLORIG, A., WARD, H. D., and NIXON, J., 1962, Damage-risk criteria and noise-induced hearing loss. In *Proceedings of a Conference on Control of Noise*. (London: HMSO.)

GOULD, J. D., and SCHAFFER. A., 1965, Eye movement patterns in scanning numeric displays. *Perceptual and Motor Skills*, **20**, 521–535.

HARRIS, D. H., 1968, Effect of defect rate on inspection accuracy. *Journal of Applied Psychology*, **52**, 377–379.

ILLUMINATING ENGINEERING SOCIETY, 1973, *The I.E.S. Code of Practice*. (London: The Society.)

JERISON, H. J., 1967a, Signal detection theory in the analysis of human vigilance. *Human Factors*, **9**, 285–288.

JERISON, H. J., 1967b, Activation and long term performance. In *Attention and Performance* (Edited by A. F. SANDERS.) (Amsterdam: NORTH-HOLLAND.) Pp. 373–389.

JERISON, H. J., PICKETT, R. M., and STENSON, H. H., 1965, The elicited observing rate and decision processes in vigilance. *Human Factors*, **7**, 107–128.

KOGI, K., 1972, Repeated short indifference pauses in industrial vigilance. *Journal of Human Ergology*,**1**, 111–121.

LOEB, M., and BINFORD, J. R., 1968, Variation in performance on auditory and visual monitoring tasks as a function of signal and stimulus frequencies. *Perception and Psychophysics*, **4**, 361–366.

MACKWORTH, J. F., 1968, The effect of signal rate on performance in two kinds of vigilance tasks. *Human Factors*, **10**, 11–18.

MACKWORTH, N. H., 1950, *Researches in the Measurement of Human Performance*. (Medical Research Council Special Report 268, London: HMSO.)

POULTON, E. C., 1973, Unwanted range effects from using within-subject experimental designs. *Psychological Bulletin*, **80**, 113–121.

SHEEHAN, J. J., and DRURY, C. G., 1971, The analysis of industrial inspection. *Applied Ergonomics*, **2**, 74–78.

SMITH, R. L., and LUCACCINI, L. R., 1969, Vigilance research: its application to industrial problems. *Human Factors*, **11**, 149–156.

SWETS, J. A., 1964, *Signal Detection and Recognition by Human Observers* (New York: WILEY.)

WALLACK, P. M., and ADAMS, S. K., 1969, The utility of signal detection theory in the analysis of industrial inspector accuracy. *AIIE Transactions*, **1**, 33–44.

WARE, J. R., KOWAL, B., and BAKER, R. A., 1964, The role of experimenter attitude and contingent reinforcement in a vigilance task. *Human Factors*, **6**, 111–119.

WARGO, M. J., 1967, Human operator response speed, frequency, and flexibility: a review and analysis. *Human Factors*, **9**, 221–238.

WEYMOUTH, F. W., 1958, Visual sensory units and the minimum angle of resolution. *American Journal of Ophthalmology*, **41**, 102–113.

WILLIAMS, L. G., and BOROW, M. S., 1963, The effect of rate and direction of display movement upon visual search. *Human Factors*, **5**, 139–146.

The analysis of an inspection task in the rubber industry

R. W. Astley and J. G. Fox

1. Speed and accuracy of inspection

The emphasis in applying ergonomics to quality control is not unnaturally directed towards improving fault detection. That, after all, is the fundamental point of the quality control function: and in the almost ubiquitous paced-inspection situation, accuracy is the only performance criterion. However, there are some inspection tasks where the job is self-paced, or only indirectly paced by virtue of a bonus scheme based on throughput. In such circumstances another realistic criterion will be speed. This will have two components: speed of handling the items to be inspected and speed of inspection: of these the former is a novel factor in most discussions of inspection performance.

Whether machine-paced or self-paced, speed of inspection will, of course, influence accuracy of fault detection. Given an infinite time to inspect the items, one could expect near perfect fault detection. On the other hand with a series of rapid, and hence necessarily cursory, scans of the items, one might expect a very low level of fault detection. In fact, in these two extreme cases, these expected results do not demonstrate themselves in quite such a clear cut fashion in every case. However, in general, the concept of high speed and low accuracy, and vice-versa, holds and there is a trade-off between speed and accuracy between these extreme conditions. The contribution of ergonomics to this problem, is to give the inspector the perceptual conditions to operate with the necessary sensitivity to faults, so that he can inspect efficiently at the greatest possible speed.

In a self-paced situation, however, the upper limits of speed of inspection as they affect fault detection may have little relevance for an inspector's performance if he does not have the necessary conditions for handling the items at high speed: i.e. the method of handling may restrict the inspection speed to a level well below the critical upper limit. A study of handling methods is therefore an additional factor in the discussion of self-paced inspection tasks.

The determination of the swiftest and smoothest method of handling the items to be inspected is determined by standard method study techniques. But if the inspector is to execute these optimum movements then he must be free of any constraints to his movements imposed by a workplace design that is incompatible with his anatomical or biomechanical requirements. For example, the most effective horizontal movements of the hand, wrist and forearm will be when these limbs are at right angles to the perpendicular line of the body: but about 50% of people will not be able to take up this position seated at a table whose top is greater than 30 in. high. Ergonomics data from anthropometry and biomechanics as it relates to workplace design is, of course, relevant to all inspection jobs as it affects well-being: but when inspection is unpaced and there is a large handling element it can be extremely pertinent to the inspector's performance.

Handling the items will have two major components: bringing and removing the material to be inspected in and out of the line of sight: and handling it during the period of inspection. This latter activity brings an interaction between handling and the perceptual conditions for inspecting with maximum speed and accuracy. For example, the method of handling will interact with the position and intensity of illumination to determine the contrast conditions between the object to be inspected and its immediate surrounds: a crucial factor in visual acuity.

The effect of handling on perceptual performance may be even more subtle if the items are small and it is possible to handle more than one at a time. Inspecting the items in a symmetrical array rather than individually, apart from increasing the speed of inspection, may in fact assist in fault detection since such a method of handling allows a visual display which is compatible with the innate perceptual organizational functions of the human visual system. It allows a display which provides the most effective fault/background relationship for fault detection. It is, in fact, easier to detect a fault in one of a batch of items held or placed closely adjacent to another and scanned, than it is to detect a fault when the items are inspected serially. The discussion of this phenomenon has been noted and used to good effect by, for example, Scott Blair and Coppen (1942), Thomas (1962) and Fox (1975).

Thus, methods of handling and hence workplace design interact with the more obvious determinants of inspector performance in various ways.

A very direct interaction between workplace design and illumination is established by the eye–hand distance which will be a key dimension and which will depend on the visual acuity allowed by the illumination conditions: this interaction will be extended if a lens is necessary to detect faults. The dimensions and position of the visual aid have to be considered as an integral part of the workplace dimensions; and the illumination, handling motions and degree of magnification have to be harmonized for effective performance.

The relationships between these ergonomics factors has been demonstrated in a study of a quality control group engaged in inspecting rubber seals of various dimensions in a plant of an international rubber company.

2. The basis for the study

The inspection group were, by any standards, effective in fault detection. An average batch of seals entering the department contained 25·5% defective seals. On average approximately 92% of these would be detected at a cost of falsely rejecting 3% of good seals. This meant that just under 3% of seals going to the customer were defective: and that about 9% of scrap could in fact have gone to the customer and been accepted. It was not considered that an investment in work to improve fault detection would produce results which were economically significant. A preliminary analysis did show, however, that it might be possible to increase throughput in the department by improving the inspectors' handling techniques when inspecting. Subsequently using standard method and time study principles a new method was synthesized which it was predicted would increase throughput by around 25% This was not an inconsiderable saving when it is realised that approximately one million rubber components were inspected each week. Unfortunately, it was then found that the synthesized 'ideal' method could not be implemented at the actual inspection points because of the constraints imposed by the anthropometrically incompatible dimensions of the benches and chairs.

An analysis of the requirements for acceptable workplace dimensions was undertaken. It was necessary to ensure that any recommendations which might result from the analysis would not disrupt the stability of the total system which was achieving acceptable fault detection results. Mindful of the points which have just been made above, the analysis, therefore, examined illumination and magnification parameters in addition to workshop dimensions.

The aim of the study thus became to optimize on these three factors, both individually and with respect to their interactions, so that speed of inspection could be increased by use of the 'ideal' method of handling: at the same time ensuring that if inspection accuracy was not improved by changes in these factors, it was certainly not diminished.

Figure 1. A typical inspection point before the study.

3. The inspection of the seals

3.1. *The task*

Seals came from production to quality control in polythene bags to be allocated to any of the inspectors who worked at a bench as illustrated in Figure 1. A bag might contain a batch of any one of over 100 different types of seals which might number between a few hundred and a few thousand. They were examined, if necessary, under a lens attached to a lamp unit which was adjustable. After inspection, good seals were placed in one bag and rejects in one of two other bags depending on the fault. Samples of the good bags were further checked by audit inspectors and if the faults in a sample exceeded the A.Q.L. the bag was returned to the inspector, the faults found were pointed out and the bag had to be reinspected. A variety of methods of handling the seals were used by the inspectors.

3.2. *The new method of handling*

As a result of the method-time study and perceptual considerations of the type already noted a new 'ideal' method of handling the seals rapidly and accurately was evolved. Described at its simplest, this new method of viewing was to hold a seal in each hand and examine them side by side, under a lens and lamp unit if necessary. This simple method of handling and inspecting the seals during viewing allowed the optimum method of bringing the material in and out of the line-of-sight; particularly in that it allowed the bilateral arm movements so fundamental to method study practice.

4. The redesign of the workplace

The major ergonomics commitment to the redesign was the application of anthropometric and biomechanical data to the physical dimensions of the workplace. This, however, could not be the starting point of the study.

The crucial factor in dimensioning the workplace was the hand–eye distance which allowed optimum visual acuity when using the magnifying lens. With the hand and the eyes, and thus the head-position, fixed, degrees of freedom for the position of the whole body would be considerably reduced as would the dimensional considerations of the bench and chair.

The hand–eye positions were, of course, dependent on the optical characteristics of the magnifier: and these in turn were related to illumination parameters for optimum visual acuity.

The order of factors considered was thus illumination, magnification and workplace dimensions.

4.1. *Illumination*

The illumination in the inspection department was provided by a symmetrical co-planar array of 5 ft. twin fluorescent tubes in reflector fittings: by windows on both sides of the A-frame roof running the length of the room: and by further windows in the walls above head height. The wall windows were usually covered with blue polythene. To reduce the heat in the room the roof windows were usually coated with green paint at the beginning of summer. This general illumination was supplemented at each bench with light from a 100 watt tungsten filament reading lamp. The immediate surrounds of the target seal were the inspector's fingers: the general surround being the bench top covered in cream coloured laminated plastic, partly covered by piles of seals and polythene bags containing seals.

These conditions gave the following values of the three important parameters of illumination as follows.

Intensity: The luminance of the seals was 46 lumens/sq. ft. which meant they were somewhat under-illuminated for the requirement was 83·7 lumens/sq. ft.

Contrast: The value of the contrast between the seals and their immediate surrounds was 1 : 15 which compared badly with the required 10 : 3 (50 : 15).

Glare: The *Glare Index* was calculated as being 21. This was considerably higher than the recommended maximum of 10 (IES 1973).

An immediate task was thus to make recommendations which would improve the illumination conditions.

The factor which demanded the greatest physical alterations was glare. Recognizable sources of glare were the roof windows and the fluorescent tube fittings which produced multiple images in the magnifier and high luminance of the bench tops and polythene bags. Reduction in glare, therefore, could be achieved progressively in several ways.

(1) Reduce the transmissibility of the roof windows by using a coating or eliminate them altogether.

(2) Replace the reflector fittings with diffuse fittings.

(3) Decrease the reflectance of the walls and ceiling by painting them with more light absorbent paint.

The question of contrast was much more difficult. The *object : immediate surrounds* contrast ratio was governed by the fact that since the operator was holding the seals, the amount of incident light on the fingers was the same as that on the seal and as the former reflected more light, the contrast condition was the reverse of that required. The job itself thus made the problem of contrast virtually intractable. A narrower beam of illumination was possible, or the inspectors could have worn low reflectance gloves. Both these solutions had to be rejected. The latter for obvious reasons. The former, because a narrower beamed lamp would have prevented flexibility in positioning the hands and arms: and the need to position the seals within the beam would have significantly increased the handling time. The immediate contrast problem therefore had to be left unresolved. The luminance of the general surrounds, however, was open to treatment and a reduction in its value would contribute to a more favourable *object : surround* contrast ratio. The bench top and polythene bags had high reflectance. An improvement was thus possible simply by removing the polythene bags from the bench top: and by replacing the formica top with dark, possibly baize material. This reduced the reflectance of the bench top from 0·8 to 0·01 and changed the contrast of *object : surround* to 10 : 11·6 (13 : 15). This was a reasonable improvement even if it fell short of the optimal value.

Except that it interacted with suitable contrast conditions, the question of intensity was satisfied by providing local illumination which would supplement the general illumination to the required level. The more localized this additional source could be, the more effective would be the illumination conditions. The physical means of achieving the intensity could not, in fact, be separated from questions related to the magnifier and in this respect illumination and the magnifier were considered together.

4.2. *The magnifier*

The use of the magnifier was a significant aspect of the visual task. There seemed to be little in the ergonomics literature, however, which gave guidance on the use of magnification to enhance visual performance. But a number of general points were noted on the basis of observations in the inspection department.

The most serious was that the magnifier in use distorted the edge of the image when two seals were viewed side by side. This effectively precluded the operation of the 'ideal' handling movements. It was also found that the focal length of the lens was such that the way the viewers used the lens in terms of eye–hand (seal) position often meant that some viewers did not view a magnified image: and would have been better off without the lens.

An improved magnifier was required which would have
less distortion,
greater magnifying power, compatible with an acceptable eye–hand position.

4.2.1. *The optimum means of magnification and illumination*

The question of distortion was resolved by an examination of magnifiers commercially available. This gave a short list of instruments of varying magnifying power. To arrive at optimum values for these two factors a small experiment was carried out. In the same experiment the optimum means of physically providing the illumination was examined.

A simulated inspection unit was used having the glare and contrast conditions which have been noted as the best possible in the prevailing physical conditions. The subjects inspected specially prepared batches of seals which included known numbers and types of faults. Four magnification conditions and two means of illumination were tested as follows.

Using no lens: a lens of focal length 12 in. and magnification 1·8: a lens of focal length 7 in. and magnification 2·4: and a lens of 18 in. and magnification 1·5.

Illumination from a single 24 watt mushroom parabolic diffused reflector lamp plus two 9 in. 6 watt fluorescent tubes attached to the magnifier: illumination form two 24 watt lamps fitted to the magnifier.

Performance was significantly better with the combination of lens of 18 in. focal length and magnification 1·5 and the 24 watt lamp supplemented by the two 6 watt tubes (which gave an intensity of 90 lumens/sq. ft. at the seal). The two 24 watt lamp arrangement provided a narrow beam of intense light, consequently they had to be accurately orientated for the seal to be held in the high illumination area. This reduced the flexibility of posture which was desirable.

4.2.2. Determination of eye–hand distance

Having determined the magnifying power of the lens to be used within the range of equipment which was commercially available it was possible to determine the value of the eye–hand distance which was the hub of the whole study. As it had to be obtained from first principles in the course of which more general data was generated it seems of value to give consideration to the elucidation of the problem.

The ability of the eye to detect detail on an object is determined by the angle subtended by the object at the eye. From Figure 2, an object held at a distance of $(a+g)$ from the eye will subtend an angle of x'' at the eye. If a convex lens is introduced between the eye and object at distance g from the lens so that g is less than the focal length (f), a virtual image is produced which is further away from the eye (distance A), than the object, but which is so much bigger that the angle it subtends (x) is greater than x''.

A measure of the effectiveness of introducing the lens is given by

$$m' = \frac{x}{x''}.$$

It can be shown that

$$m' = \frac{f(a+g)}{f(a+g) - ag}.$$

Figure 2. The relationship of the parameters when an object is viewed through a convex lens.

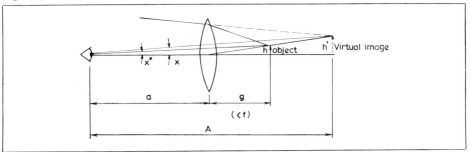

The usual measure of magnification, m, is the ratio of the angular subtense of the image (x) with the angular subtense (x') of the object held at the least distance of distinct vision $(D$, the 'near point').

Thus

$$m = \frac{x}{x'}.$$

It can be shown that

$$m = \frac{fD}{f(a+g) - ag}.$$

The relationship between m, m', a and g (for a given focal length) is shown graphically in Figure 3. The value of m' increases with increase in a and/or g (provided that g is less than f). It is clear that the further the object is held from the eye, the greater the value of interposing a lens. If, however, the object is a long way from the eye, say 16 in., the improvement made by introducing a lens such as that recommended (focal length 18 in.) is not as great as the improvement achieved by bringing the object close to the eye, in terms of the angular subtense at the eye. Thus the lens is only being used to maximum efficiency when the distances a and g are such as to give a value for m greater than 1.

Figure 3. Variation in magnification with variation in eye–lens (a) and lens–object (g) distances for a lens of focal length (f) of 470 mm, and taking the least distance of distinct vision (D) as 250 mm.

The upper values are values of m which is the conventional measure of magnification being the angular subtense of the image (x) compared with that of the object with the latter at the least distance of distinct vision (x'). The lower values are of m' which is the ratio of x to the angular subtense (x'') of the object at ($a+g$), i.e. with the object at the same distance from the eye as it is when viewed through the lens.

Below the line $a+g=250$, m' is not applicable as the object is too near the eye to be clearly seen.
Below the line $A=250$, neither m nor m' are applicable as both object and image are too near the eye.
Above the line $m=1$, viewing through the lens is less effective than holding the object 250 mm from the naked eye.

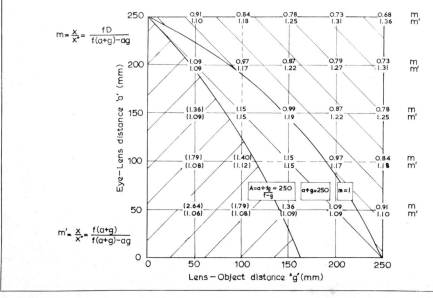

If the eye-to-object distance ($a+g$) is very small then the eye-to-image distance (A) may be less than the least distance of distinct vision so that the inspector will be unable to see the object clearly, and the eye muscles will become fatigued.

The average person has a near point at approximately $A = 10$ in. (250 mm).

It can be shown that $A = a + \dfrac{fg}{f-g}$, and the curve representing $a + \dfrac{fg}{f-g} = 10$ in.

(250 mm) is plotted in Figure 3. This indicates the combinations of values of (a) (eye-to-lens) and (g) (lens-to-object) distances which would produce an image too close to the eye.

Thus the unshaded area in Figure 3 contains the combinations of a and g values which allow the lens to be used comfortably and to maximum effect. In fact this area is further limited by the fact that neither a nor g is likely to be less than, say, 2 in.

260

All the combinations of a and g values which lie in this optimal area, produce values for $(a+g)$ which is the eye-to-object distance within the range 8 in. to 12 in.

Thus the critical feature for anthropometric considerations was not a single value but lay in a range of 4 in.

4.3. *Bench and chair dimensions*

The dimensions of any workplace are important simply in terms of reducing overall body fatigue. They were especially important in the present case for the most efficient handling patterns were dependent for their success on adequate postures. The derivation of the optimum workplace dimensions for the inspectors was therefore given prolonged attention and the following critical dimensions were identified.

4.3.1. *The principal posture factors*

The lens and eye–hand position

The power of the lens determined the distance between the hands and the eyes. To obtain the greatest benefit from the new lens without overtaxing the muscles of the eye, the hands had to hold the seals between 8 in. and 12 in. from the eye.

For the hands to be held this distance from the eye, the upper arm had to be held extended well forward of the trunk and the elbow flexed considerably, or the head had to be inclined sharply forward. Both of these positions are uncomfortable if they have to be maintained for any length of time. To allow the arm and head positions to be contained within comfortable limits, the arm must be supported to offset fatigue in the supporting muscles. Such fatigue would cause tremor and 'drifting' of the hands, and the operator would have to vary her posture by lowering her hands away from the eyes. Consequently the angle subtended by the image of the eye would be reduced, causing a reduction in visual acuity and, therefore, inspection efficiency.

The upper bench surface height

The arms needed to be supported by the upper surface of the bench at some point between the elbow and the mid-point of the forearm. If the bench was lower, the inspector would lower her elbow onto it thereby increasing the eye-to-hand distance unless she flexed her elbows and inclined her head at undesirably acute angles. If the upper surface of the bench was higher, it would provide less efficient support and would interfere with manipulation of seals at bench-top level.

The lower bench surface height

The height of the lower surface of the bench was only important if it did not provide sufficient clearance for the larger inspector to sit with her lower leg vertical. This is desirable for comfort when sitting for long periods with an upright posture, and when entering or leaving the workplace.

Leg space

In addition there had to be no obstruction below the bench top which would prevent sufficient clearance forward of the leading edge of the bench for the inspector's knees, lower legs, and feet.

Seat height

Seat height was, of course, important in that it had to support the inspector in the correct height relationship to the bench, so that she could support her arms on the upper surface and at the same time have sufficient thigh clearance between the lower surface and the seat. In addition, the seat could not be so high that the small inspector's feet could not reach the floor. Excessive seat height is extremely undesirable in that it causes excessive pressure on the underside of the thigh which is uncomfortable because it inhibits blood circulation.

Body dimensions

The workplace dimensions were obviously determined not only by the posture of the inspector but by her body size. People do vary greatly in size so that bench and seat heights acceptable to a large inspector can be uncomfortable for —even unusable by—a small one. However, users of this equipment were (and were likely in the future to be), women, which reduced the range of body sizes to be considered. Nevertheless, unless women were to be selected on the basis of size, it was necessary to design the equipment to accommodate as wide a range of sizes as was practicable.

The total range of sizes for any body dimension is very large. In fact one cannot state absolute limits because one cannot be sure of finding the single largest person or the smallest. But if a big enough sample of the population is measured the frequency distribution of people across the size group is approximately normal. This means that most women are near the average size, and towards the extreme there are fewer people. By ignoring a few per cent of the smallest and largest people, one can considerably reduce the range of sizes that have to be accommodated in the design.

The dimensional constraints for this equipment were developed using the 5th to 95th percentile range of body size data for adult British females obtained from Gaebler (1964). The dimensions and values used are given in Table 1.

Table 1. External body dimensions (inches). (After Gaebler 1964.)

Dimension	5th percentile	95th percentile
Eye height (above seat)	26·5	31·5
Cervicale height (above seat)	22·0	27·0
Shoulder height (above seat)	19·0	24·0
Elbow (rest) height (above seat)	7·5	9·5
Height of top of knee (above floor)	18·0*	21·0*
Height of back of knee (above floor)	14·5	16·5
Shoulder to elbow	11·5	14·5
Elbow to middle-finger-tip	15·5	19·5
Abdomen to front of knee	10·0	16·0
Buttock to front of knee	20·0	24·0
Buttock to back of knee	16·5	19·5
Elbow circumference	9·5	13·5
Forearm circumference	7·5	11·5

* Plus 1 to 3 in. for shoe heel.

The biomechanical model

These design constraints were further modified using a simple biomechanical model. This consisted of regarding the inspector as a system of rigid segments articulated at the major joints (see Figure 4). These segments represent a

Table 2. Segment lengths: i.e. distances between major joints (inches). (After Gaebler 1964, Murrell 1965, Wisner & Rebiffe 1963.)

Dimension		5th percentile	95th percentile
	Eye-to-axis of head	3·5	3·5
(eye height minus cerivale height)	Eye-to-cervicale (along axis of head)	4·5	4·5
(cervicale height minus shoulder height plus 2 in.)	Cervicale-to-shoulder	5·0	5·0
(external dimension—1·5 in.)	Shoulder-to-elbow	10·0	13·0
(elbow to fingertip, external minus 5 in.)	Elbow-to-centre of hand	10·5	14·5
(shoulder height minus hip joint height—see Table 3)	Shoulder-to-hip	13·6	17·9
(buttock to front of knee minus 6·5 in.)	Hip-to-knee	13·5	17·5
(knee height minus 4·5 in.)	Knee-to-ankle	13·5	16·5
(ankle height)	Ankle-to-sole of foot	3·0	3·0
		+1–3 inches for shoe heel	

simplified view of the spine and the long bones in the limbs. The segment lengths can be estimated from the external dimensions (Table 1) as shown in Table 2.

Where the body comes into contact with equipment it is necessary to know the depth of tissue and clothing surrounding the joint or segment. These dimensions were again estimated from the data available for external dimensions (Table 1) as shown in Table 3.

Table 3. Relevant body depth dimensions (inches).

Dimension	5th percentile	95th percentile
Elbow joint-to-tip of elbow (after Gaebler 1964) (Estimated as elbow circumference/2)	1·4	2·2
Hip joint-to-underside of buttock (vertical) (after Wisner & Rebiffe 1962)	3·5	4·0
Forearm thickness from centre (after Gaebler 1964) (Estimated as forearm circumference/2)	1·2	1·8
Knee joint-to-top of knee (after Gaebler 1964) (Estimated as height to top of knee minus (knee-to-ankle plus ankle-to-sole of foot)	1·5	1·5

The determinants of posture in the biomechanical model are the angles between the segments. The relevant angles in this case were those labelled in Figure 5. The ergonomic literature contains data, not only on the maximum possible ranges of angular movement, but on the angles which people find comfortable to maintain for prolonged periods. From this data, minimum and maximum values were selected and these are tabulated in Table 4.

4.3.2. *Designing for the small inspector*

The biomechanical model now had a range of sizes (Tables 2 and 3) and a range of postures (Table 4). The procedure now was to insert the 5th percentile size values into the model and use it to determine the ranges of values for principal equipment dimensions which would allow the small inspector to work with a reasonably comfortable posture. This was done graphically as shown in Figures 6, 7 and 8.

Figure 4. The biomechanical model.

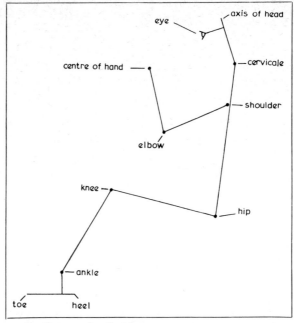

Table 4. Intersegmental angles: comfort limits.

	Angle	Minimum	Maximum
A	Inclination of the head forward of the axis of the trunk (after Murrell 1965)	0	40°
B	Extension of the upper arm forward of the trunk axis (after Rebiffe *et al.* 1969)	−15°	35° if supported
C	Elbow flexion (after Rebiffe *et al.* 1969)	80°	160°
D	Inclination of the trunk to the vertical (after Wisner and Rebiffe 1963 and others)	0	25°
E	Inclination of the thigh to the horizontal (after Wisner and Rebiffe 1963)	0	15°
F	Flexion of the knee (after Wisner and Rebiffe 1963 and others)	90°	120°
G	Ankle flexion (after McCormick 1970)	90°	120°

Figure 5. Intersegmental angles.

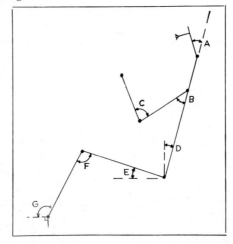

Figure 6. The relationship between the arms, the head and the trunk for the 5th percentile inspector.

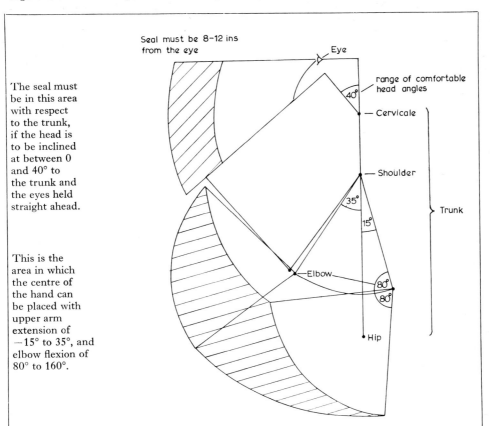

The seal must be in this area with respect to the trunk, if the head is to be inclined at between 0 and 40° to the trunk and the eyes held straight ahead.

This is the area in which the centre of the hand can be placed with upper arm extension of −15° to 35°, and elbow flexion of 80° to 160°.

In side view the seal is held in approximately the centre of the hand. As the two shaded areas do not overlap, the two sets of postural constraints (relating to the eye position and the hand, relative to the trunk) are incompatible. The shaded areas do, however, nearly meet. If the upper arm is extended slightly further forward to 38° to the trunk, and the elbow is flexed to 79° instead of 80°, the hand can hold the seal at approximately the near point (10 in.) with the head inclined at 40°.

Figure 6 shows that in order to hold the seal at the optimal distance from the eye, the 5th percentile must adopt a head and arm posture at the extremes of the comfort limits. The head must be inclined at about 40° to the trunk, the upper arm must be extended 38° forward of the trunk, and the elbow flexed to about 79°. It should be noted that this head and arm position is related to the trunk. Assuming for the moment that the lens is sufficiently adjustable in position, then this head and arm posture can be maintained whatever the inclination of the trunk to the vertical (within the range 0 to 25°).

As previously mentioned, the arm required support from the upper surface of the bench at some point between the elbow and halfway up the forearm. The position of the arm is fixed relative to the trunk as shown above, but the trunk can be inclined to the vertical over a range of 25°. Consequently the position of the lower portion of the forearm can vary in space. This affected the range of

Figure 7. Determination of the bench height (upper surface) above the hip for the 5th percentile.

Minimum: The lowest point at which the bench surface can support the arm is under the elbow. The elbow is at its lowest when the operator is sitting upright. Consequently the bench surface must be at least 4·3 in. above the 5th percentile hip. Such a bench height would not provide support for the inspector's arms if she leaned back in her seat.

Maximum: An upper bench surface 9·1 in. above the 5th percentile's hip would provide comfortable support whether she sits upright or leans back 25°. If it were any higher she would find difficulty handling seals at bench level.

Optimum: A bench surface 6·6 in. above the hip would provide the most comfortable support over the range of trunk inclination and would offer little obstruction to arm movement over the bench.

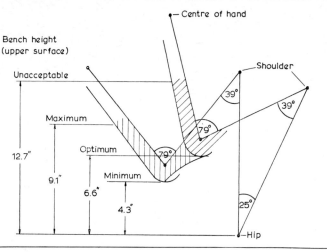

Figure 8. To determine hip height above the floor for the 5th percentile.

The inspector must be able to sit with her feet on the floor, her lower leg vertical and her thigh at an angle of between 0 and 15° to the horizontal.

For the 5th percentile this means a hip height of 14 in. to 17·5 in. As the distance from the hip joint to the underside of the buttock is 3·5 in. (Table 3), the height of the compressed seat should be 11·5 in. to 14·0 in.

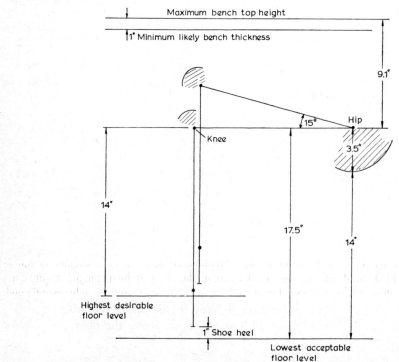

Figure 9. The relationship between the arms, the head and the trunk for the 95th percentile.

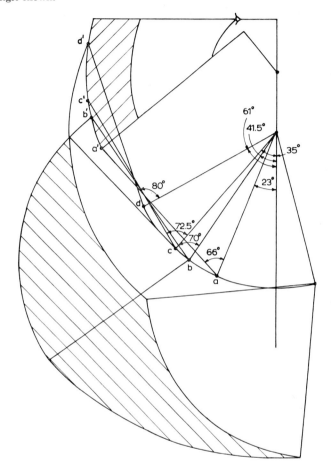

a′, b′, c′, and d′, are the hand positions corresponding to elbow positions a, b, c and d, with the elbow flexed at the angle shown.

The 95th percentile cannot hold the seal within the desired range of the eye, and maintain arm positions within the recommended comfort limits. To reach the upper shaded area the inspector must either extend her upper arm up to an angle of 61° to her trunk, or flex her elbow to 70° or some less extreme combination of both.

In fact, if the forearm is supported, a higher degree of elbow flexion would be more comfortable than increased extension of the upper arm.

bench heights acceptable to the 5th percentile as shown in Figure 7. The upper surface of the bench had to be between 4·3 and 9·1 in. above the 5th percentile inspector's hip (optimally 6·6 in.).

The next stage of development was to determine the comfort limits for the height of the 5th percentile inspector's hip above the floor. These are shown in Figure 8 to be 14·0 in. and 17·5 in., corresponding to a seat height range of 11·5 in. to 14·0 in. A 5th percentile operator should not be required to sit on a seat higher than 14 in. for any length of time for reasons previously mentioned.

As the bench top had to be between 4·3 and 9·1 in. above the 5th percentile's hip, and the hip can be between 14·0 and 17·5 in. above the floor, it appeared

Figure 10. Determination of the bench height (upper surface) above the hip for the 95th percentile.

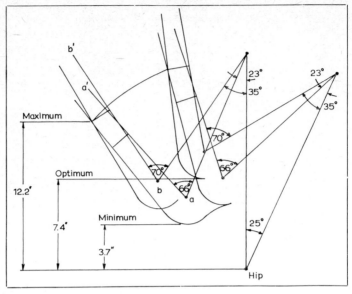

Figure 11. **To** determine hip height above the floor for the 95th percentile.

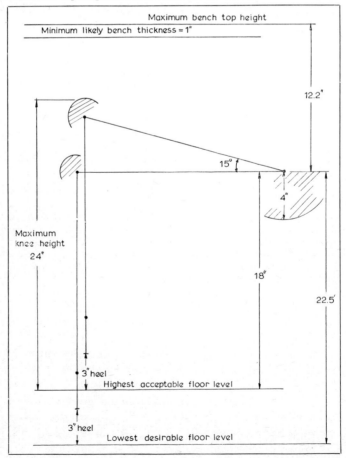

that the maximum range of bench top heights above the floor (given an appropriate seat height) would be 18·3 in. (14+4·3) to 26·6 in. (17·5+9·1). There
was, however, the requirement that the inspector should be able to draw her feet
back so that her lower legs were vertical (to vary her posture and to facilitate
standing and sitting). The maximum knee height of a 5th percentile woman
wearing a 3 in. heel is 21 in. (Table 1). Assuming a minimum bench thickness of
1 in. then the minimum bench top height for the 5th percentile was 22 in.

4.3.3. *Designing for the larger woman*

Having determined the ranges of seat and bench heights acceptable to the 5th
percentile values, the procedure was repeated for the 95th percentile values,
as shown in Figures 9, 10 and 11.

According to the model, the 95th percentile women must hold her arms
considerably flexed at the elbow in order to bring the seal within the desired
range of the eye (Figure 9). She can extend her elbow if she extends her upper
arm as well as raising her elbow: whilst she may wish to do this occasionally to
vary her posture, it could not be taken into account when determining bench
height. A bench which supported the forearm at great height would be difficult
to use when picking up seals, or in fact depositing them. From this point of view
it was desirable that the bench be as low as possible, provided it was high enough
to support the arms in a comfortable viewing posture. Because of bench top
handling, the maximum height considered was that which supports the middle
of the forearm when the upper arm is at 35° to the trunk and the trunk is vertical.
This is illustrated in Figure 9 as elbow position (*b*) and hand position (*b'*).

Because she must adopt excessive elbow flexion to hold the seals within 12 in.
of her eye, the 95th percentile operator may wish to increase the flexion even
more by 4° (70° to 66°) in order to reduce her upper arm extension by 12°
(35° to 23°). This would have the effect of reducing muscle load, because more of
the arm's weight would be taken by the shoulder and the bench (since the
upper arm would be nearer the vertical and the forearm nearer the horizontal).
This is the position *a*, *a'*, in Figure 9. It was thought that this would be a fairly
comfortable posture compared with the others available to the 95th percentile
woman. Position *a* was therefore taken as the minimum desirable elbow level
in Figure 10.

From Figure 10, the upper surface of the bench must be between 3·7 in. and
12·2 in. above the 95th percentile hip (optimally 7·4 in.).

From Figure 11 it appears that the 95th percentile woman requires a seat height
between 14·0 in. and 18·5 in., producing a hip height of between 18·0 and
22·5 in.

The knee height of a 95th percentile woman wearing 3 in. high heels is
24·0 in. This was the minimum height for the lower surface of the bench.
Assuming a minimum bench thickness of 1 in. the minimum height of the upper
surface was 25·0 in.

As a bench top was required at between 3·7 in. and 12·2 (optimally 7·4 in.)
above the 95th percentile hip: and the hip had to be between 18·8 and 22·5 in.
high, the bench top had to be between 25·0 and 34·7 in.

4.3.4. *A summary of dimensions*

These considerations allowed the following specific recommendations to be made.

Seat height

If the seat to be used is non-adjustable it should be 14·0 in. high. Any adjustable seat must be adjustable to 14·0.

Bench height

The upper surfaces of benches should be between 25·0 and 26·6 in. high, whether they are used with fixed height or adjustable chairs. The lower surface must be at least 24·0 in. in height.

Seat height adjustment

The maximum useful range of seat adjustments is 12·6 in. to 18·5 in.

Seat pan

The seat pan should be at least 16 in. wide, and between 10 in. and 16 in. long from the front edge to the backrest.

The pan should not be 'contoured' but should be upholstered having a compressibility of 1–2 in. under a body weight of approximately 130 lb.

Backrest

A backrest should be provided which is between 10 in. and 13 in, wide. to provide adequate support without obstructing the elbows. It should be at least 4 in. deep, vertically. It may be curved or flat but must not have a radius of curvature less than 13 in.

The lower edge should not be less than 5 in. above the compressed seat surface, to allow lumbar support above the buttocks.

The optimum height of the centre of the backrest is approximately 9·0 in. A vertical adjustment of $\pm 1·5$ in. is desirable. It is also desirable that it should be pivoted in the vertical plane, or adjustable in rake. If fixed it should be vertical or inclined backwards at not more than 20°.

Leg space

To allow the 95th percentile to sit up to the bench the vertical knee clearance of 24·0 in. must be extended at least 16·0 in. forward of the edge of the bench.

It is, of course, desirable that the inspector should be able to extend her lower leg. To accommodate this, leg clearance should be extended up to 32·0 in. forward of the edge of the bench although vertical clearance may be reduced.

The essential knee clearance of 24 in. vertically and 16 in. forward should extend laterally to a minimum width of 16 in. Where possible, the extended leg space should also be of the same or greater width.

4.4. *Validation*

Two prototype inspection stations designed according to the recommendations which have been discussed were introduced into the inspection department. Results of performance at these stations showed considerable variation which was to be expected as they were used by different inspectors who were faced with a new method of handling as well as new equipment. Direct observation and the subjective reactions of inspectors resulted in a few minor modifications. An example of the final design from two points of view is shown in Figures 12 and 13.

Further inspection stations were established over a period of months and inspectors retrained in the new method.

Figure 12. A general view of the redesigned inspection bench.

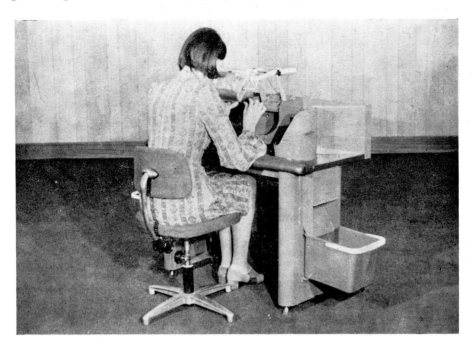

Figure 13. A redesigned bench viewed from above.

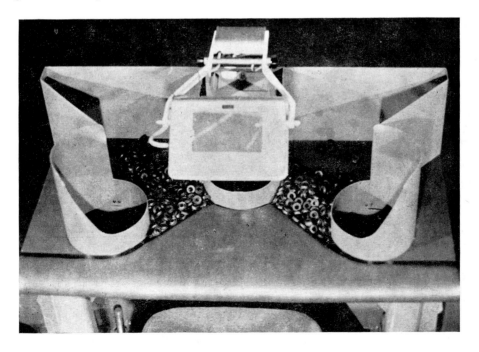

After a further several months performance seemed to have stabilized and the audit inspector's records were sampled over a twelve week period and compared with a similar period when the old handling method and the old bench, chair and magnifier had been in use.

From this comparison it seemed that: the percentage of defectives accepted had gone up slightly by 1·5%: and the percentage of acceptable seals rejected had decreased slightly by 0·2% Thus there was no significantly effective difference in the fault detection performance of the inspectors. However, this fault detection performance was achieved at considerably greater speed. From the data it was estimated that the throughput of 28 inspectors was now achieved by 21 inspectors. Because of increased production and a changing of the agreement with the principal customer with regard to quality, the availability of seven inspectors for additional inspection was of genuine economic significance to the company.

5. Conclusions

The relationship between workplace design and the speed and accuracy of inspection which was argued at the beginning of this paper would seem to have been sustained by the tangible benefits just noted. It is worthwhile noting that physical results may only be the tip of the iceberg. To quote the company report on the project—and not the present authors—' . . . benefits to be derived from implementation of the recommendations are . . . Improved working environment which will influence labour relations, turnover, absenteeism and recruitment '.

The authors wish to thank Mr. R. Hampton, Senior Consultant, Group Industrial Engineering, and Mr. V. McConville, a Chief Inspector of the Company who commissioned the study: also Miss Tan Guat Lin for her assistance while a member of the Ergonomics Information Analysis Centre staff.

Fox, J. G., 1975, The inspection of newly minted coins. In *Human Factors in Work, Design and Production*. (Edited by J. S. Weiner and H. G. Maule.) (London: Taylor & Francis.)

Gaebler, F. S., 1964, *Anthropometric Data for Designers*. (Warren Spring Laboratory Research Report No. RR/ES/58.)

Illuminating Engineering Society, 1973, *The I.E.S. Code of Practice*. (London: The Society.)

McCormick, E. J., 1970, *Human Factors Engineering* (3rd Edition). (New York: McGraw-Hill.)

Murrell, K. F. H., 1965, *Ergonomics*. (London: Chapman and Hall.)

Rebiffe, R., Zayana, O., and Tarriere, C., 1969, Determination des zones optimales pour l'emplacement des commandes manuelles dans l'espace de travail. *Ergonomics*, **12**, 913–924.

Scott Blair, G. W., and Coppen, F. M. V., 1942, The subjective conception of the firmness of soft materials. *American Journal of Psychology*, **5**, 127–139.

Thomas, L. F., 1962, Perceptual organization in industrial inspection. *Ergonomics*, **5**, 429–434.

Wisner, A., and Rebiffe, R., 1963, Methods of improving work place layout. *International Journal of Production Research*, **2**, 145–167.

Glass inspection

G. J. Gillies

1. Introduction

Technological advance, over the years, has produced glass of higher quality at a faster rate. The development of automatic inspection has not been as rapid. As a consequence a large amount of inspection is still manual and requires the examiner to inspect for smaller faults which occur less frequently. It is therefore not surprising that ergonomics has been seen as an important contribution to improving inspectors' performance.

A general understanding of glass inspection is best obtained by considering it in the context of the manufacturing process.

The first stage of any glass product is the conversion of the raw materials (mainly silica) into molten 'metal' or glass. Most faults inside the glass, 'body' faults, are introduced here. A well known fault is 'bubble' produced by the trapping of minute quantities of furnace gas inside the molten glass. Other faults such as 'black speck' and 'ream' are caused by inclusions and poor mixing respectively.

The next manufacturing stage dictates the product and gives rise to a number of characteristic glass faults. Both 'body' and 'surface' glass faults can be introduced by this second or product stage of the process. Pilkington, where the studies to be described have been undertaken, have five product operating divisions namely: Flat Glass, Pressed Glass, Fibreglass, Safety Glass and Optical Glass, each demanding a different specification and hence a different quality criteria.

After forming, all glass has to be annealed. This is achieved by using a conveyor to transport the product through an enclosed conveyor (lehr) at the correct temperature regimes at the right speed. This is referred to as 'lehr time'. Lehr faults are normally gross such as breakage and dimensional faults. The first stage of detailed inspection is normally at the 'lehr end'. Typical of the inspection is that for the Float Process. It is worth describing this in detail since it illustrates the glass inspection problem.

The Float Process which produces a continuous ribbon of glass is of major commercial significance. Lehr end examination of the glass ribbon is for body and surface faults. Manual inspection is by 'shadowgraph'. Figure 1 shows how monochromatic divergent light is passed downwards through the glass ribbon and falls on a white screen below. Bubbles, inclusions and other faults cast dark shadows on the white screen. The faults move towards the inspector at fixed speed across the white screen about 1800 mm away. The inspector scans a defined area. The faults are magnified 1·3 to 1·4 times actual size and this has been found acceptable for clarity of image, and is a trade off between scanning area and fault size. Rejectable size faults (greater than 0·8 mm for the motor trade) are inked by the examiner.

273

Glass inspection

Glass speeds have increased and more efficient production techniques have reduced the fault incidence rate. These factors have made the manual inspection task more difficult and sustaining vigilance is a major problem. It is hardly surprising that this inspection is now automated on several lines and this removes a 'boring' job. Where human inspection is still involved, the inspectors alternate every half hour.

Figure 1. Shadowgraph inspection.

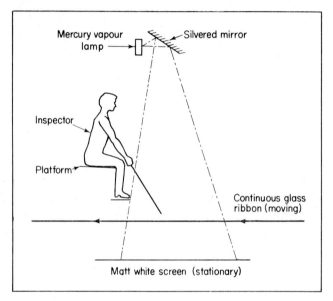

An alternative to the manual shadowgraph is to reflect strip lights from the glass ribbon and view the surface at a shallow angle of incidence against a dark background. This shows glass faults by a distortion effect which enhances the actual fault size by 8 to 10 times. The magnification varies across the ribbon width and for the position of the fault in the glass body. Since only fault magnification occurs the effective scanning area is less than for the shadowgraph and the speed of travel of the fault is the glass ribbon speed. This method is more sensitive for fault detection ('d'' in signal detection theory has been increased) but it is difficult if not impossible to make decisions on an accept or reject basis.

Float glass ribbon has to be cut into sheets and this can produce 'cutting faults' such as pieces absent or pieces protruding on corners or 'shelling' which is local chipping of edges. Tolerance on edge faults can vary from 12 mm to 1·5 mm depending on whether the edge is to be removed subsequently or not. Edge inspection is often done by the glass 'pick–off' men at the end of the conveyor. Here the glass is stationary for a fixed period. Where automatic packing is installed inspection is upstream with plates moving past the examiner.

When the inspector takes glass off a conveyor it is viewed stationary at very close proximity and no magnification is required to show up possible faults. Glass sheets are often viewed with the glass at a small angle of incidence to the observer and use is made of reflected strip lights. Faults stand out mainly due to distortion. Larger sheets are supported in frames or held on support posts and the lighting often consists of a number of fluorescent tubes on a black background.

The inspector looks at the glass against this background and moves his viewing position during inspection. Mosts faults are easily spotted. The glass surface is also viewed at a shallow angle to investigate distortional features. Lifting and handling the glass creates an active work component for the inspector and this should tend to stimulate the mental functions and help vigilance.

Another very important technique is the use of light for crack detection. This is of particular interest for pressed products. Cracks produce intense concentrations of light but the effect is very localised as the cracks are very sensitive to light direction. They are best seen against a dark background. Experiments with polished wired glass has shown that 'weld bubble' is detected much more effectively using this principle than with the shadowgraph technique. This is due in part to the low signal/noise ratio for the shadowgraph caused by the bubble shadow against the unwanted wire shadow. Also the bubbles are often partially masked by the wires. Inspection for 'weld bubble' can only be made with the plate stationary.

Whilst the methods of inspection require close scrutiny the organisational factors are often more important. Most inspection methods are reasonably successful since they have stood the test of time. It is fairly clear from the ergonomics (human factors) literature that organisational factors are often given insufficient attention or are changed without a full awareness of their effect on inspection performance. Two key factors in this context are the use of feedback and/or feedforward of information and whether or not standards exist and are kept close to the point of inspection. The checking of inspector performance is important and is often amply justified for high cost, high volume products. No inspector can claim never to have incorrectly rejected good products. The monitoring of individual performance and feedback of results reduces such occurrences. The length of the inspection work period can have important influences on inspection performance due to vigilance decrement. Finally considerable external pressures can be applied to inspection groups if production personnel are paid on the basis of the inspection results.

The Ergonomics Department in Pilkingtons have conducted a number of major inspection studies in both methods and the organization of inspection. Two are reported in this paper. The first illustrates the steps taken to produce an alternative inspection method, and gives some findings from a broad based inspection system study. The second shows how the Department approached a future product application and outlines the results obtained.

2. Application 1

The objective was to reduce the manual handling effort and skill required to inspect a heavy shaped precision glass product: and to appraise the lehr end inspection system with a view to change. (One aspect, only, of this broad based study is presented.)

2.1. *Inspection method change*

The existing inspection facility comprised an exposed fluorescent strip light above a vertical black and white board. The inspection method was as follows:

1. Inspect general features	Product resting flat on wooden rail at side of lehr.
2. Inspect outside surface using reflected light	
3. Inspect side and edges using transmitted light	Product held in the air and rotated in a vertical plane.
4. Inspect features on side in more detail	Product held in the air supported by one hand and turned by the other in the horizontal plane.
5. Inspect inside surface using reflected light	Product rested on lehr rail.
6. Inspect main area using transmitted light	Product held in the air.

A large part of the inspection involved lifting the heavy product (about 12·7 kg) to head level. The older men found the inspection physically tiring.

The inspectors examined from the side of the lehr having access to about half an hour's production. They examined for 32 possible visual faults comprising 6 tank furnace, 24 process and 2 lehr faults. Approximately half the faults are discretionary, 2–3 reclaimable, and the remainder rejectable if present. Some examination was made at the process end but the first major inspection was at the lehr end. Further processing is done when the product leaves the lehr end and this is followed by a final inspection and quality control check.

Rejects are disposed of at the lehr end and the inspection information entered. From this, hourly breakdowns are made in order to correct adverse variances as soon as possible.

2.1.1. *Approach*

Preliminary discussions were held with management and shop floor personnel and the inspection method was observed. Yield and fault data were obtained from previous production runs. This showed that 80% of the rejects were caused by less than 20% of the faults. This information indicated the relative importance of each fault in the long term. This also showed where technical effort needed to be directed.

Faults were divided into discretionary and non-discretionary since most incorrect decisions would be associated with the former. Study of the existing method showed the means of detecting each fault. At this stage a procedure was set up to collect additional samples for the study and those already in the Training Department were re-organized to make them readily accessible for the experiments.

The best lighting arrangement was investigated for each fault category. The direction, type and intensity of lighting was varied. A structured approach was used and several judgements obtained at crucial stages. This work suggested two separate lighting arrangements, one for cracks and surface defects and one for body faults.

At this stage it was possible to say that all faults could be detected with the product mainly horizontal with the lighting deployed in the correct manner. A rotating ring support was designed by the Department and constructed by the workshop.

Some general findings were as follows:

(*a*) Cracks 'sparkle' best from tungsten filament lamps against a black background.

(*b*) Bubbles could be detected against a black background as a white shadow, or on a matt white background as a dark shadow.

(*c*) Other surface faults could be seen by fluorescent light reflected off the surface.

(*d*) The effect of unshielded light was to create glare which reduced the signal/noise ratio. All strip lights were shielded except the underneath light for bubble detection.

(*e*) The rotary ring support allowed the product to be examined easily with the minimum of physical effort.

The inspectors were involved at key stages in this project and direct comparisons were made between the existing and proposed inspection method. Some small faults were not seen by either method until they were pointed out to the inspector.

The recommended inspection arrangement is shown below Figure 2. The sequence by which different parts of the product are inspected can be varied. The method is described in terms of what each light does.

Figure 2. New inspection method.

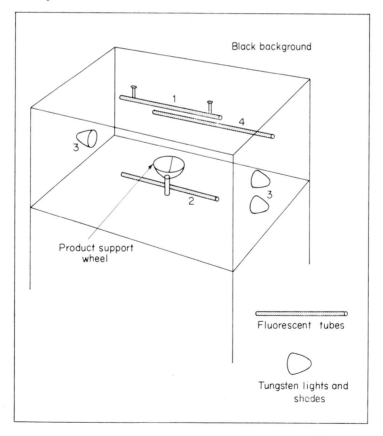

Black background

Product support wheel

Fluorescent tubes

Tungsten lights and shades

2.1.2. *The new inspection method—Overhead fluorescent light*
The product is supported on its outside face. This light is used to inspect the inner surface of the product. The product is tilted on the stand and the reflection of the overhead light is run from one end to the other (this is called banding).

Under fluorescent light. The product is supported on its outside face. This light allows the face and radius of the product to be inspected using transmitted light. The product is rotated (using the stand) allowing each part of the product to pass over the fluorescent tube.

Tungsten lights. The product is supported on its outside face. Three tungsten lights and shades are used to inspect the side and radius of the product. These lights should be directed to shine parallel with the fluorescent tubes, so that they do not shine into the inspector's eyes.

The far edge of the product is inspected as it passes between these lights. Any cracks sparkle at some point as they pass between the lights.

The near edge of the product is inspected by looking down at it. Cracks appear as sparkling lines. One fault can appear as a dark line.

Back wall fluorescent light. The long wall of the product rests on the stand. This light is specifically installed to help detect two particular faults. The product is held resting on its long edge so that the light is transmitted through the product face. The outside surface is viewed. The product can also be turned over on the ring if necessary to inspect the outside surface in more detail.

2.1.3. *Implementation*
The revised inspection method was designed primarily for a new layout but the booth was fitted into one of the existing inspection areas.

Fifteen inspectors were used in an extensive production trial using the revised inspection method. Less than 1% of the rejects were missed by the new method and all these were clearly visible when re-shown to the inspector. Some checks were also made on the 'good' product and this showed that a very small number of faults detectable by the new method were not visible by the existing method.

The inspection method was accepted by management and an implementation programme was adopted to ensure a smooth transition into the system.

2.2. *Lehr end inspection system*
The inspection needs of the product were considered in detail and led to the following objectives being formulated.

2.2.1. *Total system objectives*
To ensure that lehr end inspection was part of an effective total inspection system. This implied consideration of the function and effectiveness of each inspection point in the process and not treating the lehr end in isolation.

To produce a lehr end system suited to the needs of the factory within the constraints laid down by Management for such factors as manning levels, costs and function. Also with regard to future demands and new products.

2.2.2. *The objectives for any lehr end inspection system*
The purpose of setting out these objectives was to allow proper evaluation of alternative proposals and to highlight the project aims.

Independent of system

1. To improve the method of inspection.
   (*a*) Reduction in manual handling.
   (*b*) Improved lighting arrangement.

2. Re-check and re-set lehr end standards.
   (*a*) Consideration of re-work for some faults.
   (*b*) Closer tie up with customer standards.
   (*c*) Involvement of all affected parties. For example production, quality control as well as the Lehr End Department.

3. A means of improving inspectors' performance by training.
   (*a*) To ensure inspectors have an adequate knowledge of standards and ready access to standards.
   (*b*) To ensure inspectors have the skill to identify all faults adequately.

4. To ensure the training of lehr end inspectors is effective.

5. To ensure all lehr end personnel recognize the full importance of their job and their role in the system.

6. General considerations were also included, viz:

   Safety
   Fire hazard
   Maintenance
   Related rest and canteen facilities

Dependent on system

1. Improved effectiveness (efficiency) of lehr end inspection.

2. Improved environment (social and physical).

3. Improved communication within and between lehr end and other departments.

4. The production of accurate fault information for longer term technical or system modification.

5. To minimize handling damage to product.

6. To facilitate re-examination of rejects and good products as classified by the inspectors. Access had to be provided to production and possibly to an independent Q.C. check.

7. To give the Production Department more confidence in the lehr end examination.

8. Provision of an effective means of identifying deficiencies in inspector performance: also in any other functions within the 'lehr end'.

9. To provide an effective means of updating standards where appropriate so that all inspectors are informed.

10. To ensure all inspectors have the relevant skill and knowledge of faults before they are transferred from one product type to another.

11. To ensure that the direct supervision of the lehr end is fully effective. This took account of

    (*a*) the role of the foreman and chargehands with respect to lehr end personnel.

    (*b*) the role of the foreman with respect to warehouse management.

12. Improved accounting to enable

    (*a*) accurate recording of the number of items in each category of product; such categories could be accept, reject, re-work and bonded product pending decision;

    (*b*) achievement of budget cost.

    For this it was necessary to establish the correct functional roles between the Lehr End Department and other departments such as Production and Quality Control.

2.2.3. *Production studies*

Production studies were made to obtain more information on lehr end inspector performance. Statistical batch samples were taken in which the classification of the product into 'good' and 'reject' was known. The product was then re-examined by lehr end inspectors and differences in decisions as high as 10% for 'good in reject' and a mean of 9% for 'reject in good' were found.

In other production studies the inspectors had to circle each reject. The rejects were then re-examined by experienced inspectors when less than 1% 'good in reject' was found. From this it was concluded that marking the rejects and re-checking the product tended to minimize incorrect decisions.

The existing system was self corrective for rejects since those missed at the lehr end were detected at final inspection. No formal checks existed for 'good in reject' though the high cost and volume of production indicated a need.

The re-checking of lehr end inspector performance and feedback of information was thus identified as a key objective.

2.2.4. *Effect of check inspection*

A representative control period was taken near the end of the previous production run. Check sorting was introduced at the start of the succeeding production run. The first full months' data was taken after production start-up to enable a fair comparison.

Lehr end yield variation was markedly reduced (significant at the 5% level) after the change-over to check inspection. Figure 3 gives the final inspection results (showing lehr end rejects undetected). The reject levels at final inspection are lower (average 5·0% before, 3·9% after check sorting) and a reduction in variability has occurred (very nearly significant at the 5% level). No appreciable trend is seen for the 'good in reject' or 'reject in good' for the lehr end sampling scheme (see Figure 4). The overall predicted percentage rejects for final inspection corresponds fairly well to the actual reject level.

Monitoring inspector decisions of 'good' and 'reject' products has significantly reduced the variation between inspector's judgements. This is demonstrated by final inspection and indicated by lehr end yield. The fact that rejects, in particular, are now being checked has reduced losses due to incorrect decision

Figure 3. Final inspection percentage rejects before and after check inspection.

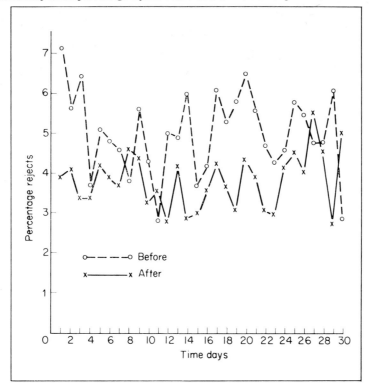

Figure 4. Lehr end inspection performance shown by check inspection scheme.

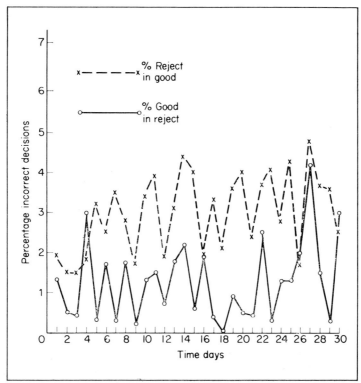

associated with rejecting a good product. This in turn means that the process yield has been increased.

Improvement in inspection performance and yield can be ascribed to

the effect of checking performance and feeding back this information to reduce incorrect decisions;

the checking of performance motivating the inspectors to make fewer errors;

borderline cases now getting full attention and often being found to be acceptable;

the system now being self corrective for both reject and good product.

2.2.5. *Outcome*

Thought is now being given to applying the monitoring principle and feedback of information to the total inspection system. This indicates the need for a central team of check inspectors. Sampling rate could be increased as desired at any point if output is low or too many incorrect decisions are found.

3. Application 2

3.1. *Objective*

The purpose of this study was to investigate the effect of conveyor speed on manual edge fault examination for glass cut sizes: and to investigate at what conveyor speed 95% (correct decisions) performance can be achieved.

3.2. *Background*

This work was required to aid the decision making on whether manual or automatic inspection should be used for a future line. Figure 5 shows how manual inspection would take place on a conveyor side leg off the main float line.

Figure 5. Plan view of proposed scheme.

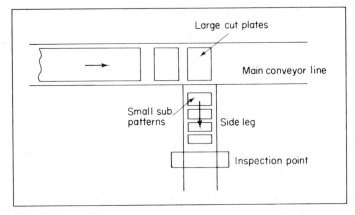

The side leg conveyor speed could be well above line speed. The inspector would look upstream and examine the glass coming towards him.

3.3. *Approach*

A list of all cutting faults was obtained and information on their overall percentage contribution to cutting rejects. The overall level of cutting rejects was less than 5%.

Figure 6. 'Corner on', 'Corner off'.

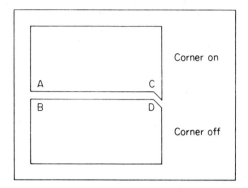

The predicted breakdown of glass sizes for the side leg was obtained together with details on plate separation and orientation. It was decided to investigate the single fault case using 'corners on/off'. (See Figure 6.)

3.4.   *Experiment 1: the search time for stationary targets*
Two stationary cardboard sheets were used and a range of fault sizes 6·4 mm, 9·5 mm, 12·7 mm (standard), 15·9 mm, 19·1 mm. The faults were introduced in matching pairs in A and B or C and D positions. The 'no fault' situation was also used. With two subjects it was found that a search time of about 0·9 sec was required. No appreciable difference in performance was found between viewing from 2·4 metres or 4·8 metres or for the two angles of vision 21° and 28° from the horizontal.

3.5.   *Experiment 2: the inspection time (search plus decision time)*
The same subjects were used but this time decisions were recorded as to acceptance or rejection of the faults. Knowledge of results was given and the inspection time (search plus decision) was about 1·4 sec.   Accuracy and speed were traded off and about 80% correct decisions were scored.

3.6.   *Experiment 3: glass on a conveyor*
Only one conveyor was available and this allowed only two plates to be inspected at once with a gap of 2 to 3 minutes before the next pair could be sent through. 'Corners on/off' were made on glass sheets and the same inspectors performed this task with the glass coming towards them at 3810 m/hr. A 1·5 sec viewing time indicated similar results for the static target experiment.

3.7.   *Experiment 4: simulation of glass cutting faults*
It was necessary to place the inspectors in the more realistic situation with sub-patterns of cut sizes continuously passing by at constant speed. There was a need to investigate performance over a speed range. As a result of these requirements a novel simulation was devised. Cut size plates were represented by scribed outlines on cellulose acetate. Templates enabled 'corners on/off' to be constructed. The cellulose acetate roll was pulled across an overhead projector screen and the image focused on a white screen on the floor. Speed could be varied by using pulley combinations. The subject stood on a 305 mm platform

915 mm from the viewing area. The 'glass' plates were presented moving towards him. Masking tape was placed on the cellulose acetate against plates with faults. This was used to interrupt light passing to a photocell, and generated a signal every time a fault was present on the screen.

Two experiments were carried out both using 80 plates and with fault sizes 9·5 mm and 15·9 mm. Firstly, detection was investigated using 3 subjects (2 trials at each speed) and secondly, decision making. The results are given in Table 1.

Table 1. Detection and decision preliminary data.

Speed m/hr	% overall correct detections (20% F.D.)	% overall correct decisions (10% F.D.)
2592	88%	75%
3048	78%	83%
3810	81%	75%
4422	75%	66%

F.D. = Fault density

Correct decisions exceed correct detections for the speed of 3048 m/hr. This is attributed mainly to the very significant learning effect, and in part to the fault density differences. The length of experimental run was much shorter for higher speeds.

3.8. *Experiment 5: improved simulation of glass cutting faults*
The aim of this study was to further investigate the effect of conveyor speed on inspection performance, using a longer period of inspection.

The method was as for Experiment 4 but with the following differences.

(*a*) Run length extended to 320 plates, consisting of 36 'rejects' and 27 acceptable faults, i.e. 'corners on or off' of less than 12·7 mm. Nominal fault sizes of 9·5 mm and 15·9 mm were used, although some fell between 9·5 mm and 15·9 mm and some were larger than 15·9 mm.

(*b*) A second inspection station upstream was provided, with the same relevant dimensions as that downstream. This enabled two subjects to be used simultaneously. Also it provides data on whether inspection performance was superior with the plates either approaching or receding from the inspector.

(*c*) The bell indicating a correct rejection of a faulty plate was disconnected. so as not to interfere with the second examiner. Two subjects (shop floor personnel) participated in each trial. Each speed was repeated for each subject in the upstream and downstream positions.

At the slowest speed 1026 m/hr, 320 plates took 18½ minutes to pass. Previous trials had investigated decision making for the speed range 2592 m/hr –4422 m/hr. Inference was drawn for the lower speed range from the results of fault detection (no decision accept or reject required). The run length was increased by four times for these experimental runs.

Figure 7 gives the combined subject performance for % correct rejects, % correct accepts, and % correct decisions (% correct rejects + % correct accepts).

Performance is expressed as a percentage of the total number of plates in each category excluding all the 'good' plates with no faults on. This allows one to investigate subject performance more closely without fault density having a masking effect. It appears that performance was roughly constant at 85% and 87%, for speeds up to 3048 m/hr for % correct rejects and % correct decisions respectively. A linear fall takes place above 3048 m/hr. Percent correct accept appears to be fairly steady over the whole speed range.

Figure 7. Effect of conveyor speed on correct decisions.

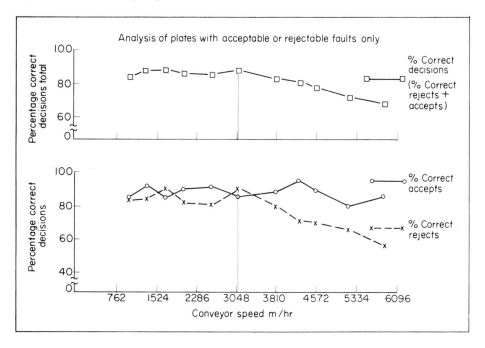

Figure 8 gives the % correct rejects and % correct decisions against transit time. This shows more clearly the rapid drop in inspection performance for speeds above 3048 m/hr. The shaded box shows the times and performance range for decision making for static targets. It is interesting to see how closely the dynamic and static data agree.

The flat characteristic of the performance curve for speeds up to 3048 m/hr is interesting. It is felt that for the low speeds (probably below 2286 m/hr) the inspector is bored. At speeds between 2286 m/hr and 3048 m/hr the task becomes more of a challenge and extra mental capacity is utilized. Above 3048 m/hr the task is evidently becoming progressively more difficult as the speed increases. Table 2 gives detailed results.

There is some evidence to show that if the effect of depth perception can be overcome when locating a faulty plate on the reject wire, then inspection upstream may be superior to inspection downstream. This finding if substantiated

Glass inspection

Figure 8. Inspector performance versus transit time.

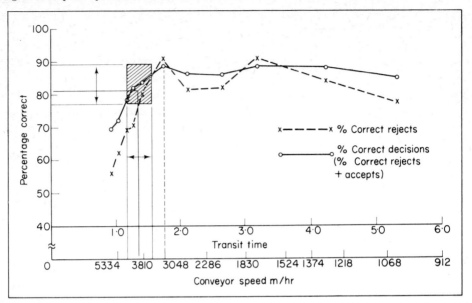

Table. 2. Simulation results Experiment 5.

	Downstream				Upstream					
8.10.73	Subject 1					Subject 2				
Rejected rejects	Missed	Rejects late	False alarms Accept	Good	Rejected rejects	Missed	Rejects late	False alarms Accept	Good	Speeds m/hr
33	3	0	7	0	32	3	1	4	0	1716
31	5	0	2	0	31	5	0	4	0	1296
31	5	0	2	0	34	2	0	7	0	2058
26	10	0	0	0	27	9	0	0	0	2592
26	10	1	0	0	28	8	0	0	0	1026
8.10.73	Subject 2					Subject 1				
*13	2	0	2	0	14	1	0	0	0	1716
26	10	0	1	0	33	3	0	2	0	1296
27	9	0	1	0	26	10	0	1	0	2058
31	5	0	0	0	33	3	0	10	0	2592
31	5	0	0	0	36	0	0	17	0	1026
10.10.73	Subject 1					Subject 2				
36	0	0		7	34	1	1		5	3114
31	4	1		4	30	5	1		6	3834
22	14	0		8	24	6	6		9	5238
31	5	0		3	32	4	0		6	4602
14	22	0		4	21	14	1		9	5880
28	8	0		4	27	9	0		7	4266
10.10.73	Subject 2					Subject 1				
24	12	0		1	35	1	0		4	3114
22	14	0		0	29	7	0		4	3834
17	19	0		1	24	11	1		6	5238
15	21	0		2	20	14	2		2	4602
17	19	0		2	25	9	2		2	5880
16	20	0		0	29	6	1		3	4266

1. Tests are in chronological order.
2. Total number of plates = 320.
* Only half the number of plates are recorded.

3. Total number of rejectable faults = 36.
4. Total number of acceptable faults = 30.

286

by further trials would be surprising since intuitively a fault approaching the inspector appears to be a stable feedback situation.

3.9. *The limitations of the experiments*
This series of experiments had several limitations, namely: only a single fault was possible; simulation had to be used; there were few subjects; and the experiments were of limited duration. The results should be examined with this in mind. However if the manual inspection of cut sizes is still considered feasible having seen this data, then a multi-fault experiment should be conducted.

4. Concluding remarks
These two studies are only brief indications of attempts to improve inspector efficiency in the examination of glass products. But from them the following points will have emerged.

1. The identification of losses and associated costs together with a quantification of inspector performance is an essential preliminary in understanding the inspection problem.

2. Inspection is the essential means of achieving correct product quality. Inspectors differ in their subjective judgements and the monitoring and feedback of their performance removes a large amount of this subjective variation. This mechanism also allows for any standard changes to be quickly effected.

3. The most effective deployment of inspection manpower should be a major aim.

I would like to thank the Company Management who have given every assistance. Also I would like to acknowledge the valuable contribution made by my ergonomics colleagues Dr. J. W. Hill, Mr. B. J. Giddings and Miss M. Sims.

Visual inspection of integrated circuits: a case study

H. A. Froot and W. E. Dunkel

1. Introduction

This paper will discuss two case histories of problems encountered in the visual inspection of semiconductor microelectronic computer components. First, some background will be presented describing the manufacturing process and the nature of the visual defects that the inspectors were required to detect.

1.1 *Manufacturing process*

A large number of components (chips) are simultaneously made on a single slice of silicon, called a wafer (Figure 1). The active devices, diodes, transistors, resistors, etc., are made by selectively diffusing materials into appropriate areas on the wafer. These devices are then interconnected by thin metallic conductors called 'lands'. The interconnection pattern on each chip determines its function. A chip may contain anywhere from a very few active interconnected areas to many thousands. Basically, repeated photolithographic processing is

Figure 1. Example of a chip (magnified 30 ×).

used to define the areas where diffusion will occur, as well as to define the interconnections. The lands are electrically connected to the chip carrier (substrate) through evaporated metallic hemispheres called pads, located around the periphery of the chip. The entire face of the chip, except the pads, is covered with a protective layer of glass. The completed individual chips are cut from the wafer by a dicing process.

1.2. *Defects*

Defects in the semiconductor industry fall into two classes. *Time zero defects* cause an immediate malfunction of the component and can be detected at final electrical test. *Reliability defects* are related to the lifetime of the component and cannot be detected electrically. It is this latter type that is searched for during final visual inspection. An example is a pinhole in the glass covering the chip, which exposes a small area to environmental attack during use. A reliability defect is potentially detrimental to the lifetime of the chip only if it is above a certain minimum size and is in or near an active area. These two criteria, size and location, are common to all reliability defects.

2. Case study 1

Problem. Chip lots that had passed final visual inspection when inspected by manufacturing inspectors were being rejected when resampled by quality control inspectors. Reinspection by both groups failed to resolve the conflicts. *Analysis.* This problem illustrates one of the pitfalls in the visual inspection of microminiature parts. Because the components are so small, the inspectors must examine an enlarged image. Procedures had been generated which specified the magnification at which each type of defect was to be viewed; these ranged from 50X to 800X. Manufacturing and quality control inspectors both followed the same procedures, but used different microscopes, which had the same magnification but not the same ability to resolve details. Thus, the quality control inspectors could see defects that the manufacturing inspectors could not. Once the differences were resolved, the problem disappeared.

Optical inspection stations generally tend to be designed by trading off magnification, cost, availability, and throughput, which is related to the field of view. The field of view determines how much of the product is visible at any one time, and varies inversely with the magnification. Certain equally important optical parameters, however, have often been ignored by the designers.

Magnification: The ratio of a lateral dimension in the image to the same dimension in the object.

Resolving power: The fineness of the detail that is visible—that is, the minimum separation between two small structures that can be distinguished from each other. This is inversely related to the numerical aperture.

Numerical aperture: The size of half the included angle of light collected by a lens times the refractive index of the medium between lens and object.

Contrast: The relative reflectivity or transmission of adjacent structures.

Depth of field: In a three-dimensional structure, the sum of the distances on either side of ideal focus at which images will still be acceptably sharp.

Depth of field, like resolving power, is inversely related to the numerical aperture.

In a microscope, the resolving power depends on the numerical aperture of the first element of the objective. Its significance relative to magnification can best be illustrated by a photographic analogy between a negative and an enlarged print from it. A certain amount of the detailed information on the negative may not be readily seen from a contact print. Continuously increasing enlargements will make more and more details visible, up to the point at which all the information on the negative can be seen. Additional enlargement increases the size of these features but presents no new features to view. Likewise, increasing the total magnification of a microscope might make details more apparent but cannot reveal details that were not passed by the objective lens.

Contrast too plays an important role in finding defects. The higher the contrast between the defect and its surroundings, the more readily it can be seen.

In optimizing an optical system for visual inspection, then, one must carefully define the defect and then determine which optical parameters must be controlled. Too low a resolving power would be unacceptable. But too high a resolving power forces the inspector to judge whether the anomaly is large enough to be called a defect. Ideally, the numerical aperture of the objective should be chosen so that only anomalies large enough to be potential reliability defects will be visible to the inspector. For defects with very low contrast, visibility can be improved by decreasing the numerical aperture. This in turn increases contrast, at the cost of some sacrifice in clarity. Another method of increasing contrast is to use dark-field illumination, which makes all smooth reflective surfaces appear dark while all rough reflective surfaces appear bright. This method is particularly suited to the detection of scratches on highly polished reflective surfaces.

A word of caution is in place here. For the sake of mechanical interchangeability, manufacturers have standardized many dimensions of the microscope, such as the diameter and thread of the objective. The optics, however, are not interchangeable; hence mixing parts made by different manufacturers can very often severely degrade the image, and also give rise to severe eye strain after moderate use.

There are some other potential causes of eye strain. The usual tendency of a person using a microscope is to use excessively intense light. The effects are not noticeable at first, but after prolonged viewing will cause severe eye strain. The proper technique is to set the light intensity at the minimum for comfortable viewing.

Further, normal eyepieces are designed for use by persons who do not require eyeglasses. Simple near- or far-sightedness can be compensated for by adjusting the eyepiece, but astigmatism cannot. When an inspector attempts to use a standard eyepiece with eyeglasses, his eye is forced to accommodate for the increased viewing distance, and severe eye strain results; moreover, he cannot see the entire field of view. Inspectors with astigmatism should use high-eye-point eyepieces, which are offered by all manufacturers.

Optics that are not scrupulously clean will cause eye strain and also degrade the image. An out-of-focus image of any dust, facial oil, or dandruff on the lens is superimposed on the image as darker spots, which can mask defects.

3. Case study 2

Problem. In general, the computer industry has moved towards smaller, denser circuits, to reduce the cost per circuit and to increase the speed of operation. Rapid technological advances have significantly decreased the time between development and production. As a consequence, inspection efficiencies often must be defined before chips are available in numbers large enough for experimental determinations.

Analysis. Whereas the first case discussed had to do with optimizing inspection equipment, this second one deals with the problem of inspector efficiency as a function of product complexity. A method developed by J. D. Gould and J. W. Schoonard, both of IBM's Thomas J. Watson Research Center, makes it possible to predict the accuracy of visual inspection of integrated chips.

Since the manufacture of integrated circuits relies on photolithography, the masks for a chip are usually available months before the chip itself is to be manufactured. The mask used is usually that of the interconnection pattern, since this is where most of the visual defects occur.

An empirical curve is developed by the following procedure. First a positive print of the mask is made, and from it sixty slides are prepared. Half have no defects. On each of the rest, one defect is introduced by placing a rectangular piece of paper, either black or white, on the print before photographing it. Thus one quarter of the slides contain one 'black defect' each, and one quarter contain one 'white defect' each. All sixty slides are inspected by a group of people.

From the results of the inspections, the ratio r_1 of the number of parts accepted is determined. This ratio is divided by $r_2 = 0 \cdot 5$, the ratio of the number of defective parts to the total number of parts in the original population; the result is the slide inspection accuracy x_1.

This experiment is now repeated with real chips, and the chip inspection accuracy y is determined. A plot is drawn with x_1 as the abscissa and y as the ordinate. The experiments are repeated for various levels of complexity.

The result is an empirical curve. To predict the inspection accuracy for a chip of a given complexity, slides of the chip mask are prepared and the experiment is run. The y-coordinate of the point on the curve corresponding to x_1 is found, and the chip inspection efficiency is taken to be $1 - y$.

4. Conclusion

In spite of the increasing automation in the manufacture of semiconductor devices, and in spite of their increasing complexity, visual inspection is going to be with us for a long time to come. The two cases discussed here have illustrated what should be the two principal concerns of ergonomists designing inspection methods and stations. In the first case, the solution was concerned primarily with the optical design; in the second, human factors had to predominate because of the low signal-to-noise ratio of the devices inspected. Which concern is more important depends on the problem, but neither should be neglected.

292

Industrial applications

Quality control to detect manufacturing faults, whether it be to protect the customer, to provide process control information or to generate information for payment systems, is clearly a major activity in any production system. It would seem reasonable to conclude from the papers in this section that the human inspector using his basic senses to detect faults is the crux of current quality control activity. The papers cover a broad span of industries and services and yet they are only representative of a larger number of studies of the role of the human inspector: a full list might have included, for example, textiles (Rothe 1969 and Bakos 1971), horticulture (Stevens 1969), lamp filaments (Bessonova and Nikitin 1970), radiography (Gregg 1969 and Goldstein and Mobley 1971), or bottles (Saito *et al.* 1972).

The evidence from all these papers gives strong grounds for claiming that the dominant position of the human inspector in future quality control systems is assured. In the present state of technology he offers the most economic method.

Unfortunately, the advantages of using the human inspector cannot be accepted without the inspector's limitations. He is rarely perfect in either detection or diagnosis. Carroll's (1969) summary of the situation seems reasonable when he says that in examining a complex product the inspector may be expected to miss 15% of the defects present: and this viewpoint ignores the percentage of good items erroneously rejected.

There is then a price to be paid for utilizing the advantageous characteristics of the human inspector. As the earlier sections of this volume must surely testify, much human factors' effort has been extended to reducing this cost by the study of the factors which determine the inspector's basic efficiency in detecting and diagnosing faults. It would not seem unduly pretentious on the evidence from the *Applications* that the current position is such that the human factors specialist using data from these studies can make a significant contribution in practice to reducing the cost of the human inspection device by specifying the physical conitions for his optimum performance.

Many factors have presented themselves in the papers: the obvious such as visual acuity and illumination in visual inspection; and the less obvious, such as feedforward of sample production quality data to inspectors. Some are common to all inspection systems, others to particular industries or products.

Figure 1 has gathered these factors into a Checklist for the quality control engineer or manager. Most of the elements of the list have been discussed in

Figure 1. Human factors in quality control checklist

1. Criteria definition
    discretionary faults
    non-discretionary faults
    limit standards
    multiple fault/first fault decision
    a priori fault probabilities
    costs and values of decisions and errors

2. Job analysis and synthesis
    sensory requirements
    decision requirements
    physical requirements

3. Display
    perceptual organization
    search and scanning
        display size
        structure
        overlays
    pacing
        maximum speed
        optimum speed
        tolerance zone

4. Illumination
    intensity
    contrast
    direction
    colour
    sequence

5. Visual aids
    magnification
    resolution
    numerical aperture
    contrast
    depth of field

6. Job aids
    instructions
    perfect specimens
    limit standards
    written procedures

7. Workplace design
    anthropometry
    motion analysis

8. Systems organization
    feedforward of quality information from production to
        inspection
    feedback of performance information to inspectors
    length of inspection period
        rest pauses
        job enlargement
        extraneous stimulus
    organizational position of inspector
    financial incentives

9. Selection
       sensory acuity
          static
          dynamic

10. Training

11. Measurement of performance
       time and errors
          percentage of defects detected
          percentage of acceptable rejected
          movement times (P.M.T.S.)
       reliability of action sequences

the presentations in this book and it is perhaps sufficient to say that if in any system an element is relevant and yet has not been explicitly related to the task then the system's efficiency is at risk.

However 'Criteria definition' and 'Job analysis and synthesis' perhaps deserve a little further consideration. Being explicit in the foregoing discussion, they received little or no treatment. They are, however, crucial to the successful application of human factors data. If the criteria have not been defined and the job analysed, then the relevance of the human factors data applied to the inspection task may be a chance affair.

Criteria definition

In the first instance the set of criteria for faults will be built up between the manufacturer and customer. It is no part of this discussion to pursue routine aspects of quality control procedures. But for the systems to be eventually effective it is to be stressed that no variance should exist between the manufacturer's and the customer's view of quality. Yet there are many stories less than anecdotal of manufacturers genuinely accepting items subsequently rejected by the customer only to have the latter accept items which the manufacturer's inspectors had classed as rejects. The inevitable extension of this type of situation was provided by one of the case studies in this volume when the manufacturer was successful in meeting the A.Q.L. of the customer because the customer's inspectors were at a considerable disadvantage not having the necessary magnification equipment available to the manufacturer's inspectors.

The technical criteria firmly established, they must be transposed to terms of human functioning. Only then can a human factors intervention be effective. This obvious point bears re-iteration, for often it is more obvious by its absence than its presence in inspection considerations. In more than one study it has been found that technical specifications could not be met under the existing conditions for the inspectors. There is little point, as has been found in practice, of specifying '0·001 in. diameter superficial hole' as the maximum acceptable size of defect if no magnifiers are available. Human visual acuity is such that a $\times 6$ magnification would be required for such fault discrimination. The need for the additional hardware would have been the more obvious if the technical criteria for faults had also been available in terms of human functions. Here it would be the visual angle subtended by the largest allowable sized hole: which in turn could be related to the maximum resolving power of the human eye.

At a latter stage in the system, during training, these standards must be transmitted to the inspectors. In anticipation of this, the standards of acceptance and rejection should be clearly specified in yet another form. That is one which based on standard terminology can be interpreted unambiguously and yet with facility by the inspector. In this last respect, it may often be more advantageous to relate the largest acceptable defect to 'the size of a pin head' rather than the more exact '0·01 in. diameter hole': his concept of the former being more clearly established than that of the latter.

Given the criteria we essentially have the requirements of the system and they form the basis for a job analysis and synthesis which will describe the demands of the system on the human inspector and which will in turn specify the physical conditions for his optimum functioning.

Job analysis and synthesis

It is important in the appraisal and design of any inspection system to carry out a job analysis and synthesis before proceeding through a checklist and attempting to provide what intuitively may seem to be conditions for optimum inspector performance. There are nuances in both system's requirements and performance which will not come out if the analytical activity is omitted: and thus the system may be unnecessarily expensive or performance unaccountably poor.

To give an example. Visual acuity will always be considered a necessary prerequisite for visual inspection tasks. Thus, there was some consternation in one study when it was discovered that, unknown to management, one inspector had only one-eyed vision. Consternation heightened when an investigation of inspectors' performance showed that she could be rated the fourth best inspector in a group of twenty-seven where inspection performance was high. This apparent anomaly was probably explained by the fact that the inspector was only concerned with surface blemishes on the product and her one-eyed visual acuity was adequate for the task. The story would have perhaps had a different twist if the inspector had been concerned with faults where depth perception was important; where two eyes are usually better than one.

Measurement of performance

The theoretical formulations of Section I gave models for predicting inspectors' performance, allowing the construction of more realistic quality control systems. They also gave structures for an understanding of the various physical and organizational factors which influence performance and which were discussed in Section II and seen to be applied in this final section. In addition these formulations gave the means of a more realistic and accurate measure of performance which is necessary if the benefits of the application of human factors is to be truly evaluated in practice.

Signal detection theory may have been over-subscribed in this volume. However, it would be difficult to deny that it makes it clear that the false rejection of good items by an inspector, often found in practice, is an inevitable feature of his performance and that it is not a casual random process, but is related to the inspectors fault rejection performance. It is thus imperative that in any measure of inspector's performance we use the basic measurement parameters highlighted by the theory to give the real cost of his actions. An acceptable value of the single measure 'faults detected' is of little consequence if it carries with it unacceptable costs from false rejections. Often in measuring the effect of an ergonomics intervention, changes in the rate of false rejections may be the only sensitive parameter. For example, in one of the case studies in this section, human factors applications showed little effect when measured against increased detection efficiency. However, measured against reductions in false rejections, the Company's savings were in the region of £23,000 per year on a group of approximately thirty inspectors.

The use of this more sophisticated measuring stick demands familiarity with the concepts d' and β. How these signal detection theory parameters can be extracted from production-inspection data in a form amenable to management interpretation has been demonstrated by Drury and Addison (1973).

The checklist

The checklist in Figure 1 may not be complete but using it with discretion along with the relevant data from what has gone before in this volume it should be possible for the practicing quality control engineer to influence the physical and organizational variables to improve inspection performance and the inspector's well-being.

References

BAKOS, I., 1971, Psychological investigation of the strain imposed on fabric inspectors by the colour characteristics of the fabrics under examination. *Magyar Taxtiltechnica*, **23**, 152–155.

BESSONOVA, A. N., and NIKITIN, V. D., 1970, Evaluation of visual conditions of work during the inspection of incandescent lamp filaments in a lamp factory. *Gigiena Truda i Professional' nye Zabolevanija*, **14**, 7–11.

CARROLL, J. M., 1969, Estimating errors in the inspection of complex products. *AIIE Transactions*, **1**, 229–235.

DRURY, C. G., and ADDISON, J. L., 1973, An industrial study of the effects of feedforward of fault density on inspection performance. *Ergonomics*, **16**, 159–169.

GOLDSTEIN, I. L., and MOBLEY, W. H., 1971, Error and variability in the visual processing of dental radiographs. *Journal of Applied Psychology*, **55**, 549–553.

GREGG, E. C., 1969, *Visual Response of the Interpreter*. (Report No. N70–39358: 00–78–225; CONF700516–7 Scientific and Technical Aerospace Reports.)

ROTHE, O., 1969, Identification of faults in textile materials. *Ingenieria Textile*, **36**, 569–583.

SAITO, H. *et al.*, 1972, Studies on a bottle inspection task. *Journal of Science of Labour*, **48**, 239–260, 445–454, 475–525.

STEVENS, G. N., 1969, The human operator and quality inspection of horticultural produce. *Paper presented to the Institution of Agricultural Engineers Autumn Open Meeting on Ergonomics in Agriculture, Loughborough University of Technology.*

The inspector in the future:
his efficiency and well-being

C. G. Drury and J. G. Fox

The industrial inspector does not have to grapple with the sophistication of modern technology or the complexity of management of a modern industrial system. The basic skills he requires for the task have not to be trained to accommodate external structures, but are innate and should only require development rather than the modification required for the successful completion of more complex tasks. It must thus be a cause for wonder that such a volume of human effort in research and industry has been devoted to an understanding of what at first sight is overtly man operating in one of the simpler of his repertoire of roles.

The stimulus of interest has had three starting points. Firstly, the inspector by virtue of the apparent simplicity of his task offered a vehicle for research and explanation of the more fundamental performance of human mental processes. Secondly, for philosophic reasons, by its nature, inspection has proved an exciting vehicle for ergonomics. In one direction it has offered scope for applied research: in the other it has provided opportunities for the application of research results with easily measurable pay-offs: and it has demanded the multi-disciplinary approach which marks an ergonomics problem. Thirdly, in industry the interest has, not unnaturally, been economic: it is estimated that some 10% of manufacturing costs are often earmarked for maintaining quality standards and as was pointed out in the *Prologue*, and surely reinforced in subsequent papers, much of this cost would show no return if human error was left unattended. In addition to these three interests in human inspection performance, much data has come from inspection·type tasks which have been the special concern of the military.

Whatever the stimulus for the interest, there would seem to be merit in the effort.

This tiny mundane aspect of human activity has provided psychologists with a wealth of data explaining some facets of the human mental processes. It should add weight to the argument that we are unlikely to understand or have an explanation of human behaviour in one grand model: and that we have much to learn about basic mental functions before we can hope to understand the behaviour of man when he has to interact with the complexities of equipment which, paradoxically, he can design to extend these very functions.

But it is in industry that the most concrete and most immediate benefits of this thirty years of work must accrue. This collection of papers must surely have sustained the argument that ergonomics philosophy, models and data can do much to make the 10% of costs devoted to product inspection a more effective investment: allowing greater prediction of the inspector's performance: increasing his fault detection efficiency: and improving his well-being in a task which intrinsically may give little job satisfaction being repetitive, impersonal, often relentlessly paced, monotonous and often appearing trivial.

Thus the matter stands. But what of the future?

Given limitless freedom of action, which modern society rarely allows, the evidence would strongly suggest that the wise manager or designer would attempt to design-out the majority of the inspector's functions (particularly fault detection and criterion evaluation) in any future system, leaving the inspector to make decisions on simple unambiguous signals. Many sophisticated methods of quality control do exist which would achieve this aim and many more will appear. But for the immediate future, the position of the inspector as the hub of quality control activity seems assured for social, economic and technological reasons. For example, he is unlikely to be surpassed economically, or technologically, in detecting faults when a whole array based on multiple criteria is possible, or in taking action when a new, unspecified defect appears.

However, if there appears to be a future role for the human inspector it is equally clear that if the problems of using human inspectors remain unattended they will get worse rather than better. In some industries increasing mechanization and the steady improvement in manufacturing efficiency will add to the problems as the faults become fewer and more difficult to detect. In other industries it seems that faults are likely to increase with faster modern equipment. Difficulties of recruitment and the deployment of the older worker to this type of job will further enlarge the problem.

It thus seems reasonable to accept the argument of the *Prologue* with respect to human factors in any future inspection system. This being so, development in both research and practice in this area gets its justification.

Clearly, the hope and expectation for the future, if this volume is to have any meaning, is for the extensive use of the human factors data and philosophy currently available which in turn means the extensive and common practice of collaboration between the human factors and quality engineer. In the longer term it is to be hoped that as their data make their contributions more significant for 'man-at-work', other behavioural specialists would participate in this collaboration. The economic value of such an approach must be unmistakable.

Improved practice will, of course, only be sustained by further research.

For the more applied researcher there is much to be done in the empirical investigation of factors affecting inspection efficiency. For example, there seems little likelihood that conveyor inspection will come to an end in the near future in industry so that this relatively unglamorous field still has considerable scope for study with benefits to all concerned.

In more fundamental research the development should be towards the production of general predictive models. The simplest method of using the theoretical formulations currently available is to use them as the basis for a methodology to combine with local calibration to determine performance in a given situation. This, of course, only represents an interim step in the development of a general predictive model and the task of the human factors specialist in the future should be directed to developing methods of predicting performance (in terms of P_1, P_2 and time) for a wide range of realistic conditions. If there is to be progress beyond measuring performance in each individual circumstance and using theories to describe qualitatively the effects of changes in external variables, then current theories need to be improved to the point where the contribution to total performance made by the parameters they describe may be combined as the standard industrial engineering technique of P.M.T.S. can be used to predict the time required for each step in the action sequence following a decision.

Ultimately a macro theory may be evolved from these component parts. A good model for such an integration can be seen in work physiology. Here separate theoretical models exist which will predict individually the effect of a number of external variables on such measures as temperature or heart rate of the worker. Recently, however, these separate mathematical models have begun to be integrated so that performance and individual stress can be predicted under a wide range of environments, clothing assemblies and work rates. By analogy the work on visual search, vigilance and decision making requires to be integrated into higher level theoretical structures. Starts have already been made on this as Bloomfield noted. But at this stage the integrated theories have yet to incorporate a vigilance component, the dynamic effect of changes in variables they measure (such as changes in input fault rate), and indeed the effects of a large number of external variables on inspection performance.

However, 'grand' theories of human behaviour have been notoriously unhelpful in describing the human at work and a macro theory of human inspection performance may have to remain a pipe dream. Certainly it could still at best provide only a partial description embracing the 'mechanistic' psychological functions. The variance provided by as yet ill-defined social and sociological parameters in the total situation preclude any other possibility. Nevertheless such an integrated theory or model should fare better than its predecessors in the general psychological framework being based on a broader range and better established models of single facets of human performance. It could well be that the nucleus of the psychologist's counterpart to the 'Theory of Relativity' lies in the humble industrial inspector.

Author index

Subject index